SOFTWARE ENGINEERING
PRINCIPLES AND METHODS

COMPUTER SCIENCE TEXTS

CONSULTING EDITORS

K. J. BOWCOCK
BSc, FBCS, FIMA
Department of Computer Science and Applied Mathematics
Aston University, Birmingham

C. M. REEVES
MA, PhD, FIMA
Professor of Computer Science
University of Keele

K. WOLFENDEN
MA
Emeritus Professor of
Information Processing
University of London

COMPUTER SCIENCE TEXTS

Software Engineering Principles and Methods

B. RATCLIFF

BSc, MSc
Department of Computer Science and Applied Mathematics,
Aston University, Birmingham

BLACKWELL SCIENTIFIC PUBLICATIONS

OXFORD LONDON EDINBURGH

BOSTON PALO ALTO MELBOURNE

Copyright © 1987 by
Blackwell Scientific Publications

All rights reserved. No part of this
publication may be reproduced, stored
in a retrieval system, or transmitted,
in any form or by any means, electronic,
mechanical, photocopying, recording or
otherwise without the prior permission of
the copyright owner.

First published 1987

British Library
Cataloguing in Publication Data

Ratcliff, B.
    Software engineering: principles and
    methods.
    1. Computer software—Development
    I. Title
    005.1′2   QA76.76.D47

ISBN 0–632–01459–8 Pbk

Blackwell Scientific Publications
Editorial offices:
Osney Mead, Oxford OX2 0EL
    (*Orders*: Tel. 0865 240201)
8 John Street, London WC1N 2ES
23 Ainslie Place, Edinburgh EH3 6AJ
52 Beacon Street, Boston
    Massachusetts 02108, USA
667 Lytton Avenue, Palo Alto
    California 94301, USA
107 Barry Street, Carlton
    Victoria 3053, Australia

Printed in Great Britain by
Billings & Sons, Worcester.

Library of Congress
Cataloging in Publication Data

Ratcliff, B.
    Software engineering : principles and
    methods / B. Ratcliff.
        p.   cm.—(Computer science texts)
    Bibliography : p.
    Includes index.
    ISBN 0–632–01459–8 (pbk.) : £12.95
    1. Computer software— Development.
    I. Title. II. Series.
QA76.76.D47R37 1987
005.1—dc19   87–23712

Contents

In memory of my mother and father.

Preface

The emergence of software engineering in recent years has been in response to the manifest need to transform software development and its attendant activities from being a cottage industry based on an *ad hoc* collection of unprincipled techniques and inadequate tools into a rigorous, cohesive discipline that rests on firm theoretical, computer-scientific, methodical, methodological and managerial foundations. The extent of the problem that software engineering addresses is now almost universally appreciated:

* That, even nowadays, much of the software produced is of (sometimes appallingly) low quality for a variety of well known reasons.
* That many of the applications for which a software solution is required are overwhelmingly daunting in their size and complexity.
* That, as software costs escalate and schedule overshoot is the norm, the demand for (quality) software increasingly outstrips the ability to supply.

This latter situation is exacerbated by the fact that there is already worldwide a severe shortage of appropriately knowledgeable, trained and highly skilled personnel needed to tackle the ever-present 'software crisis'. The main objective of this book is to contribute to the educational effort needed to reduce that shortage.

Software engineering is a wide-ranging, complex amalgam of related topics, and the book is intended to provide general coverage of the whole area in sufficient depth and detail that it can adequately function as a main text for software engineering courses at both undergraduate and postgraduate levels (and their equivalents). It is also hoped that the book will be of equally direct relevance to software engineering courses taking place in an industrial or commercial environment. If necessary, for courses of an introductory or scaled-down nature, it should be possible to subset the book's content to cater for most teaching requirements.

The book's material is structured around the traditionally perceived major components of software engineering – requirements analysis and definition, specification and design, implementation, etc. This structure acts as a convenient paradigm for organization of the material, but should not be taken to mean that the conventional 'life-cycle' model of software development is in any way espoused by the author. A synopsis of each chapter follows.

Chapter 1 'sets the scene'. The main theme is to characterize software engineering in terms of the major issues it has to tackle, e.g. dealing with large scale, the need for a coherent organizational framework for software production, software quality, the problems of keeping to schedule and budget, the immense diversity of software as regards application, implementation, etc.

The first section of Chapter 2 discusses how software applications and (sub)systems originate. A small example problem is also introduced that is used as the main illustrative base in the book; it is in effect the book's 'case study', which is interspersed at relevant points throughout subsequent chapters. For easy reference, the various components of the problem and its (partial) solution developed in the text are brought together in an Appendix. Keeping track of the case study is certainly instructive, though by no means essential; most of those parts of the text that deal specifically with the case study can easily be bypassed.

The remainder of the chapter deals in detail with the nature of software requirements, their analysis and definition in requirements documentation, and their validation and verification (V&V). Section 2.3 includes a brief overview of various requirements definition techniques, as well as the definition of some example requirements for the case study using an author-developed syntax. The final section of the chapter, which deals with requirements V&V, concentrates on prototyping and executable specifications.

The intention in the first five sections of Chapter 3 is to sketch a general picture of the main fundamental concepts and techniques associated with software specification and design at the 'system' level of scale and complexity. Although some of the material in these sections is fairly basic and may already be familiar to some students, its assimilation in the context of system development is of fundamental importance. The fuzziness conveyed by the text in differentiating between 'specification' and 'design' is deliberate – in the opinion of the author, the two should be seen as representing a continuum of transformation in which it is artificial to separate out (technical) specification as some kind of distinct, separate preliminary to design.

Following this general discussion, Section 3.6 briefly surveys some of the major contrasting approaches to specification and design using the case-study problem for illustration, before the penultimate three sections devote themselves in detail to the case study using one particular system development technique, namely JSD/JSP. The author has no particular axe to grind here – lack of space precludes detailed comparison of different development approaches, and JSD/JSP is a reasonable choice (for the reasons given in the text) to illustrate system specification and design 'in action'. However, reading of these sections could be entirely omitted, if desired.

Chapter 4 represents a natural continuation of Chapter 3, considering concepts and techniques of design either unmentioned or only touched upon there. The emphasis is still on software architecture – modularity, abstraction, structure, etc. – but at the more concrete level of detailed program design. The penultimate two sections employ a contrived mini-problem extracted from the case study to illustrate and contrast two well-established approaches to program design: design by (step-wise) refinement and Structured Design. Again, these two sections (4.5 and 4.6) could be regarded as optional reading. The last section of the chapter deals with the topic of software component reusability.

Including a separate chapter devoted entirely to formal methods of software development is, of course, a direct reflection of the author's view that their importance to software engineering is such that the topic deserves this prominence. Whilst the techniques still arouse controversy in some quarters, there is no doubt as to their increasing influence on, and gradual incorporation into, 'everyday' software development (though to what ultimate degree yet remains to be seen). Chapter 5 outlines the rationale for formal methods, and then concentrates on the latter's two main components: specification and design verification. A survey of some of the support (tools, languages, etc.) that formal methods presently enjoys is then presented, before the chapter concludes with a few provisos concerning the current applicability of the techniques.

This chapter could be omitted in its entirety in courses of an introductory nature; however, Sections 5.1, 5.2 first subsection, 5.3 first subsection and 5.5 could be covered without undue difficulty.

Many textbooks on software engineering devote considerable attention to features of modern programming languages and the support they provide for good software engineering practice. The orientation of Chapter 6 is slightly different, being more in keeping with the spirit of the book's 'model' of software development – that it is a series of transformations starting with requirements definition that eventually produces an executable end-product. This chapter therefore looks at various transformations on designs needed to produce executable software, but without going into significant detail about the characteristics of particular languages (only Ada receives a modicum of attention, this being in 6.5 and 6.8). The topics covered range from straightforward coding, through optimizations to complex transformations on abstract network architectures. As regards the latter, Sections 6.6 and 6.7 inevitably have been influenced by the choice of method used to illustrate the case study development. What is important, though, is for the reader to grasp the general points being made in these two sections.

The chapter concludes with two sections that respectively deal with compilation/library issues from an Ada perspective, and portability.

Reliability is the first main topic covered in Chapter 7. The emphasis of the discussion is on designing robustness into software via appropriate data error and exception handling techniques, the Ada model being used to illustrate the latter. The main bulk of the chapter is then given over to quality control techniques, which have been divided into V&V techniques (walkthroughs, inspections, etc.) and machine testing. The chapter concludes by dealing briefly with the activity of debugging.

Chapter 8 brings together major aspects of managing a software project from the planning stage through to maintenance inclusive. The objective is to give a reasonably in-depth coverage of management of the following: resources (money, time and their estimation), people (team functions and structures, etc.), software configuration, maintenance, quality (i.e. quality assurance) and information (documentation). Although documentation is not, of course, directly a project management issue, the beginning of Section 8.7 presents a rationale for ncluding it as a topic of this chapter. Section 8.6 on quality assurance includes a discussion of software metrics.

The final chapter, Chapter 9, attempts to give the reader a feel for the evolution of software engineering by discussing previous advances that have been made, surveying its current status and taking a look into the future. The chapter includes sections on software tools and support environments, and the relationship between Artificial Intelligence and software engineering.

As regards references and bibliography, the author has attempted to make them as up to date and wide-ranging as possible. The intention has been to enable the reader to follow up any particular topic arising in the text to greater depth without any difficulty. Only texts from mainstream publishers and papers in established journals, periodicals and conference proceedings have been quoted – reference to obscure or potentially hard-to-get technical reports, PhD theses, etc. has been deliberately avoided.

The book is a culmination of giving lecture courses in software engineering at postgraduate level over the last decade. Inasmuch as it is a product of that process, the author would like to thank all students who have taken the course over that period and thus have been the main vehicle for its continual development and improvement. As other authors will undoubtedly testify, the conversion of a set of annually mutating lecture notes into a viable textbook is a highly non-trivial transformation. It is here that due acknowledgement must be given to those who, one way or another, have helped me along this arduous path. Firstly, thanks must go to colleague Peter Coxhead for the initial encouragement more than two years ago that prompted me into action. His subsequent valuable comments on early drafts of many of the chapters were also much appreciated. Other people who chipped in included Ted Elsworth, Peter Bates and Jawed Siddiqi. Particular thanks must go to Michael Jackson of Michael Jackson Systems Ltd for furnishing me with some timely(!) advice when it was needed, and also for his encouragement after inspecting the draft manuscript. I am especially indebted to the referee, who somehow found the time to read the draft manuscript in depth and suggest numerous improvements, which I have incorporated. Nevertheless, whatever omissions, inaccuracies or other types of defect still remain are of course my sole responsibility.

Finally, I would like to thank my wife Jan and daughter Alice for all their love and much-needed support throughout the project, especially during the latter stages when deadlines had passed, evenings were a rarely unbroken sequence of prolonged conversations with a word processor, and worry and exhaustion continually dominated the psyche of the author.

Bryan Ratcliff,
Aston University

ACKNOWLEDGEMENTS

In putting together a book such as this, one draws upon considerably the accumulated wisdom and knowledge embodied in other sources. The author would like to offer thanks to all those whose works have been consulted and have provided invaluable material and/or inspiration; they have all been duly acknowledged at the appropriate points in the text.

The text was prepared entirely by the author on word-processing facilities available on the Harris computing system at Aston University. It is here that I must express my thanks to Philip Findon and Eric Richards of Aston University Computing Services for always being willing to provide prompt help when it came to laser-printing the draft, no matter at what inopportune moment I chose to seek it.

The following names appearing in the text are trademarks and have been acknowledged as such at the first instance of the use of each name:

(TM)Ada is a trademark of the US Department of Defense (Ada Joint Program Office).
(TM)Ina Jo is a trademark of SDC, a Burroughs Company.
(TM)Occam is a trademark of the Inmos Group of Companies.
(TM)SADT is a trademark of Softech Inc.
(TM)Smalltalk is a trademark of Rank Xerox Corporation.
(TM)Unix is a trademark of AT&T Bell Laboratories.
(TM)Miranda is a trademark of Research Software Ltd.

Chapter 1

Software Engineering:
An Overview

1.1 WHAT IS 'SOFTWARE ENGINEERING'?

The technological revolution of computers is just a few decades old, and yet within that rapid advance a number of significant, separately identifiable subrevolutions have taken place. First and foremost from a person-in-the-street perspective, the age of microelectronics has wrought a dramatic change: it has transformed a large, mysterious beast lurking in some remote, guarded, air-conditioned room (often producing non or misinformation, occasionally with unfortunate consequences) into a carry-home-under-the-arm machine obtainable from one's local electrical hardware or department store. As a consequence of this domestication of computing power, a fundamental side effect has occurred: computers have at last been 'demystified'.

This demystification helps people to place computers in their proper context. For, whether the computer plays games with you at home, controls your washing machine, produces your gas bills, keeps track of your credit rating, helps manage your business or guides the aircraft in which you fly, it should be seen for what it basically is: a tool, albeit the most powerful and sophisticated ever invented, but a tool nevertheless. Moreover, since the infrastructures of developed or developing societies are becoming increasingly dependent on computer systems for their proper functioning, it follows that the quality of life, in part at least, is directly affected by the software that controls and harnesses the computer's power and sophistication. Whilst some software is intended to improve the human interface and accessibility of computers (e.g. operating system, network and communications software), from the point of view of users, the basic function of software is to configure the general-purpose machine into special-purpose tools and applications that (it is hoped) satisfy particular requirements. Unfortunately, the past is littered with counter-examples; software has often manifestly failed to achieve basic levels of quality and user satisfaction.

This past failure of software (or, perhaps more accurately, the people responsible for its development) to 'deliver the goods' is often referred to as the 'software crisis' – a term now firmly embedded in software folklore, yet still to some extent relevant today. This term refers to the fact that software frequently:

was delivered way behind schedule;
cost far more to produce than original budget estimates;
failed to meet user requirements;
was unreliable;
proved to be virtually impossible to maintain;
lacked other quality criteria (e.g. was difficult to use).

This is not to imply that all software in the past suffered from every conceivable deficiency. However, as far back as the late 1960s the prevailing abysmal state of much software was sufficient for the term 'crisis' to be apposite rather than exaggerated.

The crisis was revealed and subsequently heightened by another subrevolution preceding that of the personal and home computer – the fact that, as hardware got smaller, it also became more powerful, cheaper, and more reliable. The general-purpose tool increasingly opened up ever-widening vistas of complex and sophisticated applications. Largely, software was unable to meet the challenge, for one simple reason: any principles, tools and techniques that were applied to software development were generally *ad hoc* and inadequate – they lacked an underlying rationale and theoretical basis, and there was little, if any, method or methodology in their application. Software development was an enigmatic process, practised by many but understood by very few. Thus, the parallel revolution in software technology needed to match its hardware counterpart failed to materialize.

Clearly, there was an urgent need to remedy the situation by placing software development on sound theoretical, methodological and practical foundations. The concept of 'software engineering' arose directly from this need. The relevance of the term 'engineering' can be appreciated by enumerating the major activities that contribute to the formulation, design and manufacture of almost any complex, reliable product; these activities are:

(a) *Analysing* a problem.
(b) *Specifying* the requirements for a solution.
(c) *Designing* a solution to match the specification.
(d) *Implementing* the design.
(e) *Assuring* the quality of the end product.
(f) *Maintaining* the end product.
(g) *Planning* and *controlling* (a) to (f).
(h) *Selecting* and *applying* (sometimes even creating) principles, tools, techniques and materials to effect (a) to (g).

Such a comprehensive discipline of activities, embedded in a coherent methodological framework, is just as important to software development as to all other forms of engineering. However, as Michael Jackson† has pointed out, the engineering analogy should not be overstretched. Software production deals with strings and patterns of symbols that are constantly being rearranged, combined, modified and transformed into different representations – manipulations that the computer itself is uniquely geared to perform. Compare this with the manufacture of an automobile, for instance, which is an amalgam of a bewildering array of components that have been separately produced by quite different techniques from a variety of materials. In other words, software production – hence software engineering – possesses attributes that make it stand apart from other forms of engineering and that we should attempt to exploit to our advantage.

Use of the term 'software engineering' can be traced back at least as far as a 1968 NATO conference held in Garmisch, West Germany, the proceedings of which (together with the follow-up conference held near Rome, Italy, in 1969) can be found reprinted in Naur *et al.* (1976). In a survey of the current 'state of the art' and overview of software engineering, Boehm (1976) defines software engineering in terms of the application of 'scientific knowledge' to the development of programs and their associated documentation. Interestingly, Boehm (1981) offers a similar definition but with the extra proviso that software engineering should make '... the capabilities of computer equipment ... *useful* to man ...' (author's italics) – a point made previously by Hoare (1978a). The notion of 'usefulness' will be the central theme of Section 1.4.

As our own definition, we will say that:

Software engineering is the disciplined utilization of a systematic, coherent set of principles, tools and techniques within a planned organizational framework, the objective of which is to achieve the on-schedule, cost-effective development of quality software for a diverse range of non-trivial applications and environments.

The essential ingredients of – or rather, questions begged by – this definition are:

★ What principles, tools, etc.?
★ What is meant by 'non-trivial'?
★ What constitutes a planned organizational framework?
★ What is software 'quality'?
★ What issues affect schedule and cost?
★ What diversity of application, etc.?

† Seminar, held in the Department of Computer Science and Applied Mathematics, Aston University, Birmingham, UK, on 22 January 1986.

One main purpose of this book is to describe some of the possible answers to the first question. To provide a backdrop, the remaining issues will be discussed briefly in the rest of this chapter, and some of these will also receive more detailed treatment in later parts of the book.

Before leaving this section, it is worth mentioning a third subrevolution that has been gaining momentum for some time now and should continue to do so for the foreseeable future – that of Artificial Intelligence (AI). AI is already here in such forms as 'expert systems' and is envisaged as being a major component of fifth-generation computer technology. AI could have a considerable impact on software engineering in the future. It seems appropriate to discuss issues of the future in the last chapter.

1.2   PROBLEMS OF SCALE

A small problem might be 'non-trivial' in the sense of being intellectually demanding to solve due to inherent properties of the problem itself, even though it yields a simple, elegant program solution. Our definition of software engineering uses the term 'non-trivial' more in the sense of being demanding to solve due to largeness of size. One metric that enables the relative size of software development tasks to be appreciated is to give a rough estimate of the effort required to carry them out. Effort is an estimate of how many persons P over what timespan T a development task would take to complete from inception to some form of operational capability (note: we shall return to the problem of estimating effort in Chapter 8). It is instructive to examine in terms of effort the breadth of the spectrum of size-related complexity that exists. One need go no further than the familiar world of data processing. Here is a list of examples:

(a) A subprogram to locate the position of a record, given its key, in an ordered sequence of such records.

$P \times T \rightarrow 1$ person in a day at most if starting from scratch with 'inside-the-head' knowledge of a familiar search algorithm; alternatively, minimal effort will need to be expended if a module to perform the task is already available in some utility library.

(b) A program to update a master file of accounts given a set of transactions, producing update and error/exception reports.

$P \times T \rightarrow 1$ person in a day, or a few days or weeks, depending on the actual size of the task and the software development tools available.

(c) A complete, partly online subsystem that handles all transactions of a major banking firm's current account customers nationwide.

P × T → 1 person in a considerable number of months, almost certainly spanning at least a year, and probably much longer.

(d) A total system for handling all of a major banking firm's business, both national and international.

P × T → 1 person in a lifetime, perhaps; in practice, many people in a few years.

(e) A general-purpose, multi-user operating system capable of organizing a mainframe environment on which the previous system (amongst others) could run.

P × T → 1 person in many lifetimes; in practice, a large number of people in several years. (For an account of salutory experiences gained in precisely this type of project, read Brooks 1975.)

Yourdon (1975) has some apposite names for the categories to which these examples belong: example (e) would be a 'nearly impossible program'. There is, however, a more extreme category still – that of 'utterly absurd' programs (millions of high-level source-code instructions in size) as exemplified by some real-time military applications. For one person's view of a particular program considered by him to reside in this category (and his view of the current and future limitations of software engineering), read Parnas (1985).

It is obvious that development tasks such as (e) and (a) bear absolutely no relation to one another in terms of effort required – the difference is many orders of magnitude; as a rough comparison, 100 person-years is approximately 2.5×10^4 person-days. This illustrates the essence of the basic problem that confronts software engineering – the fact that many of the tasks to which computers are being applied are potentially overwhelming in their size-related complexity. We can elaborate upon the difficulties involved:

★ How can we understand initially what the problem is and determine what the requirements for a computerized solution to it are? How should we define those requirements?

★ How can we cope with the complex intellectual task of specifying, designing and implementing a product to satisfy a given, possibly incomplete, set of requirements?

★ How can we ensure, as far as is possible, that the eventual product actually works, is delivered on time within reasonable sight of cost estimates, satisfies the original requirements and is of high quality in other important respects?

★ How can we cope with the complex organizational task of managing people and emerging product (including documentation) in such a way

that all objectives are met and the project reaches satisfactory completion?
★ How can we achieve acceptable solutions to all these problems given the constraints (i.e. finite resources – time, financial, people, machine) under which we have to work?

What is being emphasized here is that the difficulty of cost-effectively producing quality software rises acutely and disproportionately with increasing size. However, it should not be inferred that software engineering is concerned solely with large-scale tasks. Software can exist in a variety of forms – routines, modules, libraries, programs, systems, environments; and even software at the humble end of this spectrum, such as the library module, must be well engineered and has a vital role to play in the overall scheme of things.

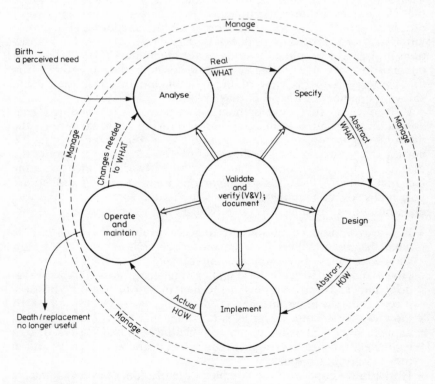

Fig. 1.1.   The software life cycle: major activities.

1.3 A FRAMEWORK FOR SOFTWARE ENGINEERING

The lifespan of a software product begins, naturally, with a realization of its need. It ends when the product, having been developed, used and possibly subjected to significant modification since its first release, reaches the end of its useful life and is discarded, usually to be replaced by a totally new product. In between, a framework needs to be established in advance in which the product's formulation, development, use and maintenance can be organized and successfully accomplished. The 'software life cycle' (or similar terminology) is the umbrella phrase generally used to describe the conventional model of the overall organizational framework relevant to software engineering. We have already suggested such a life cycle in the previous two sections, and Fig. 1.1 gives a broad impression of it in terms of the major activities involved.

* An *analysis* phase initially establishes the need for, and the feasibility of developing, a computerized system, a replacement for an existing one, or some software product. The 'output' from this phase will include a set of defined *requirements* that must be satisfied by the software component of the planned development.
* A software *specification* is then constructed that will meet those requirements. This can be regarded as translating a real-world (i.e. user/customer) view of WHAT is required into an equivalent abstract, computer software view of the same.
* A *design* is then derived from the specification, the former being in effect a prescription of HOW the latter will be satisfied. This WHAT-to-HOW progression can be perceived elsewhere in the life cycle and is useful in understanding the nature of certain transformational processes that take place in various phases of software development. It is within the design phase, and to some extent the specification phase, that perhaps the largest slice of insight, imagination and engineering creativity is concentrated.
* The design itself will not normally be directly operable in the intended target environment(s). By 'target environment' we mean minimally a machine together with, usually, an operating system, though other software might be involved in specific instances, such as a database management system. Thus, a further HOW transformation must take place on the design to obtain a 'realization' or *implementation*, i.e. a product that is actually executable.
* Finally, the implemented product, once validated and accepted, must be 'cared for' during its operational lifetime. In other words, it will generally undergo *maintenance* from time to time in order to preserve or enhance its usefulness before it is eventually discarded or superseded.

Figure 1.1 also depicts three other major activities, which are indicated as being 'global' to the whole life cycle. Each phase generates its own products or 'deliverables' that must be subject to *validation* and *verification* (V&V) and *documentation*. V&V is a vital life-cycle discipline contributing to the assurance of quality in the final product. Documentation defines, describes and records (meetings, decisions, deliverables, etc.), and promotes effective communication between all parties involved. V&V and documentation help 'bind' the various phases together and facilitate effective *management* of the entire complex development process.

Note that the cycle has been depicted as a closed loop (which is, of course, consistent with using the word 'cycle'). Large systems in particular are rarely static during their operational lifetime; they must evolve to meet changes in their surrounding environment. These changes may be due to unpredictable external factors or may be suggested as a result of user experience with the system. This experience may highlight required modifications to the software that were difficult, if not impossible, to foresee originally (e.g. because the system is aimed at a new, innovative application area). Nevertheless, it is highly desirable to minimize the likelihood of changes being requested to the final released version of a product – software crises are often due to developing a product that, even if it does 'work', is not what users wanted.

Modelling the lifespan of software as a simple cycle comprising a number of distinct but interacting main phases is over-simplistic as it stands. There are several reasons for this:

★ At a more detailed level, software development is highly iterative and parallel in nature and does not proceed in a simple, clear-cut sequence of the phases indicated. This is because:

There are potential feedback loops at various points (for clarity not shown in Fig. 1.1); the reader will no doubt already be familiar with the (frustrating!) implementation iteration of {CODE → TEST → DEBUG}. More generally, as a result of validating each deliverable generated, errors and inconsistencies may be detected that have filtered through from earlier stages. For example, specifying the system may reveal problems with the stated requirements; design may reveal problems with the specification (or, worse, requirements, if earlier validation procedures have not been carried out effectively). Similarly, changes necessary to the implementation or even design may become apparent as a result of using the system. System development cannot be 'monolithic' – a term applied pejoratively to the indefensible strategy of developing non-trivial software in a way that involves no significant breakdown of the task at any stage into smaller parts. Thus, particularly during design and the early part of the implementation phase, there is potential for a high degree of parallel development of system components that are subsequently combined together according to some integration strategy being employed.

★ The boundaries between the various phases are not as distinct as suggested. The main reason for this is because such terms as 'specification' and 'design', and the activities they describe, can possess slightly different interpretations in different contexts. Some of the 'boundary' problems include the following:

Where does software engineering proper begin? Is requirements analysis a software-engineering task? Is specifying a system an analysis task?

What is the dividing line between specification and design? Is specification purely a WHAT concept, or does (should?) it contain a HOW element?

Where does design stop and implementation begin? If the degree of abstraction separating a design and some target environment is large, then surely a significant amount of 'design' will inevitably be involved in achieving an implementation?

To some extent, this is just terminological wrangling. But it does serve to indicate that life-cycle nomenclature is relative rather than absolute, and that notions of 'specification', 'design', etc. are somewhat blurred and intertwined, and vary slightly according to the development method being used.

A further aspect of the software life cycle, merely implied by Fig. 1.1, is that each major transition in development can be viewed as a transformational process T on 'the system' – see Fig. 1.2a inset in Fig. 1.2, the latter showing T exploded into greater detail (note: arrows indicate inputs and outputs to development activities, which are designated in circles; items in open rectangles represent retained data). Interpreting software development in this way has a certain appeal in that the essence of each transition is the same:

★ The system (or any component of it) Xf is transformed from one domain of conceptualization and representation into Yf as described (specified) in another such domain. Broadly, the overall life-cycle sequence is: requirements (user WHAT domain)–> specification (abstract WHAT domain)–> design (abstract HOW domain)–> implementation (actual HOW domain). Note also that a major transformation such as designing may itself be composed of a number of subtransformations.

★ The system (or a system component), as expressed in each new target domain, is a deliverable that can be documented and subjected to

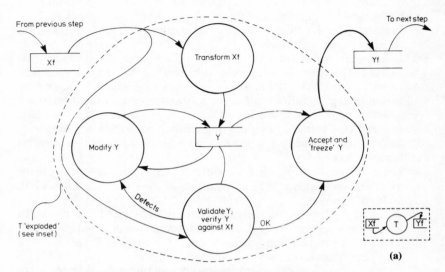

Fig. 1.2.   A general transformational step in software development.

some form of validation and verification against its immediately previous representation. Naturally, there could be many iterations involving modification and V&V before the new representation is accepted. Hence, the eventual completion of a transformation also represents a 'milestone' against which development can be monitored and recorded.

This transformational view highlights some of the main areas of direct concern to software development, namely the need for:

★ Appropriate descriptive mechanisms and formal languages for expressing requirements, specifications, designs and implementations.
★ Transformations for mapping one representation into another, possibly automated by appropriate software tools.
★ Techniques for validating an emerging or transformed product and verifying its correctness against its previous representation.

Where appropriate in this book, we will continue to place emphasis on software development as a series of transformations, some of which can be (partially) automated, e.g. designs into implementations, and some of which are as yet largely effected by the application of human intellect and ingenuity, e.g. requirements into specifications.

(Note: the reader will have observed the separate usage of the terms 'validation' and 'verification'. The distinction between the two is clarified in Section 7.1.)

There exist several variations of the life-cycle model which, in part, is evidence for the fact that the model may need to be tailored to suit the characteristics of a particular software engineering project such as the size and complexity of the problem to be solved, the development method to be used, the management and control functions to be applied, etc. The model of Fig. 1.1 is sufficient to capture the essence of the process, though the rigidity, over-generality and inappropriateness of the traditional life-cycle concept have been criticized. McCracken and Jackson (1982), for example, argue that it is of little use in solving problems of communication between users and developers, or involving the former in system development, for which *prototyping* provides considerable potential. Basically, prototyping is rapidly building some 'rough and ready' version of the intended software, or some of its components, for early evaluation purposes, especially with respect to requirements. Detailed discussion of prototyping will be left until the next chapter, where the possible perturbations its inclusion has on the life-cycle model of Fig. 1.1 will be described.

Although each phase named in Fig. 1.1 conceals a wealth of detail, this applies especially to 'maintenance', a term that covers all the repair, care and evolution of a software product occurring from its first release to its obsolescence. This evolution can be vastly more extensive (and expensive!) in time, effort and cost than the original development. Indeed, it has been observed that, generally:

★ A software system undergoes continuous change until it becomes more economical to replace it.
★ The 'entropy' of a software system increases as it evolves, i.e. the quality (orderliness) of its structure decreases.
★ Surprisingly, over the maintenance lifespan, such factors as the rate of development and degree of change between releases remain approximately constant.

These observations and their implications underpin the laws of 'program evolution dynamics' formulated by Lehman and Belady, much of whose work over the years on the processes of software change can be found published in Lehman & Belady (1985).

1.4 SOFTWARE QUALITY

The central goal of software engineering is to develop software products that possess 'quality'. The notion of software quality may at first seem somewhat difficult to crystallize. However, one approach is to start with the observation that, ultimately, software engineering must generate products that are *useful*. The implication is that software quality can be articulated in terms of a product's 'usefulness'.

(Note: the term 'product' is being used in its most general sense here. It is sometimes used more narrowly to apply to 'product software'. Product software, unlike bespoke (tailor-made) software, is applications software, ranging from library components to stand-alone packages, that is designed to be of use to computer users in general. We shall distinguish between these two categories only when the context demands.)

Using the symbol $--\!>$ to mean 'depends on' or 'is a function of', we can start with the idea of 'total usefulness' of a software product and subdivide it thus:

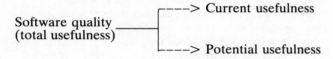

Software quality
(total usefulness)
└----> Current usefulness

└----> Potential usefulness

In effect, the first component of usefulness relates to the product's capability in the specific environment(s) in which it is currently operational; the second relates to the product's potential capability to operate successfully within contexts – applications, operational environments, changing requirements, etc. – other than those for which it is currently configured. Figure 1.3 breaks these two major components down further; the 'quality characteristics tree' depicted is an adaptation of that found in Boehm *et al.* (1978).

We shall now elaborate upon the more concrete aspects of quality in terms of which 'current usefulness' and 'potential usefulness' are expressed in Fig. 1.3.

Characteristics Contributing to Current Usefulness

Reliability

Ideally, software should behave without deviation from its specification at all times when operating under conditions consistent with that specification. In practice, the difficulty of achieving anywhere near 100% reliability with some large systems is, to date, insurmountable. This is somewhat disturbing, since many of the largest systems that exist (e.g. in military applications) could cause catastrophe if they malfunctioned in some unpredictable way. This situation should be contrasted

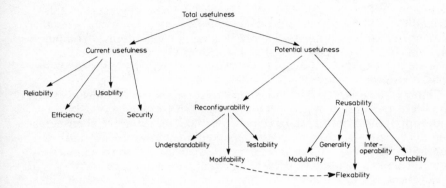

Fig. 1.3. High-level software quality characteristics.

with other large systems (e.g. operating systems) where poor reliability is extremely irksome but not potentially disastrous. Product software should fare better in respect of reliability, since it can undergo extensive testing and trial usage before being advertised and sold for general usage. With bespoke software, the exigencies of keeping within budget and meeting agreed deadlines tend to be more acute, with consequent pressure to effect product release prematurely.

Efficiency

The demand made by a product on resources (processor time and processor/backing store) is perhaps one of the more obvious criteria by which to judge software quality. However, given the ever-decreasing hardware unit cost ratio with respect to processing power and storage capacity, efficiency is nowadays a far less important consideration than it used to be. Even so, efficiency cannot be dismissed as no longer relevant. Firstly, there is no justification for any software being incompetently inefficient and merely relying on user tolerance. Secondly, response times of certain components of a system, particularly a real-time system, may have to lie within critical limits that must be adhered to. More generally, the performance (primarily a function of processing load, storage utilization and input/output activity) of any proposed system may have to satisfy certain minimum requirements in order to obtain user acceptance.

Usability

Usability refers to the ease of use and human engineering ('user friendliness') of a software product. For a detailed examination of the issues relevant to (the design of) usable, 'people-literate' computer systems, the reader can consult a text such as Gaines & Shaw (1984) or the paper by Gould & Lewis (1985). Briefly, we will make the following observations.

Firstly, the quality of the human interface will have a significant effect on users' perception of product usefulness. It is the degree of clarity and appropriateness of this interface that can make the difference between a product being an excellent tool, or tedious, error-prone and very unsatisfying to use. Of relevance here are such aspects as the commands and formats to be used for presenting input data, and the readability and relevance of output generated by the system. These considerations apply, of course, regardless of whether or not the product is used online. However, with today's high-capacity, powerful mainframes, large populations of online users do not present such an efficiency problem any more. Couple this with the explosive growth at the microcomputer end of the market and it is not surprising that the trend is increasingly towards interactive software.

Interactive communication possesses its own quality problems, not least because of the variety of different possible forms it can take. Some of the more commonly used methods include:

⋆ Inputing data using a special command language, or as prompted by messages or screen displays.
⋆ Presenting options via (possibly 'pull down') menus.
⋆ Employing 'windows' to display simultaneously, or to overlay, disjoint sets of relevant information.
⋆ Displaying facilities, options, etc. pictographically via 'icons'.
⋆ Achieving screen cursor positioning via a key-pad or 'mouse'.

Of course, any combination of these methods might be used. The choice in practice depends on a judicious balancing of such factors as application area, whether users will be novices or experienced at using computer systems, and whether the interaction will be primarily user driven or product driven.

There are other aspects to usability as well as the quality of the user interface. For example, a 'friendly' system would possess 'help' facilities to provide users with immediate online information about the system, should they require it. Usability is also affected by the degree to which the functionality of the software satisfies the needs of the application and of its users. Especially with product software, there can be quite major differences between separate products targeted at the same area.

For example, one word processor might possess a column-delete facility, whilst with another the same function might be less satisfactorily achieved via repeated substring deletion over the lines involved. Generally, the more complete and sophisticated the facilities offered, the better, though there may be a price to pay for sophistication – a greater effort in learning, or greater investment involved in training people, in order to use the product effectively. This sort of consideration is important when judging the appropriateness of a system's functionality with respect to the intended type of user. Thus, end-users who are (and will to all intents and purposes remain) inexperienced at using computer systems will be satisfied with an adequate subset of all possible facilities; others will expect a more comprehensive capability.

Security

A software product should be secure against misuse in at least two important ways. Firstly, it should be (almost) impossible for the product to be corrupted deliberately in any way by mischievous users. Secondly, appropriate levels of protection should be built into the product so that access to sensitive or confidential data (or programs) is strictly controlled. Security of software systems is becoming more and more problematic, particularly with the trend towards networks and distributed systems, and the increasing sophistication of methods of electronic espionage being used to gain unauthorized access to computerized databases.

Characteristics Contributing to Potential Usefulness

Reconfigurability: ---> Understandability
           ---> Modifiability
           ---> Testability

Essentially, we are referring to the ability of software to be changed successfully in any required way and for any reason whatsoever with minimal cost and effort commensurate with the scale of the change. If the software is operational, then the more specific term 'maintainability' can be used. However, software must be reconfigurable during development as well as after release. Either way, it is clear that:

(a) Nothing can be changed if it is not appropriately described and the description comprehensible: *understandability*.
(b) Small changes of enhancement, extension or adaptation should not necessitate large, or even total, redevelopment: *modifiability*.

(c) The specification, design and documentation of software must permit effective application of normal rigorous validation and verification procedures when changes have been made: *testability*.

Of all the many factors that in turn influence these reconfigurability subcharacteristics, perhaps the most important is *structure*, by which we mean:

★ *Logical* structure, i.e. the abstract make-up of a system as expressed in terms of various specification and design concepts that will be discussed in later chapters.
★ *Physical* structure, i.e. the physical representation of a system in terms of routines, modules, programs and the way in which these are maintained in files, libraries, databases, etc.

It is relevant to note here that successful reconfiguration also depends on effective 'configuration management'; this topic is examined in Chapter 8.

Reusability: ---> Modularity
                        ---> Generality
                        ---> Flexibility
                        ---> Interoperability
                        ---> Portability

Reusability is primarily a quality of product software and refers to the extent to which such software can be (re)used in as many operational environments and applications as possible, within a given application area, with minimal alteration or further development. The whole point about reusability is to avoid unnecessary and wasted effort in 're-inventing the wheel'. Clearly, this partly depends on making potentially reusable products available. *Portability* – target environment independence – is obviously an important consideration here; but availability can be enhanced by developing several variants of a product specifically configured for different target environments.

For self-contained products, reusability also means building in functional relevance but with plenty of scope for user 'tailoring'. For software components, reusability depends upon more technical characteristics such as *modularity* and greater *generality* achieved via mechanisms such as generic abstraction. These issues are covered further in Chapter 4.

Interoperability refers to a product's ease of interfacing harmoniously with other software with which it will operate in concert. Potential for reuse is also enhanced if a new capability can be easily added to a product, or an existing capability easily suppressed, eliminated or adapted; the majority of code can then be incorporated into the new application without rewrite. We have used the general term *flexibility* to cover all these possibilities. As Fig. 1.3 suggests, flexibility is subsumed by modifiability, which represents a software product's overall facilitation of cost-effective revision to accommodate changes, regardless of their nature.

End Note

Other software quality schemas are possible, as well as the one we have described. One alternative is to partition quality characteristics into the following four categories:

★ Application specific: e.g. data security, which would be crucial only for certain kinds of system involving access to sensitive or confidential information.
★ General, but needing an application-specific definition: e.g. efficiency, which would apply to all systems but would be defined in different ways for an operating system, say, compared to a transaction processing system.
★ General, and application independent: e.g. reliability.
★ Related to the software production process: e.g. testability.

This particular classification is given by Kitchenham & Walker (1986).

Our quality schema has deliberately not included every conceivable characteristic that could be deemed desirable in software; for example, we have not gone down to source-code levels such as readability. Rather, the aim has been to give the reader a qualitative feel for the major quality issues involved, and to demonstrate that, whilst 'software quality' is a complex phenomenon, it can be understood in terms of a hierarchy of desiderata that represent realistic and tangible objectives for software engineering.

1.5 SCHEDULE AND COST

Software is big business. Already by the mid 1970s the cost of software production in the United States was being measured in billions of dollars. Boehm (1981) states that the annual cost of software in the United States in 1980 was around $40 billion (about 2% of the GNP). Boehm (1986) quotes the annual software cost in 1985 to be about $70 billion in the United States and over $140 billion worldwide; this U.S. figure is based on an estimated average 12% annual growth rate since 1980. Moreover, in the acquisition of complete computer systems, it is estimated that, nowadays, software alone can account for up to 80% of the costs – a situation that existed in reverse in the late 1950s when hardware was the major cost factor. We have thus arrived at a situation where hardware is, in effect, not much more than the inexpensive packaging that surrounds a very costly software product or 'bundle'.

Such high software costs can be attributed partly to the fact that software development is inevitably going to be relatively expensive. This is because it is labour intensive, involving trained and highly-skilled (hence highly-paid) people, possibly in very large numbers over a considerable timescale (i.e. many years). Yet high costs also result from inadequate planning with respect to schedule and budget, which are difficult parameters to estimate and control, particularly for large-scale, long-term projects. Over-ambitious projects undertaken within unrealistic timescale and resource estimates are major causes of software crises. Furthermore, schedule and cost are interlinked – if a project 'slips', costs will automatically increase. Thus, two important questions arise here:

★ How can schedule and cost be planned and estimated in advance with acceptable accuracy?
★ What factors cause schedule and cost to overrun during the life cycle and how can such factors be eliminated or at least their effect significantly reduced?

The first issue will be dealt with later when we will have a more detailed understanding of what software development involves, and thus how schedule and cost can be realistically estimated. At the heart of the second issue lies quality.

An 'axiom' of software engineering is that the earlier in the life cycle a defect occurs and the longer the delay in detecting it, the greater will be the cost and effort needed to rectify the defect. This axiom has long been well established by experience, and Boehm (1976) provides firm evidence to support it. Thus, the cost and effort of (and hence delay caused in) getting rid of a requirements error discovered during acceptance testing, say, will generally be out of all proportion to eradicating a design error detected before coding – the developer might just be 'lucky' with the change needed in the first case, but it is unlikely. In short, effective quality assurance must be carried out throughout the life cycle.

Having to reconfigure software is the major 'black hole' activity of the life cycle as far as resources are concerned. Maintenance alone can devour typically at least 50% of budgets, though figures much higher than this are by no means uncommon. It follows that:

(a) The need to reconfigure should be reduced as much as possible.
(b) When reconfiguration is necessary, it should be effected with as little cost and time slippage as possible.

The software quality of 'reconfigurability' has already been overviewed in the previous section. It is again worth pointing out that any reconfiguration necessary must also be controlled and managed effectively, if disasters are to be avoided. Sound 'configuration management' is essential for successful project execution.

Obviously, resources spent on maintenance that could have been avoided, or spent on repeatedly iterating round subcycles such as (RE)DESIGN $\rightarrow$ (RE)IMPLEMENT $\rightarrow$ (RE)TEST, are resources wasted. Moreover, overshoot on estimated costs and deadlines severely disrupts projects scheduled for the future. Productivity can decrease sharply as precious resources have to be diverted from elsewhere to support existing developments that are in trouble, which in turn adds further twists to cost and time inflation. Thus, the whole process can feed on itself; and dealing with customer dissatisfaction and alienation will not be the least of the developer's problems.

Basically, the issues of cost and schedule are intimately tied up with applying principles, tools and techniques that have a proven track record in achieving good quality (or, at least, are regarded as being some of the best currently available). Moreover, as new methods are introduced that possess a sound theoretical basis or well-argued rationale, there must be commitment to apply them in practice, especially when they supersede older, well-established methods. Nothing ventured, nothing gained. The benefits may not be immediate but longer term. If an extra X% spent during the early development phases in being more rigorous and disciplined later saves Y% on reconfiguration costs where $Y \gg X$, then the risk and extra investment will be worthwhile. From a customer point of view, the situation is very similar – you generally get what you pay for.

1.6 SOFTWARE DIVERSITY

In terms of size, complexity, application, response and physical organization, software systems exhibit a vast diversity. As regards size and complexity, a system could comprise a single small program handling a couple of files, say, or it could comprise a multitude of processes interacting in highly intricate ways via complex data objects. With respect to application and response, the two largest general categories of system are data-processing systems and real-time systems. Although the reader may already be familiar with either type of system, a brief juxtaposition of their essential characteristics is worthwhile.

Data Processing Systems

These systems are predominantly concerned with the processing of data associated with the structure and operation of an organization or institution, be it industrial, commercial, educational, governmental or whatever. Typical commercial applications, for example, would include payroll, orders and invoicing, stock control and the like. Such systems form an integral part of an organization's infrastructure, being essential to its day-to-day functioning and hence successful operation. Often, specific data-processing applications are but components of a larger information system, typically centred on a database that maintains all data relevant to the organization's needs. Such a database will not only support all data processing requirements but will also provide appropriate visibility of data to all levels of management (management information systems) facilitating more effective control and planning ('decision support').

As regards response, data processing systems can be purely online, purely 'detached' (i.e. 'batch' or 'background'), or any mixture of the two. Online software processes data as and when it enters the system, rather than the data being collected for processing at an intentionally delayed date, when 'response' could be measured in terms of hours, days, weeks or even longer. With interactive or conversational online systems where there is a two-way communication between system and users, system response should be within the limits of user tolerance, preferably 'a few seconds' at worst.

Real-Time Systems

In one sense, any system can be said to be 'real-time' if it is desirable that its response is as rapid as possible to data generated by external events. Thus, on this basis, an airline reservation system, for example, could be classed as a real-time system. However, in its more specific sense, 'real-time' implies an absolute need to respond to events within specified, time-critical limits. Such systems are typified by embedded and process control systems. The term 'embedded' is used to describe the fact that the software forms part of a (typically micro) computer system that is itself but a component of a larger electromechanical system, as in medical support, processing plant and air navigation systems, for example.

'Process control' implies that the functional essence of the system is to sense, and then in some way apply control to, its surrounding environment. These characteristics set such systems quite apart from other categories of 'real-time', transaction-processing software. In the latter case, if a response is still to be forthcoming after half a minute when it was expected in a few seconds at most, frustration and impatience may well set in; but nothing worse than, perhaps, economic loss is possible. If, however, a medical support system fails to respond appropriately and immediately to deleterious changes in the respiratory rate of a critically ill patient, the result could be tragic. This latter example of an unwanted outcome is somewhat extreme; but it serves to illustrate that if a 'true' real-time system fails to respond as it should, the result will generally be 'very bad', rather than merely being annoying.

Naturally, not all systems are catered for by these two major classes. For example, science and engineering applications are generally characterized by their numerical processing requirements, performing statistical or analytical manipulations on numerical data that can demand vast amounts of processing resources, as in weather forecasting and image processing, say. Likewise, AI systems are sufficiently distinct to warrant being placed in their own separate category; in particular, they can be combinatorially problematic with respect to both time and space requirements.

An alternative way of categorizing systems is in terms of their implemented physical organization. The two main possibilities are:

Centralized

The system is implemented on a single actual machine; for simplicity, we will regard a cluster of tightly coupled processors as a single machine in this context.

Distributed

The system is spread across two or more actual machines that communicate with each other as nodes in some network topology via sequential message passing.

Some of the potential benefits mentioned by Alford (1985a) that are obtainable from distributed systems are:

★ Increased performance due to parallel processing and greater memory capacity, giving faster execution rates and response times.
★ Improved cost-effectiveness due to economies of scale, since it may be cheaper to manufacture, install and maintain a number of small-scale machines than a large-scale machine with equivalent performance.
★ Better hardware availability, since a faulty component (e.g. node or communication link) no longer means that the whole processing resource is disabled.

* Increased system reliability and robustness, since the system may be able to recover from component failure by reconfiguring and rescheduling processes on available nodes whilst the fault is repaired, or the faulty component is replaced by a spare part.
* Extensibility in size and performance via the addition of extra processing nodes and communication links, providing the software can be reconfigured to take advantage.

The development of network and communications technology in recent times makes distributed implementations a practical alternative, despite he greater complexities associated with their specification, design and implementation.

We could dwell on the variability that exists in other system features. But the purpose of this section has merely been to give an overall impression of the multifaceted diversity of software that software engineering has to deal with. Despite this diversity, a great deal of what can be said about the principles and methods of software engineering is independent of the 'variability' factors outlined, as the remaining chapters attempt to demonstrate.

BIBLIOGRAPHY

A number of general texts on software engineering are currently available. These include Jensen & Tonies (1979), Pressman (1982), Sommerville (1985), Fairley (1985) and Macro & Buxton (1987). Shooman (1983) is also in this category, possessing a bias towards software complexity, testing and reliability, which receive quite a detailed mathematical treatment. Birrell & Ould (1985) give a comprehensive, life-cycle coverage of current software development practices and methods. Vick & Ramamoorthy (1984) contains much useful material relevant to this book, although the early chapters are more theoretical in nature (dealing with complexity, modelling, graphics, etc.). Although these works between them contain a wealth of references and extensive bibliographies, Yourdon (1982) provides a quick route into some twenty-five important papers in software engineering that have appeared in the last two decades or more.

As regards periodicals, etc., *IEEE Transactions on Software Engineering* is indispensable. Another important publication is *ACM SIGSOFT Software Engineering Notes*. Papers and articles of interest on software engineering can frequently be found in *IEEE Software, Computer* and (to a lesser extent) *IEEE Transactions on Computers*. Other journals such as *ACM SIGPLAN Notices* and *Software Practice and Experience* should also be consulted regularly. 'Mainstream' journals such as

Communications of the ACM and *ACM Computing Surveys* from time to time publish papers on software engineering topics. Lastly, the recently introduced *IEE Software Engineering Journal* should prove an invaluable source of material.

If the reader wishes to obtain a quick, general appreciation of software engineering before immersion in textbooks, then papers such as Boehm (1976), Zelkowitz (1978) and Ramamoorthy *et al.* (1984) should be read. Slightly more advanced, though providing an up-to-date account of software engineering techniques that support 'programming in the large', is Ramamoorthy *et al.* (1986).

Chapter 2

Software Foundations

2.1 SYSTEM ORIGINS

A development task might be purely 'soft', consisting of either development of stand-alone product software or bespoke software. Often in the second case, however, the software is but part of a larger, computer-based system to be developed that itself could be just a component required in an even larger task or 'mission'. A computer-based system thus arises by one of the following routes:

as a component of a set of 'operational requirements' to accomplish some overall mission;

by computerization of an existing real-world manual or mechanized system comprising people and/or devices but not computer hardware.

A software-based system therefore arises either:

as a component of a computer-based system; or

as a complete system development product running on existing hardware; or

as (part of the) replacement for an existing computerized system that is approaching obsolescence.

A computerized system in its entirety – the hardware, software, possibly firmware (i.e. programs in ROM, or read-only memory), and people (e.g. computer operators) – does not function in isolation. Rather, it is a subsystem embedded in some surrounding real-world environment with which it interacts via often highly complex patterns of communication – monitoring, controlling, informing, servicing, even adapting that environment (see Fig. 2.1). Thus, in the most general sense possible, all computer systems are 'embedded'. This viewpoint can be compared with the notion of 'E-type' software in Lehman's (1980) classification of programs into three basic types:

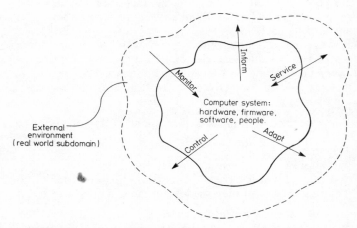

Fig. 2.1. Computer system-real world interactions.

S programs

An S program satisfies a fixed problem that admits to precise, formalizable specification. An S program can, in principle, be verified against its specification and does not evolve once developed. An example would be the 'Eight Queens' program (see Wirth 1971).

P programs

A P program needs to evolve because, although its specification may be precise, it involves approximation to the universe of discourse that it addresses; e.g. a chess playing program. The evolution of a P program is thus concerned primarily with improving its acceptability or validity in the (real-world) context in which it is used.

E programs

An E program computerizes some external world system that it (inadequately) models. This results in the program unpredictably changing the environment in which it becomes embedded. E programs must therefore evolve to remain useful. Moreover, 'correctness' of an E program can be evaluated only with respect to the adequacy of its behaviour and performance under operational conditions.

Lehman postulates that all P and E programs can be partitioned into S-type components – an echoing of the fact that the behaviour of a complex system is much more than, and cannot be predicted by, a mere summation of its parts.

Taking a real-world 'environmental' view of computer systems forms the basis of *systems analysis*. Systems analysis is that extensive set of preliminary fact-finding and analysis activities in the genesis of a new computer system, the objectives of which are to seek answers to such crucial questions as:

* Is a computerized system (or replacement for the current one) really needed?
* If YES, then:
  What should be its desired characteristics?
  What impact will it have on its surrounding environment?
  What resources and plan of development will be needed?

Pressman (1982) gives a useful overview of the issues and techniques involved in systems analysis. A taxonomy and brief descriptions of some of the main analysis methodologies are presented by Wood-Harper & Fitzgerald (1982). Ceri (1986) discusses analysis phases and objectives and also reviews and compares current analysis methodologies applicable to information systems development. As systems analysis is a large topic in its own right, its detailed discussion is not intended to lie within the scope of this book. Nevertheless, we shall present a brief summary of some central analysis issues that have a profound influence on the viability and success of software engineering projects. Inadequate systems analysis leads inevitably to inadequate computer systems; and the latter foster confusion, disillusionment, dissatisfaction and alienation amongst (most definitely) users and (probably) development staff as well. The main areas of concern, and associated problems to avoid, are as follows:

The Need

Avoid: – computerization for the sake of it;
          – developers starting with a ready-made solution looking for a non-existent problem.

Once a need for computerization has tentatively been perceived, systems analysis seeks to:

* Understand and define the problem in a total system context, i.e. analyse the current system, identifying its defects and thus the desired improvements.

★ Propose and evaluate alternative solutions.
★ Select the most appropriate solution and justify the proposal. Computerization should bring tangible benefits, such as improvements in one or more of the following areas: job satisfaction, cost-effectiveness, timeliness of information, efficiency, accuracy, accessibility/visibility of data, or management control.

The Commitment

Avoid: – rash commitment to an over-ambitious proposal.

Thorough analysis and evaluation must be performed to ensure, as far as is possible, that the proposed solution is feasible. All projects are subject to constraints of various kinds – temporal, financial, technological and legal amongst others. It must be determined whether or not the proposal lies within the 'feasibility window' defined by whatever constraints exist. In particular, commitment to unrealistic timescales and budget estimates must be avoided. Thus, estimation of likely costs and resources is essential, as well as planning and scheduling the development of the system and its subsequent implementation.

The Consultation

Avoid: – insufficient (at worst, non-existent) consultation with relevant parties.

Fact-finding, feedback and evaluation are essential ingredients of systems analysis. In order to acquire relevant information about the existing system and thus determine the desired characteristics of its replacement, access to any current system documentation will be necessary. In addition, consultation with users at all levels will need to be carried out via interviews and questionnaires. Regular meetings and reviews should be held with user authorities to help resolve conflicting opinions and solidify half-formed ideas, and to provide feedback and the opportunity for user evaluation of the analyst's conclusions and recommendations. It is meaningful and sympathetic user consultation and participation during the various stages of systems analysis that foster user confidence in the competence of the developers and in the fact that they (the users) will be supplied eventually with something that adequately satisfies their needs.

The Documentation

Avoid: – inadequately documented records (of meetings, etc.), recommendations, definitions and specifications.

Documentation can be inadequate for a number of possible reasons,
e.g. it might be incomplete, inconsistent, ambiguous, irrelevant, incomprehensible, poorly structured or stylistically incompetent. Where user
approval is also needed, it should be user comprehensible, rather than
being a morass of technical detail that can be penetrated only by
computer specialists. This can be quite a difficult problem to overcome
if what is being documented is technical in nature. We shall return to
this issue later.

Note: naturally, a customer organization might perform its own analysis
studies, derive a set of requirements and then survey the software
market. It is quite possible that the requirements could be satisfied by
existing applications packages that are commercially available. Thus, we
are assuming for the purposes of our present discussion a customer-
developer relationship involving bespoke software development. As
regards terminology, 'customer' (or 'client') can imply anything from
one individual to a complex organization where there may be many
potential users of the system. The term 'user' will be applied interchangeably with 'customer', though of course a given user will not
necessarily have contractual responsibility for the system. The term
'developer' will be used both corporately and generically on an individual basis to cover systems or requirements analysts, software
engineers, designers, programmers and so on. The reality of the
distinction between the roles of such people is a fuzzy boundary
problem that is largely a matter for actual developer organizations to
resolve. Note also that 'customer' and 'developer' might be part of the
same organization.

Once a project has passed its feasibility review, the first main deliverables of the analysis process will be two distinct sets of documentation:

(1) System Definition: this will set out the salient features of the desired
computer system, such as:
  ☆ broad definition of problem addressed;
  ☆ system objectives and envisaged benefits;
  ☆ description of the environment that the system will service;
  ☆ system functionality described in the most general terms and
    distributed amongst various subsystem elements;
  ☆ customer-specified criteria for accepting the system.

(2) Project Management Plan: whereas the System Definition describes overall WHAT is to be achieved, the Project Management Plan (PMP) describes overall HOW it will be achieved. That is, it will set out in as much detail as possible the 'software engineering framework' within which the project will be executed. The main contents of the PMP (e.g. see Metzger 1981) will be:

☆ *breakdown*: of development work into phases/activities with associated milestones, deliverables, review points;
☆ *organization*: of staff and their allocated responsibilities;
☆ *estimates* (to be refined and revised later as appropriate) of, for example:
    effort required, e.g. how many person-months
    timescale
    cost
    computing resources needed
    distribution of effort, time, etc. over various phases
    scheduling of activities, development work products, etc.
☆ *techniques*: any special development tools or methods to be used;
☆ *plans* for:
    quality assurance
    configuration management
    validation and *verification*
    system and *acceptance testing*
    delivery, installation and *maintenance* of product.

We will return to a detailed examination of the main ingredients of project management identified above in later chapters.

The phase of analysis that follows the feasibility and system definition stages belongs to the realm of software requirements engineering, i.e. determining and specifying in sufficient detail what the system software component should be. We have assumed in our discussion so far a 'total system' project involving hardware, etc. as well as software. For a project that is entirely 'soft', the functionality described in the system definition is mainly a detailed description of software requirements (see following sections).

It is at the software requirements stage that analysis and software engineering begin to overlap. Before discussing the analysis and definition of software requirements, we shall present an example of a system development problem. The example, which is realistic though very modest in its scope and complexity, is intended to provide an illustrative base for subsequent material.

Example Problem Scenario

The University's computer science department possesses a Nirvana hypermini that can support a large number of online users. The machine is used primarily for teaching purposes, especially to support Pascal programming courses which form part of several first-year undergraduate degree programmes. The Pascal system implemented on the Nirvana, named PATSY (PAscal Teaching SYstem), includes a special-purpose screen editor. The editor accepts Pascal source code, generates an internal, tokenized representation (from which the original source is easily recompiled), and in so doing carries out simple low-level syntax checking. Tokenized forms, correct or otherwise, whether of partial or complete programs, are automatically saved by PATSY for future editing. Complete tokenized programs can be translated down to machine code by the main compiler and optionally run if a clean compilation is obtained.

At a departmental staff meeting, it is decided that it would be worthwhile developing a system to monitor student performance and usage of PATSY.

Brief Analysis

This has been carried out by staff involved in teaching Pascal. Their deliberations have led them to the following consensus conclusions:

(a) At present, there is absolutely no feedback about usage of the PATSY system, either in general terms (e.g. patterns of loading throughout the day, or on different days of the week), or specifically with respect to individual students. The latter is seen as particularly desirable when judging a student's perceived performance (via coursework, say) against his or her actual usage of the system. The only way to obtain the desired information would be by implementing a 'bigbrother' monitoring system on the Nirvana.

(b) The new system, codenamed SUMS (Student Usage Monitor System), would obviously impose additional overheads on an already heavily used machine. However, estimates suggest that SUMS will be relatively small (at most a few thousand lines of high-level source code) and could be scheduled to run, in part, at times of low-volume Nirvana usage.

(c) SUMS will clearly need to interact with the PATSY system, which will therefore have to be modified with possible consequent degradation in its performance. However, the source code of PATSY (written largely in Pascal) is available for maintenance purposes; and the modifications required are envisaged as being relatively minor.

Furthermore, any performance degradation is likely to be apparent only during peak loads, and is considered to be worth the price.

(d) The development task, which is completely 'soft' and requires no additional equipment, is estimated to be about 1 person-year. Two of the department's research assistants are requested to carry out the development work in order that it is completed well before the start of the next academic session, when the department wants SUMS operational. The research assistants involved are capable, experienced with Pascal and STOPS – the Nirvana's Single Tasking OPerating System – and familiar with the idiosyncracies of the Nirvana and PATSY.

Overall Conclusion

Determination of the exact requirements for the system and subsequent development of the necessary software and its associated documentation should go ahead immediately. A member of staff will function as 'project manager', who will hold reviews with the two research assistants at regular intervals (yet to be determined) to monitor progress, perform quality assurance checks, etc.

2.2 SOFTWARE REQUIREMENTS ANALYSIS

We have seen that, in a computer-based system development project, analysis will result in a preliminary allocation of certain system elements to software as specified within the system definition. Analysis must also determine detailed requirements for the software component; in a 'soft-only' development task, this might represent the bulk of the analysis task. The overall objective of software requirements analysis can be stated as follows:

To determine a complete, consistent and realizable set of properties and constraints for the intended software that will adequately satisfy user needs and objectives.

Whether the eventual system is 'adequately satisfactory' will be judged by customer representatives (users) during acceptance testing.

Software properties and constraints can be partitioned into several different kinds. The illustrative examples in the categorization that follows have been expressed informally in natural language – a point for the reader to reflect back upon in Section 2.3.

Domain Requirements

As already stated, no computer system exists in isolation but, rather, is embedded in some real-world environment with which it has to interact. Domain requirements capture the relevant 'subject matter' of that environment. Using two completely different kinds of system – one data processing, the other real time – as examples, this subject matter might include:

(a) customers, orders, payments etc.; or
(b) engine, gears, exhaust flow, etc.

Although there are different methods of describing real-world subject matter, it is analysis of real-world 'entities', their properties and the relationships that exist between them that forms the basis for building a stable, well-structured system – that is, a system that in some sense adequately reflects or *models* the nature of the environment it services. As will be seen, permanent system data such as a system database is derived from domain requirements.

Functional Requirements

This category is concerned with the functionality that the software must possess in order that it performs the services required of it and so interacts with its environment in a meaningful manner via inputs and outputs. 'Function' is unfortunately a somewhat overloaded term in software development. For now, we will merely note that, at a more detailed descriptive level, many internal software functions will not be directly concerned with capturing real-world input or generating real-world output. However, from the 'macroscopic' viewpoint of users, it is precisely through input and output interaction that software functionality is experienced and utilized. Here are two examples:

(a) On request, a list of all customers whose accounts are in debit must be displayed.
(b) Average fuel consumption must be computed and displayed at regularly clocked intervals.

Exception Requirements

Although really part of the functionality of software, exception requirements merit separate consideration, pertaining as they do to a system's response to erroneous or unpredictable events. Determining exception requirements could be regarded as contingency planning, for the reliability of a system hinges very much upon whether, and how, such events are handled. For example:

(a) If the BREAK key is pressed during a transaction on the accounts database, the transaction should be aborted and no associated update(s) committed.
(b) If no reading is being received from the odometer, a message to that effect should be generated, indicating that average fuel consumption figures can no longer be displayed.

Interface Requirements

These requirements relate to the form in which information is to be presented to, and received from, a system – an area where there exists enormous scope and variety; a brief overview of some of the main possibilities has already been given in Section 1.4. Interfaces should be engineered for people where people are involved – a simple statement whose validity some actual systems do not appear to uphold. Thus, determination of user-interface requirements should be very much user driven – it is the human interface, as well as other properties such as reliability, by which users judge system quality. Here are two simple examples:

(a) The database choice menu should be displayed vertically in the centre of the screen and comprise the following options formatted as shown:

> ENTER   (to create new tables in database)
> QUERY   (to interrogate the database)
> UPDATE   (for processing transactions)
> SPECIAL (special subsidiary functions)
> HELP   (to get more information)
> RETURN   (to return to the main menu)

User choice is to be made by the mouse, positioning the cursor anywhere over the desired option name, which is to be displayed with its description in reverse video.
(b) The average fuel consumption should be displayed thus:

> Av. fuel cons. is D*D.D l/km;
> Dist. travelled is D*D.D km.

$(D^* = 0$ or more D's; D = numeric digit)

Performance Requirements

Performance, or 'non-functional', requirements define the time and space criteria – operational constraints – that the system must satisfy. These constraints relate to such factors as:
* The timeliness of information that is processed.
* The timeliness of system responses.
* The storage bounds within which the system must operate.
* The online load the system must be able to handle.
* The processing rate the system must be capable of.
* The data-flow rates that must be handled across the system boundary.
* The frequency of malfunctioning, i.e. reliability.

For example:

(a) The system should be able to process an average of 100 database transactions per second during the peak 8-hour period 09.00 to 17.00 hours.
(b) Average fuel consumption should be updated and displayed automatically at default intervals of 1 minute and relate to the total journey so far undertaken.

Requirements analysis thus involves identifying and dealing with an extremely complex set of interrelated issues and problems, solutions to which have to be formulated, specified, validated, agreed upon and subsequently adhered to. In many ways, requirements analysis is the hardest part of the software life cycle because customer views concerning the system might be vague, ill conceived or in conflict; and there might be a general lack of understanding of what the system is supposed to do if the problem domain that the system addresses is complex or innovatory. Difficulties can be encountered even when replacing an existing system with a new version. Heninger (1980) discusses the rewriting of the requirements for an existing real-time aircraft flight program and reports that:

* No requirements document existed for the current program.
* None of the current documentation was entirely accurate.
* No one individual knew the answers to all questions asked.
* Different answers to the same question were received from different people.
* Some answers could be obtained only by experimenting with the existing system.

Requirements analysis is also the most critical part of the life cycle, because if the eventual delivered system is not what users want, it is essentially worthless, irrespective of other desirable characteristics that it might possess. Unwanted systems foster and entrench user cynicism towards computerization and also damage the reputation of the developers. In practical terms, extensive redevelopment may be required to repair requirements defects in a delivered product. This redevelopment will be both time consuming and costly, though who pays will depend on contractual agreement; in extreme cases, legal action might ensue, probably with each side apportioning blame to the other. As Brooks (1986) states: 'The hardest part of building a software system is deciding precisely what to build. ... No other part of the work so cripples the resulting system if done wrong. No other part is more difficult to rectify later.'

It follows that extensive customer participation in the requirements engineering phase is of paramount importance and is the key to successful systems. Both sides have their responsibilities – the developer to involve users appropriately, and users to co-operate constructively in their requested involvement. As to the actual extent to which user participation can occur, both in analysis and design, Mumford (1980) defines three levels that are relevant in different contexts:

'Consultative':   Users are consulted but they have no say in the system design itself, e.g. when senior management seek to obtain approval from the workforce for future strategy.

'Representative': User representatives become involved in defining the boundaries and broad form of a future system.

'Consensus':   There is appropriate continuous participation of all users throughout the system design process.

We shall not discuss the practicalities and methodological implications of building in high levels of user participation into systems development (see Mumford *et al.* 1978). Suffice it to say here that the main way of achieving high levels of user participation in system design is to provide users with software tools that allow them to build and experiment with prototypes – a topic dealt with in Section 2.4.

However, regardless of the analysis philosophy adopted, the trained and experienced analyst will know the most effective way to elicit the relevant information from users, depending on the kind of customer organization involved and system required. Also, the successful analyst must function as a dual personality, being able to appreciate system problems both from a user's perspective and from a developer's viewpoint. As Ceri (1986) concludes, analysts who are technicians '... should recognize the importance of organization and human problems ...' and analysts who are social experts '... should accept the fact that ... requirements descriptions should contain enough technical information to enable subsequent design phases'. Certainly, the ability to communicate effectively with all parties concerned, from end-users to software engineers, is essential. What users want does not always match with what is cost-effectively or technically realizable, practical or consistent. So, for example:

A domain-functionality inconsistency

Well, in principle you can have a system function that interrogates discount purchases made by employees, but employees have not been included in the system domain.

An impossibility

It is not possible to distinguish between accidental, as opposed to deliberate, pressing of the BREAK key.

More cost-effective choice available

The colour graphics interface you are suggesting is fine in principle, but due to the cost of the special hardware needed together with the extra software complexity involved, we would recommend that you consider simpler alternatives.

A conflicting requirement

If you want combined customer, product and sales data to be immediately accessible and displayed in the manner described, then transaction processing rate is unlikely to meet your stated minimum acceptable level even during non-peak loading.

The analysis process must detect and then filter out or repair all such requirements anomalies. Deciding what is realizable is a matter for professional judgement, though completeness (or lack of it) from a user viewpoint can only be discovered by review. However, technical inconsistencies and conflicts may be easier defects to check for, since some requirements methods support automated verification to an extent, and this acts as a valuable adjunct to review procedures. We shall look at requirements validation and verification in more detail after the next section.

2.3 EXPRESSING REQUIREMENTS

Requirements Documentation

Appropriate documentation of the results of requirements analysis is clearly crucial to the success of a project, for once validated and agreed upon, this documentation becomes the defining top-level reference for all subsequent software development and maintenance. Important issues here are the notations and languages to be used in expressing requirements, together with the degree of 'computer system detail' contained therein. The importance is due to the fact that requirements need to be conveyed to, and understood by, two quite different sets of people: users and developers.

In one sense, any expression of requirements can be regarded as a '(system) specification', since it will inevitably contain at the very least a top-level WHAT description of the complete system. Moreover, it is frequently argued that a statement of requirements should be purely WHAT and not contain any HOW (design or implementation detail). Yet actual requirements specifications, particularly those that are developer-oriented and hence are technical documents largely expressed in terms of formalized notations and concepts, sometimes do contain a certain degree of HOW descriptive detail. In practice, when comparing development methods, there may be no real difference of content between a 'requirements specification' (or definition) of one development method, a 'system specification' of another method or even 'system design' of yet another. As Section 1.3 indicated, the fuzziness associated with interpreting certain nomenclature is partly a product of the somewhat over-generalized view of software development embodied in the conventional life-cycle model.

For our purposes, we shall regard a 'requirements specification' as a 'software (i.e. system or program) specification'; that is, it is primarily a technical document intended to function as the top-level reference from which all subsequent software development ensues. Whether or not users also are able to comprehend such a document raises the general question: can a single requirements document suffice for both user and developer? The problem here is that users are unlikely to be familiar with the formalisms used in developer-oriented specifications. Moreover, the latter may contain much technical detail that is irrelevant and incomprehensible to users – users are concerned only that the stated requirements adequately embody all system attributes that will satisfy their real-world aspirations for the new system. Unfortunately, though users will understand narrative description, natural language is the worst vehicle for achieving precision in any form of specification because:

* It is inherently very complex.
* It is unreliable, i.e. its use is frequently, and unintentionally, imprecise, ambiguous or inconsistent.
* Its syntax and semantics are clumsy and inappropriate for the
expression of abstract concepts and relationships needed to specify
software requirements.

In practice, the best compromise, where compromise is necessary, is to
have two documents:

(A) A narrative-based requirements document that is user oriented and
could be termed the 'user requirements definition'.
(B) A technical requirements specification that is mainly for developers, though knowledgeable users might be party to its contents.

Document (A) might be prepared by the customer organization itself,
possibly with outside professional help. The important point is that the
user requirements definition should express the system requirements
from an external, user viewpoint in terms that are user-comprehensible.
This is not to say that such a document necessarily employs only
narrative description – some formal diagrammatic notations and languages understood by trained users could be used. Indeed, there might
well be some commonality of formalism between (A) and (B). Furthermore, if there is essentially a one-to-one correspondence between (A)
and (B) (which is not necessarily the case – they merely have to be
consistent), and all formalisms used in (B) are user-comprehensible,
then the need for two separate documents disappears. Usually though,
it will be necessary to construct a separate requirements specification
that correctly satisfies the user requirements definition. It may even be
the case that requirements analysis is followed first by the production of
document (B) in advance of (A). Indeed, it will generally be easier to
construct an adequately precise informal description from a formalized
specification, than vice versa. There is also one other advantage to this
'backwards' mapping from (B) to (A): the process can be automated to
an extent. Naturally, users must rely on the competence of the developers to construct a software specification that preserves all aspects of
their articulated requirements. Again, the process of user consultation
can be employed as the vehicle for explaining to users in terms of their
requirements definition the ramifications of a technical specification. It
may even be preferred to merge (A) and (B) into a single document;
thus, the text of (A) becomes informal explanatory insertions for users
in (B). There is also another route to user comprehension of technical
specifications that is described in the next section – namely, specification
execution.

Techniques for Expressing Requirements

A variety of notations and methods exist for the expression of require-ments. We will not be concerned here with purely informal techniques, even though use of natural language dominates user requirements definitions. Instead, we shall briefly survey the main characteristics of a number of different techniques that possess varying degrees of formality, from some formal syntactic structure to complete mathe-matical rigour (Roman 1985 includes a classification of requirements methods in terms of key attributes such as their scope, degree of problem domain specialization, level of formality etc.). Some of the techniques we shall mention are usable within user requirements definitions; others are suitable only for technical requirements specifi-cations. The survey is representative rather than comprehensive, and intentionally contains no detailed exposition or example usage of any technique; the references quoted will enable the interested reader to follow up a particular technique in more depth if desired. Many of the techniques mentioned here, and others besides, are described in some-what greater detail in Birrell & Ould (1985).

SADT(TM)

SADT (Structured Analysis and Design Technique – see Ross 1977; Ross & Schoman 1977; Ross 1985) is a graphical-based method aimed primarily at hierarchical description of the structures of systems, com-puterized or otherwise. It also provides a methodology for project management and control, e.g. organizing personnel, recording the results of reviews, etc. The formal graphical language is relatively easy to learn and comprehend and so is suitable for application in user requirements definitions.

Requirements are expressed in SADT via hierarchies of diagrams called 'models', possibly supplemented by explanatory text. A model, which can either be process oriented or data oriented, represents one individual's or group's 'viewpoint' of the desired system. If there are several viewpoints, they must of course represent consistent models of the same system. It should be noted that the notation and methodology is suitable for both requirements specification and system design. Therefore, it is not surprising that the boundary between these two phases is somewhat blurred in SADT.

SREM

SREM (Software Requirements Engineering Methodology – see Alford 1977; Bell *et al*. 1977; Alford 1985b; Scheffer *et al*. 1985) is part of an overall methodology (SYSREM) for the development of time-critical, distributed real-time systems. Like SADT, a special graphical notation is used, requirements being specified in terms of diagrams called R-NETs. An R-NET depicts the functional processing that is 'stimulated' by arrival of a given input through to the eventual 'response' (outputs) produced. Inasmuch as an R-NET specifies such detail, R-NETs therefore capture a degree of high-level design.

SREM also incorporates a Requirements Statement Language (RSL) and automated tool support. More specifically, R-NETs can be expressed equivalently in RSL, to which additional material can be added, such as textual description. RSL specifications are then translated and stored in a relational database to form an ASSM (Abstract System Semantic Model). Automated tools can then interrogate the database to check the requirements for completeness, consistency, etc. and produce error reports. It is also possible to generate automatically from the database simulations of the specified system in order to carry out requirements validation.

The specialized role of R-NET/RSL notation – to define the stimulus-response processing needs of a real-time system – suggests that it is less suitable for general use in expressing user requirements than other (semi-)formalized notations.

PSL/PSA

PSL/PSA (Problem Statement Language/Problem Statement Analyser – see Teichrow & Hershey 1977; Winters 1979) is, as its name suggests, a combination of a language for expressing requirements and a support tool. Its main use in practice tends to be as front-end requirements definition support for a variety of development methods, although it can be used for documenting design as well. In a similar manner to RSL of SREM, system requirements are specified (modelled) in PSL and then translated and stored in a database that can then be interrogated by the PSA tool-kit of report generators. The amenability of PSL descriptions to database representation is perhaps reflected by the fact that PSL models systems in terms of 'objects' that possess 'attributes', objects being connected to form a complete system by various 'relationships' (which is familiar database terminology, although objects in PSL can be events, processes, etc. as well as data).

Although PSL is substantially formal, with some training users could become accustomed to PSL-type descriptions in user requirements definitions of information systems, for which application domain PSL is probably best suited.

Structured Systems Analysis (SSA)

SSA is not to be confused directly with SADT, though they share much in common, as their names suggest (see also Mullery 1979 for a similar graphically based method called CORE). SSA is an overall method encompassing a collection of useful modelling and descriptive tools that can be applied to initial phases of the life cycle. The graphical notation in particular can be applied to the description of systems in general, whether computerized or not (in fact, the notation has already been applied in Fig. 1.2 of Section 1.3). The notation is easy to learn and understand, and so can be used not only as a vehicle for analyzing an existing system, but also for specifying the requirements of a proposed system in a user-comprehensible manner. A requirements specification in SSA represents a functional model of the proposed system. Because of its importance as a specification method and as a front-end to sister methods like Structured Design, SSA will be described in more detail in the next chapter. Definitive works on the method include DeMarco (1978), Weinberg (1978) and Gane & Sarson (1979).

Data Analysis

Whereas SADT or SSA, say, model the *functionality* of an existing real-world system to act as a basis for deriving a functional specification of the proposed system, data analysis techniques develop non-functional models of the real world (compare also Jackson System Development, introduced below). Data analysis can be regarded as a systems analysis technique that:

★ Acquires relevant information (by standard systems analysis procedures) about the organization that the new system will service.
★ Models this information in terms of 'entities' (real-world objects of interest) and their relationships and attributes (properties) to build a 'conceptual schema' that will later be used to derive a database supporting functional requirements.

Although the approach is geared towards developing information systems with database, it is also of general use in determining and specifying in an abstract, implementation-independent manner the data requirements of any proposed system. Moreover, the concepts and notations used are easily understood by users. The general approach to systems development that data analysis supports will be discussed in the next chapter. Data analysis can be found described in Howe (1983), for example.

Programming Languages

The utilization of a programming language as a means of introducing formality into requirements specification is an obvious possibility to be explored. However, apart from unsuitability for user requirements definition (unless users happened to be familiar with the language used – unlikely), there is one major drawback: programming languages are generally too low level. As a result, they would:

be unable to express the high level of abstraction needed in requirements specification;
unavoidably imply implementation detail.

Nevertheless, Ada$^{(TM)}$ (DoD 1983) has been under scrutiny in recent years precisely for this purpose; this is due, no doubt, to the fact that its specification capabilities transcend those currently offered by most other commonly used procedural languages. Goldsack (1985) explores the potential of Ada both as a specification language and as a means of modelling systems as collections of interacting 'objects'; an Ada-derived language (Dad) for general systems specification is also introduced. The general conclusion is that Ada, whilst versatile in some aspects of specification, is inadequate in meeting all the requirements of a specification language. One way to make Ada more suitable for specification is to modify and augment it appropriately, as with the specification language Anna (Luckham & von Henke 1985).

Formal Specification

Completely formal specification requires a specification language that is mathematically precise in both syntax and semantics. Arguably, certain methods of formal specification are able to offer a degree of abstraction that allows specifications to be constructed that are purely WHAT, containing no HOW detail whatsoever. Formal specification is intimately tied up with formal verification (of design correctness). Together, these two activities constitute what are usually termed 'formal methods' of software development. The importance of formal methods is such that a later chapter is devoted entirely to their discussion. Obviously, formal specification lies outside the realms of user requirements definitions, and so translation from formal specifications to informal definitions is required here (see also 'executable specifications' in Section 2.4). For a general coverage of formal specification issues and techniques, Gehani & McGettrick (1986) can be consulted.

An Example: Requirements for the SUMS System

The aim of this example is to create an impression of what might be contained in a combined user/technical requirements specification comprising a mixture of formal and informal notation. The example details a partial set of requirements for the SUMS system that was defined in outline in Section 2.1. The requirements are partitioned according to the five categories enumerated in Section 2.2. In the first category (domain requirements), the technique associated with Jackson System Development (JSD) has been used (Jackson 1983; Cameron 1986). Other requirements categories are dealt with mainly in a manner that is not method specific, although some of the descriptive structures used in the second category (functional requirements) have been influenced by JSD characteristics. Emphasis has been placed on domain and functional requirements, as these will be central to the illustration of system development to be given in the next chapter.

SUMS domain requirements

A real-world domain in JSD is dynamic rather than static. It is described not in terms of passive data relationships, but in terms of actions performed or suffered by real-world entities constituting the domain of interest and which characterize the behaviour and experience of those entities through time. Naturally, there are certain ground rules to apply in determining whether some feature of the real world is a proper entity or action and, given that it is, whether it should be included in the domain requirements, e.g. on grounds of relevance or feasibility; developers can provide users with suitable guidance in these respects. The eventual outcome is a user-specified list of entities (more usually, entity types), their associated actions, and for each action a preliminary list of attributes, which are data elements that characterize the properties of an action. In the following specification, action names are in upper case and are followed by an informal description in braces; a tentative list of attributes (the lower case names) is given for each action.

Entity type STUDENT

REGISTER {become an allowed user of the Nirvana machine in
                general, and hence the PATSY system in particular}
   name, date, department, course, log_on_code
TERMINATE {cease to be an allowed user of the Nirvana machine}
   name, date, log_on_code
ENTER {initiate use of PATSY}
   log_on_code, date, time
QUIT {leave PATSY}
   log_on_code, date, time
CREATE {create a new program within the PATSY system}
   log_on_code, prog_idr, date
EDIT {use the PATSY editor to alter an existing program}
   log_on_code, prog_idr, date
COMPILE {request a program to be compiled}
   log_on_code, prog_idr, date
RUN {request a cleanly compiled program to be executed}
   log_on_code, prog_idr, date
DELETE {erase a program from the PATSY system}
   log_on_code, prog_idr, date

Entity type PROGRAM

CREATE {the program comes into existence via use of PATSY
                editor}
   log_on_code, prog_idr, date
DELETE {the program is erased from the PATSY system}
   log_on_code, prog_idr, date
COMPILE {the program is compiled}
   log_on_code, prog_idr, date
RUN {the program is executed}
   log_on_code, prog_idr, date
EDIT {the program is modified}
   log_on_code, prog_idr, date

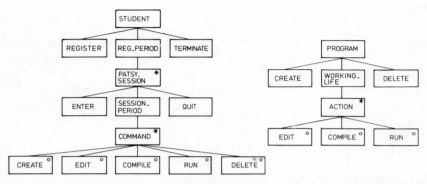

Fig. 2.2. JSD time-ordered entity structures: entity types STUDENT AND PROGRAM.

Notes

(a) The decision to model students and programs separately is an important one. By 'separating our concerns' in this way, we avoid unbridled complexity that would soon become apparent in subsequent development.

(b) All instances of an entity type in the real world must be uniquely identifiable by some means. We have assumed that student log_on_ codes are unique, and that for programs, log_on_code of student owner combined with the program identifier prog_idr will be unique.

(c) The attribute lists do not have to be complete or accurate at this stage – they are merely tentative and may be modified at a later date.

The next step is to structure each set of actions into a sequential ordering that defines their real-world time relationships over the life-span of the entity – this in effect captures the dynamics of the behaviour or experiences of the entity. This information is specified via a particular hierarchical diagrammatic notation, as illustrated in the 'entity structures' for STUDENT and PROGRAM given in Fig. 2.2. An asterisk in a box denotes iteration of the item indicated (e.g. SESSION_PERIOD is a repetition of COMMAND) and the degree symbol denotes unordered alternatives (e.g. ACTION is either EDIT or COMPILE or RUN); otherwise, strict left-to-right sequential ordering is being specified (e.g. STUDENT is REGISTER followed by REG_PERIOD and then TERMINATE). Although users in general will not be familiar with such notation initially, only a small amount of training should be necessary to make them skilled at interpreting such diagrams. Note how, in order to construct an entity tree structure, it is necessary to introduce non-primitive, intermediate lifespan components (e.g. REG_PERIOD, WORKING_LIFE etc.).

SUMS Functional Requirements

The functions defined below are expressed in a language devised by the author that permits the inclusion of natural language description. The main elements of the language are as follows:

★ Functions are 'triggered off' to produce output by some event that is specified by:

> **on** <event description> => <action(s) to be performed>

Possibilities for <event description> include:

> <action performed or suffered by some entity>, OR
>
> <message received> **from** <source>, OR
>
> <time grain marker received> **is** <time grain magnitude>

(Note: a 'time grain marker' is a message transmitted to a system at regular real-world time intervals.)

★ Entities can be referred to:

> individually, e.g. EMPLOYEE (i.e. *any* actual employee), OR
>
> universally, e.g. **all** EMPLOYEE (i.e. all employees currently within the domain of the system), OR
>
> as a subset, e.g. EMPLOYEE **selectedby** <filter>

The <filter> is a predicate that acts as the decision procedure for membership of the subset. If a name is placed in square brackets after the entity name in the latter two cases, e.g. EMPLOYEE[N], it is considered to be instantiated to the cardinality of the (sub)set.

★ A structured object is described by a list of component names between { ... }; a component can be described, if required, by a **descr** clause.

★ Components of objects are selected by dot notation, i.e. <object>. <component name>. If <object> is a set, the selection operates on all set members, thus creating a set of the selected components. If <component name> specifies a structured object, each component of the latter acts on <object>.

★ If a name appears on its own not preceded by '<object>.', it is deemed to be an action or attribute of the 'nearest' entity type. The latter can be determined by tracing back outwards through the nest of naming scopes implied by the syntactic structure surrounding the occurrence of the name in question.

★ A set can be partitioned via a **groupedby** qualifier into disjoint groups; all set members with the same value of the specified qualifier form a particular group. A group is considered to be a structured object of two components: its identification (i.e. the qualifier value common to all group members), and the set of its members. If G is a group, G.#<name> selects (i.e. instantiates <name> to) the group identification; selection of the member set is achieved by omitting the '#' mark. Furthermore, if GS is a grouped set, GS#<g_idn> selects the member set whose group identification is the value of <g_idn>.

★ A set can be ordered by an **orderedby** qualifier which specifies the ordering criterion to be applied; (+) and (−) denote increasing and decreasing order respectively.

★ A **where** clause introduces a retrospective definition.

★ A '**let** <name> **be** <object>' clause introduces for notational convenience a naming abbreviation for the <object> specified.

★ An **asin** clause references a separate interface requirement where the external presentation required of the data (input or output) to which the clause is attached is specified.

★ A **constraints** clause references one or more separate performance requirements.

★ The name USER denotes an online message source or destinaton; the name PRINTER denotes a hard-copy device.

★ The verb **do** specifies one or more actions that must be accomplished as a side effect of satisfying the functional requirement in which the **do** clause occurs.

★ Informal text can be included by a **descr** clause; the text itself is enclosed between a matching pair of delimiters (the delimiter symbol must not appear in the text itself).

Using this language, four possible functions for the SUMS system are now defined:

function FR1 **is**
  descr
    "Whenever a student quits PATSY, the totals of compilations and runs performed during that session by the student, together with the session time length, are to be appended to a file QLOG_LIST"
  on STUDENT.QUIT =>
    write STUDENT.PSN_INFO **asin** OUTR1 **to** QLOG_LIST
    where PSN_INFO **is**
    {log_on_code,
     NCOMPS   **descr** "number of compilations initiated by the student during the PATSY session just quit",
     NRUNS   **descr** "number of executions initiated ... ditto ...",
     PS_LENGTH **descr** "the length of the PATSY session just quit in minutes and seconds"
    }
  constraints PR1
end FR1;

function FR2 **is**
  descr
    "On enquiry from a terminal, the number of students currently
    within PATSY, and who they are, should be displayed"
  on E_ENQ **asin** INR1 **from** USER =>
    let SN **be** STUDENT[N] **selectedby** entered_PATSY = **true**
    write E_DSP **asin** OUTR2 **to** USER
    where E_DSP **is**
      {N, SN.LOGINFO
        where LOGINFO **is**
          {name, dept, course, log_on_code}
      }
  constraints PR2
end FR2;

function FR3 **is**
  descr
    "On request, automatically delete all program files not accessed
    within the last 180 days. List to a file FLUSH_REP the names
    and the last access dates of all such files deleted. The files listed
    should be grouped according to student owner, the latter being
    identified by log_on_code. Groups should be lexicographically
    ordered by log_on_code, and program file names within each
    group should be ordered by decreasing last access date"
  on F_REQ **asin** INR2 **from** USER =>
    let
      SP **be** PROGRAM **selectedby**
      F_REQ.date – last_access_date) >180
      GSP **be** SP **groupedby** log_on_code
    do SP.DELETE
    write F_RPT **asin** OUTR3 **to** FLUSH_REP
    where F_RPT **is**
      GSP.GRP_DESCR **orderedby** (+)LOC
      where GRP_DESCR **is**
        {#LOC,
         PROGSET.PROG_DESCR
         orderedby (−) last_access_date
        where PROG_DESCR **is**
         {prog_idr, last_access_date}
      }
  constraints PR3
end FR3;

function FR4 **is**
  descr
    "At the end of each month, print out certain details of each
    student currently registered on the Nirvana machine. Per stu-
    dent, these details are to comprise:
    ☆ the student's name, course and log_on_code;
    ☆ the total number of compilations, edits and runs initiated, and
        total PATSY time consumed, during the past month;
    ☆ the names, lexicographically ordered, of all program files
        owned by the student.
    These details are to be alphabetically ordered by student name"
  on TM **asin** INR3 **is monthly** =>
    let GPROGS **be all** PROGRAM **groupedby** log_on_code
    write MSP_RPT **asin** OUTR4 **to** PRINTER
    where MSP_RPT **is**
      all STUDENT.ST_DETAILS **orderedby** (+)name
      where ST_DETAILS **is**
        {name, course, log_on_code,
          NCOMPS **descr** "total number of compilations initiated
                      by student during the last time grain
                      interval"
          NRUNS   **descr** "total number of executions initiated
                      ... ditto ..."
          TP_TIME **descr** "total amount of time spent in PATSY
                      during ... ditto ... "
          (GPROGS#log_on_code).prog_idr
            orderedby (+)prog_idr
        }
  constraints PR4
end FR4;

SUMS Interface Requirements

In the example that follows, a special 'user interface definition' language is employed. We shall suppose that MAIN_TITLE is a component of requirement OUTR3 (associated with function FR3) that is being defined separately as OUTR3/1:

interface OUTR3/1
   defines OUTR3.MAIN_TITLE **where**
      MAIN_TITLE **is** \i, centreTD(BOX)
      BOX **is** centreLR(BAR, BAR1, TITLE_LINE, BAR1, BAR)
      BAR **is** "*" * chrsize(TITLE_LINE), \l
      BAR1 **is** "*", " " * (chrsize (TITLE_LINE)−2), "*", \l
      TITLE_LINE **is** "* FLUSH REPORT ON: ", date("dd/mm/yy"),
                       " *", \l
end OUTR3/1

Briefly, the language used possesses the following features:

★ The constituent composition of an interface component X is specified by a clause of the form: X **is** D.
★ D is a list of one or more ITEMs separated by commas (commas specify concatenation), parenthesized if necessary, where an ITEM can be:
   the name of a previously defined or yet-to-be defined interface component;
   a format control specification ' \x', which is interpreted as "move to the start of the next x"; e.g. x can be: i {= image}, l {= line}; literal text delimited by a pair of double quotes;
   a replication of the form ITEMS * R, where ITEMS is replicated R times, R being an integer expression;
★ Certain built-in functions are available, e.g. 'chrsize' (gives the size in characters of its argument), 'date' generates the date in a form according to its string argument, and 'centreTD' (or 'centreLR') specifies that its argument should be placed centrally from top to bottom (or from left to right) in an image.

The example specification is relative, being expressed in terms of 'images', which could correspond to screens, pages, or whatever is desired. Image layout requirements like this could also be specified on special forms, or alternatively via software tools designed specifically for the purpose. For users, the latter method is by far the most flexible.

SUMS Exception Requirements

Generally, an exception requirement will specify:

★ The nature of the exception.
★ What is to be done when the exception occurs, e.g. recovery actions or 'graceful closedown' actions.
★ If appropriate, what to do, or conditions to ensure are satisfied, when the system is restarted.

Here is one example:

exception EX1 **is**
  PATSY_SYSTEM_CRASH **descr** "the PATSY system becomes inoperable whilst being used"
  on PATSY_SYSTEM_CRASH => **fatal**
  on restart =>
    descr "When subsequently re-entering PATSY, a student who was in PATSY at the time of the event will be deemed to have QUIT at the time of the last action he or she performed, namely: ENTER, CREATE, EDIT, COMPILE, RUN or DELETE"
  end EX1;

Note: **fatal** means that no actions of any kind can be taken by the system when the exception occurs.

SUMS Performance Requirements

An example:

constraint PR4
  relatesto FR4
  PR4/1 **descr** "Information generated should be up to date with respect to 21.00 hours of the TM day"
  PR4/2 **descr** "Output should be ready for inspection by 9.00 hours the next working day"
  end PR4;

End Comment

All identified requirements, appropriately expressed, will be brought together to form a user requirements definition. This definition will vary greatly in size, depending on the scale and complexity of the system required – it could be a single document of a few pages in length, or possibly run into several volumes for a large real-time system, say. Its exact content, the notations and languages used therein, and the document's relationship to more technical software requirements specification and subsequent system design will depend very much on the requirements method and development method adopted. Other items possibly included in a requirements definition would be:

★ Information concerning the environments in which the product will be developed, used and maintained.
★ Priorities for implementing the system in an incremental manner, and envisaged enhancements.
★ Criteria for accepting the system, especially tests for validating that the software adheres to its stated functional and performance requirements.

The importance of requirements and their definition/specification cannot be overemphasized – they represent the 'baseline' against which the acceptability of the software end product will be judged.

2.4 REQUIREMENTS VALIDATION AND VERIFICATION

It is vital that software requirements are validated and verified as thoroughly as possible. As previously stressed, any requirements defects that are not detected until a later stage are likely to prove extremely costly to repair. Validation and verification (V&V) in general imply a process of 'detecting defects in ... '. With respect to requirements V&V, users and developers will have different viewpoints:

User validation
    Do the requirements express what we really want?
    Are they complete, i.e. does the requirements definition capture all that we desire of the new system?

Developer validation
    Are user needs consistent and non-conflicting?
    Can the requirements realistically be satisfied?

User/developer external verification
    Are the requirements consistent with the functionality stated in the system definition?

Developer internal verification
    Does the requirements specification possess any technical anomalies of syntax or semantics?

For large systems or innovative applications, these questions can be extremely difficult to answer satisfactorily. The main V&V techniques available for software requirements are as follows:

Reviews

Reviews are an important form of group V&V activity in software engineering (see Section 7.3). A review of any kind involves subjecting some form of documented deliverable to human scrutiny for the purposes of validation, verification or both. The people involved in a requirements review would be user and developer representatives; the latter will include analysts, software engineers and quality assurance and configuration management personnel. Developers will separately conduct their own internal reviews on technical requirements specifications. The objectives of an external requirements review will be mainly concerned with validating the requirements from user viewpoints and, where appropriate, verifying them against the system definition. As regards the developer's viewpoint, the majority of unrealistic, conflicting or inconsistent requirements will have been filtered out at earlier meetings by the time the final review takes place. The culmination of this review will be the signature of the user authority to some requirements definition document.

Automated Verification

Although reviews can be used for validating and verifying deliverables of any kind, the formalized expression of requirements facilitates the development of software tools that perform various automated checks. Apart from verifying syntactic legality, more importantly internal semantic consistency can be checked across various system elements – data (structure, flow), functions, input/output interfaces and communication, etc. As we have seen with the SREM and PSL/PSA methods, a translation tool builds up a database from the requirements specification; the database can then be interrogated by software tools to check consistency, generate reports, and so on (see Fig. 2.3). Automated internal verification is thus one advantage that accrues from formalizing requirements specifications. Obviously, the extent to which automated processing of informally expressed requirements is possible is limited to standard natural language text analysis techniques. However, such analyses might provide useful back-up material for documentation purposes and requirements reviews.

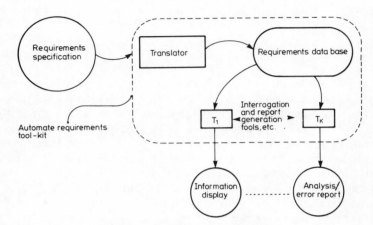

Fig. 2.3. Automated requirements verification and documentation.

Prototyping

The term 'prototyping' means rapidly building an implementation for
trial purposes. The primary objective is to provide users with a working
example of the proposed system (or components of the proposed
system) that they can evaluate and that will help them to identify and
define their requirements more precisely. As such, prototyping is mainly
concerned with evaluating functional and human interface requirements
and therefore pays little, if any, attention to other aspects of system
quality (thus, prototyping should be distinguished from system simulation, for example, which is basically used for performance evaluation).
Once it has served its purpose, a prototype may be discarded in favour
of developing what will be the actual system. However, there are several
reasons why a prototype might be retained, rather than being regarded
merely as a 'throw-away' work product in a 'do-it-twice' approach:

★ The prototype may represent the first stage in the 'evolutionary'
   development of an innovative system; that is, it may function as an
   experimental base for further development.
★ In some development environments (e.g. a 4GL environment – see
   below), the finalized prototype may be the product from which the
   required applications program is directly generated.
★ The prototype may act as an important component of the requirements definition itself.

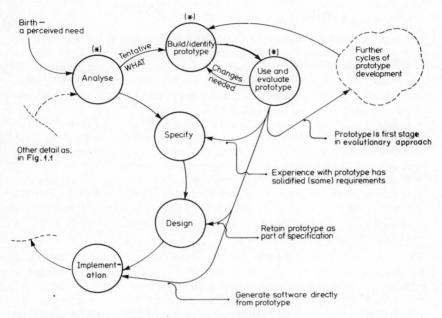

Birth –
a perceived need

(*)

(*)
Tentative
WHAT

Build/identify
prototype

Analyse

Changes
needed

(*)
Use and
evaluate
prototype

Further
cycles of
prototype
development

Other detail as,
in Fig. 1.1

Specify

Prototype is first stage
in evolutionary approach

Experience with prototype has
solidified (some) requirements

Design

Retain prototype as
part of specification

Implement-
ation

Generate software directly
from prototype

Fig. 2.4. The effect of prototyping on the traditional life cycle.

In terms of the software life cycle, prototyping creates a subiteration in the early stages of software development. This is shown in Fig. 2.4, in which the activities marked (*) are those where heavy user involvement is possible; note, therefore, how users can contribute to the specification and design of a system, as well as to identifying requirements. Increasingly, prototyping is being espoused as a technique that ought to become a standard activity of the software development process; see Dearnley & Mayhew (1983), for example. However, prototyping should be regarded as an option, not an obligation – whether or not to prototype must be a decision based on the envisaged benefits outweighing the extra costs incurred. Naturally, the same considerations also apply when deciding how many iterations of the prototyping subcycle can be afforded before users are called upon to 'freeze' their requirements – users may be tempted to 'play around' with a prototype for longer than is beneficially necessary. In fact, the main argument used against prototyping in the past has been that its associated overheads are too expensive to justify when compared with the cost of developing the actual system. However, some of today's powerful development tools enable prototypes to be quickly built and easily modified, thus transforming prototyping into a more cost-effective, advantageous technique. The advantages are as follows:

★ Users can discover, and/or experiment with, requirements ideas in an environment that corresponds closely to that which will be experienced with the eventual real product. Moreover, as a means of investigation and fact-finding, it can be far more efficient than traditional analysis methods, enabling greater quantities of information to be processed in a much shorter space of time.
★ It fosters a greater sense of participation and co-operation between users and developers. In addition, it can be educationally beneficial, providing valuable hands-on experience for users who have had little, if any, contact with computer systems previously.
★ Since a computer system will inevitably 'perturb' the environment it services, prototyping can to an extent discover in advance what the short term effects of introducing a computer system might be. The results can then be used to influence subsequent development of the system proper.

The last point is related to the system theoretic notion of an 'emergent property' of a system – that is, a property that cannot be attributed to any system component but rather to the system as a whole. Emergent properties materialize only when the complete system is operational, which is why it is extremely difficult to predict what impact a computer system will have on its surrounding environment. This in turn leads to the argument (e.g. McCracken & Jackson 1982) that system development based on a traditional life cycle model is inadequate. What is needed is a more evolutionary approach, where specification, design, implementation and evaluation are iterated throughout the system's lifespan from conception to eventual discontinuation.

The key to cost-effective prototyping is thus a rapid build plus ease-of-modification capability. The implication for a prototyping language is that it must be very high level, enabling functional and interface requirements to be easily and correctly expressed. The programming language APL, with its terse syntax, dense semantics and interactive support environment, has been used successfully by Gomaa (1983) for prototyping purposes; Gomaa presents the general rationale for, and method of, rapid prototyping as well as the specific case study. However, perhaps the greatest prototyping potential is currently offered by so-called 4GL ('fourth generation language') systems. A 4GL system – or 'applications generator' – is applicable to data processing and information system prototyping in particular. Although 4GL systems form a very broad range of development environments, varying considerably in facilities offered, application scope and intended users (anything from data processing professionals to inexperienced end-users), the make-up of a fully fledged 4GL system is typically:

★ A database management system, usually relational, with associated query and update language.
★ A data dictionary for recording and maintaining definitions of objects of relevance to the proposed system.
★ Comprehensive facilities for specifying screen formats, e.g. for data input, validation and display.
★ A sophisticated report generation facility.
★ Various other capabilities, e.g. information retrieval, graphics, decision support (statistical analyses, spreadsheets, etc.).
★ Full tool support for application program generation, with translation into conventional high-level languages.

The attraction of a 4GL system lies not merely in its prototyping capability but in the fact that actual applications can be quickly constructed and modified at a very high level, with the 'user-friendly' 4GL software reducing much of the tedium normally attached to specifying human interface requirements by conventional techniques. The general characteristics and virtues of 4GL systems can be found described and extolled in Martin (1985); Horowitz *et al.* (1985) examine application generators, including actual systems that are available.

Executable Specifications

Prototype construction provides a general means of requirements validation, particularly from a user viewpoint. However, if the development method employed generates requirements specifications that are executable, then execution ('animation') of a specification presents a direct means of validating various aspects of the requirements expressed therein. This is useful especially for users, who will generally be completely unfamiliar with the formalisms used to construct specifications that are executable. In fact, specification animation represents probably the most fruitful way of demonstrating the requirements content of a formalized specification to users. Note that, in this method, the specification is itself the prototype and there is no need for any language support for prototype construction above and beyond the specification language itself. All that is required is the development of the appropriate software tool-kit, including an interpreter for specifications written in the specification language.

Because of its advantages, executable specification is increasingly being used as a mainstream software engineering technique. Examples of methods which support this particular route into prototyping and requirements validation are:

OBJ

The OBJ language (Goguen & Meseguer 1982) and associated support system is a tool for writing and animating formal specifications of the so-called 'algebraic' variety (discussed in Section 5.2). Part of a specification in OBJ is a set of equations that can be viewed as 'rewrite' rules, and which can be executed by the OBJ interpreter, thus providing the desired capability.

Prolog

Davis (1982) shows how Horn clauses (i.e. 'X if Y' type statements, as in Prolog) can be used to derive a runnable specification from one that has been algebraically expressed.

Gist

Gist is a language designed for the specification of system behaviours (Balzer *et al.* 1982). Gist specifications function as direct prototypes – the language is operational (see below), being based on a number of 'freedoms' from implementation concerns.

PAISLey

The PAISLey language (Zave 1982; Zave & Schell 1986) has been developed to support the construction of executable specifications for real-time embedded systems. PAISLey specifies systems as sets of asynchronous processes, with the internal logic of processes being expressed in a functional (applicative) style.

Me-too

The Me-too language and method (Henderson 1986) provide a rapid prototyping capability via formal executable specifications expressed in a functional programming style. Alexander (1986) has used an extension to Me-too to prototype human-computer interaction.

Clearly, for a specification to be executable, it must embody a certain HOWness. This behavioural description, however, will be at a level of abstraction that is divorced from conventional target environments. More generally, constructing an executable specification is the first stage in the so-called 'operational' approach to software development. Zave (1984) favourably compares the operational method with conventional (i.e. standard life-cycle orientated, top-down decompositional) software development. The method comprises three broad stages:

(a) Develop an operational specification XS by an intimate mixture of requirements analysis and abstract specification and design. XS will be problem-orientated, implementation-independent and executable.
(b) Apply transformations as necessary to XS to yield XS', where XS' takes into account the actual constraints imposed by the target environment, e.g. processor and storage resources, scheduling regimes, etc.
(c) Finally express XS' in the source language(s) of the target environment to achieve a runnable system.

Advantages of the method include:

* Step (a) automatically provides a prototype (the specification).
* Many of the transformations of step (b) possess potential for automation.
* Requirements changes can be accommodated by suitably modifying XS and then reapplying the same transformations, which gives better maintainability.

Chapter 3

Software Specification and Design

3.1 PREAMBLE

Our purpose in this and the next two chapters is to explore in detail the specification and design phases of software development. We shall do this both in terms of general concepts and with respect to specific development methods. In this chapter, we shall concentrate on software development at the system level.

As indicated in the previous chapter, 'specification' is taken to mean constructing an abstract, computer-oriented representation of a set of user requirements. 'Design' is the iterative problem-solving activity of deriving a solution, expressed down to some predefined base level of representation, that satisfies a given specification. However, designing can be regarded as 'specifying in more detail', and so design products themselves are then simply more detailed specifications – a point of view echoed in Goldsack (1985). As Sommerville (1985) states, 'the activities of software specification and design are so closely connected that it is impossible to separate them'. Certainly this is true of some development methods in which there is no clear-cut transition or distinction between 'specifying' and 'designing'. Swartout & Balzer (1982) argue that specifying and 'implementing' (i.e. realizing a previous specification) are inevitably intertwined. This intertwining results because, in practice, implementation rarely achieves a true realization of a specification – rather, attempting the former highlights inadequacies in the latter which are then repaired; thus, the process of implementing generally initiates specification modification.

The specification and design components of software development still remain largely within the province of human intellect, insight, intuition and imagination though automated tools can help to reduce the 'housekeeping' load involved. Specification and design are essentially creative activities, though not entirely so; the skilled software developer is partly one who, through (long) practice and experience, acquires an increasing number of design 'paradigms' that are useful for future application to stock problem situations. Acquisition of a useful collection of standard paradigms (algorithms, etc.) reduces the tendency to 're-invent the wheel'. Reducing unnecessary development effort is also achieved by the construction of reusable software – a topic discussed in the next chapter.

In order to handle the potentially unlimited complexity and diversity that software displays, a relatively small set of underlying software concepts is needed to form the basic tool-kit of the specification and design processes. This tool-kit needs to be sufficiently general so that:

★ We have a common basis for dealing with systems of seemingly quite disparate kinds, e.g. data processing and real-time embedded systems.
★ We can exploit whatever commonality exists at all levels of software, enabling a uniform treatment to be applied where possible throughout the entire fabric of a software system.

The latter point simply reflects the realities of software architecture. For example, there is no difference in principle between two instructions in a program communicating via a shared variable and two processes in a system communicating via a database – what difference there is relates only to complexity and level, not concept. This is not to deny, however, that certain concepts and techniques may be more suitable than others at a given level of software architecture. Indeed, much of the skill of software development lies in judiciously selecting the tools and methods most appropriate to tackle the nature, scale and level of abstraction of the task at hand.

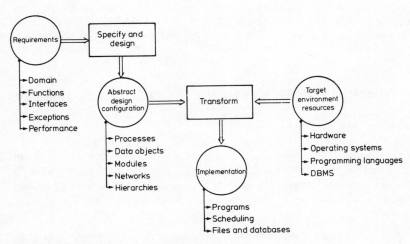

Fig. 3.1. Software development: an overall view.

The overall view of software development we shall adopt as our basic model for discussion purposes is illustrated in Fig. 3.1 (the terminology used in the diagram will be explained subsequently). The process is regarded as essentially one of abstraction and conceptualization, as captured by the joint activity of specifying and designing, followed by transformation into target machine environments, as characterized by source languages, operating systems and so on. This division into two main phases has the following advantages:

★ There is a more obvious break between specifying/designing and implementing (as we view it) than between the processes of specification and design themselves.
★ The model envisages the construction of a single 'design configuration' which can then be transformed into any number of different required implementations; there is then a clean separation between the abstract 'solution space' of the design and the numerous actual solution spaces of various target environments.

Although this model of software development is an overgeneralization that leans towards the operational approach described in Section 2.4, most development methods can nevertheless be mapped on to it with reasonable comfort. The model is also in accord with a large slice of current thinking and research in which there are two essential elements to software development: constructing a formal(ized) specification, and then implementing it, possibly via automated transformations. The 'specification' may be largely the product of what is conventionally regarded as 'design', but that is immaterial. Our aim is to portray implementation as a transformational activity in which target environment considerations have been maximally isolated from previous development phases.

3.2 SOME FUNDAMENTALS OF SYSTEM DEVELOPMENT

Modelling

It has already been mentioned in the previous chapter that a system must in some way reflect, or model, that part of the real world with which it interacts, if it is going to provide a reliable, stable service to that environment. The reasons for this principle of system construction are as follows:

(a) A system cannot meaningfully interact with a real-world environment, hence also cannot be useful or understood, unless it has some model of that environment built into it – that is, a representation in some form of the objects in that environment which the system affects, and of the behaviours that those objects exhibit or experience. For example, if a system that is intended to deal with employees' wages, say, is going to function appropriately, it must *necessarily* somehow model the employees concerned (e.g. by their names, employee numbers, tax codes, current wage rates, etc.) and their relevant behaviours (e.g. clocking in and out, taking sick leave, working overtime, getting promoted, etc.).

(b) Software systems are rarely static over their operational lifetime (Lehman 1980: the first law of program evolution states they never are – see again Sections 1.3 and 2.1). This is because real-world environments, and particularly user requirements within them, are rarely unchanging, and because introduction of a computerized system inevitably perturbs its surrounding environment anyway. Thus, a system must appropriately respond to real world changes if it is to remain useful. If a system adequately models its environment, then it is much more likely that the system can be adapted successfully to accommodate changes occurring to that environment. Furthermore, the more adaptable a system, the more maintainable it is.

Thus, the issue is not 'should real world environments be modelled in systems?', but 'how?'. As we shall see, different system development methods describe realities, and then model those realities in systems, in different ways. In Section 2.2, descriptions of (certain aspects of) realities for systems were termed 'domain requirements'; in Section 2.3, the modelling of those requirements according to one particular method (JSD) was seen in action.

Abstraction

Complexity caused by the sheer size of a problem is at its most severe in the early stages of software development when least is understood about the problem or the system required to solve it. Here, abstraction is the key tool. Abstraction facilitates the conquest of complexity by emphasizing what is relevant and suppressing what is not. It can do this in three different ways:

* Discarding, i.e. omitting irrelevant detail.
* Hiding, i.e. not revealing, or not determining, detail, knowledge of which would be unnecessary and immaterial at a given stage.
* Generalizing, i.e. capturing the common 'essence' of a collection of similar or related objects by a single description.

The process of discarding applies basically to the real-world modelling part of system development, for it is here that decisions are made as to which features of the real world are to be reflected in the system and which are not. Discarding is thus primarily an analysis, rather than a software development technique, but we include it here because the specification that results from real-world modelling is fundamental to the rest of a system's development. As an example of discarding, note that in SUMS system domain requirements specified in Section 2.3, the following (amongst others) were omitted from the model on the grounds of irrelevancy:

> members of staff and the project manager;
> students' age, sex, marks obtained in coursework, etc.;
> operating system commands;
> PATSY commands other than those specified.

It is deciding what is, and what is not, relevant that is the hardest and most critical component of the modelling process.

In the preliminary stages of specification and design, it is important not to be overwhelmed by too much detail or to concentrate unnecessarily on aspects of the system that can, and should, be left until later. Detail hiding plays its role here in two ways:

★ Existing detail can be hidden by structuring it into one or more abstract objects that in effect state WHAT, but do not reveal HOW.
★ Unrealized internal detail of an abstract object can remain hidden by temporarily deferring its realization.

The first strategy encapsulates, and has a masking effect, on previously realized HOWness. The second strategy is one of delaying decision-making on HOWness until a point is reached where such decisions can properly, or must, be made. The general principle at work in this second strategy might be described as: do not prematurely force an issue that can be resolved more satisfactorily at a later date. With either strategy, however, the end result is the same: the abstraction represents a specification that is realized by its 'implementation'.

The process of generalization simplifies. It does this by reducing to a single description what would otherwise be a proliferation of separate descriptions. Obviously, the descriptions must possess a sufficient degree of commonality for the generalization to be possible via some notational mechanism of the descriptive language employed. This exploitation of commonality can, by a variety of techniques, be applied to advantage at various stages of software development. It has already been applied to real world modelling in Section 2.3; there, a large number of different students, for example, are being modelled by a single action-attribute structure.

Composition and Separation

We can represent the make-up of all systems, regardless of their complexity, in terms of two basic kinds of component:

data objects ('data' in brief);
processing objects ('processes' in brief).

Data conveys information around a system, or to and from the real world; the data relates to either objects and events within the system itself or in the system's external environment. Processes are 'data transformers'; that is:

★ Generally, they accept (import) data from one or more sources (though, in rare circumstances, all the data that a process needs might be internally self-generated).
★ They carry out some 'function' (in the widest possible sense of the term).
★ They generate (export) one or more data objects destined for other parts of the system or real world.

Note that we are using the term 'process' in preference to 'program', say. This is because of our desire to be abstract at this stage. A process is an abstract imperative, functional or declarative prescription that can be interpreted (executed) by some virtual processor. Such objects as programs are manifestations of processes in implemented systems that are executed by real machines. Similarly, implementations of data – buffers, files, tables in a database, or whatever – do not presently concern us either.

Clearly, then, one main function of data in a system is to bind processes together to form an interacting communicational structure, where the exports of some processes become the imports of others. Thus, we might say that:

A system is a collaboration of one or more processes that communicate with each other and the real world via data objects.

The term 'collaboration' is intended to imply that, viewed as a functioning whole, the system components accomplish some meaningful overall task or set of tasks. System development is therefore concerned with deriving an aggregate of *appropriately separate* process and data objects *composed* together in such a way that they function to satisfy a given set of requirements. Obviously, precisely how this separation and composition is arrived at depends on the actual development method employed – in particular, the way the method models realities into system architecture and the abstraction techniques it adopts. As we shall see, three main architectural abstractions applied in software specification and design are:

  networks;
  hierarchies;
  modules.

These software architectures are discussed in turn in the next three sections.

Modelling Revisited

We can now see that aspects of the real world are modelled into systems by two means:

★ System data: any data permanently retained by a system models objects ('entities') in the real world (contrast this with data that transiently exists within a system merely to effect communication of occurred events from one part of the system to another).
★ System processes: processes provide a way of modelling the dynamics of events that take place in the real world.

One immediate implication is that any change in the reality modelled by a system must be followed by an equivalent change to the corresponding model component within the system – either to its retained data, or to a process that models real-world dynamics. In this way, what might be termed 'semantic consistency' is maintained between the system and the reality it models. It is the breakdown of such consistency that is a frequent cause of systems failing to perform reliably according to expectations.

3.3 NETWORKS

A network provides one possible conceptualization of system architecture. Figure 3.2 is an example, where simple diagrammatic conventions have been employed – boxes for processes, directed arcs to define flow of communication, arc labelling to indicate the data communicated. Note that a network model of software architecture is applicable at all levels – the processes in the diagram could equally well be components of a program.

  It is important to appreciate that a network diagram as in Fig. 3.2 says nothing specific about the timing relationships of process executions – the arcs merely indicate direction of communication and not passage of time (although, of course, flows of data will imply broad 'arrows of time'

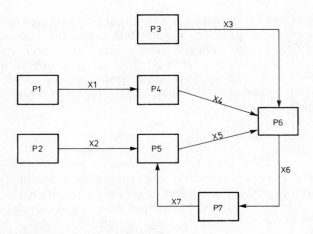

Fig. 3.2. A network of connected processes.

through a network). In fact, processes in a network are to be regarded as *asynchronously concurrent*. The term *asynchronous* means that processes operate at their own conceptual speeds – there is no notion of process executions being 'in phase' or synchronized in any way. *Concurrent* means that process executions overlap during some finite segment of time.

There are in fact substantial benefits to be gained from exploiting asynchronous concurrency as a specification and design tool:

Modelling

The real world is full of parallelism and indeterminacy. The former fact should be obvious; for example, at any given moment there could be many credit-card holders using their credit cards to effect a purchase. However, we frequently experience or unquestioningly accept indeterminacy without really being conscious of it; for example, if a credit card is used late in the month, one cannot be certain whether the charge will appear on the next statement of the one after. In other words, the timing of arrival of data generated by real-world events often cannot be predicted exactly. In interacting with their external environments, computer systems have to cope with this parallelism and indeterminacy. Asynchronous concurrency provides a basis for modelling parallelism and indeterminacy of real-world event timing in the architecture of systems.

Specification and design

As already explained, during system specification and design there is the greatest need for abstraction and flexibility, and the least need for commitment to specifics. Thus, process scheduling – deciding when to effect process executions relative to one another – is a concrete aspect of operational systems, i.e. it is an implementation issue. Concurrency enables systems to be described that are not constrained to conform to any particular scheduling regime.

Implementation

Concurrency provides a natural opportunity for exploiting certain powerful implementation tools and target environment characteristics, such as high-level languages that permit direct expression of concurrency and distributed implementations on multi-node networks, where true parallel execution is possible. Even if a given target environment provides no direct support for concurrent implementations, it is far easier to transform a system description containing concurrency into an implementation that does not, than vice versa.

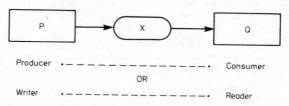

Fig. 3.3. Two connected processes.

Consider the simple case of two connected processes, as shown in Fig. 3.3. Process P could be periodically updating data object X, components of which from time to time are being read by process Q (that is, X is a component of retained system data). Alternatively, P could be a producer process generating a stream of items X that are to be consumed by Q (that is, X is 'transient' data). If P and Q are concurrent, care must be taken in the implementation to avoid certain calamities such as simultaneous access to the shared data resource X. In fact, concurrency gives rise to a number of special correctness considerations that need careful handling. For example, two general properties that system processes should exhibit are:

Safety

Informally – 'nothing bad will happen'; e.g. *mutual exclusion* is always ensured between the *critical sections* of concurrent processes (those sections of processes that access a common resource) so that simultaneous access never occurs.

Liveness

Informally – 'something that is supposed to happen will happen'; e.g. whenever a process needs to access a shared resource, it will eventually be able to do so – it will never be permanently 'locked out'.

Readers who wish to know more about concurrency than we have space to detail in this book should consult a text such as Ben-Ari (1982) or a tutorial paper such as Andrews & Schneider (1983).

If processes are connected neither directly nor indirectly through a chain of communicaton, then problems of shared access to a data object disappear. Unconnected processes are said to be *collateral*, e.g. processes P1 and P2 in Fig. 3.2. Since there is no communicational structure to preserve in the implementation, the timing relationship of a set of collateral processes is inconsequential and, by definition, unspecified.

Absence of concurrency or collaterality inevitably results in sequentiality. Sequentiality imposes a specific time ordering on the processes involved. Thus, if this were the case in the example of Fig. 3.3, P would definitely finish before Q started, by which time X would be updated, or exist, in its entirety, and so there would be no safety or liveness problems associated with access to the resource X. Sequentiality on its own, however, would be far too limiting as a process-structuring tool, generating software designs containing varying degrees of overspecified process scheduling. As a side issue (at the moment), sequential structuring can actually be broken down into three important categories:

concatenation – 'straight' or simple sequencing;
selection – expressing the idea of alternatives;
iteration – expressing the idea of cyclic execution.

In fact, these structures have already been applied in the entity structure diagrams of Fig. 2.2 in Section 2.3. However, since sequentiality is more predominant at the descriptive level of programs, further discussion of these three process substructure types will be left until the next chapter. (Note: it should be appreciated that whereas iteration is exclusively a sequential concept, expression of the concept of alternatives is not limited solely to sequential environments.)

Although it may seem that data and time are quite separate issues, nevertheless a strong connection exists between the two. A data structure implicitly maps a timing relationship on to any set of processes intended to access its constituent data objects. (It also defines creation, modification and inspection operations, for example, but this does not concern us here.) Thus, a data structure can be either:

random access – constituent data objects are all accessible for processing during any segment of time; examples include direct-access files, arrays;

or:

sequential access – constituent data objects are accessible for processing only successively one by one in some strict sequence; examples include serial files, lists.

Thus, a sequential-access data structure constrains time-wise the processes that manipulate its components, whereas the components of a random-access data structure can (in principle) be manipulated concurrently. In practice, however, most widely used programming languages lack the concurrency capability needed to exploit the processing of random-access data structures to advantage.

3.4   HIERARCHY IN SOFTWARE DESIGN

Hierarchical models are applicable whenever the make-up of a composite object is being analyzed – that is, an object that is describable in terms of one or more simpler objects, possibly via many intermediate levels of decomposition, down to some predefined primitive level of description. Naturally, the terms 'composite' and 'primitive' are purely relative, and depend on the 'basis set' of objects towards which representation of a given hierarchy is targeted.

Hierarchy is readily discernible in software architecture. For example, from its external environment a system can be viewed as a single complex process. As we descend through the system architecture, many kinds of hierarchy can be seen in processes and data (the distinction below between systems and programs is used as a convenient intermediate division between levels of architectural complexity).

For processes:

{At the system level} System −−> subsystems −−> programs
{At the program level} Program −−>subprograms, algorithm struc-
                                    tures −−> instructions

For data:

{At the system level} Database $--> $ subschemas $--> $ tables (say)
{At the program level} File $--> $ records $--> $ fields

The most appropriate descriptive mechanism for hierarchy is a tree diagram, as illustrated in Fig. 3.4. Note that such simple level-by-level description of composition does not indicate the nature of the structuring that binds objects together; e.g. it tells us that M is a composition of A, B, C and D but not what the nature of that composition is. However, there are certain forms of tree diagram that include this information. As an example, the reader is referred again to the domain requirements specification in Section 2.3 and Fig. 2.2 in particular – here, the structures indicated in the two hierarchies are the three basic forms of sequential structuring: concatenation, selection and iteration.

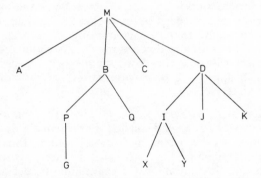

Fig. 3.4. Simple tree diagram of hierarchy.

Hierarchy plays a role, to a greater or lesser extent, in virtually all software development methods. The importance of hierarchy, accompanied by other notions such as modularity (see next section), is that it represents one of the most simple, yet powerful, conceptual tools that can be applied to the understanding and organized representation of complex objects. In software design, it can be exploited in two basic ways.

Top-Down Design

This is one of the most widely used general design strategies; it can be applied to the design of any composite component of a software architecture, whether at the system or program level. As the name implies, design begins at the highest, most abstract level of a problem (i.e. with a specification) and proceeds 'downwards' towards some prescribed base level. More specifically:

★ The problem solution is first represented as a single abstraction (e.g. M in Fig. 3.4). This will trivially complete the design if a solution to the problem already exists; e.g. the problem might require the development of a subprogram, say, that is already available in some library.
★ The abstraction is then expressed as some structure of new, simpler objects (M is expressed in terms of A, B, C and D); in effect, this represents a decompositional transformation ('refinement') of a specification of WHAT into a specification of HOW (a 'realization').
★ This process is successively applied, level by level, to each new composite object that emerges, until all leaf objects in the design tree are target primitives (A, G, Q, C, X, Y, J and K).

This continual progression from WHAT to HOW, creating a hierarchy of abstract design 'layers', each being realized by objects in the layers below, and by the same token providing objects to realize the layers above, is the hallmark of top-down design. It is widely acknowledged that design based within a top-down framework represents a sound general approach applicable to a wide variety of problems. Its main advantages are that:

★ It enables the size problem to be handled in a simple, effective manner; at any step, one need consider in principle only a single, yet-to-be-realized object in isolation from all others, thus significantly reducing the intellectual load (if such isolated reasoning is not possible, the implication is that constituent objects are not 'well separated' and that the design possesses some structural inadequacy).
★ Although the design at any stage prior to completion will contain abstractions of yet-to-be-realized representation, it will nevertheless encompass a total solution to the problem – a fact that can be exploited to advantage, e.g. during software testing (see Section 7.4).

However, top-down design alone should not be regarded as the panacea for all software development. There are a number of reasons for this viewpoint:

(a) The target level may be too low, or lacking in certain respects, making top-down design unnecessarily arduous, long-winded and prone to error.
Solution: Augment top-down design with some bottom-up design (see below) in order to 'raise' the target level appropriately.
(b) Much of the critical decision-making in design tends to reside at the highest levels. Hence, top-down design forces some of the most

important decisions to be made very early on when least is understood about the problem. This may be inappropriate, or even impossible, especially when a complex problem contains 'untrodden ground'. Thus, top-down design seems best applied to problems that 'one already knows how to deal with'.

Solution: Adopt a more flexible approach. For example, develop the software in an evolutionary manner, prototyping through various stages of development, reserving top-down design for non-innovatory components of the problem.

(c) The largeness of a project may be such that top-down development cannot cope with the 'requirements drift' that may occur during the extensive timescale involved. Appleton (1986) expresses the problem aptly: 'It is impossible for a project team to get to the bottoms and to build and assemble them before the top moves.'

Solution: One possibility is to adopt an incremental approach, developing a scaled-down version of the system initially and then 'growing' it in a series of major enhancements.

(d) The complexity of large systems often tends to be spread out 'horizontally' across processes and their communication structuring. In these circumstances, networks, rather than hierarchies, will be better suited to the modelling of system architecture. This implies that top-down design is not always the most suitable approach to system development (though at the program level, where programs are 'simpler' objects than systems and the emphasis is more on hierarchical algorithm structuring, there is a much better fit).

Solution: Adopt a compositional design approach with a 'sideways' orientation to the development of system architecture.

(e) The top-down method, without further qualification, is a very broad strategy that supplies no specific guidelines for working out, or deciding upon, the 'best' decomposition when alternatives exist. A colleague of the author's† has expressed this lack of 'tactics' in the general top-down method with words to the effect that 'whilst we may have a knife, we are not necessarily sure of how to carve'. The dilemma is nicely highlighted by the juxtaposition of Descartes and Leibniz:

> (Descartes): 'Divide each problem that you examine into as many parts as you need, to solve them more easily.' (Rene Descartes, *Oeuveres*, vol. VI, *Discours de la Methode*, Part II.)
>
> (Leibniz): 'This rule of Descartes is of little use, as long as the art of dividing ... remains unexplained. By dividing his problem into

---

† I am indebted to Jawed Siddiqi both for the 'knife' metaphor and for discovering the quotes from Descartes and Leibniz.

unsuitable parts, the unexperienced problem solver may increase his difficulty.' (Gottfried von Leibnitz, *Philosophische Schriften*, vol. VI.)

Solution: Augment the top-down approach with additional design criteria. This can be achieved in a number of ways:

☆ Pragmatic – keep decomposition structures as simple as possible and do not attempt too much decomposition 'in one go'. As far as possible, each decomposition should be 'self-evidently' correct or able to be informally argued to be correct.

☆ Formal – use techniques associated with formal verification methods to steer the decompositional process so that realizations of proven correctness are achieved (see Section 5.4).

☆ Evaluative – employ criteria, which can be rationally argued to be reasonable quality indicators, to judge the 'goodness' of a decomposition. For example, a method such as Structured Design (Yourdon & Constantine 1979) possesses a strong top-down element and uses additional criteria (module 'coupling' and 'cohesion') to provide measures of design quality.

A further point to be made is that people do not necessarily think in an orderly top-down manner; that is, problem-solving 'inside the head' tends to take place in a more chaotic fashion. There are many who support this view; Green (1980), for example, employs the metaphor of programmers who '... leap intuitively ahead from stepping stone to stepping stone, following a vision of the final program'. This, of course, is not a refutation of the usefulness of top-down design; but it does suggest that the latter is more of an organizational tool that is applied *after* primary problem solving has taken place.

Bottom-Up Design

As with top-down design, this method can be applied at any level to any kind of software object (network, process, data). It is the mirror-image of top-down design, involving the structuring of progressively higher levels of abstraction. Thus, bottom-up design is a process of synthesis rather than decomposition that hides, rather than reveals, detail. However, as a general method of development, it has disadvantages over a top-down approach:

★ It is harder to maintain correctness in an approach that involves continually structuring new higher-level sets of abstractions that eventually (it is hoped) converge towards some original specification.

★ The actual design product never exists in its entirety until the final

synthesis step (except possibly only in the mind(s) of the designer(s)!); at all lower levels, the design is merely a collection of components.
★ The general method does not lend itself well to augmentation by design-quality evaluation criteria of any kind when it comes to the design of complex objects possessing numerous intermediate levels of abstraction.

Nevertheless, despite these caveats, bottom-up design should not be regarded as in any way inferior to top-down design, provided it is appropriately applied. In fact, a bottom-up element is a desirable, useful and essential adjunct to any other systematic design approach. Firstly, especially where complex, innovatory system development is involved, bottom-up design may provide the only way 'into' the problem – often in such circumstances, certain components can be quickly identified and tackled, before an overall architecture begins to emerge. Secondly, the basis layer of a design is sometimes inadequate and needs its level of abstraction raising by augmentation with more powerful primitives that can be developed from the current basis set – a technique illustrated in more detail in Section 4.3.

3.5 MODULARITY

All systematic development yields software whose architecture is in some sense 'modular'. This is because modularity is a natural conse-quence of applying abstraction via various forms of structuring, hier-archy, etc. However, different development methods applied to the same problem will yield software solutions that possess different kinds, and degrees, of modularity. The quality of modularity in a system (as judged by certain criteria) is directly related to the way in which a system is separated out into process and data objects, and, equivalently, to the internal composition of those objects.

Associated with modularity are two fundamental notions that we shall explain initially by reference to single processes.

Visibility

It is possible at various levels of software to encapsulate not only the description of a process but also its component data objects, creating a private 'local environment' that is masked from all external processes. For example:

★ At the system level: many job-control languages allow the con-struction of macros (operating system procedures controlling the scheduling of user programs and other operating system processes) that can possess their own local variables.

★ At the program level: the data objects of a high-level language program are always hidden from its external environment.

★ At the subprogram level: most high-level languages allow the construction of subprograms possessing local environments.

★ Below the subprogram level: some languages – typically hierarchical, 'algorithmic' languages, e.g. C and Ada (but not Pascal) – permit local environments at any composite algorithm level; the textual program unit involved is commonly referred to as a 'block'.

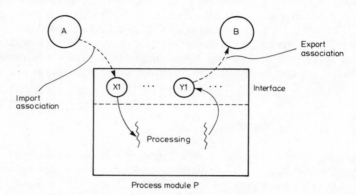

Fig. 3.5. Communication via parameters.

Interface

The interface of a process is its 'window' with any external environment, providing a means by which the two communicate without sacrificing the internal privacy of the process's local environment. Process interfaces are specified by *parameterization*. Parameters in the simplest case are special components of the local environment of a process that act either as import sources or export sinks, or in some cases both. Thus, it is possible for a process to communicate with its external environment indirectly via one or more parameters, rather than by directly accessing data objects in the latter. The simple example in Fig. 3.5 should make this clear. Here, X1 is an import parameter of P, Y1 an export parameter; the actual import and export involved happen to be respectively A and B in this instance, but could be other suitable data objects on other occasions. (Note: as to the association or 'correspondence' that is obviously required between A and X1, and between Y1 and B, it is a function of the underlying processor to apply an appropriate mechanism to achieve this; for example, correspondence 'by value' or 'by reference' are mechanisms commonly employed for subprogram parameters.) Examples of parameterization are:

★ At the system level: job control languages with a macro capability normally allow macros to be parameterized.
★ At the program level: languages have various means by which a program's input and output interface can be parametrically specified.
★ At the subprogram level: parameterization is allowed by virtually all high-level languages.

The overall principle at work here is that of masking internal detail, or 'information hiding' – see Parnas (1972a) for an early discussion of this essence of modularity, based on the need to isolate and hide difficult, or likely-to-change, design decisions from one another. In particular, if a process's own environment is made strictly private and its interface completely parameterized, then this removes any dependency it might otherwise have on a particular external environment – it is modular, a 'black box', and can be embedded and utilized in any environment which provides the necessary imports and exports. Quite apart from the obvious benefits bestowed by localization and self-containedness – e.g. secure, controlled communication, lack of subtle side effects on external objects, total abstraction, etc. – independence of environment is particularly important as regards software reusability, a point amplified in Section 4.7.

For simplicity, the above discussion has concentrated on single process abstractions as modularity units in a system. However, more powerful modular objects can be constructed that possess the following general composition:

★ A set of one or more operations (processes) that, from an external viewpoint, are themselves strictly modular, i.e. only their names and interfaces are visible.
★ A set of one or more data objects on which (some of) the operations of the module act.
★ Possibly an initializing process executed once-off when use of the module is first instigated.

Thus, modules of this type are not themselves executable objects but export processes and data that other objects in the system can access and make use of as 'building blocks'. An extremely important subcategory of this general type of module arises by imposing the following restrictions:

★ The internal representations of the module's data objects are completely invisible externally, just as the internal composition of the module's operations are.

★ The function of the module's operations is to provide the sole permitted means by which the data objects are manipulated.

This kind of modularization is termed *data encapsulation*. A classic textbook example is that of a module for handling a stack data structure. The module's operations, informally described, might be:

create {an empty stack}
push {a new element on top of the stack}
top {obtain a copy of the top element of the stack}
pop {remove the top element of the stack}
is_empty {test for empty stack}

which operate on some data object representing a stack, such as an array or linked list, that is hidden within the module's implementation.

More usefully, however, a stack-handling module might be constructed in such a way that, along with the stack operations, it exports a stack data type instead of owning a stack data structure. This enables any number of stack objects to be created and manipulated, rather than the module's operations acting on one single encapsulated instance of a stack. In effect, then, the module defines a stack data type in terms of the specification of stack operations. Such a module is referred to as an *abstract data type*. Abstract data types (see Liskov & Zilles 1974, for example) are an extremely important modular concept. Apart from being of general applicability in any development method, data abstractions play a significant role in 'formal methods' and 'object oriented' design.

Although data abstraction will be discussed further in later material, it should be noted for now that its usefulness lies not merely in defining simple objects such as stacks. In fact, it is possible to model a complete system on a data abstraction basis. To see this, note that, externally, a system's functionality is manifested to users by visible operations (representing the user interface) that permit:

creation
construction
modification
inspection
deletion

of the (hidden) system data, which, at this level of abstraction, can be thought of as a single complex data object or (loosely) 'database'. The implementation of the operations and representation of the database

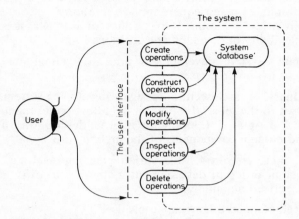

Fig. 3.6. A system viewed as an encapsulated data object.

are, of course, completely invisible to users. In other words, the system behaves as an encapsulated data object, as shown in Fig. 3.6.

3.6 METHODS OF SYSTEM DEVELOPMENT

The preceding sections have given an overview of the basic conceptual tools that are utilized in software specification and design. It will be useful at this point to give a summary of what those tools are:

★ Basic building blocks
   processes
   data objects.
★ Structuring concepts
   networks (connection, data flow)
   hierarchy (decomposition, synthesis)
   modularity (separation, detail-hiding – process and data abstraction).
★ Techniques
   top-down decomposition (hierarchical, abstraction-decreasing)
   bottom-up synthesis (hierarchical, abstraction-increasing)
   'sideways-on' development – compositional but non-hierarchical.
★ Criteria
   reflect real world environments in systems;
   utilize abstractions to:
   ☆ discard irrelevant, or ignore not yet needed, detail
   ☆ combat complexity

☆ avoid unnecessary constraints expressed in specification or design
   that impinge on subsequent implementation
generally delay commitment to specifics for as long as is possible to
retain flexibility in development decisions.

Conventionally, system development prior to coding, etc. is often
separated into two main phases:

(a) 'Preliminary' or 'architectural' design – developing system architec-
    ture down to the level of modules, data flows and retained data.
(b) 'Detailed' design – developing the internal descriptions of process,
    data and module components of the architecture.

In practice, there is considerable variation in approach amongst the
large number of different development methods that exist, with each
being characterized mainly by:

★ The diagrammatic and language tools used.
★ The emphasis which the method places on particular concepts, criteria
  and techniques.
★ The way in which elements of the software architecture are created,
  specified and designed.

An extensive comparison of all the major development methods would
require at least one whole book in itself. We content ourselves here with
a modest survey and overview of a few well established methods that
provide some measure of contrast. We shall then use one method in
detail to develop a system solution satisfying the SUMS domain and
functional requirements defined in Section 2.3. Further design concepts
and techniques will be discussed in Chapter 4. In addition, Chapter 5 is
devoted entirely to formal methods of software development and so no
exposition of the topic will occur here. A more comprehensive and
detailed survey of development methods can be found in Birrel & Ould
(1985).

Database approaches

Especially suited to the development of information systems, the
emphasis of a database approach, as the name implies, is on data
modelling of the real world. The main objective of the data analysis
phase is to:

★ Analyse the real-world data pertinent to an organization's data
  processing or information system needs; this is termed *data analysis*
  (e.g. see Howe 1983).
★ Construct a *conceptual model* of that data by identifying and specifying

the various properties of, and relationships that exist amongst, its components.

Tsichritzis & Lochovsky (1982) give an in-depth treatment of the many different techniques of data modelling that exist. One main approach for constructing conceptual models is the Entity-Relationship (E-R) approach. In E-R modelling, the main ingredients of a data model specification are:

Entities

An entity is any active or passive real-world concept or 'object' of interest and relevance.

Attributes

An entity's attributes are a set of data elements that sufficiently characterize (the properties of) that entity.

Relations

A relation is an association that exists between two entities; an association can be one-to-one, one-to-many, or many-to-many.

Fig. 3.7. E–R data model for the SUMS system.

As a simple example, Fig. 3.7 is an E-R model for the SUMS system (recall that one student can own many programs). Attributes of the two entities would include those given in the JSD entity analysis of Section 2.3.

The conceptual model, or conceptual 'schema', can be regarded as an abstract system data specification. It is now necessary to transform it into an equivalent *logical schema* that is suitable for database implementation. The logical schema, which is in effect an abstract system data design, might be constructed so as to be directly compatible with some available DataBase Management System (DBMS). However, if there are no suitable DBMS tools available, then subsequent design and implementation of the *physical schema* (file structures, etc.) for the database will also be necessary, along with an appropriate DBMS interface. Common types of logical schema are *relational, hierarchical* and *network*. The relational approach in particular is often favoured, partly because it is completely independent of any physical organization of the data, and partly because it is the most easily understood – relationally modelled data is logically arranged in terms of tables, which are one of the commonest ways of structuring data in everyday life. For further description of logical schemas and database architectures, a standard text on databases such as Date (1986) should be consulted. Also, Claybrook *et al.* (1985) show how formal data abstractions can be used to define database schemas and architectures.

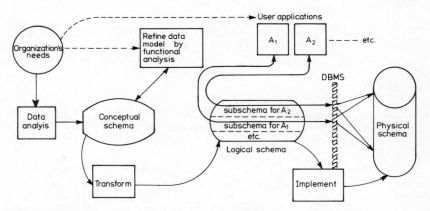

Fig. 3.8. A data analysis and database approach to software development.

The overall development method being outlined here is summarized in Fig. 3.8; a more detailed account can be found in Avison (1985). The functionality of the desired system is specified and designed only after the logical model has been established, although functional analysis in advance can help determine whether the data model will be adequate in supporting what are envisaged to be the eventual functional requirements. Depending on the implementation tools available in the target environment, e.g. a 4GL system, it may be possible to prototype or implement various functions and applications rapidly once the database exists. Note that each application will process only its own 'subview' (subschema) of the overall logical database.

Structured Systems Analysis

There exists a family of virtually identical methods with the title 'Structured Systems Analysis' (SSA), particular variants being described by DeMarco (1978), Weinberg (1978) and Gane & Sarson (1979). The overall approach is as follows:

Using the descriptive formalism of *data flow diagrams* (DFDs) that is described below:

★ model the system as it currently physically exists and then convert this physical DFD into a logically equivalent DFD, i.e. where processes and data flows do not necessarily correspond directly to the physical system; the logical DFD is accompanied by associated process and data specifications (also see below);
★ as appropriate, modify the logical DFD and specifications (by adding or deleting processes, data objects, data flows, etc.) to capture the requirements for the new system;
★ evaluate alternative implementations and choose one; this will partly involve defining on the DFD the boundary around the part of the system that is to be computerized.

The rest of the design – modular architecture and internal logic of modules – is then carried out according to the related method of Structured Design, which is described in the next chapter.

A DFD is a graphical representation that models a system as a set of *functional transformations* (the processes) and *data stores* (retained system data) connected by *data flows* (transient data). The main elements of a DFD are:

Interface

Rectangles for data sources or sinks at the boundaries of the total system.

Processes

Circles (or 'soft' boxes) for functional transformations.

Data

Labelled directed arcs for data flows; open rectangles for data stores.

Figure 3.9 gives an example, which represents a top-level logical

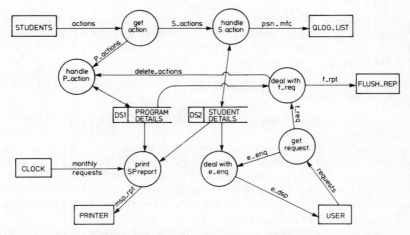

Fig. 3.9.   First level logical data flow diagram of the SUMS system.

description of the SUMS system. The retained system data is represented by the data stores DS1 and DS2, to which various system functions have read access or read-write access as indicated by the access arrows. The functional requirements FR1 to FR4 inclusive defined in Section 2.2 are realized respectively by:

handle S_action (which also deals with all student actions (in the sense described in Section 2.3) and all updates to DS2, where appropriate details of every student are kept);
deal with e_enq;
deal with f_req (which also generates delete actions, to be handled by *handle P_action*, for those programs to be flushed out of PATSY's filestore);
print SP report.

In addition, *get action* and *get request* perform auxiliary input, and *handle P_action* deals with all actions on programs (in the sense described in Section 2.3) and all updates to DS1, where appropriate details of every student's program are kept.

A DFD as in Fig. 3.9 provides a view of system functionality at the highest level. If necessary, a process can be functionally decomposed into a subordinate DFD, though it is usually unnecessary to carry out decomposition beyond one or two levels. Basically, any process will be sufficiently primitive if its 'top-level logic' can be completely and concisely specified by one of the process specification tools that SSA employs. These are:

★ 'Structured English': an algorithmic 'pseudocode' with syntactic templates for selection and iteration, and processing steps described in terse, precise natural language. For example, using an extended form of structured English, the process *handle p_action* might be specified as:

```
HANDLE P_ACTION(in P_ACTION)
   case P_ACTION.TYPE of
      CREATE   => CREATE PROGRAM ENTRY
      DELETE   => DELETE PROGRAM ENTRY
      COMPILE  => UPDATE PROGRAM ENTRY
      EDIT     => UPDATE PROGRAM ENTRY
      RUN      => UPDATE PROGRAM ENTRY
   endcase
```

★ Decision trees and decision tables: descriptive mechanisms particularly useful for specifying processes comprising non-trivial decision (selection) logic.

Composite data flows and data stores are specified in terms of their data structures and constituent data elements in an implementation-independent hierarchical manner; if desired, relational modelling techniques, say, can be applied to data store specification. For example, the data flow *msp_rpt* might be specified as follows (as usual, a '*' indicates unbounded repetition):

```
MSP_RPT
   STUDENT_DETAILS* {increasing order of NAME}
      STUDENT_HEADER
         NAME
         COURSE
         LOG_ON_CODE
      STUDENT_USAGE
         N_COMPS
         N_EDITS
         N_RUNS
         TOTAL_PTIME
      PROG_IDR* {increasing order of PROG_IDR}
```

All such specifications (data and process) are held in a data dictionary. The data dictionary acts as a central repository for all definitions that, together with the logical DFD, constitute the 'structured functional specification' of the system – the main deliverable of SSA.

Note: a data dictionary is a useful documentation tool in any system development method for recording definitions, specifications and their interrelationships. A data dictionary might be nothing more than a simple text file manipulated by a standard editor. Alternatively, it might be a sophisticated tool that is an integral component of some database or 4GL system.

Object-Oriented Design

A number of texts on software engineering have recently appeared in which the main design method espoused has been 'object oriented' (Booch 1983; Wiener & Sincovec 1984). This is perhaps a reflection of the perceived increasing importance and popularity of the method. One slight problem is interpreting precisely what 'object oriented' means. Loosely, it can be regarded as a design method that typically, though by no means exclusively, models relevant 'objects' in the problem environment as encapsulated data objects or abstract data types. However, as Rentsch (1982) emphasizes, the object-oriented paradigm is more than just a method that exploits modularity and data abstraction. We shall return to the topic of object-oriented architecture in Section 4.2.

Following Booch (1986), object-oriented development consists of the following steps:

Identify objects and their attributes

Identification in object-oriented design needs a set of requirements in some form to work from. In system development, an analysis technique such as SADT or SSA will be needed to develop a specification that is sufficiently rich to facilitate object identification; in smaller 'programming' problems, a top-level outline design can be derived from the requirements definition to feed the identification process. In essence, it is nouns and their associated adjectives, which respectively indicate objects and their attributes, that will form the basis of the 'reality model' in a system.

Identify the operations suffered or performed by each object

Similarly, it is adverbs and verbs appearing in the specification, and the nouns with which they are associated, that indicate a particular object's attributes and the operations it performs or suffers. An object can be classed as either an actor (it performs operations), a server (it suffers operations) or an agent (it does both). Moreover, an operation primitive is basically one of three types: a constructor (which alters the state of an object), a selector (which inspects or evaluates the current state

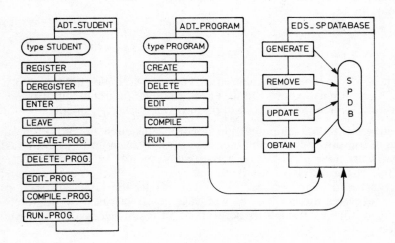

Fig. 3.10. A (partial) object-oriented view of the SUMS system.

of an object) or an iterator (which visits every part of an object).

Establish the visibility relationships of objects

The hierarchy of objects is determined by deciding for each object what it imports and which object(s) the imports are obtained from. Figure 3.10 gives a partial object-oriented view of the SUMS system in terms of two abstract data types ADT_STUDENT and ADT_PROGRAM, and one encapsulated data structure EDS_SPDATABASE; the arrows between the objects indicate the 'used by' relationships. In practice, many other objects of varying complexity would enter into the SUMS design, such as:

an object to zeroise, update and display counts: used by ADT_STUDENT and ADT_PROGRAM, for example;

an object to perform screen output: used in satisfying interactive output requirements of the SUMS system;

an object to satisfy each main SUMS functional requirements.

Establish the interface of each object

Each object is now specified in terms of a name and a specification of each of its exports. To express object specifications precisely requires a suitable formal language, and Ada (DoD 1983) amongst others is commonly used.

Implement each object

Each object is then implemented by choosing suitable (hidden) representations for its exports. In addition, the overall architectural framework into which the objects will be integrated is determined.

Object-oriented development thus incorporates elements of bottom-up design, top-down design and hierarchy. It is bottom-up in the way that objects are first identified and then subsequently integrated into an overall structure. It is top-down in the sense that objects are first specified and then realized – an act of decomposing abstractions into representations. There will also exist a used-by hierarchy amongst objects, though its determination is not necessarily achieved decompositionally.

Real-Time System Development

Petri Nets

Petri Nets (e.g. Peterson 1977 and 1981) are a graphical representation technique particularly useful for specifying concurrency in systems – hence their relevance to real-time systems development. A Petri Net comprises (see Fig. 3.11):

★ A number of *places*: a place is depicted by a circle that contains zero or more tokens; a single token is usually represented by a dot, but if necessary the number of tokens held by a place can be specified by an integer.
★ A number of *transitions*: a transition is depicted by a straight line.
★ A number of directed arcs: an output arc from a place node becomes an input arc to a transition node, and similarly, an output arc from a transition node becomes an input arc to a place node.
★ A *marking*, which is an allocation of token counts to the places in the net.

In effect, a transition corresponds to a processing step or event within

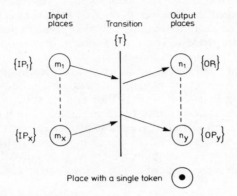

Fig. 3.11. Petri Net notation.

the system. The set of input places and output places of a transition captures something about the state of the system prior to the transition 'firing' and after the transition has fired, respectively. A transition T can fire if it is enabled. It is enabled if all its input places IPi, $1 <= i <= x$ hold at least one token. After T fires, all its input places each lose one token and all its output places OPi, $1 <= i <= y$ each gain one token.

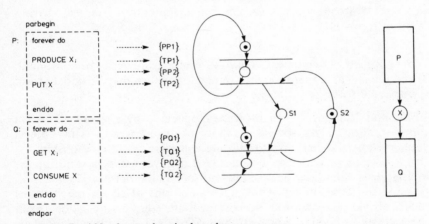

Fig. 3.12. Petri Net for synchronized producer–consumer.

To illustrate the use of a Petri Net, Fig. 3.12 describes a simple producer-consumer relationship where the two processes are synchronized; i.e. the critical resource X holds one item only – producer P will be blocked at TP2 if X is not empty, and consumer Q will be blocked at

TQ1 if X is empty (the reader should check that places S1 and S2 ensure the correct behaviour of P and Q as regards their access to X). Figure 3.12 also gives a diagrammatic and textual representation of the joint producer-consumer process. The text, as given, is incomplete; we shall return to the example in Section 4.2.

One main use of Petri Nets is as an early specification and modelling tool in the development of concurrent and distributed systems. An advantage of using Petri Nets is that they can be subjected to various analyses that enable the behaviour of the modelled system to be studied, e.g. with respect to important correctness properties such as safety and liveness. In later stages of system development, a Petri Net can be transformed into a system design expressed in terms of Ada tasks (DoD 1983) or communicating sequential processes (Hoare 1985), say.

MASCOT

MASCOT (Modular Approach to Software COnstruction and Test; e.g. Simpson & Jackson 1979; Budgen 1985; IEE/BCS 1986) is a development method for real-time systems that encompasses architectural system design through to acceptance testing. Its main features are as follows:

(a) System architecture is specified independently of target environment in terms of:

  activities (processes);
  data objects of two types: *channels* – message queues to be consumed; and *pools* – data that is not consumed, but which may be updated and inspected from time to time.

In familiar fashion, the architecture is specified by a simple graphical representation using special symbols for process and data objects connected by directed arcs to indicate communication relationships.

(b) Access by activities to a data object is governed by a set of *access mechanisms* – modular operations that specify the permitted manipulations of the data object. The implementations of access mechanisms deal with mutual exclusion, synchronization, etc. and are hidden from the accessing activities. In effect, then, MASCOT data objects and their access mechanisms represent data abstractions and bear close resemblance to the 'monitor' concept described in Section 4.2.

(c) Architectural design is followed by detailed design (of activities and data objects), and then coding and testing, which takes place in standard bottom-up fashion (see Section 7.4), i.e. data objects, access mechanisms and activities are individually tested before integration into subsystems, etc.

A major feature of MASCOT is that it possesses its own support environment, which provides tools for system construction and testing and a suitable run-time environment under which MASCOT-derived applications can be exercised.

Jackson Methods

For our detailed illustration, we shall use Jackson System Development (JSD). This choice has been influenced by the following considerations:

★ JSD covers the development cycle from requirements analysis through to implementation and therefore provides a coherent illustrative base threading the book.
★ It is a recently exposed method (Jackson 1983; Cameron 1986) that is operational in nature and therefore provides a contrast with more traditional (analysis −> specification −> design −> implementation) approaches and top-down techniques.
★ It is a semi-formal approach, possessing a balanced mixture of diagrammatic and textual description.
★ It has a wide application domain, e.g. data processing, 'dynamic' information systems (i.e. where data is time dependent) and real-time process control and embedded systems.
★ It has a wide implementation domain: implemented JSD-specified systems can be with or without database, can be subject to any desired scheduling regime (e.g. pure 'batch', pure online or any mixture of the two) and can be centralized or distributed.

We shall now apply Jackson methods – JSD and its sister design method JSP (see Cameron 1983) – to develop an operational specification of a system satisfying the SUMS domain and functional requirements specified in Section 2.3.

3.7 REFLECTING REAL-WORLD DOMAINS IN SYSTEMS

Broadly, the JSD approach can be broken down into a sequence of distinct phases:

Specify system = specify model −> specify functionality
                                  −> specify constraints

Here, 'functionality' can be taken to include user interface, error handling, etc. The following should be noted:

★ 'Model' pertains to an abstract description of salient aspects of a real-world environment – NOT of the system architecture itself. For the rest of this chapter, we shall use the term 'model' in the former sense, unless otherwise stated.

★ The rationale for dealing with model before functionality is that the former provides a more stable system foundation than the latter because:

> A real-world model acts as a conceptual basis for subsequent functional specification. By resolving all aspects of the model first, there can be no doubt as to whether the system can or cannot support a proposed function. However, by starting with functional considerations, there is a less reliable basis for determining what future modifications to a system's functionality can be accommodated, and at what cost.

> By basing systems on real-world models, one is building in robustness and flexibility with respect to future 'requirements drift' in functionality. Of course, the real world might change too, but then no system development method can provide immunity to the possible upheavals that this could cause. At least with a model-based approach that generates models possessing good separability, there is a much better chance that the effects of a real-world change can be localized, thus avoiding costly, large-scale redevelopment.

★ The term 'function' should be interpreted more narrowly in JSD. A JSD function is primarily concerned with providing information (outputs) to the real world, and occasionally to the system model component itself, though this is somewhat rarer. This is less general than the notion of a function as a data transformer – that is, *any* process that effects a transformation of imports to exports, regardless of whether or not system output is involved.

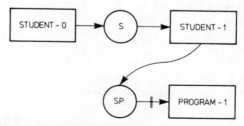

Fig. 3.13. The SUMS system: model processes.

In JSD, specifying the model component of a system is a relatively simple procedure. Basically, it involves translating the domain requirements (entities with their sequential action structures) directly into system processes. Figure 3.13 specifies this graphically for our example SUMS system. Conventionally, the name suffixes −0 and −1 refer to 'level−0' (= the real world) and 'level−1' (= the system model process level) respectively. Such diagrams are deceptively simple, as they implicitly convey a considerable amount of information:

(a) Firstly, the notation has the following interpretation: square boxes are strictly sequential processes (no hidden concurrency) and circles are 'data (message) streams'. A data stream is an idealized (i.e. potentially infinite) FIFO buffer (queue). The communication protocol of two processes connected by data stream is briefly as follows:

☆ the producer process is the instigator of the communication and can never be blocked on writing;
☆ the consumer process must read every message of the data stream in the order written by the producer and will be blocked on a read if the queue is currently empty;
☆ the consumer cannot affect the behaviour of the producer in any way.

The only other type of connection allowed in a JSD network is 'state vector inspection', shown in Fig. 3.14. Here, the process Q gets a copy of the state vector – the set of local variable states SVP – of the process P. Q is the initiator of the communication, not P, which is always 'unaware' of any such inspection. Note that there is a certain indeterminacy here – P is constantly updating its local variables as it executes at its own speed, and so the values obtained by Q depend on exactly when the inspection is effected. Moreover, P never keeps a 'backlog' of information to enable Q to catch up on any updates that have occurred since the last inspection.

Fig. 3.14. State vector inspection.

(b) All processes in a JSD specification operate at their own conceptual speeds, i.e. they are asynchronously concurrent – either on an idealized producer-consumer basis when connected by data stream, or a writer-reader basis when connected by state vector inspection. Data stream is normally appropriate for level−0 −> level−1 connections – it is more usual for real-world entities to generate streams of messages as they perform their associated actions. However, especially with embedded process control systems, it is quite common for model processes to have to inspect the states of electromechanical devices, making state vector inspection the appropriate communication mode. State vector inspection plays a greater role in connecting functions to model, as the next section will illustrate.

(c) Figure 3.13 – the beginnings of a System Specification Diagram (SSD) – implicitly specifies a crucial multiplicity that applies to all level−0 −> level−1 connections: the fact that every real-world entity is modelled by its own corresponding process in the system (remember that STUDENT and PROGRAM are entity types). Thus, if there are 509 students currently possessing 2346 Pascal programs within PATSY, then the SUMS system model component will contain 509 corresponding STUDENT−1 processes and 2346 corresponding PROGRAM−1 processes.

Clearly, then, JSD specifications can incorporate vast numbers of processes. Obviously, whatever other merits and virtues a particular abstract specification method possesses, there must be effective ways of transforming the specifications it generates into implementable systems of acceptable performance, otherwise the method is of theoretical use only. Implementation transformations for dealing with process multiplicities of this kind will be discussed in Chapter 6.

(d) The purpose of a model process is to 'track', though inevitably always lag behind, its real-world counterpart. Each entity action generates data that arrives at, or can be detected at, the system boundary and subsequently causes a corresponding reaction within the model process. The lag occurs because, no matter how fast this action and reaction happens, it will always take a finite amount of time for data to reach the system boundary and the model process to respond.

Note that, in our example, the actions performed by STUDENTs include all those that are suffered by the passive PROGRAMs. Hence, PROGRAM-1 processes receive their real-world data streams indirectly via STUDENT-1 processes: in JSD parlance, PROGRAMs are 'marsupial' entities of STUDENTs. The double bar across an arc indicates a 'many' relationship – here, each STUDENT-1 process will contribute to the data streams of many PROGRAM-1 processes.

(e) All JSD specification processes are 'long running', i.e. they – and hence the whole system – are considered to execute once only. A process starts up when the system is first initiated and data begins to arrive. It then continues to execute throughout the lifetime of the system (though it could be blocked into idleness for long periods) until the system is dispensed with, or the process has to be deleted for some reason, as when an entity leaves the real-world domain, e.g. a student deregisters from the Nirvana machine or a Pascal program is deleted – hence, the corresponding model process must be eliminated from the system. Note, therefore, that a model process with its state vector in effect represents a dynamic historical 'track record' within the system of the real-world entity to which it corresponds.

This summarizes the main features of JSD model specification. One other task to be accomplished is to specify the texts of each model process. This is done by translating each entity structure diagram into JSD structure text, syntactic details of which are briefly summarized below in BNF-style notation for the main composite process types:

<sequence> = <NAME> **seq** <process_list> <NAME> **end**

<selection> = <NAME> **sel** '(' <condition> ')' <process>
{<NAME> **alt** '(' <condition> ')' <process>}
<NAME> **end**

<iteration> = <NAME> **itr while** '(' <condition> ')'
<process>
<NAME> **end**

Note that a process <NAME> label is consistently substituted by the same identifier throughout a structure. The structure texts for STUDENT−1 and PROGRAM−1 processes are as follows:

```
STUDENT−1 seq
  read S;
  REGISTER; read S;
  REG_PERIOD itr while (not terminate)
    PATSY_SESSION seq
      ENTER; read S;
      SESSION_PERIOD itr while (not quit)
        COMMAND sel (create)
          CREATE; write CREATE to SP[prog_idr]; read S;
        COMMAND alt (edit)
          EDIT; write EDIT to SP[prog_idr]; read S;
        COMMAND alt (compile)
          COMPILE; write COMPILE to SP[prog_idr]; read S;
        COMMAND alt (run)
          RUN; write RUN to SP[prog_idr]; read S;
        COMMAND alt (delete)
          DELETE; write DELETE to SP[prog_idr]; read S;
        COMMAND end
      SESSION_PERIOD end
      QUIT; read S;
    PATSY_SESSION end
  REG_PERIOD end
  TERMINATE;
STUDENT−1 end
```

(Notational note: SP[prog_idr] denotes the data stream for the PROGRAM-1 model process corresponding to program prog_idr; recall that prog_idr is a data element of all program actions.)

```
PROGRAM-1 seq
  read SP;
  CREATE; read SP;
  WORKING_LIFE itr while (not delete)
    ACTION sel (edit)
      EDIT; read SP;
    ACTION alt (compile)
      COMPILE; read SP;
    ACTION alt (run)
      RUN; read SP;
    ACTION end
  WORKING_LIFE end
  DELETE
PROGRAM-1 end
```

Actions at this stage are treated as primitive operations (semicolons are used to terminate primitive actions only). Read operations are included on a systematic basis – one at the start of the process text, and one after each action except the last; a read operation is deemed to obtain the next message from the specified data stream. As functionality is added in the next stage, the model generally becomes embellished as a consequence, with further read, write and update logic being inserted into level-1 processes. As a result, their local environments become enriched with extra variables. It is these variables – model process state vectors – which represent the important 'attributes' of corresponding real-world entities that, analogously, are determined in the entity and attribute analyses of E-R data modelling techniques, for example.

3.8   ADDING FUNCTION TO MODEL

The second major stage of the JSD specification phase is to satisfy functional requirements. The model processes of the system act as a basis for supporting functions, the latter being specified by: (a) showing graphically how they connect to the model, and (b) giving their structure texts. There are in fact a number of different, basic ways in which the model can support functionality, and these are illustrated by the following examples, which refer to the functional requirements FR1 – FR4 inclusive defined in Section 2.3. For the reader's convenience, the informal description of each requirement is given again.

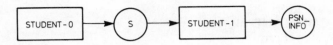

Fig. 3.15. Satisfying requirement FR1 – an embedded function.

Function FR1

"Whenever a student quits PATSY, the totals of compilations and runs performed during that session by the student, together with the session length, are to be appended to a file QLOG_LIST"

This is representative of the simplest function type in JSD – an 'embedded function', so called because it can be supported directly by inserting primitive operations in model processes (here, the STUDENT-1 processes). The SSD has been elaborated to show this in Fig. 3.15. Implicitly, the PSN_INFO outputs of all the STUDENT-1 processes going to QLOG_LIST are deemed to be 'rough merged'; that is, the separate outputs are merged as a single data stream, the merging taking place purely on the basis of when records become available from the separate producers. Rough merging of data streams represents another means by which indeterminacy arises in system networks – the merging is dependent purely on the speeds of the producing processes, and on no other factor.

The structure text of STUDENT-1 becomes:

```
STUDENT-1 seq
  read S;
  REGISTER; read S;
  REG_PERIOD itr while (not terminate)
    PATSY_SESSION seq
      ENTER seq
        entertime := ENTER.time;
        ncomps := 0; nruns := 0;
      ENTER end
      read S;
      SESSION_PERIOD itr while (not quit)
        COMMAND sel (create)
          CREATE; write CREATE to SP[prog_idr]; read S;
        COMMAND alt (edit)
          EDIT; write EDIT to SP[prog_idr]; read S;
        COMMAND alt (compile)
          COMPILE seq
            ncomps := ncomps + 1;
          COMPILE end
```

```
        write COMPILE to SP[prog_idr];
        read S;
      COMMAND alt (run)
        RUN seq
          nruns := nruns + 1;
        RUN end
        write RUN to SP[prog_idr];
        read S;
      COMMAND alt (delete)
        DELETE; write DELETE to SP[prog_idr]; read S;
      COMMAND end
    SESSION_PERIOD end
    QUIT seq
      sessionlength := QUIT.time − entertime;
      write log_on_code, ncomps, nruns, sessionlength to
          PSN_INFO;
    QUIT end
    read S;
  PATSY_SESSION end
  REG_PERIOD end
  TERMINATE;
STUDENT−1 end
```

In this instance, all operations required to create the function have been allocated appropriately to action primitives (which have been duly expanded into sequences as a result), introducing new variables as and when necessary.

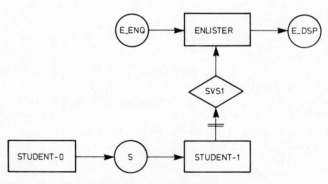

Fig. 3.16. Satisfying requirement FR2 – an imposed function.

Function FR2

"On enquiry from a terminal, the number of students currently within PATSY, and who they are, should be displayed"

This function is incorporated into the system network as shown in Fig. 3.16. In this case, a new process (ENLISTER) is required to realize the function since the latter is 'triggered' by an extra non-model input enquiry. Note that, like model processes, all function processes are longrunning. Thus, E_ENQ represents the total stream of enquiries processed by ENLISTER over the lifetime of the system, and similarly E_ DSP the total stream of responses generated.

The function ENLISTER is said to be 'imposed' – that is, it obtains the information it needs by state vector inspection of the appropriate part of the model (recall that the double bars indicate that ENLISTER must inspect the state vectors of many STUDENT-1 processes). Note the appropriateness of state vector connection here – clearly, the initiative for the communication lies with ENLISTER, not STUDENT-1 processes. However, in order to realize the function, there has to be a component of each STUDENT-1 state vector that indicates whether or not a student is currently within PATSY. This can be achieved by a new variable – 'entered_PATSY', say – that suffers 'entered_PATSY := true;' during the execution of action ENTER and 'entered_PATSY := false;' after the first 'read S;' and during the execution of action QUIT. The structure text for ENLISTER must also be specified. However, we shall leave this and the detailed design of the following two functions until the next section.

Function FR3

"On request, automatically delete all program files not accessed within the last 180 days. List to a file FLUSH_REP the names and last access dates of all such files deleted. The files listed should be grouped according to student owner, the latter being identified by log_on_ code. Groups should be lexicographically ordered by log_ on_code, and program file names within each group should be ordered by decreasing last access date"

In order to satisfy this requirement, we need a function (FLUSH) that:

is 'woken up' by an input request (F_REQ);
inspects the state vectors of all PROGRAMs to see when they were last accessed;

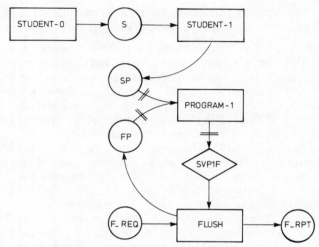

Fig. 3.17. Satisfying requirement FR3 – an interactive function.

decides which programs should be deleted and automatically generates the necessary model delete actions (FP);
produces a report (F_RPT) written to FLUSH_REP of the programs
that will be flushed out of PATSY's filestore.

Diagrammatically, this is shown in Fig. 3.17. Note two aspects: (i) the
double bars between FP and PROGRAM-1 – the data stream FP is of
course read by many PROGRAM-1 processes; (ii) the rough merging of
FP with the main model input stream SP.

FLUSH is an example of an 'interactive function'. This means that it
generates output (DELETE actions in this case) destined directly for
the system model component, i.e. it 'interacts' with the model. There
has to be an attribute (last_access_date, say) of PROGRAM-1 processes that enables FLUSH to determine whether or not deletion should
occur. The modified structure text of PROGRAM-1 is:

```
PROGRAM−1 seq
  read SP;
  CREATE seq
    last_access_date := CREATE.date;
  CREATE end
```

```
WORKING_LIFE itr while (not delete)
  ACTION sel (edit)
    EDIT seq
      last_access_date := EDIT.date;
    EDIT end
    read SP;
  ACTION alt (compile)
    COMPILE seq
      last_access_date := COMPILE.date;
    COMPILE end
    read SP;
  ACTION alt (run)
    RUN seq
      last_access_date := RUN.date;
    RUN end
    read SP;
  ACTION end
WORKING_LIFE
DELETE
PROGRAM-1 end
```

The user definition of ENLISTER implied that no particular 'access pathway' was required to STUDENT-1 state vectors, i.e. the access required was non-selective, ungrouped and in no particular order. This is not the case with FLUSH, where the access pathway is selective (on last_access_date) and where certain groupings and orderings must be present in F_RPT. This is also true of the next function. We shall defer consideration of state vector access pathways for the moment.

Function FR4

"At the end of each month, print out certain details of each student currently registered on the Nirvana machine. Per student, these details are to comprise:

the student's name, course and log_on_code;

the total number of compilations, edits and runs initiated, and total PATSY time consumed, during the past month;

the names, lexicographically ordered, of all program files owned by the student.

These details are to be alphabetically ordered by student name"

We note the following features:

★ The output required is to be produced on a regular (monthly) basis, not via *ad hoc* requests.

★ Monthly summaries of certain information are needed from the STUDENT part of the model, but model processes must not be structurally modified to support functions – a strict JSD rule.

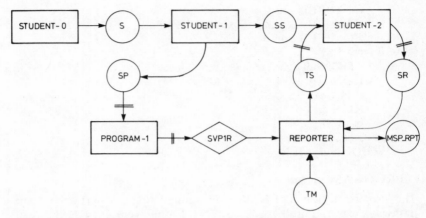

Fig. 3.18.   Satisfying requirement FR4 – a function needing a level–2 process.

Graphically, the function is realized as shown in Fig. 3.18. A number of new processes have been introduced to realize the function:

STUDENT-2

This is an example of a level-2 process – that is, a structural reworking of a level-1 process in order to accommodate a function (we could not build into STUDENT-1 the notion of a monthly interval without restructuring it). Each STUDENT-2 process, on receipt of a TS message, provides a monthly accumulation of number of edits, runs, etc. for the REPORTER process by writing a data stream message SR containing the relevant information. The information each STUDENT-2 process needs to accumulate monthly is obtained from its STUDENT-1 parent during each month via the data stream messages SS, generated by an operation:

    write ncomps, nedits, nruns, sessionlength to SS;

inserted into QUIT of STUDENT-1. Note the rough merge of SS and TS.

REPORTER

This is the process that actually generates the desired real-world output. The data stream TM is a 'time grain marker' stream, i.e. a data stream where messages signal the passage of regular real-world time intervals – here, each calendar month; in a real-time system specification, the time granularity could be a fraction of a second, and it might be appropriate to show explicitly a clock process that generates the actual timing pulses. REPORTER, on receipt of a TM, writes a TS to each STUDENT-2 in the order required by requirement FR4. On writing a TS, it awaits the SR reply before performing the necessary state vector inspections, generating another portion of MSP_RPT and then writing a TS to the next STUDENT-2 in turn, etc.

Other Considerations

There is often more than one way of incorporating a function into a network. For example, the solution for FR4 is not very sophisticated because of its reliance on a single sequential REPORTER process to generate MSP_RPT with the required orderings. We could increase the concurrency, hence decrease the timing constraints, in the specification by splitting REPORTER into a class of concurrent REPORT functions, connected one-one by data stream to each STUDENT-2. Thus, a given REPORT process would contribute information concerning one particular student to the production of MSP_RPT. The 'price' to pay for less specificity in a network is more rough merges and/or more processes. The gain is greater freedom in the choice of possible implementations.

There are, of course, further aspects to a system specification besides model and functionality that JSD, like any other development method, must take into account. These include:

★ Data collection and error handling, which is handled by an 'input subsystem' comprising processes that act as error filters and repairers between real-world and level-1 processes.
★ Other exceptional events and conditions besides data errors.
★ Interface details, e.g. message formats of internal data streams and data streams coming from, or going to, the real world.
★ Performance criteria and constraints: timeliness, etc.

There is no specific way of covering the last two in JSD. The first two are covered by extra process specifications and special escape structures within process texts. Figure 3.19 gives the full SSD for the SUMS system as far as we shall develop it.

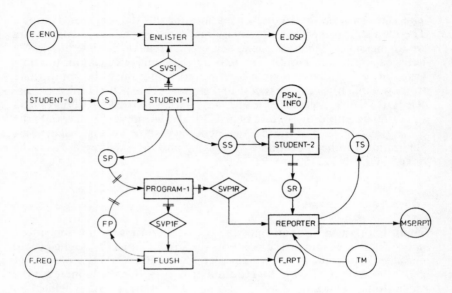

Fig. 3.19. The complete SUMS system network architecture.

3.9   DETAILED DESIGN

The detailed design method of JSD is Jackson Structured Programming
(JSP) (Jackson 1975; Ingevaldsson 1979; King & Pardoe 1985). It is
important, however, for the reader to appreciate that we are being
slightly artifical in our discursive approach, partly for convenience and
partly to accommodate the conventional partitioning of design into two
major phases. In reality, JSP is not a separate end activity of JSD but
permeates all of the specification stage; that is, design of network
architecture and process texts occur together in the construction of a
system specification.

The Basic Method

The design notations used – structure diagrams and equivalent structure
texts – have already been covered in Sections 3.7 and 3.8. We shall
illustrate the basic steps of the method by developing the process text
for STUDENT-2 in the SUMS network (see Figs. 3.18 and 3.19).

1. Model the problem structure

Structure, or 'data usage', diagrams are drawn for each input and output stream. The intent here is to adequately reflect in each structure its contribution to 'what the problem is about', rather than to provide a mere physical interpretation of each data stream (particularly an input stream), the inadequacy of which would in any case be revealed in step 4. In general, the leaves of structure diagrams will be logically primitive data items – records, lines, characters, screen images or whatever is sufficiently rich in detail to support later steps in the method.

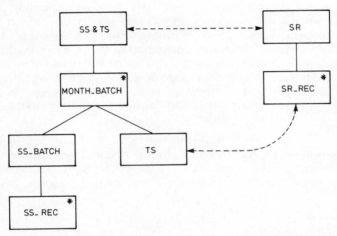

Fig. 3.20.   Data usage diagrams (with correspondence) for the STUDENT–2 process.

The data usage diagrams for STUDENT-2 are given in Fig. 3.20 (the two arrowed lines should be ignored for the moment). Note that data streams SS and TS are rough merged in the network and so are treated by STUDENT-2 as a single data stream. The important point in SS&TS's structure is to model the notion of a monthly interval.

2. Derive a process structure

This is achieved by coalescing the separate structures into a single structure. The following points capture most of the main ingredients of this compositional step:

☆ Each output component must ultimately be generated from some input component(s) and the main objective is to identify these functional correspondences. Thus, if each instance of ouput component B is derived from an instance of input component A in the same order and number, then they are combined to give a single component cAgB ('consume A generating B') in the process structure. However, A and B do not have to belong to the same structure type. For example, consider the arrowed lines in Fig. 3.20, which indicate the correspondences between the structures SS&TS and SR. Note the correspondence TS $<-->$ SR_REC* in particular; this is correct because TS is a component of an iteration and TS and SR_REC messages possess an ordered 1–1 relationship – the crucial test for a correct correspondence.

☆ Not all components in general will undergo such direct correspondence in this structural merging and these have to be appropriately placed in sequences in the single structure. This may necessitate creating additional sequences in the combined structure that are not present in any of the separate structures. The important point is that the process structure must possess all components of the problem structure as embodied in the separate data usage diagrams. A way of verifying this is that each original separate structure should be obtainable from the process structure by deleting or collapsing appropriate parts of the latter.

The essence of this whole step is to derive a single structure in which input and output are 'in harmony'. However, sometimes such harmony is unachievable – not because of a defect in the design, but because of an irreconcilable 'clash' between structures caused by some inherent

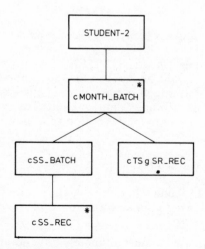

Fig. 3.21. Structure of process STUDENT–2.

characteristic of the problem. This situation will be briefly covered later. The harmonious composition of structures SS&TS and SR is given in Fig. 3.21.

3. Determine function

A list of functional primitives is made (e.g. reads and writes, assignments, read-access 'getsv' operations for state vector inspections) that need to be inserted into the process structure in order to obtain a complete design. Whilst there is no foolproof way of guaranteeing a complete list, a systematic method is to start with necessary output operations and then work backwards through intermediate calculations to input operations. The list of operations for STUDENT-2 is given in Table 3.1.

Table 3.1 List of operations to be allocated to STUDENT-2

1. read SS&TS	6. totmptime := 0
2. write SR_REC to SR	7. totmcomps := totmcomps + ncomps
3. totmcomps := 0	8. totmedits := totmedits + nedits
4. totmedits := 0	9. totmruns := totmruns + nruns
5. totmruns := 0	10. totmptime := totmptime + ptime

4. Add function

Each operation identified in the previous step is now added to its appropriate component in the process structure. 'Appropriateness' is determined by finding the component that must include the operation in question as part of its execution, so that the operation is performed once for each execution of the component. Figure 3.22 shows the allocation of the operations of Table 3.1 to STUDENT-2's structure. Read operations on each input stream are allocated on an 'ahead' basis – one as soon as the stream is opened (we have assumed SS&TS will be open at the start of STUDENT-2) and one immediately after each message of the stream has been consumed.

Step 4 is a crucial step in that it serves as a validation mechanism for the design. If no appropriate component can be found for an operation in the process structure, the design is defective and the data usage structures, or their correspondence, need to be reappraised.

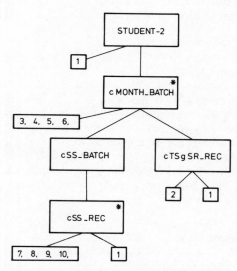

Fig. 3.22. Allocation of operations to STUDENT–2's structure.

5. Convert to structure text

At this point, the design is still expressed in diagrammatic form. Although translation to textual form is not obligatory, it generally clarifies matters to do so, particularly when non-trivial implementation techniques subsequently need to be applied. In shifting to textual format, the predicate expressions controlling selections and iterations are expressed to a sufficient degree of detail to convey their precise meaning. The text for STUDENT-2 is as follows:

(Minor note: we need an extra STUDENT-2_BODY component because the allocation of operation 1 to STUDENT-2 in the diagrammatic form creates a new sequence to be expressed in the text.)

```
STUDENT-2 seq
  read SS&TS;
  STUDENT-2_BODY itr {for lifespan of system}
    cMONTH_BATCH seq
      totmcomps := 0; totedits := 0;
      totmruns := 0; totmptime := 0;
      cSS_BATCH itr while (not TS message)
        cSS_REC seq
          totmcomps := totmcomps + ncomps;
          totmedits := totmedits + nedits;
          totmruns := totmruns + nruns;
          totmptime := totmptime + ptime;
          read SS&TS;
        cSS_REC end
      cSS_BATCH end
      cTSgSR_REC seq
        write SR_REC to SR; read SS&TS;
      cTSgSR_REC end
    cMONTH_BATCH end
  STUDENT-2_BODY end
STUDENT-2 end
```

The end result of all these steps is an operational specification of a process in the abstract design language. As with JSD at the network level, there is a clear separation in JSP between design and implementation; any techniques associated with the latter are deliberately disregarded during the former.

The Design of Other Processes in the SUMS Network

Although the design of the other function processes in the network may appear more complex due to multiple input or output streams and state vector inspections, the basic JSP method outlined above is still applicable. We shall use the text of FLUSH, given below, to make some additional points. FLUSH has one input data stream, one state vector inspection and two output data streams; the data usage diagrams and their correspondence, leading to the design of FLUSH, are in Fig. 3.23.

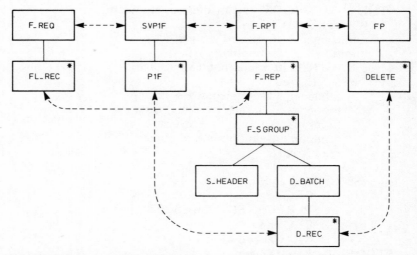

Fig. 3.23. Data usage diagrams and correspondence for the FLUSH function.

```
FLUSH seq
  read F_REQ;
  FLUSH_BODY itr {for the lifespan of the system}                    (a)
    cFL_RECgF_REP itr while (not end of log_on_codes)                (b)
      gF_SGROUP seq
        write S_HEADER to F_RPT;
        getsv(P1F);                                                  (c)
        gD_BATCH itr while (not end of P1Fs)                         (c)
          cP1FgD_REC&DELETE seq
            write P1F_details to F_RPT;
            write DELETE to FP[prog-idr];
            getsv(P1F);                                              (c)
          cP1FgD_REC&DELETE end
        gD_BATCH end
      gF_SGROUP end
    cFL_RECgF_REP end
    read F_REQ;
  FLUSH_BODY end
FLUSH end
```

As regards the contribution of the state vector inspection SVP1F to the structure of FLUSH, we have treated SVP1F as a simple data stream. In doing so, we have assumed that SVP1F, for each F_REP generated, consists only of those PROGRAM-1 state vectors grouped, ordered and selected as required by the access criteria (a), (b) and (c), namely:

(a) grouped by student log_on_code;
(b) groups ordered by increasing student log_on_code;
(c) within each group, selected by (F_REQ.date − last_access_date) >180, ordered by decreasing last_access_date.

This data structure is defined in Fig. 3.24 and is basically the same structure as F_RPT, as the annotations indicate. This is a diagrammatic way of describing the access pathway structure of state vector inspections. We would ensure in the implementation that the access pathway would actually be realized.

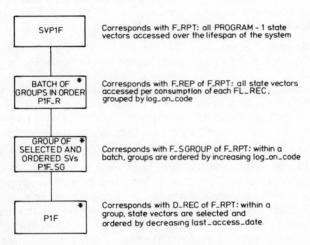

Fig. 3.24. Data structure diagram for SVP1F access pathway.

The handling of SVP1F and F_REQ represents a 'fixed merge' (compare rough merge); i.e. their processing is interleaved in a fixed way that is predetermined by the problem structure – here, for each FL_REC message read, a whole batch (P1F_R in Fig. 3.24) of PROGRAM-1 state vectors must then be inspected. Another type of merge is a 'data merge' as typified by collation processing of several input streams – see Jackson (1975 or 1983) for more details.

The text of REPORTER will be similar in structure to that of FLUSH – it will have an innermost iteration based on state vector access to the programs of a given student embedded in an iteration that deals with all students (repeat: write a TS message, receive an SR message and carry out the state vector inspection loop, generating another chunk of

MSP_RPT). The text of ENLISTER is simpler since, within its body (like REPORTER, an iteration over system lifespan), a single iteration is needed per message in E_ENQ to access STUDENT-1 state vectors selectively (on 'entered_PATSY = true'). Derivation of the two texts is left as an exercise for the diligent reader.

Closing Remarks on JSP

Space constraints preclude discussion of the more advanced features of JSP. We shall briefly mention just one – 'structure clashes'. A *structure clash* occurs when some physical constraint on an input stream cannot be mapped on to the logical input-output correspondence needed by the design. There are three types of structure clash that can arise in JSP designs (none of which occur in the SUMS network):

* Ordering clashes, caused by a misordering in an input stream; these are generally resolved by sorting, though a simpler solution is sometimes possible.
* Boundary clashes, which occur with blocked inputs when logical data entities straddle physical message boundaries.
* Interleaving clashes, which occur when logical sequences (tuples) of data are intermingled amongst one another in an input stream.

Structure clash resolution always involves the modularization of the clashing structures into separate processes communicating via extra intermediate data streams. Typically, at least one process appropriately 'reorganizes' the input stream causing the trouble into one or more non-clashing data streams. With interleaving clashes, JSP begins to encroach upon the realms of system development. Systems abound with interleaving clashes as a multitude of real-world entities perform or suffer their actions in an intermingled manner throughout the lifetime of the system. JSD takes care of this interleaving automatically by associating a separate system process with each individual instance of an entity, or by separating out 'marsupial' entities from their parents, e.g. separating PROGRAMs from STUDENTs. For further details of JSP's approach and other aspects of JSP not covered here, particularly so-called *recognition difficulties* and *backtracking*, consult one of the references quoted.

3.10   CONCLUDING REMARKS

If the JSD specification method is viewed in terms of the general concepts and tools summarized in Section 3.6, the following analysis emerges:

★ Building blocks
   sequential (single thread) processes;
   ideal FIFO data streams; state vectors.
★ Structuring concepts
   processes are connected by data stream or state vector inspection;
   networks are asynchronous, but processes strictly sequential
   internally;
   hierarchy exists within processes;
   modularity:
   (i) processes are strictly modular; state vector inspection does not
   violate this – it merely obtains a 'copy' of the state of a process;
   (ii) there is a well-defined separation between model processes and
   function processes;
   (iii) model processes are well separated by previous 'entity analysis';
   (iv) functions are largely orthogonal.
★ Techniques
   the building of networks is 'sideways on' – there is no hierarchy in a
   JSD network;
   there are some bottom-up elements in the early stages, e.g. entity
   actions are determined before being 'structured into' higher levels;
   there is a top-down element to detailed process design in the
   development of data-usage structures, but also a compositional
   element (process design is achieved by coalescing structures) and
   modular separation ('clashing' structures are kept apart).
★ Criteria
   reflect real-world models in system architecture *before* functionality;
   create abstract operational specification devoid of implementation
   detail.

JSD is of course but one viable development method out of a pool of
many possibilities. The dual purpose of the last three sections has been
to illustrate a modern system development method in action, and to
convey some desirable general properties that system specification and
design should possess, such as:

★ The method should facilitate user involvement. For operational
   methods like JSD, the separation of requirements analysis from
   system specification implied by Chapters 2 and 3 is somewhat artificial
   – the two are thoroughly interleaved.
★ The method should be divided into a number of well-defined steps,
   each step possessing a clear development objective and interface to
   other steps.
★ The method should be based on rational, defendable principles
   (e.g. develop 'model' before satisfying functionality; achieve clear

separation between 'specification' and 'implementation') and employ abstract software concepts.

★ The method should facilitate the application of other software engineering activities. For example, JSD supports:

incremental development: e.g. only part of the model or eventual complete set of functions might be specified and implemented initially;

automation: JSD possesses the potential for rapid prototyping since its specifications are largely 'executable', and for partial automated implementation since many of the transformations required to map specifications into implementations are mechanically definable.

Naturally, every development method has its protagonists and its detractors. The reader should appreciate that there is no such thing as 'the best' development method (the concept is probably not meaningful anyway). Each method possesses strengths and weaknesses, debatable claims, arguable rationales, etc. From a practical standpoint, the important thing is to:

(a) Choose a method that suits your type of application(s) and which you have the resources and commitment to support.

(b) Having made your choice, stick to its principles and techniques with 100% discipline, adapting it only when there exist watertight reasons for doing so.

Chapter 4

Further Design Issues

4.1 SYSTEMS AND PROGRAMS

There is some basis for making a distinction between 'system-sized' problems needing 'system' solutions and 'program-sized' problems needing 'program' solutions. For example, the external data objects (files, etc.) to be processed by a program will be described in its requirements specification. Thus, a 'programming' problem, unlike a system development problem, involves no file or database design apart from temporary working storage needed by the program itself. However, differences between programs and systems get easily blurred for the following reasons:

* Externally, any system can be viewed operationally as a single program. Indeed, many (even highly complex) systems are implemented as single programs.
* Equally, many programs written are extremely large and, in terms of sheer size alone, are far more complex than a lot of so-called 'systems'.
* Basic software principles and concepts discussed in the previous chapter (e.g. hierarchy, abstraction), and many of the development techniques that exploit them (e.g. top-down and bottom-up design), are applicable to all levels of software specification and design.

Nevertheless, despite a certain artificiality in distinguishing between systems and programs, such a distinction helps avoid discussing specification and design as one large monolithic topic. Furthermore, some aspects of software development are concerned specifically with design at the program level.

It will be recalled that, strictly, we are regarding a 'program' as an implementation object. A program can be defined as 'the smallest kind of stand-alone implemented module that can be submitted to a target environment for execution'. Programs are the executable end-products of the late stages of the software production process, whereas processes are the conceptual specification and design objects from which programs are derived. However, for simplicity in this chapter, we shall use the term 'program' loosely to cover both cases. Thus, the

term 'programming', if it means anything, can be interpreted as
either:

(a) designing (then implementing) individual modules as part of a
    system development task, i.e. 'detailed design'. In Section 3.9, we
    have already illustrated detailed design in this context using the JSP
    program design method. Or:
(b) taking a problem in its entirety as captured in a requirements
    definition and judging the problem to be of a nature, size and
    complexity such that development can proceed on a single program
    basis.

In this chapter, we are not concerned with discriminating between these
two development contexts – from specification through to testing, they
are identical anyway.

All that has so far been stated in previous chapters concerning
requirements definition and specification applies equally to 'program-
sized' problems, and so no further elaboration of these issues will occur
in this chapter, except to note the following:

★ In case (a) above, a requirements specification for a module emerges
  as part of the specification and design of system architecture.
★ In both cases, a 'real-world domain' exists inasmuch as it is already
  modelled in the data objects that the module or program is required to
  process.

We shall concentrate now on program design, firstly by further explor-
ing aspects of software architecture, modularity and abstraction, then
looking at some specific program design methods, and finally elaborating upon the notion of 'reusability' in software.

Note: in various parts of this chapter, we shall make use of an Ada-
influenced abstract 'program design language' or PDL (for Ada, see
DoD 1983). The reader should appreciate that there is not a complete
equivalence between our PDL and Ada in all aspects of syntax and
semantics.

4.2 FUNDAMENTAL PROGRAM ARCHITECTURES

Sequential Architectures

The following three basic kinds of structure for describing non-primitive
processes represent a sufficient set for specifying the architecture of any
sequential process – a fact that possesses some theoretical basis (Bohm
& Jacopini 1966).

(a) Straight sequencing (concatenation):

X1; X2; X3; . . .

(b) Selective sequencing: The minimal form of this is the binary decision structure, one representation of which is:

if C **then** X1 **else** X2 **endif**

Note that this represents the two possible straight sequences:

<C; X1> or <C; X2>

(c) Iterative sequencing: A minimal form of this is the indeterminate repetition structure represented by:

while C **do** X **enddo**

This represents the infinitely many straight sequences:

<C; [X;C]*> where [. . .]* means "repeat 0 or more times".

The symbols C and X stand for arbitrary Boolean expressions (conditions) and process components respectively. The structural forms in (b) and (c) have been described by well-known syntax. Both forms are general purpose – that is, any arbitrary selective or iterative structuring can be expressed by the given if-form or while-form respectively. In practice, however, use of these forms alone would prove cumbersome and delimiting in terms of elegance and expressiveness. Thus, they are usually augmented by the use of other related structures for reasons of appropriateness and clarity; for example:

★ 'Multi-choice' forms of selection structuring, with syntax and semantics along the lines of the following two possibilities:

if C1 **then** X1 **elseif** C2 **then** X2 . . **elseif** Ck **then** Xk [**else** X0] **endif**	(Such structures are ordered; i.e. evaluation of the Ci takes place i=1,2 . . . etc., until a Ck is found that is true, or otherwise the optional else-part is selected if present.)

case E **of**
  T1 ==> X1
  T2 ==> X2
    .
    .
  Tk ==> Xk
  [**else**   X0]
  endcase
	(The component Xi, $1 <= i <= k$, which is selected is the one whose 'tag list' Ti contains a value matching that yielded by the selecting expression E; if there is no match, then the else-component X0 is selected by default provided it is present, otherwise the outcome is unspecified.)

★ Other iterative structures, which include most commonly:

do X until C enddo

This is another indeterminate structure in which the 'loop body' X, unlike in the while-form, is executed *before* the controlling condition C, whose evaluation to true, rather than false, halts the iteration.

for I in S do X enddo

In essence, X is repeated $|S|$ times where $|S|$ = the cardinality of the specified index set S. S is determined once-off before execution of the first cycle begins. Per cycle, the loop index I takes on a different value in S (I is non-updatable within X), so that all elements of S are eventually covered precisely once by the iteration. There are many variations on this basic determinate iterative theme that are found in high-level languages, but these need not concern us here.

An important point is that all three types of process structuring have their equivalents in data structuring, as Table 4.1 indicates:

Table 4.1 Correspondence between process and data structure

Type of structure	Data structure equivalent
Straight	Records†
Selective	Record variants†(e.g. Pascal) Unions (e.g. Algol-68)
Iterative	(unbounded) Sequences (e.g. serial files, stacks, queues) (bounded) Arrays†

The fact that there exists this correspondence between process and data structure is not merely worth noting for its own sake. The important implication for program design is that, for any kind of data structure in Table 4.1, there exists a 'ready-made' sequential process (algorithm) structure for dealing with it – a fact that any form of 'structured programming' will exploit in some fashion. In short, 'data structures steer the design of algorithms'.

Non-Determinism

The above selection and iteration structures are deterministic in the sense that, given values for the controlling conditions and expressions, the execution path through a selection or cycle of iteration can be uniquely worked out. Dijkstra (1975, 1976) advanced a more general form of selection and iteration in which this determinism does not necessarily hold. The form of the selection structure is the 'guarded command':

if C1 −> S1
 □ C2 −> S2
.
.
□ Ck −> Sk
endif

This selection differs semantically from the conventional multi-arm conditional as follows:

★ Firstly, all guards (the conditions Ci, i=1,k) are evaluated; the alternatives Si, i=1,k whose guards are true are then available for selection.
★ One such alternative is then selected, the choice being made non-deterministically; if no guards are true, program execution is aborted.

Syntactically, the iterative form is obtained by replacing **if** . . . **fi** by **do** . . .**od**. On each cycle of the iteration, a non-deterministic choice is made as described previously. The iteration stops when all guards evaluate to false. Note that if the loop body comprises a single guarded alternative, the iteration reduces to a conventional while-form.

The advantage of using these forms is basically that the non-determinism imparts an extra 'degree of freedom' to the designer. The decrease in specificity frees the designer from commitment to certain explicit kinds of decision-making that would otherwise be imposed in a purely deterministic environment. The result is that alternative programs possessing trivial differences can be mapped on to a single non-deterministic solution. As a simple example, consider:

if x >= y −> max := x
 □ y >= x −> max := y
endif

Note that when x=y, both guards will be true and so either alternative can be selected to give the correct outcome. The structure takes care of four different conventional 'if C then . . . else . . . endif' solutions to the same problem, where C can be either 'x>y', 'x>=y', 'y>x' or 'y>=x'. In effect, each of the four deterministic solutions represents a correct implementation of the non-deterministic version.

Object Architectures

Whilst the sequential structures discussed previously represent the basic architectural components of sequential programs, they are not sufficiently powerful mechanisms for achieving proper modularity and abstraction. Moreover, some design methods such as object-oriented design, outlined in Section 3.6, are based on an 'object' view of software architecture that could not be supported without more general abstraction mechanisms. We shall defer discussion of these mechanisms until the next section.

The term 'object-oriented' has been interpreted with considerable flexibility in the literature and is often equated with design based on data abstractions and modules. However, 'true' object architecture is characterized by the following main features:

classes and objects;
message communication;
inheritance.

A *class* defines a table of operations (with hidden implementations) called 'methods' or 'behaviours' and a set of variables. *Objects* are instances of classes. Each object possesses its private data space corresponding to the variables of its class. An object's class defines at runtime the operations allowed on it. Note that this is a departure from the norm imposed by most languages, which insist on compile-time binding of types to operands and implementations of operations to operators.

Things get done in an object-oriented environment by the latter selecting and telling objects what to do, which in turn tell other objects what to do, etc. This is often referred to as 'message passing', although, as Cox (1984) observes, the terminology gives the somewhat misleading impression that object architecture is a natural choice for distributed systems. In fact, sending an object a message is equivalent to nothing more than a function call – the message selects one of the object's operations.

The property of *inheritance* enables progressively more specialized classes to be constructed from existing ones. Thus, new classes can be created from existing ones by the former inheriting the variables and behaviours of the latter and adding their own new specific features; moreover, new features can, if desired, override what has been inherited. This simple but powerful scheme has important implications for reusability, as discussed at length by Cox (1986), who shows how the 'true' object-oriented paradigm can be grafted on to conventional programming languages to form an enriching, evolving partnership. Figure 4.1 summarizes our brief overview.

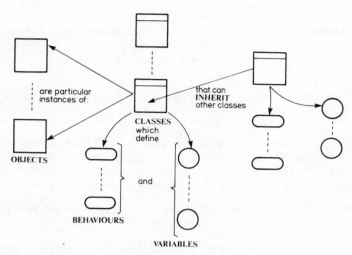

Fig. 4.1. An object-orientated environment.

Concurrent Architectures

Concurrency was introduced in Section 3.3 as a powerful tool in the specification and design of system architectures as asynchronous networks. However, this architectural model usually enjoys a much less comfortable fit at the program level. The reason has already been hinted at in Section 3.3, namely that conventional machine architecture, with its sequential von Neumann (vN) basis, has inevitably been reflected in the languages – program design and implementation languages – that 'sit on top of' that machine architecture. Amongst other characteristics, the vN model of computation:

★ Tends to de-emphasise connectivity and data flow.
★ Separates 'process' into a procedural element and local data environment.
★ Prematurely imposes sequential scheduling on procedural components.

The languages in common usage that break away from this tradition are in the minority, though gaining ground. However, inability to exploit concurrency frequently leads to impoverished program designs containing a high degree of over-specified sequentiality. For example, the data structures marked † in Table 4.1 are actually random access, although a purely sequential environment precludes any possibility of exploiting this characteristic. Thus, for example, ideally we might wish to specify:

||P(Ai),**forall**1<=i<=n {|| stands for concurrent structuring, where P is some process to be applied to each of the n elements of an array A}

But usually in practice, the language we are using forces us to specify:

for i **in** [1 . .n] **do** P(Ai) **enddo**

Collaterality is also worth exploiting, since it is a further mechanism by which a design is allowed to remain uncommitted with respect to scheduling decisions. A language such as Algol-68 (e.g. Lindsey & van der Meulen 1977) provides a general-purpose 'collateral clause':

begin X1, X2, . . . Xk **end** (the comma separators specify unordered elaboration of the Xi)

However, expression of collaterality need not require special structures. If desired, it can be defined implicitly to exist in syntactic contexts where no particular order of execution or evaluation should be assumed anyway; for example:

★ Evaluation of actual parameters or operands of any applied occurrence of a function, procedure or operator, as in F(X,Y,Z) or X @ Y.
★ Evaluation of components of the 'display' of a structured data object, as on the right-hand side of: X := (A, B, C).

This means, of course, that no connectivity should exist between, for example, members of an actual parameter list of a procedure call; if some connectivity does exist, the semantics of the call are indeterminate – the exact side effects cannot be predicted because no particular order of evaluation of the actual parameters may be assumed.

Expression of concurrency in design requires special structures and mechanisms. A number of different methods exist:

Semaphores

The P and V semaphore operations of Dijkstra (1968) represent a low-level mechanism for achieving mutual exclusion and synchronization (data transfer) between concurrent processes accessing shared data. A *binary semaphore* S is a special two-state variable on which the only allowed operations are:

P(S):
  if S = FREE **then** S := BUSY
                         {and execution of the process issuing P(S)
                         is allowed to continue}
              else {execution of the process issuing P(S) is
                   suspended}
  endif

V(S):
  if one or more processes are currently suspended on S
  then reactivate one of them
  else S := FREE
  endif

These operations are indivisible with respect to one another – the above definitions are merely intended to convey their effect. As an example of their use, consider the simple producer-consumer problem depicted in Fig. 3.12 in Section 3.6. The places S1 and S2 in the Petri Net in fact correspond to semaphores, with S1 initialized to BUSY and S2 to FREE. If we have:

S1, S2 : SEMAPHORE;
S1 := BUSY; S2 := FREE;

and position P(S2) and V(S1) around PUT X (the critical section of P) and P(S1) and V(S2) around GET X (the critical section of Q), then the textual description of the producer and consumer processes is complete. This will:

★ Achieve synchronization between P and Q, i.e. they will behave in a PUT, GET, PUT, GET ... manner.
★ Ensure mutual exclusion between P and Q (the 'safety' aspect) so that S1 and S2 cannot both be FREE at the same time, which would otherwise allow simultaneous access by both processes to X.
★ Ensure absence of deadlock (the 'liveness' aspect) so that S1 and S2 cannot both be BUSY at the same time, which would otherwise eventually result in P and Q waiting indefinitely for each other to signal release of X.

The main problem with using semaphores is that, being low level and 'unstructured', they are (rather like the 'goto' – see later) easy to misuse and can be hard to understand.

Monitors

The *monitor* concept of Hoare (1974) bears considerably on notions of modularity and data abstraction. To illustrate, suppose that several processes are accessing a shared resource. The resource is encapsulated inside a monitor, and the operations allowed on the resource by the processes are only those visibly exported by the monitor. A monitor, like a data abstraction (say), is therefore a static, non-executable object, though it can possess initialization actions automatically executed once-off when control enters the scope of the program in which the monitor is declared. Moreover, mutual exclusion is implicitly guaranteed in monitor semantics – only one process at a time is allowed to 'enter' a monitor in order to access one of its operations.

Synchronization is achieved by special monitor 'condition variables' (similar to semaphores) on which two commands, executed as appropriate within monitor operations, are allowed. Suppose C is a monitor condition variable; then:

wait (C)   causes the process accessing the monitor operation that issues the wait command to be suspended on a FIFO queue, and releases mutual exclusion on the monitor;

signal(C)   causes the process at the head of the wait queue for C, if any, to re-enter the monitor and continue the monitor operation on which it was suspended.

Thus, a wait command frees the monitor for entry by another process. Moreover, a signal(C) command gives priority to processes suspended on C over processes that are waiting 'outside' the monitor to access a monitor operation. It simplifies matters if a monitor operation issuing a signal command does so only at the end of its execution – the monitor is then released immediately (this restriction is actually unnecessary but we shall not cover the more general case).

The rendezvous

The *rendezvous* represents a mechanism for synchronized message passing, i.e. a sender process waits for a receiver process, or vice versa, to reach an appropriate point so that data transfer can be effected between them. The synchronized message passing of CSP – Communicating Sequential Processes (Hoare, 1978b and 1985) – is achieved by special read and write commands:

Q ! X   {send message X to process Q}
P ? X   {receive message X from process P}

These synchronization points can act as guards in a guarded command structure (see 'Non-determinism' above) that is incorporated into CSP. Thus, a send guard is 'true' if the named process is waiting to receive a message; a receive guard is 'true' if the named process is waiting to send a message. A process is suspended on a send or receive command until the other specified process involved 'catches up' to complete the rendezvous and enable the data transfer to take place. After message passing has taken place, both processes continue executing concurrently. Our simple producer-consumer example expressed in CSP notation would be:

*[x:item; producer?x −> consumer!x]

The rendezvous machanism of concurrent processes − or *tasks* − in Ada (DoD 1983) is a more powerful form of synchronization that enables one task (the 'caller') to rendezvous with another (the 'called' task) without the latter knowing who the former is. Here is our example coded in Ada:

```
task PRODUCER;
task body PRODUCER is
  -- local declarations
  procedure PRODUCE (Z : out ITEM) is
    -- internal details of PRODUCE (not given)
  end PRODUCE;
  X : ITEM;
begin
  loop
    PRODUCE(X);
    CONSUMER.TRANSMIT(X);
  end loop;
end PRODUCER;

task CONSUMER is
  entry TRANSMIT(Z : in ITEM);
end;
task body CONSUMER is
  procedure CONSUME(Z : in ITEM) is
    -- internal details of CONSUME (not given)
  end CONSUME;
  X : ITEM;
begin
  loop
    accept TRANSMIT(Z : in ITEM) do
      X := Z;
    end TRANSMIT;
    CONSUME(X);
  end loop;
end CONSUMER;
```

The concurrent execution of a set of tasks is automatically initiated when control enters the program unit in which the tasks are declared. A task module is expressed as two components – specification and body. The specification defines the synchronization (entry) points, if any, in the task body – none for PRODUCER, one for CONSUMER called TRANSMIT. Task entries can be parameterized in the manner of procedures to allow exchange of data between two tasks involved in a rendezvous. A rendezvous is established when one task has issued an entry call (which is like a remote procedure call – CONSUMER. TRANSMIT(X) in our example) to another task that has reached an appropriate synchronization (accept) point. If the latter occurs before an entry call has been made, the accepting task is suspended, and vice versa for the calling task. Note that the accepting task is unaware of which task it will rendezvous with, although, in our simple example, CONSUMER can rendezvous only with PRODUCER. If several tasks independently issue the same entry call, they are suspended and queued on a FIFO basis at that entry point. When the accepting task reaches the synchronization point concerned, it will rendezvous with the task at the head of the queue. Note that, when a rendezvous occurs, the calling task remains suspended until the accepting task has completed execution of the 'body' of its synchronization point.

The above is just the barest detail of task synchronization in Ada, which contains a number of powerful features for handling multi-tasking and real-time programming, including a special 'select' statement that enables a task to choose non-deterministically between a number of alternative rendezvous points:

```
select
  accept RP1 . . . do
    . . . . .
  end RP1;
or
  accept RP2 . . . do
    . . . . .
  end RP2;
--etc.
end select;
```

In addition, the alternatives can be guarded and the selection then operates as a guarded command as described previously; a rendezvous is then possible only at one of those synchronization points whose guards are open. Further details of Ada tasking can of course be obtained from any general Ada reference, but Burns (1985) deals specifically with the topic.

An excellent comparison of Ada tasks, CSP and monitors is given by Wegner & Smolka (1983). They also touch upon coroutines, which we briefly explore in Section 6.6 as a means of multiprogramming asynchronous processes on a single processor.

Functional (Applicative) Architectures

The origins of 'structured programs' are firmly embedded in a sequential vN environment. As Backus (1978) argues, vN (i.e. imperative, state-transition) languages, and hence 'vN programming', suffer from a number of disadvantages:

★ Program semantics is too closely associated with the notion of state transition (a program changes state as the point of execution moves sequentially through its instructions and its data store suffers destructive side-effects via assignment-to-variable actions).
★ There exists an artificial division between 'statements' and 'expressions'.
★ A vN language tends to have a fixed framework that is large in comparison to the flexibility that exists within that framework for building new programs from existing ones.
★ vN languages, hence programs, do not possess simple, elegant mathematical properties.

Functional programming provides a total contrast to vN programming and overcomes the disadvantages just mentioned. In pure functional programming, where there are no vN 'impurities' present such as functions with side effects, programs are merely applications of built-in or user-defined functions that are:

side-effect free;
non-imperative (WHAT instead of HOW);
unconstraining in terms of order of evaluation.

Here is an example:

Ackermann's function *ack* can be defined as:
$$ack(m,n) \; \triangle \quad \textbf{if } m = 0 \textbf{ then } n+1$$
$$\textbf{elseif } n = 0 \textbf{ then } ack(m-1,1)$$
$$\textbf{else } \; ack(m-1,ack(m,n-1))$$
$$\textbf{endif}$$

The body of *ack* is a conditional expression that could be encoded directly in an imperative language possessing a suitable conditional form and recursion capability. However, in Backus 'FP-style' notation, for example, the definition of *ack* would become:

Def ack = eq.[hd,0] −> +.[hd.tl,1];
        (eq.[hd.tl,0] −> ack.[−.[hd,1],1];
          ack.[−.[hd,1], ack[hd,−.[hd.tl,1]]])

The body of *ack* is now a function that is itself just a multi-level structuring of simpler functions. There are in fact four kinds of 'functional form' – structures that yield new higher-level functions from their components – being used in this definition, namely:

(a) Composition:

   (f.g):x = f:(g:x)

h:x means "function *h* applied to argument *x*".
(b) Construction:

   [f1, ... fk]:x = <f1:x, ... fk:x>

Objects to which functions are applied, and which functions yield, are either atoms (e.g. integers, strings) or sequences, the latter being denoted in angled brackets, possibly using ellipsis notation to indicate some arbitrary finite length sequence.
(c) Constant:

   c:x = **if** x = ⊥ **then** ⊥ **else** c **endif**

This holds for any object *c*; ⊥ (called 'bottom') represents 'the undefined value'.
(d) Condition:

   (c −> f;g):x =   **if** c:x = T **then** f:x
              elseif c:x = F **then** g:x
                        else ⊥
            endif

The atoms T and F denote 'true' and 'false' respectively.

   Other functional forms in a Backus FP-system also exist. In the example, note that the outermost structure is the condition functional form, whose 'false-component function' is also a condition functional form. The definition uses five predefined functions: *eq* (test for equality), + (integer addition), − (integer subtraction), *hd* (head element of sequence) and *tl* (tail of sequence). All these functions are defined in such a way that they will yield ⊥ if applied to inappropriate arguments. For example, *tl* is defined as:

   tl:x =   **if** x = <x1>   **then** ø
        elseif x = <x1, ... xk> **and** k >= 2 **then** <x2, ... xk>
                                            else ⊥
        endif
ø is an atom that denotes the null sequence.

Note, therefore, how the definition of *ack* is completely 'safe', i.e. even if applied to an object which is not a sequence of two non-negative integers (its intended argument list), it will still yield a value, namely $\bot$. Also note how an FP program does not contain any references to argument names, variables, etc. – one of a number of special features of FP notation.

Functional notations play a major role in formal specification (see Chapter 5). Given also the mathematical 'cleanliness' that functional programs possess, it is clear that formal software development methods and functional programming form a natural partnership that is likely to increase in strength and importance as software engineering attempts to 'move with the times'. A Backus FP system is not the current fashionable idiom for functional programming, but we have chosen it for illustration in recognition of Backus's landmark paper; for an alternative, Turner's tutorial paper (1986) on the functional language Miranda$^{(TM)}$ is highly recommended reading. In order to delve more deeply into the functional style, the reader should consult texts such as Henderson (1980) and Glaser *et al.* (1984).

Other Possibilities

Yet a further alternative to the 'vN programming paradigm' is offered by languages like Prolog (e.g. Clocksin & Mellish 1984). The architecture of a Prolog program is *declarative* rather than functional. It consists of declarations of facts about, and relationships within, some domain of interest which are entered into a database that can then be interrogated by query operations. A language like Prolog brings an element of AI or 'knowledge engineering' into software development, and this could have important implications for software engineering in the near future; some limited progress in the marriage of AI and software engineering has already been made – see Chapter 9.

The object-oriented, functional and declarative paradigms offer radical alternatives to the vN style with or without 'bolted on' concurrency. Be that as it may, for necessary brevity we shall restrict ourselves in the rest of this chapter to the 'vN sequential paradigm', whilst recognizing that notions of good structure, modularity, abstraction, etc. apply universally to all software, regardless of the architectural form in which it is expressed.

4.3 MODULARITY AND ABSTRACTION IN PROGRAM DESIGN

The sequential structures described in Section 4.2 are 'modular' in the sense that they are 'single entry, single exit' box-like structures. However, proper modularity and abstraction is achievable only by using mechanisms of encapsulation that provide appropriate degrees of detail hiding and formalized interfaces, such as:

★ Subprograms, i.e. functions (including operators) and procedures (subroutines).
★ Modules comprising collections of specified process and data objects.

Use of these structures obviously has the effect of separating the composition of a program into a number of distinct components. This separation could be driven solely by pragmatic considerations. For example, the design of a large program might be divided up to fit in with the number, and skill, of programmers available. However, subdivision into 'modules' based on such criteria alone is very unlikely to lead to quality software, unless we just happen to be extremely fortunate. Rather, there exist a number of far stronger reasons for exploiting modularity and abstraction in program design that we shall now examine.

Adherence to a Method's Principles

Modules are generated as a result of adhering to the principles of the development method being employed. For example, construction of modules such as data abstractions is fundamental to design that can be loosely referred to as 'object oriented' (Sections 3.6 and 4.2). Similarly, the specification and design of functional modules is part of the Structured Design method described in Section 4.6. As a further example, some of the techniques associated with JSP design (specifically, resolving structure clashes) inherently involve creation of separate process modules. Whilst the modularity principles of these various methods are quite different, for example:

   object-oriented design aims for encapsulation and representation hiding;
   Structured Design strives for maximum 'cohesion' and minimal 'coupling';
   JSP requires 'problem structure' to be embodied and preserved in the design;

the objective of physical module realization in the program production phase is the same in each case – to transform an abstract design into an implementation in such a way that the modular structure of the former is faithfully mapped into the latter.

Synthesis

Subprograms provide the basic facility for the separate development of process components that are then integrated together into the framework of some higher-level structure. Modules allow several independently designed components to be brought together as a single 'resource' of components; for example:

```
module SUMS_LEVEL1AND2 is
specification
    procedure STUDENT_1  . . . . .    {its interface only}
    procedure STUDENT_2  . . . . .    {likewise ... }
    procedure PROGRAM_1 . . . . .    {likewise ... }
implementation
    {of each procedure}
endmod {SUMS_LEVEL1AND2}
```

In our PDL, a module comprises a specification part for the process and data objects it exports, and an implementation part that defines the realization of each exported object. A module's specification is its logical interface to all other software units that use one or more of the module's exports for 'building block' purposes. We can imagine a software unit acquiring a module's exports by:

using <name of module>
<text of software unit that references the module's exports>

The implementation of any export is hidden by default, unless stated otherwise. This 'hiding' aspect of module semantics represents the basis for achieving any required degree of security and control over what is, and what is not, visible and accessible.

Enrichment

The example module above provides three procedural components that are to be used to develop a more complex software unit (such as a higher-level subprogram, module or program). This 'build and integrate upwards' strategy that characterizes bottom-up development can be initiated at any level and applied through any number of successively higher levels. However, when applied as a technique to complement other program design methods, bottom-up design is generally used to enrich the base level of the target language, i.e. to augment it with new primitives. In this case, the design typically involves the creation of a number of application-related operations and data types. As an example, suppose we need a string-handling capability that is not possessed by the target language. This capability could be provided by a module whose specification is of the following kind:

```
module STRING_HANDLER is
specification
  type STRING
  NULL_STRING : constant STRING
  operator + (STRING,STRING) returns STRING          (a)
  operator + (STRING,CHAR) returns STRING
  operator + (CHAR,STRING) returns STRING
  operator + (CHAR,CHAR) returns STRING
  operator * (CHAR,NATURAL) returns STRING           (a)
  operator * (STRING,NATURAL) returns STRING
  function LEN (STRING) returns NATURAL
  procedure REPLACE (STRING,STRING, inout STRING)    (b)
  procedure GETSTR (CHANNEL, out STRING)             (b)
  procedure PUTSTR (CHANNEL, STRING)
  STRING_OVERFLOW : exception                        (c)
  {etc.}
endmod {STRING_HANDLER}
```

Notes

(a) Existing operators + and * become *overloaded*. An overloaded operator or identifier is one that simultaneously possesses two or more unambiguous interpretations.
(b) Parameter communication modes **in**, **out** and **inout** define importing (non-updatable), exporting and 'transporting' parameters respectively. The **in** mode only is allowed for functions and operators, and is also the default mode.
(c) STRING_OVERFLOW is an *exception* (error condition) that will be raised by a number of the module's routines. Exception handling is covered in Section 7.2.

Clearly, for effective application of enrichment, a generalized module capability in the target language, whilst not absolutely essential, is highly desirable. Certainly though, enrichment requires an extensible language that permits unrestrictive definition of new data types and operators on those types.

Note that a similar process of enrichment can also apply to modules themselves. Thus, a new module can be created from an existing one by inheriting the latter's exports and enriching them with additional data types, operations, etc.

Data Encapsulation and Abstraction

Although we have covered this topic previously in Section 3.5, we include it here again because of its fundamental importance in modular design. Note that a data type definition:

type <TYPE_NAME> **is** <representation for TYPE_NAME>

is an abstraction in much the same way that a subprogram definition is – it ascribes a new single name to the given representation. However, on its own in a program, the data representation of objects of type TYPE_NAME remains accessible and can therefore be exploited for any purpose. By hiding the object and/or its representation in a module and restricting access to the object or type to only those operations provided by the module itself, accessibility is strictly controlled and exploitation of 'unnecessary knowledge' is precluded – we have an encapsulated data object or abstract data type, respectively. To illustrate, we can imagine abstract data types being supported in our design language as in the following example:

```
module SEQUENCE is
specification
   type LIST is abstract                            (a)
   function NEW_LIST returns LIST
   function HD (LIST) returns ELEM                   (b)
   function TL (LIST) returns LIST
   function LEN (LIST) returns NATURAL
   function CONS (ELEM,LIST) returns LIST            (b)
   function APPEND (LIST,LIST) returns LIST
   EMPTY_LIST : constant LIST
endmod {SEQUENCE}
```

Notes

(a) That is, LIST is an abstract data type; thus, the six functions that follow are the *only* operations allowed on LIST objects (even equality testing and assignment are debarred).
(b) We are assuming here that type ELEM is imported from the module's surrounding environment. In Section 4.7, we will see that there are ways of parameterizing a module with respect to data types, thus enhancing the module's generality.

Although the example given here would also have an enrichment effect, it should be remembered that data abstraction can be used at any design level, including the top-level specification of complete systems (see again Section 3.5).

Reusability

Modularity is the essence of component reusability, since it creates the required independence from external environments that is clearly necessary for a program component to be usable without modification in a potentially unlimited number of applications. Moreover, depending on the degree of parameterization and abstraction designed into a module, increasing levels of generality and hence reusability can be obtained. Portability is also an obvious requirement for reusable software, but as this is a property of implemented software, we shall delay discussion of portability aspects until a later chapter.

The topic of reusability is discussed in the last section of this chapter. For now, it may be noted that modules such as STRING_HANDLER and SEQUENCE would be excellent candidates for inclusion in a library of reusable software.

Exploitation of Commonality

This is one of the most frequent uses of subprograms that arises in practice. If a non-trivial process appears more than once in a design, then forming it into a subprogram avoids multiple occurrences of the same (or, given the generalizing power of parameterization, essentially the same) refinement. This helps to:

★ Improve economy of effort by making the design task easier.
★ Reduce program size and complexity, in principle making it easier to understand.

There is sometimes confusion between a 'common' subprogram and one arising out of bottom-up enrichment, since an enrichment subprogram will also often be applied several times in a program. However, the two forms are quite distinct for the following reasons:

★ Common subprograms are generally not part of the base level of design primitives and hence are more sensitive to program modification that results, say, from a requirements change. Because bottom-up subprograms intended to enrich the base level *are* primitives, they are much more robust to change, since 'requirements drift' is very unlikely to affect the 'abstract machine' of the design.
★ Common subprograms are usually program (hence problem) specific, i.e. they are usually of little use outside the specific design context in

which they were originally conceived. Enrichment modules, on the other hand, may well be of use to potentially any number of other applications.

To appreciate these points, consider the example of enriching standard Pascal with a more powerful string-handling capability. Is this facility likely to be affected by a requirements modification to a problem whose solution requires string handling? Is this facility likely to be useful to Pascal programmers in general? Answers: NO and YES respectively.

Maintenance of Clarity

By forming a complex process component into a subprogram, so that its realization is crystallized away from the algorithm in which it is embedded, the size of the latter is considerably reduced and therefore its clarity enhanced. A reader will then perceive a much more compact and readily understood algorithm, rather than a bewildering mass of detailed code. For example, the overall structure of a program might be:

> *read record*
> **while** *end of file not reached* **do**
>   *validate record*
>   **if** *record* ok **then**
>   *update database*
>   **endif**
>   *read record*
> **enddo**

Given that processes *validate record* and *update database* are significantly non-trivial (compared to, say, *read record*), it would be sound practice to procedurize these components. Such 'refinement' subprogramming can be appropriate at the top few levels of a complex algorithm. However, there are no hard and fast rules to apply to help decide whether or not it is appropriate in any given instance – such decision-making is a matter of judgement that comes mainly through experience. Refinement subprograms, by their very nature, occur once-off in a program text. This in turn reduces the benefits of parameterization, but not entirely so. Except possibly in the case of a global data structure that is accessed in various parts of the program, parameterization of communication will generally enhance clarity and probability of correctness by reducing otherwise necessary reliance on non-local variables.

Isolation of Specific Features

A common example of this would be to isolate some implementation dependency that could cause portability problems. To illustrate, suppose an ISLETTER predicate is required in a program that will be ported to different target environments. Irrespective of any other considerations discussed above that might apply, it would still be appropriate to form the predicate into a Boolean function. Thus, assuming an underlying ASCII machine (the dependency feature):

```
function ISLETTER (C:CHAR) returns BOOLEAN is
begin
    return (C in ['A'..'Z', 'a'..'z'])
endfun {ISLETTER}
```

This isolates the dependency as a single instance, making the program far easier to modify than if the test were lexically embedded in the program text wherever it was required. More generally, if a number of dependency features existed, it would be eminently sensible to package them together into a single module:

```
module IMPLEMENTATION_DEPENDENCIES is
specification
    function ISLETTER (CHAR) returns BOOLEAN
    {etc. including data types}
implementation
    function ISLETTER (C:CHAR) returns BOOLEAN is
        {as above}
    endfun {ISLETTER}
    {etc.}
endmod {IMPLEMENTATION_DEPENDENCIES}
```

4.4   STRUCTURED PROGRAM DESIGN

What are 'Structured' Programs?

Few people would disagree with the view that software – from the largest system to the smallest (sub)program – needs to be 'structured' in order to be considered well engineered. Unfortunately, the term 'structured' (which is often used in the implied sense of 'well structured', as in 'a structured program') has long become rather misused, overused and overloaded (more recently, this has happened to the term 'object oriented'). It may seem somewhat tempting to construct a definition of 'structuredness', thereby providing some standard by which to judge this particular quality. For example, a structured program could be plausibly defined to be one that:

★ Has been developed according to the principles of some leading method or authority on the subject.   Or:

★ Is built only from simple sequencing, if-then-else selection and while-do repetition. Or:
★ Contains no goto statements. Or:
★ Has been developed top-down. Or:
★ Possesses an associated correctness proof. Or:
★ ... some combination of these. Or ...

The problem is that there exists no simple and *useful* all-embracing definition, even given that we are confining ourselves to sequential programs in our discussions. A popular definition is the second one above, but from a practical point of view, it is too restrictive. However, this form of structured programming has its adherents, particularly those 'purists' who are concerned with its theoretical and verification aspects, e.g. Linger *et al.* (1979). In fact, Mills & Linger (1986) go further. They advocate that, in a similar way to control structuring, data structuring should also be restricted – specifically to just sets and sequences (stacks and queues), thus avoiding the use of arrays and pointers and hence the unnecessary and complicating notion of 'place' in data objects. As evidence of the benefits of this further narrowing of the interpretation of structured programming, they quote a prototype language processor of around 20 000 source code lines built in terms of their more restrictive paradigm – design correctness was proved, the proof verified by inspection and no debugging was required on the way to full system test.

Deliberately, we wish to make the term 'structured' as broad, rather than as narrow, as possible, for otherwise we place ourselves in the difficult position of having to regard most practical methods of systematic program design as something other than 'structured' (but what?). In broad terms, 'structured' certainly means 'well-separated', 'appropriately modular', 'suitably abstract' etc. – qualities that can be obtained only by using the kinds of component discussed in Sections 4.2 and 4.3 in systematic, principled ways. This still begs questions, e.g. what exactly is meant by 'appropriate' or 'suitable'? But see below.

Thus anything that conflicts with modularity and abstraction is bad for structuredness and should be avoided. One arch culprit, long regarded as being particularly guilty of perpetrating unstructured programs, is (arbitrary use of) the 'goto statement'. There is ample justification for this view, since undisciplined use of gotos will inevitably lead to programs of poor or non-existent modularity that are difficult to understand and reason about from a correctness viewpoint. The use of gotos, in design at least, is therefore somewhat contentious. An early discussion of this issue can be found in a landmark paper by Knuth (1974). He argues the desirability of utilizing gotos – even introducing them into previously goto-less designs – typically in escape-like contexts to promote elegance and efficiency *where appropriate*. Knuth quotes Hoare as defining structured programming to be 'the systematic use of abstraction to control a mass of detail, and also a means of documentation which aids program design'.

One way to avoid the use of gotos is to utilize purpose-built escape instructions in order to exit prematurely from selections, iterations, subprograms, etc. For example, there could be a 'break' instruction to exit prematurely from an immediately enclosing iteration, a 'return' instruction to exit prematurely from a subprogram, and so on. Alternatively, a generalized escape instruction along the lines of

leave <name of structure> [**if** <condition>]

can be envisaged. The optional **if** component allows conditional escapes. Unnamed structures (loops, etc.) could be named by being tagged with a label identifier:

<identifier>: ... text
    ... of
    ... structure

However, even if a program is goto-free in design, its implemented form might not be. This outcome could be due to the weak structuring capabilities of the target language used. It could also be due to the nature of the transformation from design to implementation. The transformation may necessarily introduce gotos, albeit systematically, into the source code regardless of the structuring power of the target language (an example of this is given in Section 6.6). It is thus far too simplistic to argue from any standpoint that goto-containing programs are inevitably poorly structured. It is equally simplistic to argue that goto-free designs are by definition well structured, since their quality as judged by the kind of criteria discussed in Section 1.4 might still leave much to be desired. Consider the following problem:

At the start of what is usually the busiest period of usage of the PATSY system, a 'clock' is initiated that writes a digit character 1 to a serial file each elapsed second. Every time a student enters PATSY, a digit character 2 is written to the file. At the end of the survey period, a digit character 0 is written to the file. None of these digits can be written simultaneously to the file.

It is required to develop a program to process this data in order to determine and output the length of the longest period during which no entry to PATSY occurred.

Before reading on, the reader is invited to develop his or her own design solution to this simple problem.

One possible correct, goto-free design for the above problem could be obtained by filling in the details missing from the following outline:

```
READ(DIGIT)
while DIGIT<> '0'do
  case DIGIT
    '1' => while DIGIT = '1' do
            process 1−DIGIT
            READ(DIGIT)
          enddo
    '2' => process 2−DIGIT
            READ(DIGIT)
  endcase
enddo
```

Using '*' to indicate iteration and '|' to indicate unordered alternation, the structure of this design can be expressed as $<1^*|2>0^*$. However, there are other possible goto-free design structures, each of which would correctly solve the problem; for example:

$$<1|2>0^*, \quad <1|2^*>0^*, \quad <1^*|2^*>0^*, \quad <1^*2^*>0^*, \quad <2^*1^*>0^*$$

Is one of these versions better structured than the rest? Or are some, or all, of the versions equally well structured? Is quality of structure related in some way to how well it reflects the nature of the problem being solved? The point being made is that, even for trivial problems, there may exist a number of differently structured, correct solutions. Obviously, then, correctness is not necessarily a sufficient criterion on its own for judging the worthiness of a design that in all other respects adheres to 'structured principles'.

A further consideration related to the goto issue is that of exception handling. In many applications, mechanisms are needed to deal with exceptions in ways that violate the orderly progress and change of state that occurs with uninterrupted sequential execution. Discussion of mechanisms for handling exceptions will take place in Section 7.2, which deals with software reliability. We note now merely that it is difficult to reconcile an exception handling capability with the requirement of 'jump-free' programs.

Techniques for Deriving Structured Programs

Because of the difficulty of ascribing a usefully specific interpretation to the term 'structured', there is no single, distinct method of 'structured programming' (unless, as we have seen, it is given some overly restrictive definition). The reality is that structured programming exists in practice in a variety of guises and manifestations. Ultimately, the structuredness of a program can be assessed only in two ways:

★ How easy the program is to reconfigure and, if appropriate, reuse, ease being measured in terms of effort required to effect the reconfiguration or reuse.
★ How the program's characteristics match against a particular development method's criteria for evaluating structuredness.

A number of methods exist that approach program design in quite different ways, applying various notions of what constitutes 'good structure'. The most direct technique is 'step-wise refinement', which is basically a mildly embellished form of straightforward top-down design. This technique will be described in the next section, and some of its more formalized relatives will be mentioned in Chapter 5. Being top-down, step-wise refinement is thus a decompositional program design technique. In contrast, object-oriented design composes a system or program from abstract modular objects that are integrated into some separately derived top-level framework.

Standing apart from both step-wise refinement and object-oriented design is a method like Jackson Structured Programming (JSP), which has already been discussed in Section 3.9 in the context of developing the detailed design of function processes in a system specification. JSP is more compositional than decompositional and pays little attention to the kind of correctness arguments that are associated with formal development methods. It can be characterized as a 'data-driven' approach, since program structure (derived before detailed functionality) is obtained directly from structural considerations of data streams. However, it is not the only technique of its kind. Warnier's LCP method – Logical Construction of Programs (e.g. Chand & Yadav 1980; Gardner 1981) – also proceeds by analysing input and output streams as hierarchies of sequential structures, though the method of design composition that follows on from this analysis is different to JSP. Analagously to JSP, LCP has its system level equivalent LCS – Logical Construction of Systems (Warnier 1981).

Data also plays a first-stage role in the method of Structured Design, although the problem analysis is in terms of flow and transformation, rather than 'structure'. This approach leads to functionally decomposed designs. In that sense, Structured Design is far closer to stepwise refinement than JSP and other data-driven methods. However, like JSP for example, Structured Design can be employed as an integral element of system development (in this case, as the architectural design phase following Structured Systems Analysis) or as a program design technique in its own right. We shall choose Structured Design as our main illustration of a method that exploits and embellishes basic 'structured programming' principles with its own particular set of criteria.

4.5 DESIGN BY REFINEMENT

The concept of 'structured programming' emerged and took shape with considerable revolutionary force in the late 1960s and early-to-middle 1970s. Many of the leading papers on structured programming written during that period can be found conveniently collected together in Yourdon (1979a). The rationale for 'structured programming', as expounded by Dijkstra in the now classic work Dahl *et al.* (1972), can be summarized along the following lines:

★ As programmers, we must be humble, recognizing that our intellectual capacity for how much we can successfully handle simultaneously is extremely limited. Given that this is so, how can we tackle daunting large scale problems with any hope of developing programs that are:

understandable?
possess a probability significantly greater than zero of being correct?
can be shown to be correct?

★ The answer is:

by constructing programs in a systematic step-by-step manner, thus enabling us to avoid attempting to handle too much at once ...
... from program components that are themselves understandable and whose correctness can be reasonably easily argued without undue effort, thereby leading to programs with the same characteristics.

The simplest development method that can be claimed to fulfil these requirements is top-down design employing the sequential structures for non-primitive process components described in Section 4.2. This claim can be supported as follows;

★ As we have already seen, top-down design facilitates the decomposition of large, complex entities into a hierarchy of smaller, more easily manageable ones, thus avoiding the 'dealing with too much at once' problem.
★ The individual sequential structures are readily understandable. Moreover, we can argue the effect, and hence correctness, of an instance of any such structure in a program by fairly simple means. For example, we can trace through the effect of executing straight sequencing and selection structures by *enumeration*, i.e. arguing

through all the effects on a program that can occur when the structure's components are executed. The effects of an iteration are somewhat more complex but can be understood by *induction*, i.e. arguing through what happens on the first cycle and then generalizing this to the k $>= 0$ cycles of the structure. Such techniques in a more formal guise will be discussed in Section 5.3.

★ Top-down design will produce a tree-like hierarchy of structures representing layers of process components of ever-decreasing abstraction towards the target level. Since a non-primitive process component in any structure can itself be any structure, correctness arguments of the kind just described can be applied level by level through the entire structural framework of a program, or any part of it.

★ The static textual structure of a structured program will be in accord with the program's dynamics, thus maximizing its understandability. In other words, strict sequential progress through the text at any level also corresponds directly to progress through time of the text's execution; although iterations are cyclic, these can be mentally 'unwound' into a straight sequence of $<$cycle 1; cycle 2; cycle 3 . . . $>$.

Vessey & Weber (1984) regard the empirical evidence so far obtained to support the claimed beneficial effects of structured programming on software practice (e.g. less buggy software, greater productivity, etc.) as somewhat scant and unconvincing. Nevertheless, the precepts of structured programming are compelling and accepted by the majority of software practitioners unquestioningly.

'Step-wise refinement' (SWR) as described by Wirth (1971,1974) is the standard form of what might be termed 'top-down structured programming'. The method can be summarized as follows:

1. By considering the functional relationships between, and the structural relationships within, the inputs that have to be processed and outputs that have to be produced, an outline program design is worked out. This outline will contain as yet composite ('unrefined') process components, unless the problem is trivial. The notation used comprises:
☆ a design language, possibly the implementation language itself if suitable, possessing the necessary structures and primitives;
☆ precise natural language combined with any other notation needed accurately to convey the specification of unrefined components to a reader.

2. At some point, data structuring has to be decided upon, if it is needed. The top-level data structuring required may be 'obvious' and so can be specified before step 1. Conversely, it can be entirely non-obvious, extremely complex and present a design problem equal to, or greater than, the algorithm itself. In such cases, it may be better to delay the decision, developing as much of the algorithm as possible first until

commitment to representation (refinement) of a data abstraction is no longer avoidable. Since algorithm structure is very much consequentially affected by data structure, making an inferior decision with respect to the latter at a premature stage could prove costly in terms of later redesign.

3. Once the point is reached where data structure refinement begins, this should proceed in parallel with, though generally slightly leading, algorithm refinement, so that the latter is steered by the former.

4. The process of refinement is repeated on all emerging composite components one by one in the manner of steps 1, 2 and 3, until the complete design has become expressed in the primitives of the design language.

The order in which process refinements are tackled should in principle not matter – components will be logically highly self-contained and well separated in a good design. Necessity for a certain process refinement order indicates that there exists some undesirable interdependency between the components involved, which in turn suggests that a reappraisal of the design is needed.

As part of the design description, a systematic labelling scheme for composite components and their subsequent refinements should be adopted for cross-referencing purposes. This is particularly important because:

★ It enables the design to be tracked and understood. A stepwise refinement description represents a valuable piece of design documentation.

★ It facilitates the eventual correct consolidation of the disjoint refinement hierarchy into a single textual design unit.

★ It allows 'backup' – reconsideration of a previously made higher-level decision – to be accomplished methodically. Perhaps *the* major cause of introducing bugs into designs is *ad hoc* modification. Labelling allows the whole design subtree of the affected component to be traced through systematically to determine the full consequences of the change. For example, suppose we have the design hierarchy given in Fig. 4.2. If a change is now made to C2's refinement (to its local environment, say), then the effects of this can be traced through the whole subtree of which C2 is the root; note that it will be unnecessary to scrutinize any other part of the design.

Each decomposition step in SWR represents deriving a specification of a HOW (a 'realization') from a WHAT (an abstract specification of a requirement). In carrying out this problem-solving, decision-making process, the following guidelines can be applied to determine what a given refinement should be:

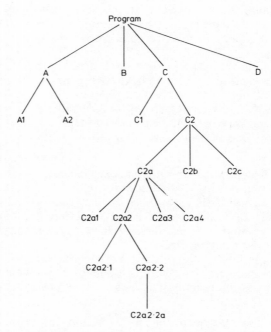

Fig. 4.2. A step-wise refinement design tree with labelling scheme.

(a) There may be no choice at all; for example, the data structure may drive, and fully constrain, the refinement needed.
(b) The skilful developer may recognize a stock situation for which he or she has a previously acquired 'design paradigm' to apply.
(c) If there is no standard paradigm to apply, a well-modularized, 'self-evidently correct' refinement must be achieved by application of problem-solving know-how and judgement.

Criticism that can be levelled against general top-down design, as already discussed in Section 3.4, applies to SWR – particularly the lack of 'sharp' design criteria for driving decomposition, though Wirth (1971) suggests that efficiency, storage economy, clarity and regularity of structure should be used as design drivers. To illustrate the point, consider the following problem, which is an elaboration of the SUMS digit-stream problem presented in Section 4.4:

The problem is exactly as stated in Section 4.4 with the additional requirement that the lengths in seconds of each interval during which no student entry occurred is to be output. The lengths are to be displayed as unsigned integer values, as many fitting on to each output line as possible subject to the following constraints:

no line is to be more than MAX (= 72) character positions long;
lines are to be filled up from the left margin;
consecutive integers on a line are to be separated by precisely two spaces, with no spaces at the start of a line;
integers are not split up from one line to the next.

The following are all outline algorithms that, with varying degrees of effort, could lead to a correct solution;

```
{V1}  READ(DIGIT)
      while not end of digit stream do                        (A)
          {see section 4.4 for at least 6 possibilities}      (B)
      enddo
      output MAX_INTV_LEN                                      (C)

{V2}  get length of next 1-digit sequence                     (A)
      while not end of digit stream do                        (B)
          deal with sequence length                           (C)
          get length of next 1-digit sequence                 (A)
      enddo
      output MAX_INTV_LEN                                      (D)

{V3}  while not end of digit stream do                        (A)
          build next line of integer output                   (B)
          output line                                         (C)
      enddo
      output MAX_INTV_LEN                                      (D)
```

We might classify these three versions respectively as 'character driven', 'sequence driven' and 'output-line driven', with at least six different variants of the first version. SWR is little help here in deciding which is the best choice. However, we could argue a case for V2 on the grounds that V1 seems too low level (it deals with characters) and V3 seems unnecessarily complex (why build a line before outputting it when the required output can be directly generated an integer at a time?). V2 seems the best match with the problem – the latter is basically concerned with sequences (representing time intervals) and V2 reflects this. Here now is a partial design based on V2:

```
(A)  procedure GET_1_SEQLEN(SL : out NATURAL) is
     begin
         ignore any preceding 2-digits                        (A1)
         obtain length of next 1-sequence                     (A2)
     end {GET_1_SEQLEN}
```

(A1) READ(DIGIT)
      while DIGIT = '2' **do** READ(DIGIT) **enddo**

(A2) SL := 0
      while DIGIT = '1' **do**
        SL +:= 1
        READ(DIGIT)
      enddo

Thus (A) in the main algorithm becomes:
   GET_1_SEQLEN(SEQLEN)

We can also see that SEQLEN will be 0 when GET_1_SEQLEN encounters the end of the digit stream. So:
   (B) SEQLEN <> 0

Whilst we procedurized (A) for obvious reasons of commonality, we would procedurize (C) to maintain a balance of clarity in the main algorithm:

   (C) **procedure** DEAL_WITH_SEQLEN(SL : **in** NATURAL) **is**
        begin
           look for new possible MAX_INTV_LEN   (C1)
           output SL   (C2)
        end {DEAL_WITH_SEQLEN}

It is at this point, we shall suppose, that we detect a fairly subtle but fatal flaw that exists in our partial design. The reader is invited to detect the flaw, repair it and complete the design; a helpful hint is given at the end of Section 4.6, if you need it.

4.6 THE STRUCTURED DESIGN METHOD

Introduction

This approach to program design has evolved and become established via the related work and publications of Myers (1975, 1978), Stevens *et al.* (1974), Stevens (1981) and Yourdon & Constantine (1979). We have already mentioned the method in the context of Structured Systems Analysis (see Section 3.6). Structured Design is perhaps a slightly unfortunate name, considering the generality of the phrase 'structured design'. Thus, for convenience and to be more specific, the method from now on will be referred to as SD.

   SD has its origins in 'classical' modular programming, where program structure is viewed in terms of a top-level control module driving a hierarchy of subordinate modules. This model of software architecture is very much a part of SD, to the extent that the main deliverable of SD is the specification of a hierarchical architecture of connected modules (that conforms to certain criteria) derived from analysis of flows of data and the transformations that the latter suffer. Overall, the method can be broadly characterized as:

Analysis of data flow —> Top-down specification of module hierarchy
—> Design of individual modules in accordance with structured programming principles.

Note that there are similarities between SD and SWR: SD possesses a significant top-down element, and SWR's decomposition process has strong, implicit functional characteristics ('how are outputs obtained from inputs?'). In SD, functional decomposition is an explicit, main driving force behind the method.

Design Criteria

The main aim of SD is to derive a hierarchy of modules that are internally as self-contained as possible and externally connected only via the systematic communication of data across formally defined interfaces; in SD parlance, the modules should be maximally 'cohesive' and minimally 'coupled' respectively. In other words, modules are as separately independent from one another as possible, the rationale for this being that:

★ Problem-solving is made faster and easier: development personnel are able to work independently on well defined components of the design.
★ Testing and debugging time will be reduced: the modular structure allows systematic test strategies to be applied and facilitates the tracking down of bugs to particular modules.
★ Modifiability is greatly enhanced: any internal changes to a module should have no 'ripple' effect on other parts of the software. Moreover, any module can be replaced by another without affecting other modules, provided the latter is functionally equivalent to the former, i.e. possesses the same interface and carries out the same transformation.
★ The cumulative effect of these previous points is to enhance reconfigurability and hence, in particular, reduce maintenance costs.

Since *coupling* and *cohesion* are SD's criteria for evaluating the quality of a modular design, it is worth examining them further.

Coupling is a general term referring to any mechanism by which one module becomes associated with another. The weakest form of coupling is the applied occurrence ('call') of one module within another – an obvious necessity. The strongest, hence worst, kind of coupling occurs when one module is able to affect directly the execution of another. Such coupling would, of course, never arise in any program that would be considered well structured. However, modules obviously must communicate, and strong coupling would result from using non-local variables, or similar, to effect communication, which would make a module's internal realization specifically dependent on external data objects. Thus, all communication should be accomplished through parameterized interfaces.

Cohesion is a complementary characteristic of coupling; that is, if the strength of one is increased, the strength of the other will decrease. There are various levels of strength of association that can exist between the internal elements of a module. The weakest possible is termed 'coincidental' cohesion, implying that there is no particular logically binding relationship at all between the module's elements, e.g. as might result from some arbitrary, unprincipled, unsystematic design manoeuvre. An example of an intermediate strength is that of 'communicational' cohesion, which means that all module elements contribute to the accomplishment of an overall task and reference the same data object(s); e.g. 'obtain student log_on record and extract log_on_ code and password'. However, the greatest cohesive strength is termed 'functional' – that is, all elements of the module contribute to a single, well—defined transformation:

$$F : X \longrightarrow Y$$

where F is the functional transformation effected, and X and Y are the import and export components of the module's interface respectively. 'Functionality' is not a property that easily lends itself to quantitative evaluation. Qualitatively, however, a useful technique is to inspect the textual definition of F – it should be a single, short imperative phrase containing just one action verb. Thus, for example, 'compute table index from student *log_on_code*' is highly functional, whereas 'compute table index from student *log_on_code*, then check and report on validity of password entered' is not.

Cohesion thus relates to the internal qualities of a module, coupling to the quality of association between modules. To complete the picture, these qualities need to be related to a module hierarchy and, in particular, its communication structure. Generally, in a hierarchy of loosely coupled, highly cohesive modules, four basic kinds of communication pattern will exist:

★ Accepting data from a lower level and passing data on to a higher level: such modules are termed *afferent* since they are primarily concerned with input transformations.

★ Accepting data from a higher level and passing data on to a lower level: such modules are termed *efferent* since they are primarily concerned with output transformations.
★ Accepting data from a higher level and passing data back to a higher level: such modules are termed *transform* since they are concerned with carrying out the computational transformations central to the problem.
★ Accepting data from a lower level and passing it somewhere else down the hierarchy unmodified: such modules are termed *coordinate* as their role is not to effect transformation but merely to control others that do.

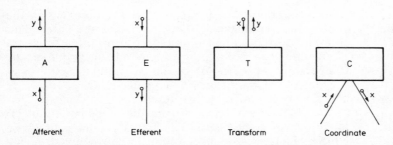

Fig. 4.3. Structured Design module types and their communication structures.

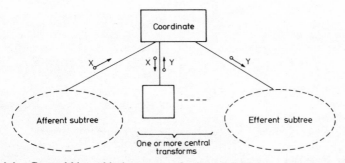

Fig. 4.4. General hierarchical structure of a Structured Design module architecture.

Diagrammatically, each module type can be described as shown in Fig. 4.3. In hierarchical terms, the more complete picture that emerges is depicted in Fig. 4.4. (the arrows in both diagrams indicate the general direction of communication). The important point concerning the general structure shown in Fig. 4.4 is that it is applicable throughout the hierarchy, i.e. any non-primitive module can be decomposed according to the structure depicted, though it is always possible that the afferent, transform or efferent component of a given module is empty.

Applying the Method

We shall use the example problem of Section 4.5 for illustrative purposes. The major steps of the method are as follows:

Analysis of data flow

The flow of data from inputs to outputs is traced, identifying all the transformational sequences that map the former into the latter. This analysis is represented in the directed graphical form, often termed a 'bubble chart', described in Section 3.6. The complete graph can be thought of as an abstract specification of the transformational flow of data that the eventual program needs to implement. Of course, in a system development problem, it is Structured Systems Analysis that generates the data flow graph. In a program development problem, drawing a data flow graph is the essential preliminary to the main phase of SD – deriving a hierarchical architecture of loosely coupled, highly cohesive modules. The bubble chart of our example problem is given in Fig. 4.5 (ignore the dotted lines for the moment).

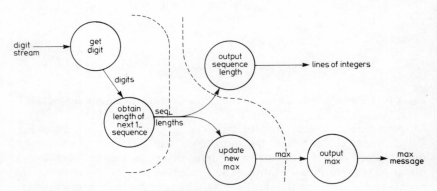

Fig. 4.5.   Sectioned bubble chart for the digit-stream problem.

Structure chart derivation

The objective of this step is to specify a module hierarchy that satisfies the data flow specification of the first step in accordance with the design criteria discussed above. The hierarchy is described in the form of a tree diagram called a 'structure chart'. In the absence of any design criteria, there would be a number of different module hierarchies that correctly realize a given bubble chart. However, application of the structural paradigm shown in Fig. 4.4 tends to steer the design towards a unique realization. The method is basically as follows:

★ The bubble chart is divided into three main sections: afferent, central transform and efferent. This is achieved by tracing inputs until a stage in the diagram is reached where they are considered to exist in their most abstract form just before suffering main computational transformations. In this manner, the afferent-central transform boundaries are delineated. Similarly, by tracing outputs backwards to a point where they are deemed to exist in their most abstract form, the central transform-efferent boundaries are established. The dotted lines in Fig. 4.5. depict this sectioning.

★ The divided bubble chart is translated into a modular realization thus: a separate afferent and efferent module for each input and output stream, together with a number of modules that deal with the transformations in the transform centre, all controlled by a top-level coordinate module as shown in Fig. 4.6. Note that, although a bubble chart contains no sequencing information, this can be depicted in structure charts as shown in Fig. 4.6. (a curly arrow indicates iteration; a diamond symbol – see Fig. 4.7 – indicates selection).

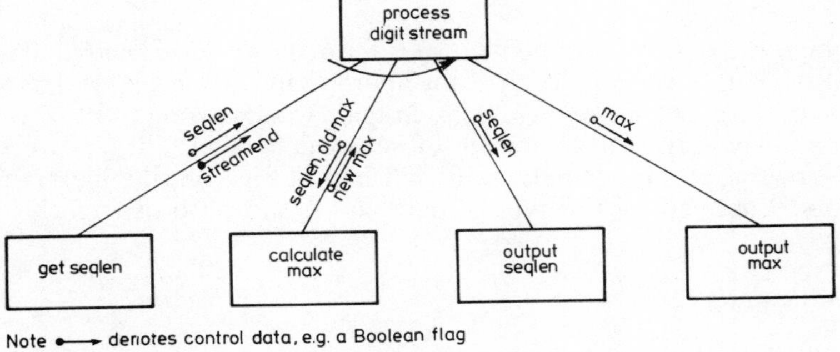

Note ●——▶ denotes control data, e.g. a Boolean flag

Fig. 4.6. First level structure chart decomposition for bubble chart of Fig. 4.5.

★ Exactly the same analysis is now applied to the remaining composite sections of the bubble chart, resulting eventually in a corresponding top-down 'refinement' of the non-primitive module sections of the structure chart. This is repeated level by level as far as is necessary until all transformations in the original bubble diagram are realized in the module hierarchy. The end product is a specification of a physical software architecture described in terms of:

a hierarchy of functional modules;
an associated data flow through that hierarchy;
appropriate sequence structuring information.

Figure 4.7 gives the full structure chart for our example design.

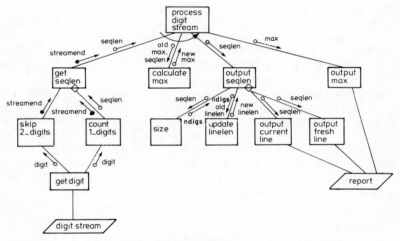

Fig. 4.7.   Complete structure chart for the digit-stream problem.

Note: the design described above is termed *transform centred*. There also exists a form of design not appropriate to the above example termed *transaction centred*. This design paradigm is relevant when an input gives rise to a number of subsequent alternative processing pathways, as for example in the left half of Fig. 4.8; the hierarchical model derived for this type of data flow is shown to the right.

Module design

Detailed design of each module in the structure chart is now carried out by applying SWR, for example. In a single program implementation,

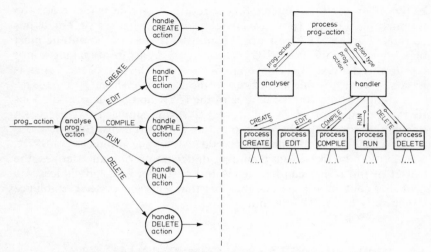

Fig. 4.8. Transaction-centred Structured Design.

the top coordinate module will be the main program module and all subordinate modules will be functions or procedures, though sometimes a module may be 'lexically included' in its parent because it is too trivial to be a subprogram. Note, however, that a structure chart does not completely constrain the implementation. For larger, system-level problems, an implementation in which the module hierarchy is divided up between two or more communicating tasks or programs may be deemed appropriate, according to considerations of target environment resources, performance, scheduling, etc.

End Comment

The flaw in the SWR design was that it assumed that 1−sequences are always followed by at least one 2−digit. However, after component (A2), we may have read the terminating 0−digit. One way to remove the flaw is to back up to the top level and modify the outline to:

```
do
    GET−1−SEQLEN(SEQLEN,EODS)                (A)
    if SEQLEN > 0
    then deal with SEQLEN                    (B)
    endif
until
    EODS
enddo
```

EODS is an extra parameter that is returned as true if (A) reads the terminating 0−digit (note that it can do this whether or not it has consumed another 1−sequence − hence the if−test in the outline must be as given and not 'if not EODS then ....'). Apart from making minor revision to the text of (A) given in Section 4.5, the rest of the design is basically what it would have been in the flawed version.

A comparison of the structures of the SWR and SD design solutions to the example problem will reveal a strong similarity. This is not uncommon for relatively simple program level problems. Both methods are based on functional decomposition. Although, in the case of SWR, we can often be faced with a number of decomposition alternatives, the subset of those that can be argued to be 'sensible' design choices will probably contain at least one member that will bear close resemblance structurally to an SD solution.

4.7   DESIGN OF REUSABLE COMPONENTS

General Considerations

Reusability has already been introduced in Section 1.4 as one of two main quality characteristics contributing to the 'potential usefulness' of software. To recap, reusability depends on:

* Modularity: self-containedness.
* Generality: the more general, the more reusable.
* Flexibility: ease of change.
* Interoperability: harmonious connection with other components.
* Portability: operational environment independence.

We shall cover the first two attributes at some length in this section. Flexibility is a broad attribute that is strongly related to encapsulation and abstraction. For example, given a set of data types, operators, etc. combined together as a modular object, then it will be easy to add new facilities, remove existing ones and adapt their implementations without the affect of such modifications propagating uncontrollably through the fabric of the object's surrounding environment. Interoperability is basically a matter of rigorous interface specification, ensuring compatibility of forms of data transmitted between components, adhering to any data communication standards and protocols that exist, and so on. Portability is discussed in Section 6.9.

On a practical level, reusability means being able to make effective reuse of an item of software because it:

★ Provides a facility, or set of facilities that, assuming sufficient availability, is useful to the computing community in general.
★ Is constructed in such a way that, where appropriate, it can be incorporated with ease as a component into other programs and systems.
★ Can be tailored with minimal effort and modification to suit the characteristics and requirements of different environments and applications.

Closely associated with reusability is the idea of a software components industry. Any practical form of engineering has its own set of standard, 'off-the-shelf' components that can be used as building blocks in the development of products. It is eminently sensible that this should also apply to software engineering via the production, maintenance and distribution of catalogues and libraries of modules that are useful in developing a wide range of applications. The benefits are obvious and potentially enormous – much-needed increases in productivity would be achieved because large amounts of time, effort and money would not be wasted rebuilding what others have already developed. However, whilst the idea is sound in principle, there are certain important practical implications, including:

(a) The need for appropriate languages and associated software tools and support systems for constructing and making available reusable software.
(b) Commitment of the computing community to using (a).
(c) Provision of a wide network for the distribution of, and access to, public reusable software.

The intention here is not to argue whether such objectives can, or will, be realized in practice, but merely to discuss certain technical aspects of building reusable software.

One way to achieve reusability in a self-contained applications product is to generalize it by building in enough functional completeness and flexibility (via default overrides, options, extensibility) to cater effectively for most, if not all, conceivable user requirements. In terms of software components – our main concern in this section – modularity is prerequisite; generality is achieved basically through parameterization of various kinds.

Note: we are treating a reusable software component as an end-product sourced in some suitable target language. However, there is no reason why abstract designs or specifications cannot be reusable, provided they can be readily refined or transformed to the required representation.

Subprogram Parameterization

To illustrate the extent to which parameterization of subprograms can be used to promote reusability, consider the following example, which begins with an obviously non-reusable version of a standard utility.

A sort procedure is to be written, performing a particular ascending sort algorithm on an array of PROFILE records:

type PROFILE **is record**
       . . .
         endrec
type SURVEY **is array** [POSITIVE *:*] **of** PROFILE
{The '*:*' denotes that any subscript range of type POSITIVE is allowed}
GROUP1, GROUP2 : SURVEY

Version 1

procedure SORT . . . {no parameters}
   {the body explicitly references GROUP1}

Clearly, SORT in its present state cannot be used to sort GROUP2 as well, though this represents exactly the same general task as sorting GROUP1.

Version 2

procedure SORT(ITEMS : **inout** SURVEY) . . .
   {The SURVEY array to be sorted is conveyed to SORT via a parameter}

SORT now has reusability in any program that wishes to sort SURVEY arrays in ascending order. In the same program, it can be 'reused' to sort any number of different SURVEY arrays. We could enhance SORT's applicability to encompass partially filled arrays by a second POSITIVE parameter that specifies the number of elements in the array to be considered by SORT (although this would be unnecessary in a target language that permits arbitrary cross-sections – 'slices' – of arrays).

Version 3

It is sometimes required to sort SURVEY arrays in ascending order, sometimes descending order. The ordering relation may also vary with usage of SORT according to different field(s) of PROFILE records acting as sort key(s) on different occasions. Despite these variations, a single version of SORT can still be constructed that caters for all these possibilities:

> **procedure** SORT(ITEMS : **inout** SURVEY
> **operator** < (PROFILE,PROFILE) **returns** BOOLEAN) ...
> {and within the body of SORT somewhere:}
> **if** PRX < PRY ..... {where the ordering test is being applied
> between PROFILE records PRX and
> PRY}

When SORT is now used, the user must supply a functional or operator parameter that defines the actual ordering relation to be applied in that instance.

Version 4

Suppose it is desired that our SORT procedure be able to operate on other types of array. Let us further suppose that our PDL allows overloaded subprograms. Then:

> **procedure** SORT(ITEMS : **inout** SURVEY
> **operator** < (PROFILE,PROFILE) **returns** BOOLEAN) ...
> **procedure** SORT(ITEMS : **inout** CHARSEQ
> **operator** < (CHAR,CHAR) **returns** BOOLEAN) ...
> **procedure** SORT(ITEMS : **inout** VECTOR
> **operator** < (REAL,REAL) **returns** BOOLEAN) ...
> {etc.}

However, this would be impractical if we wish SORT to operate on arbitrarily many different array types. To achieve this, SORT would need to be parameterized with respect to the base (element) type of the array. In most high-level languages, this would not be possible – we would already have reached the limits of generality achievable by parameterization in version 3, or even earlier.

Generic Parameterization

As a further example of why type parameterization is useful, consider the following module specification:

```
module QUEUE_SEQUENCE is
specification
    type QUEUE is abstract
    procedure ADDQ(inout QUEUE, QELEM)
    procedure REMQ(inout QUEUE, out QELEM)
    function ISEMPTYQ(QUEUE) returns BOOLEAN
endmod {QUEUE_SEQUENCE}
```

This specifies an abstract data type QUEUE composed of elements of type QELEM (obviously, QELEM will also occur in the representation of QUEUE). For some fixed QELEM, the module represents a moderately reusable component. However, its generality would be greatly increased if it could cater for QUEUEs of any element type. This would require parameterization with respect to QELEM.

The type parameterization that is needed for our two examples is possible in a few languages, Ada being one example with its *generic* capability. A generic module is merely a 'template' object from which actual modules can be 'instantiated' at compile-time by generic parameter substitution. This should not be confused with overloading, which occurs when two or more actual modules are associated simultaneously with the same symbol or name (note: this terminological distinction is not universal, e.g. procedures called 'generic' in PL/1 are actually overloaded according to our definitions).

Incorporating the spirit of Ada's capability into our PDL, the SORT and QUEUE_SEQUENCE examples are redefined below to illustrate generic abstraction:

```
generic
    type QELEM
module QUEUE_SEQUENCE is
    {As before, including the implementation – not given above –
        which is automatically covered by the generic parameter}
endmod {QUEUE_SEQUENCE}
```

Just as with (non-abstract) types in module specifications, operations on the generic type QELEM within QUEUE_SEQUENCE are restricted by default to assignment and test for (in)equality. Here are some actual instantiations from QUEUE_SEQUENCE:

```
{An actual module to handle queues of positive integers; note the
    actual parameterization}
module POSINTQS is QUEUE_SEQUENCE(POSITIVE)
{An actual module to handle queues of PROFILE records}
module PROFILEQS is QUEUE_SEQUENCE(PROFILE)

{etc.}
```

The actual modules are then used in the normal way.

If we apply generic parameterization to our SORT procedure, the situation is a little more complex:

generic
  type ELEM
  type INDEX **is discrete** {i.e. any discrete type is allowed}
  type LIST **is array** [INDEX*:*] **of** ELEM
procedure SORT(ITEMS : **inout** LIST
                operator < (ELEM,ELEM) **returns** BOOLEAN) **is**
  {As version 3 above}
end {SORT}

And some example instantiations:

procedure INTSORT **is**
  SORT(INTEGER, INTEGER, INTLIST);
  {which can be used to sort any INTEGER-element array of type
  INTLIST having any desired INTEGER index range}
procedure PROSORT **is**
  SORT(PROFILE, POSITIVE, SURVEY)
  {which can be used to sort any PROFILE-element array of type
  SURVEY whose index range is any range of type POSITIVE}

Technical note: unlike our PDL, functional, operator and procedural parameters of subprograms are not allowed in Ada and also have to be realized via the generic mechanism.

Further Possibilities

Naturally, generic modules can be used as part of everyday 'non-reusable' programming. But their main use is in the construction of generalized, reusable component software. It should be realized, how-ever, that generic parameterization, as offered by Ada, say, is not the last word in building reusable software. For example further generality can be obtained if functions and procedures can be treated as values (so that, for example, arbitrary functions are allowed not only as para-meters, but also as the results of functions). As with type parameteriz-ation, very few imperative languages possess this capability (the C language – Kernighan & Ritchie 1978 – is an exception). The way forward here appears to lie with high order functional languages, their mathematical 'cleanliness' and the correctness-preserving transforma-tions that can be applied to programs written in them. Thus, it is possible to construct a very highly generalized function that can be customized via parameter substitution to a particular application and the resulting product then transformed, if necessary, into a more efficient version via optimizing transformations. More on this can be found in Darlington (1982)

Greater generality is also obtainable if types can be manipulated as values. This would provide a more powerful and flexible 'polymorphic' (multiple type) mechanism than that obtainable by overloading or generic abstraction (read Cardelli & Wegner 1985 on polymorphism). Reusability is also an area of investigation at the formal specification level. Goguen (1984,1986) advances a generic schema more abstract and powerful than Ada's. The schema involves 'theories' (a theory is an abstract semantic description of some software component), 'views' (a view is a particular interpretation of a theory – one theory can have many different views) and both horizontal and vertical (hierarchical) composition of components. The schema is expressed in a special Library Interconnection Language used for specifying module interconnections in building large systems and can be front-ended on to, say, Ada's module capability.

Finally, object-oriented architectures offer considerable potential for reusability. This is partly because they dispense with static binding that fixes at compile time the operand types and implementations of operations. More importantly, the inheritance property allows classes to share and, where necessary, override the attributes of other more general classes, avoiding the necessity to discard and rewrite, or modify, existing software objects. Thus, inheritance greatly enhances software flexibility. As Cox (1986) says, 'the effect [of inheritance of 'Software-ICs' – a term coined by Cox for classes to highlight the hardware analogy] is to put reusability squarely in the mainstream of the software development process'.

Note: IEEE (1984) is devoted to the topic of software reusability.

Chapter 5

Formal Methods in
Software Development

5.1 FORMAL METHODS – WHAT AND WHY

The picture of software development so far expounded has been what one might describe as 'traditional', with an emphasis on engineering quality into software via rational principles and concepts underpinning systematic methods and techniques that are applied in a disciplined manner. However, there is little formal scientific basis underlying the development paradigms that have so far been described. 'Formal methods' seeks to establish a mathematical foundation for software development in two crucial and related areas where precision and rigour are of the utmost importance: *specification* and *verification*.

The fact that specification and verification are inextricably linked should be self-evident: what is inadequately specified cannot be realized without defect (unless one happens to be extremely fortunate); and lack of a proper specification does not permit a (potentially defective) realization to be subjected to the process of verification. Elaborating this statement further in the context of formal methods:

★ A central aim is to provide a framework for the development of verified software. By 'verified', we mean 'of proven correctness' in the following sense: that we have established conclusively that a software unit will not deviate from the intended behaviour expressed in its specification when it is executed by the (possibly abstract) target machine defined by its realization language. Formal verification has a number of potential advantages:

increased confidence can be placed in the reliability of software units whose correctness has been formally proved;
there is no longer any major reliance on the inadequacies and inherent limitations of testing (see Section 7.4) as a verification technique;
the need for corrective maintenance should be greatly reduced; the 'should' implies an important proviso here – there are certain practical difficulties associated with formal verification that we shall mention in Section 5.5.

★ Formal verification is the application of reasoning expressed in mathematical formalism, i.e. a formal system such as *first order predicate logic*. To achieve this with respect to programs requires the following:

(i) Programs, and therefore individual program constructs, must possess a precise interpretation to permit reasoning about their effects. That is, we must be able to reason formally about the behaviour of constructs when they are executed. This in turn requires that the realization language to which the constructs belong possesses a formal semantics.

(ii) Any formal proof argument necessarily presupposes a specification that is completely precise, i.e. that is also expressed in some formal language with associated formal semantics. Moreover, since the 'domains of representation' of a specification and its realization will in general be quite different, verification must involve showing consistency between the two – i.e. that what is deduced about an element of behaviour in the target domain 'maps back' to some corresponding element of behaviour expressed in the specification.

It is easy to feel that this 'formal methods scenario' is considerably removed from the practicalities and exigencies of 'everyday' software development – indeed, this can be seen as a major stumbling block to the uptake of formal methods. However, Fig. 5.1 – another modified version of the traditional software life cycle – attempts to place formal methods in a concrete engineering context. The diagram represents a generalised view of formal software development.:

(a) Conventional requirements analysis takes place, which establishes a set of user requirements for the intended software. It is assumed that these requirements are expressed (semi-)informally as a user requirements definition. This documentation is not to be confused with the formal specification to be constructed (see Section 2.3 again).

(b) The informal user requirements definition is then transformed by skilled personnel into a formal specification. Note that, whilst the specification can be checked for correct syntax and internal consistency, it cannot itself be formally verified – i.e. that it maps back to the requirements definition – since the latter is informally expressed. Thus, verification of formal specifications can only be attempted informally by review. Note that this aspect of adequacy of a formal specification is different from asking the question: is the specification complete, relevant, etc. from a user viewpoint? Recall that this is requirements *validation*. An apparent problem here is that users cannot validate formal specifications by review since they will be unable to understand

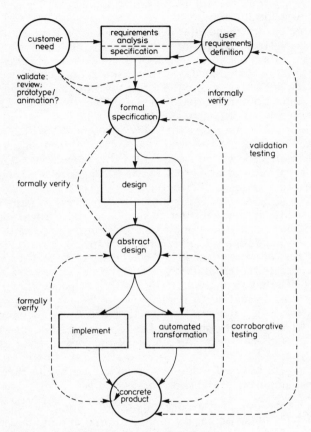

Fig. 5.1. Software development using formal methods.

them. However, the possible solutions to this problem will be found mentioned in Sections 2.3 and 2.4:

☆ A formal specification can be translated back into an informal description of requirements. Furthermore, the resulting natural language text is likely to be a clearer, more precise statement of requirements than any that was prepared during preliminary analysis. The text can be a separate document, or interspersed amongst the formal specification itself.

☆ Depending on the formal specification approach used, it may be possible to animate the specification, given the appropriate tools. Specification execution represents a direct means of prototyping and

user validation of the behavioural acceptability of the WHAT embodied in a specification.

(c) From the validated and internally verified formal specification is then
derived an abstract 'blueprint' for the program or system, whose
correctness is formally verified against the specification. This might be
achieved in more than one stage, the reason being that the abstraction
gulf between specification and the target level may be sufficiently large
to make realization and verification too difficult to accomplish in one
step. Thus, any intermediate stage will consist partly of (formal)
specifications of components that will be refined (i.e. realized) and
verified subsequently. An issue that arises is the position occupied by
the verification process with respect to the refinement steps, i.e. is
verification carried out after refinement is complete or during it? We
shall return to this question later on.

(d) Step (c) is, of course, 'designing' and it remains to implement the
proven design. The implementation must itself be verified against the
design. In fact, exactly the same techniques can be used as in step (c),
since the verified design is itself just a formal specification against which
the correctness of an implementation can be established. Thus, achieving
the final concrete representation of the software can be seen as the last
of a series of refinement steps starting with the specification. Alternatively, the transformation to implementation might be automated by
appropriate software tools (possibly acting directly on the specification
itself), in which case no formal verification is necessary for this stage,
assuming confidence in the correctness of the tools used. Either way,
testing is reduced to playing a corroborative role in the verification
process and will be used mainly in its validation role – checking out
behavioural adequacy of the end product and gaining user acceptance.

We shall now look at some techniques for formal specification and
verification. But in so doing, it should be borne in mind that our main
concern is with the relevance and appplicability of these techniques to
the software engineering process, rather than with the theoretical and
mechanistic detail of the techniques themselves. The amount of published literature on specification and verification is prodigious and so we
shall pinpoint only a few main references in the following sections. A
useful general text that covers both aspects of formal methods is Berg *et
al.* (1982).

5.2 FORMAL SPECIFICATION

Formality in Specification

Lack of formality is characterized by the use of natural language for
part, or all, of a specification. The problems associated with applying

natural language for this means – already stated in Section 2.3, but worth summarizing again – are:

* Its use can be unavoidably complex and verbose.
* Its syntax and semantics are extremely difficult to specify formally, even for subsets.
* Its syntax and semantics are inappropriate for the expression of abstract concepts.
* Its use can be unintentionally ambiguous, inconsistent, unclear and imprecise.

Meyer (1985) considers the seven deadly 'sins' of specification, to which the informal variety is particularly prone, to be:

* Noise: the presence of redundancy, irrelevancy, etc., which detracts from, and clouds, the real essence of a specification.
* Silence: omission of some part of the essence.
* Overspecification: providing details of HOW beyond necessity, thus artificially constraining implementation.
* Contradiction.
* Ambiguity.
* Forward referencing: appealing to concepts defined later in the specification text.
* Wishful thinking: inclusion of a feature, any possible solution to which cannot be realistically validated.

Meyer examines the revision of Goodenough & Gerhart (1976) of Naur's original informal specification (Naur 1969) of the so-called 'line edit problem' in order to show that, even after careful reformulation, an informal specification can still contain many 'sins'; he identifies instances of the first six above in Goodenough & Gerhart's revised specification. However, Meyer does not dismiss informal specifications but sees them as being enriched and improved by formal specification. This is also the view of Gehani (1982), who concludes from a case study that the two varieties of specification are both necessary and complementary.

The term *formal* should be interpreted carefully with respect to specification. For example, SSA and JSD specifications are largely 'formalized' in the sense that they are expressed in languages and graphical notations that admit to precise interpretation. However, there is no formal semantics defined for the specification languages and notations used by these methods, and no associated verification technique. Thus, the approaches are not 'formal' in the sense being used here.

A (very) high-level programming language might be considered suitable as a formal specification language. Yet, as stated in Section 2.3, any actual target language would be too inappropriate in form and level, and too implementation-constraining in practice, for general formal software specification. Mathematical abstraction is a prerequisite for precision and uncluttered semantics in specification – the semantics of computational objects in the concrete domains of actual programming languages and operational environments is much more difficult to specify and reason about.

There are in fact a large number of specification languages in existence and a number of formal specification methods that they support; such diversity is perhaps typical of a technology that is still some way from maturity. Apart from formality, Liskov & Zilles (1975) consider the desirable, though not necessarily compatible, characteristics of a specification method to be:

★ Constructibility: specifications can be constructed without undue effort (note: for large specifications, this requires a bottom-up and/or incremental mechanism for building largeness from smaller parts).
★ Comprehensibility: generally, the smaller a specification, the easier it is to understand – the specification method should not be verbose.
★ Minimality: the method should facilitate specification of what is interesting without the need to include extraneous (e.g. implementation) detail.
★ Range of application: the wider, the better.
★ Extensibility: a small conceptual change should require a commensurately small change in the specification (*author's note*: this is a curious use of the term 'extensibility').

Despite the variety in specification techniques and languages, there exists a certain basic commonality of features. For example, formal specifications tend to be functionally and data-abstraction oriented, i.e. they centre around statements about functions (possessing certain domains, ranges, effects etc.) and data objects on which (some of) the functions operate. Liskov & Zilles (1975) identify six categories of specification technique:

Implicit (input/output) specification

An *implicit* specification defines an operation functionally by specifying its name, domain and range – i.e. its *signature*. The specification will also define:

(when necessary) a constraint on inputs additional to that imposed by the domain specification of the operation;
a constraint relating inputs and outputs that captures the 'computational essence' of the operation.

The signature and constraints are sufficient to characterize fully the operation's intended behaviour without in any way being explicit about the latter. If the operation is 'procedural', i.e. has side effects, the specification technique requires notation to specify both the functional computation of the output and the side effects that occur. Implicit specifications play a leading role in formal verification techniques.

Operational specification

As the name implies, the specification of a function will include an explicit description of its intended behaviour in addition to its interface; this description might be recursive. However, the description of the computational transformation should be sufficiently abstract to avoid appeal to efficiency considerations or other implementation features. Recall that operational specifications have potential for direct animation, with the attendant benefits that we have previously discussed.

State-machine specification

In this approach, first taken by Parnas (1972b), the required behaviour is specified by an abstract state machine – that is, a 'state' (a set of data variables) manipulated by a class of defined operations. Generally, the operations can be divided into two kinds: those that are purely functional – i.e. value returners that observe the state but do not change it – and those that change the state, accomplishing side effects. Depending on the specific approach:

operations possessing both characteristics may be permitted;
it may be necessary to specify 'hidden' operations that are not part of the external behaviour of the state machine but which are needed internally to achieve a complete description of the state's history, i.e. dependency over time.

Abstract model specification

In this approach, a data abstraction is specified in terms of – i.e. 'modelled' by – existing data abstractions that are already formally specified, possibly as part of the axiomatic basis of the particular method used. The operations of the data abstraction can then be specified in the implicit or operational styles (or both), where necessary applying operations of the model in input and output constraints or behaviour descriptions. For example, the data abstraction to be specified might be *stack* with operations *push*, *pop*, etc., which we might chose to model in terms of, say, a previously specified abstraction *sequence* with its operations of *head*, *tail*, etc.

Axiomatic specification

As implied by the name, an axiomatic approach specifies a data abstraction in terms of a set of axioms. The axioms specify constraints on, and relationships between, the permitted domains, ranges, behaviours, etc. of the operations of the abstraction. A particular kind of axiomatic specification that has received considerable attention in the literature is:

Algebraic specification

The *algebraic* specification technique has been developed independently by Goguen *et al.* (1977) and Guttag & Horning (1978), amongst others. Discussion of the technical differences between their approaches is beyond the scope of this book. The name *algebraic* is derived from the fact that the technique's theoretical underpinning is the mathematics of 'many sorted' algebras (an algebra is a set on whose members certain operations are defined and which possess certain formal properties; the term 'many sorted' refers to the fact that the sets are heterogenous, i.e. comprise members of various types or 'sorts'). In the algebraic approach, signatures are specified for the operations of the abstraction, and the axioms are stated in an *equational* style, i.e. as a set of equations between expressions involving the operations.

These specification techniques are not mutually exclusive; a specification method may be a combination of the above approaches as the following examples illustrate.

Some Simple Examples

The specification languages used in the following examples intentionally do not correspond directly to any that are currently in use. The idea behind the examples is simply to convey to the reader a brief, general flavour of the techniques being illustrated. Our first example is of a specification in the equational algebraic style. The specification is of a parameterized abstract data type SEQUENCE. Although the object being defined is simple, the example conveys most of the elements to be found in algebraic specifications. We shall first give the example (line numbered for convenient referencing) and then explain its syntax and structure.

```
 1.  using BOOLEAN => bool with T, F, and, or
 2.  object SEQUENCE
 3.        (elem with
 4.            _==_  : elem, elem -> bool
 5.            bottom:              -> elem)
 6.  sorts seq
 7.  operations
 8.    new    :                -> seq
 9.    undseq :                -> seq
10.    hd     :          seq -> elem
11.    tl     :          seq -> seq
12.    _@_    : elem, seq -> seq
13.    _==_   :   seq, seq -> bool
14.    _isin_ : elem, seq -> bool
15.  axioms
16.    hd(undseq) = bottom
17.    hd(new) = bottom
18.    hd(e@s)  = e
19.
20.    tl(undseq) = undseq
21.    tl(new) = undseq
22.    tl(e@s)  = s
23.
24.    x isin undseq = F
25.    x isin new = F
26.    x isin e@s  = (x == e) or (x isin s)
27.
28.    new == new = T
29.    e@s== new = F
30.    h1@t1 == h2@t2 = (h1==h2) and (t1==t2)
31.    s1 == s2 = s2 == s1
32.  end object
```

Line 1 states that the specification object is accessing a previously specified object BOOLEAN; the components of BOOLEAN explicitly imported are listed after the => mark (*bool* is in fact a sort, and the others are operations, of which *T* and *F* are actually constants – see below). Line 2 gives the name of the object, and lines 3 to 5 define its parameterization. The latter is very similar to the technique of generic abstraction described in Section 4.7. SEQUENCE is thus a template from which more concrete objects can be instantiated via

actual parameters that correspond to a sort and two associated operations (whose formal parameter names are *elem*, _==_ and *bottom*
respectively).

The **sorts** section of the specification defines the one or more
new types that the specification introduces. The **operations** section (lines
7 to 14) defines the signature – name, input domain(s) and range – of
each operation of the object (note: this is sometimes called the 'syntax'
of the operations, whereas the axioms are their 'semantics'). The
number of inputs is called the *arity* of an operation. Note thus the
following:

★ Constants are treated as operations of zero arity.
★ Operations of arity two that we desire to apply in an infix manner,
  rather than functionally, are named thus: _ <op name> _.
★ Operation overloading is permitted, e.g. _==_.

The axioms that follow (lines 16 to 31) are equational relations that
capture the desired behavioural properties of the operations. Note that
the axioms are implicitly qualified by the following quantification:

forall e,x,h1,h2 ε elem
forall s,s1,s2,t1,t2 ε seq

The domain of each variable can be determined from the syntactic
context in which it is applied; in some algebraic styles, the domains of
the axiom variables are stated explicitly. Taking random examples and
expressing the equations informally:

line 17: applying *hd* to the *seq* constant *new* always yields *bottom*;
line 22: the effect of *tl* on a *seq* value is the same as the *seq* value
         involved in the immediately previous '@' operation that con-
         structed the current *seq* value;
line 26: an *elem* value is a member of a non-*new* or non-*undseq seq*
         value if either the *elem* value is the same as the *elem* value used
         in the immediately previous '@' operation constructing that
         seq value, or it is in the *seq* value involved in that '@'
         operation;
line 30: the _==_ operation on *seq* values is commutative.

Observe the complete formality and abstraction of algebraic specifications – there is no explicit or implied interpretation of symbols,
representation of sorts or implementation of operation behaviour. One
main technical problem with algebraic specifications, however, is determining that one has specified a set of axioms that sufficiently, though not
redundantly, defines all behavioural properties. This sufficiency is
obtained by specifying equations of the form:

behaviour (... constructor ...) = ...
modifier   (... constructor ...) = ...

for each possible combination of behaviour operation, modifier operation and constructor operation. *Behaviours* yield results from observing objects (*hd*, *tl*, *_==_*, *isin*). *Constructors* build objects (*new*, *undseq*, *@*). *Modifiers* yield results by changing objects, i.e. the right-hand side of the equation must partly involve the constructor on the left-hand side; there are no modifiers in the above specification.

In the next example, we combine an element of three other types of specification technique – implicit, abstract model and state machine specification. Note the change in syntax for specifying operation signatures:

```
1.  using NATURAL => natnum with _==_, −1
2.         BOOLEAN => bool with _==_, not, or, T
3.  object NAT_STACK
4.  model
5.     natst by SEQUENCE(natnum, _==_, −1) =>
6.                  seq with _==_, new, undseq, _@_, _isin_
7.  state
8.     ns : natst
9.  initial
10.    ns ε {undseq}
11. invariant
12.    inv_ns: T
13. operations
14.    newst()
15.       pre_newst: T
16.       post_newst: ns' == new
17.    push(n:natnum)
18.       pre_push: not(ns ε {undseq})
19.       post_push: ns' == n@ns
20.    pop() n:natnum
21.       pre_pop: not(ns ε {undseq} or ns == new)
22.       post_pop: n@ns' == ns
23.    isempty() b:bool
24.       pre_isempty: not(ns ε {undseq})
25.       post_isempty: b == (ns == new)
26.    isin(n:natnum) b:bool
27.       pre_isin : not(ns ε {undseq})
28.       post_isin : b == (n isin ns)
29. end object
```

Firstly, in the style of the previous example, lines 1 to 2 specify the objects accessed by this specification object, together with an enumeration of the components of each object that are imported by the specification. Lines 4 to 6 state that the sort *natst* is modelled as sort *seq* (with the specified operations) derived from the object SEQUENCE instantiated with the actual parameters indicated. The parameters of SEQUENCE have all come from object NATURAL. Note that, for the instantiation to be 'correct', _= =_ must be a (*natnum, natnum* −> *bool*) operation and −1 an operation of zero arity with range *natnum*; although _= =_ is (triply) overloaded in this specification, the syntactic context (here the parameter specification of SEQUENCE) is sufficient to disambiguate the application of _= =_. The **state** section (lines 7 to 8) specifies a (simple) state in terms of a variable *ns* of the specified sort. In general, the model section might comprise many sorts and the state section many variables. The **initial** section (lines 9 to 10), if present, defines one or more initial conditions on the state that must be established prior to any operation application (note: the set membership operator ε is deemed to be a built-in part of the specification language itself). The **invariant** section (lines 11 to 12) defines a Boolean function on the state that must always be satisfied, i.e. both initially and after the application of any operation; in effect, it is a 'factored out' common component of postconditions of operations that update the state. In our example, the state invariant is T, i.e. there is no additional constraint; we could, if we so wished, have therefore omitted the **invariant** section.

Lines 13 onwards specify the operations on the state in the implicit style. The change in syntax from the previous example is marked by:

omission of the state itself from each signature specification;
assigning names to an operation's inputs and result.

The names are required in the constraints following each operation signature that define the operation's *precondition* and *postcondition*. A precondition *pre_op*:C is a Boolean function C on the state and the inputs of the operation *op*. It imposes an additional constraint that must hold for application of *op* to be valid; if omitted, there is no such constraint, which is equivalent to writing *pre_op:T* (thus, we could have omitted the precondition for *newst*). Similarly, a postcondition *post_op*:C is a Boolean function C on the state before and after the operation, and on the inputs and result of the operation *op*; distinction between 'before' and 'after' is indicated by priming the state's name for the latter case. Note that, whereas *newst* and *push* are constructors, and *pop* is a modifier, *isempty* and *isin* are behaviours; thus, the 'after state' necessarily appears in the postconditions of the first three operations since they modify the state, but not in the postconditions of the latter two operations, since they leave the state unchanged. The application of an operation must result in satisfaction of its postcondition; this in turn is possible only if the operation's precondition has been satisfied.

We have combined the abstract model and state machine approach to specification for convenience in one example; in general, there is no direct association between the two, i.e. an abstract model specification does not have to possess state-machine elements. Likewise, we have chosen to include the implicit method of operation specification in the same example for convenience. In respect of this method, we have adopted the less conventional approach of using 'two-state' (before and after) postconditions. The technical ramifications of this will be touched upon later. Although there is no single generally accepted method of specification, the algebraic approach and model-based approach with or without state tend to predominate, where necessary using an implicit style of operation specification. A good text in which both techniques are covered is Cohen *et al.* (1986), which uses a non-trivial specification problem drawn from an electronic office scenario as the main example.

Finally, if we were adopting an operational specification approach in our second example, then the specification of *isin* (say) might appear as:

```
isin(n:natnum) bool
  if n = = hd(ns) then T
  else n isin tl(ns)
  endif
end isin
```

Although the specification implies a 'search from head to last element' behaviour, the implementation of *isin* need only be behaviourally equivalent, not identical. This brings us to the next main topic – verifying that realizations are consistent with their specifications.

5.3 FORMAL VERIFICATION

Overview

Formal verification requires:

* A formal specification S.
* A realization R that must be expressed in some suitable formal language with a formal semantics.
* A verification method, dependent upon the style of specification and the semantics of the languages used to express S and R, that enables the correctness of R against S to be formally proved or refuted.

Note: this is a slight simplification – it suggests that R is created before verification ensues. This is not necessarily so – see Section 5.4, for example.

The following gives a brief indication of what is involved in verifying a realization against each of the kinds of specification described in the previous section.

Implicit specification

Recall that an implicit specification will be of the form:

OP: Dom $->$ Rng
  pre_OP: Dom $->$ Bool
  post_OP: Dom x Rng $->$ Bool

Note: *Dom* is the cartesian product of the domains of the inputs when there are two or more.

For verification of a realization R(OP) against the specification S(OP), we must show that, for any inputs of R(OP) satisfying its signature and precondition *pre*_OP, R(OP) will terminate with an output satisfying its postcondition *post*_OP. Assuming that *Dom* and *Rng*, and hence the (axiomatic or proven) properties of objects belonging to these sets as applied in *pre*_OP and *post*_OP, are also part of the language in which R(OP) is expressed, then *pre*_OP $\equiv$ *pre*_R(OP) and *post*_OP $\equiv$ *post*_R(OP). If this is not the case, we must proceed as described below for the realized operations of an abstract model specification.

Operational specification

Given:

OP: Dom $->$ Rng
  B {a description of OP's 'behaviour'}

then, if S(OP.B) is the behavioural specification of OP, we must show that S(OP.B) and R(OP.B) are equivalent behaviours in their respective abstract machine domains, as defined by the languages in which S(OP) and R(OP) are expressed.

Abstract model specification

Given an abstract data type T modelled as M, then, for some *reification* (representation) R(M) of M – we are ignoring the simple case M = R(M) – we must show that:

★ R(M) can be 'mapped back' to M (technically that there exists a *homomorphic mapping* between R(M) and M);

★ R(M) is *adequate*, i.e. for each M object, there exists at least one R(M) object that can be mapped back to that M object (thus, every model object has at least one distinct concrete representation).

Assuming that operations are expressed in the implicit style, then verification of their realizations is carried out as follows. For each R(OP), constraints *pre*_R(OP) and *post*_R(OP) are constructed against which the correctness of R(OP)'s behaviour can be verified. It must also be shown that satisfaction of the pre and postconditions of the realization and satisfaction of the pre and postconditions of the specification are (in some formal way) directly associated, e.g. that the one implies the other.

State-machine specifications

A state-machine specification might comprise model style and/or implicit style specification components, for example. Thus, the above techniques apply. However, there is a complication – the state itself, and the fact that it has a 'history' – a value sequence that depends upon the operations that have been applied to it. One proof 'obligation' in the verification process will be to show that operations preserve the invariant on the state (if there is one).

Technical complications arise for verification methods if, for example, implicit specifications of operations refer to 'before and after' states in their postconditions. We shall not investigate the consequences of this, except to say that 'before and after' postconditions can be avoided by a style of implicit specification different from that used in the second example of Section 5.2. To illustrate, the PUSH operation might be specified instead as:

    PUSH(n:natnum)
      pre_PUSH: ns == x
      post_PUSH: ns == n @ x

We have introduced a 'ghost variable' x in the precondition to avoid reference to *ns* and *ns'* in the postcondition. It is implicit that x is universally quantified over the appropriate set (here, *natst*), which can be determined from the syntactic context(s) in which x is applied. This kind of quantification would apply to all ghost variables introduced in pre and postconditions.

Axiomatic and Algebraic Specifications

Here, verification involves showing that the axioms of the abstraction are 'preserved' in the representation. In effect, we have already stated the essence of the required verification process under abstract model specification. Thus, for example, given an algebraic specification Sa, then we must construct an algebraic specification R(Sa) for the representation and show that R(Sa) 'maps back' to Sa (technically, that there is a homomorphic mapping between the algebras of R(Sa) and Sa).

In a book such as this, there is no space to describe in detail the full range of verification techniques needed in formal methods, let alone dwell on the elegance of the underlying mathematics. We shall compromise by examining the verification process for one of the most frequently occurring types of situation – that of verifying the realization of operations specified in the implicit style.

The Axiomatic Method of Verification

The *axiomatic* method of verification stems from Hoare (1969). Being deductive, it relies on:

★ A set of axioms.
★ A set of inference rules – mechanisms by which new theorems can be deduced from existing theorems (axioms and previously verified statements).

The axioms employed are based on the semantics for the primitive operations of the realization language. Briefly, the axiomatic method of semantic specification defines the semantics of each kind of language construct X in terms of a pair of logical expressions P and Q thus:

$$|-\{P\}\ X\ \{Q\}$$

Overall, the notation can be expressed informally as: it is the case that P being satisfied (true) before X is executed ensures that Q will be satisfied (true) afterwards. The semantic rule defines the effect of executing constructs of kind X in purely general terms relative to the abstract machine represented by the language to which X belongs. In what follows, we will assume a very simple Pascal-like abstract machine (rather than, say, a functional machine, even though functional languages are mathematically 'cleaner' than imperative ones and thus enjoy a more 'natural' relationship with formal methods). As an example of a semantic axiom, consider the operation of assignment:

$$|-\{P(v:e)\}\ v := e\ \{P\}\quad \text{-- the assignment 'axiom'}$$

where $P(v{:}e)$ is a logical expression obtained by replacing all free (non-quantified) instances of v in P with e. Strictly, this is a 'generic template' that represents axioms for specific instances of assignment; but we shall continue to use our inexact terminology.

The main inference rules are associated with the structuring concepts of concatenation, selection and iteration; for simplicity, our examples will be confined to the basic forms of these structures:

Inference rule for concatenation (straight sequencing)

$$|-\{P\} \ X1 \ \{Q\} \ \text{and} \ |-\{Q\} \ X2 \ \{R\} \ => \ |-\{P\} \ X1; \ X2 \ \{R\}$$

The generalization to straight sequences of any length is straightforward.

Inference rule for (binary) selection $\quad \{ P \wedge R \} S_+ \{ Q \}$

$$|-\{P \ \text{and} \ C\} \ X1 \ \{Q\} \ \text{and} \ |-\{P \ \text{and not} \ C\} \ X2 \ \{Q\} \ =>$$
$$|-\{P\} \ \textbf{if} \ C \ \textbf{then} \ X1 \ \textbf{else} \ X2 \ \textbf{endif} \ \{Q\}$$

Note that if the else part is not present, we simply need a modified inference rule that states:

$$\ldots\ldots\ldots \text{and} \ (|-\{P \ \text{and not} \ C\} \ => \ \{Q\}) \ => \ \ldots\ldots\ldots$$

Inference rule for iteration (while form)

$$|-\{P \ \text{and} \ C\} \ X \ \{P\} \ => \ |-\{P\} \ \textbf{while} \ C \ \textbf{do} \ X \ \textbf{enddo} \ \{P \ \text{and not} \ C\}$$

The logical expression P is termed the *loop invariant* – it is true before and after execution of the loop body X (though not necessarily during it), regardless of how many times the latter is executed. Invariants represent a powerful means by which loop programs can be understood and reasoned about.

Inference rules can be specified for other selection and iteration structures. Together with appropriate axioms, they form a deductive system of proof that enables structured realizations ('structured' in the sense of 'structured programs' – see Section 4.2) to be verified against implicit formal specifications. To see this, if R(OP) is the realization of OP, then verification of R(OP) against S(OP) can be transformed into the following proof problem:

$$\{pre\_OP\} \ R(OP) \ \{post\_OP\}$$

Informally expressed, the proof problem is to verify the claim that 'if *pre*_OP is satisfied before the execution of R(OP), then *post*_OP will be satisfied after execution of R(OP) is complete' (we are simplifying by assuming that *pre*_OP ≡ *pre*_R(OP) and *post*_OP ≡ *post*_R(OP)). More generally, for the proof problem:

$$\{P\} \ X \ \{Q\}$$

P is referred to as the *antecedent* (or *input assertion*) of X, and Q the *consequent* (or *output assertion*) of X. Note that the Hoare axiomatic proof method does not permit 'before and after' two-state postconditions.

Thus far, we have deferred consideration of an important issue that verification must address – not only must we show:

{pre_OP} R(OP) {post_OP}

but also that R(OP) actually terminates.

Partial and Total Correctness

Put more explicitly, the complete proof problem is to verify that:

(a) {pre_OP} R(OP) {post_OP}.
(b) For any initial state of R(OP) that satisfies pre_OP, R(OP) *terminates* in a final state that satisfies post_OP.

This is called proving *total correctness*. If we relax our verification criteria by *assuming* R(OP) will terminate, then we are proving *partial correctness*; this is essentially part (a) of the complete proof problem. As might be expected, therefore, proving total correctness is a more onerous task than proving partial correctness. In particular, the inference rule for while-loops given above establishes partial correctness only; we shall address the problem of establishing total correctness of while-loops shortly.

The axiomatic proof technique can be broken down as follows:

Preliminary

We are given a specification S(OP):

    OP: Dom −> Rng
      pre_OP: .....
      post_OP: .....

and a realization R(OP) in the concrete language. We are required to demonstrate the total correctness of R(OP) against S(OP) as described above.

Main process

R(OP) is hierarchically decomposed level by level into its constituent primitive and structured constructs. Initially, we make a start by examining:

    {pre_OP} R(OP).X1 { ...?... }

and/or:

{ ...?... } R(OP).Xk {post_OP}

where X1/Xk are the first/last steps respectively of R(OP). More generally, for each construct X in R(OP)'s decomposition, an intermediate theorem is hypothesized of the form:

{A} X {B}

which is needed as a stepping stone in the overall proof. In effect, A must result via inferential reasoning from the original antecedent {pre_
OP} and B must be a 'useful' assertion that ultimately plays its part in inferring the consequent {post_OP}. Such intermediate theorems can be established in one of two ways:

Establishing intermediate theorems

To verify {A} X {B}, the appropriate inference rule or axiom is applied, depending on the kind of construct X. This application can either take place in 'forward reasoning mode':

We have arrived at {A} X { ... ? ... }; so we deduce {A} X {B'} via the rule for X for some B', and verify that B' => B (i.e. B' might be a *stronger* postcondition than than the desired B).

Or in 'backward reasoning mode':

We have arrived at { ... ? ... } X {B}; so we deduce {A'} X {B} via the rule for X for some A', and verify that A => A' (i.e. A' might be a *weaker* precondition than the desired A).

Implications such as B' => B and A => A' are *verification conditions* that must be proven; they represent the extra work in proofs additional to applying the appropriate axioms or inference rules for each construct X. Note that verification is creative in the sense that it is up to the verifier to 'discover' the intermediate assertions, hence theorems, that usefully lead to a proof of the given realization. This comment applies especially to the construction of appropriate loop invariants.

Verifying total correctness

Apart from malfunction of the machine (which we shall discount), non-termination can result in a 'structured' program only from infinite looping. In other words, proving that a program terminates involves proving that each of its constituent loops terminates. Thus, in axiomatic proofs of total correctness, given that we wish to verify that the theorem:

{A} X {B}

is totally correct, then we proceed as stated above, and:

★ Termination is axiomatic if X is primitive (thus all axioms are sufficient for both partial and total correctness proofs).
★ Termination is inferred if X is not a loop construct and all its components terminate, in which case application of the appropriate inference rule for X is adequate.
★ If X is a loop construct, application of the loop inference rule must be accompanied by proof of termination.

The latter requirement represents the 'extra work' in total correctness proofs. Briefly, loop termination involves finding an integer function that can be shown to decrease per cycle of the loop body down to zero (hence in a *finite* number of cycles) such that, at that point, the controlling loop predicate is false. Because proving theorems with respect to loops is particularly important in correctness proofs, it is worth describing in more detail the general method of verifying:

{P} **while** C **do** S **enddo** {P and not C}

for some hypothesized invariant P, loop condition C and loop body S:

(a) Find a candidate P for an invariant of the loop. This requires skill and understanding of the effect of the loop in question and its particular role in the program.
(b) Show that P is true before the first cycle. $= \quad i = 0$
(c) Show that, for any arbitrary cycle:
     {P and C} S {P}
(d) Show that 'not C' occurs after a finite number of cycles (proof of termination).

Steps (b) and (c) combined establish P as an invariant of the loop. Many readers will recognize here the familiar technique of proof by induction – (b) is the induction basis, (c) the induction step.

induction

Example of 'Rigorous' Verification

The example is intended to illustrate most aspects of the axiomatic method that have been covered in this section. In practice, a correctness proof is often constructed against an informal specification, the semantics of which is nevertheless deemed to be sufficiently precise to enable a proof to be constructed and subsequently accepted as being a verification on which reliance can be placed. In addition, correctness proofs are often 'rigorous' rather than being formal in the strict sense – that is, some of the 'obvious' reasoning is expressed as narrative rather than purely in the mechanics of the formal logic system employed, though it could be formalized if this was required. For simplicity, we shall start with a formal implicit specification and then give a proof in the spirit of 'informal rigour'.

We shall use the object NAT_STACK specified in Section 5.2 as a springboard for the example. Let us suppose our concrete language is Pascal and that we have reified sort *seq*, hence *natst*, as follows:

```
const MAXSEQLEN    = ..... {some chosen upper limit U};
      MAXSEQLENM1 = ..... {= U−1};
type NATNUM = 0..MAXINT;          Set
     SEQLEN  = 0..MAXSEQLEN;      set
     NATST   = record
                  SEQSP : array [0..MAXSEQLENM1] of NATNUM;
                  SLEN  : SEQLEN;
                end;
```

We shall suppose that we have proven that this is an adequate representation for sort *natst*. In the abstract specification, there is an operation *isin*:

```
isin(n:natnum) b:bool
   pre_isin: not(ns ε {undseq})
   post_isin: b = = (n isin ns)
```

In the concrete form that follows, we have parameterized the function ISIN with respect to the state also:

```
function ISIN(N:NATNUM; NS:NATST):BOOLEAN;
   var FOUND:BOOLEAN;
       POS:SEQLEN;
begin
   with NS do begin
      POS := 0;
      FOUND := FALSE;
      while (POS <> SLEN) and (not FOUND) do
         if SEQSP[POS] = N then FOUND := TRUE
                           else POS := POS + 1;
      ISIN := FOUND
   end
end {ISIN};
```

We must show that this is correct with respect to the reification NATST and that, in turn, the implicit formal specification of *isin* is satisfied. Our first task is to construct pre and postconditions for the realized ISIN, i.e. for any arbitrary call ISIN(N,NS) where N ε NATNUM and NS ε NATST. Our choices will be:

pre_ISIN: NS.SLEN ε SEQLEN
post_ISIN: ISIN = ∃i ε 0. .(NS.SLEN−1): NS.SEQSP[i] = N

Informally, we are representing 'not(ns ε {undseq})' in the abstraction as NS.SLEN ε SEQLEN in the realization – intuitively, a defined stack in the realization must have a length of 0 or greater, up to the specified limit (note: the precondition is equivalent to 0<=NS.SLEN<= MAXSEQLEN and is not intended to convey merely that NS.SLEN is of type SEQLEN, which does not of itself guarantee 'definedness'). The postcondition expresses the fact that the result if ISIN is the truth value of the assertion that there is at least one element of the array representation SEQSP of NS that is the natural number N being searched for. We will assume without proof that verifying:

{pre_ISIN} ISIN(N,NS) {post_ISIN}

establishes that ISIN satisfies its implicit specification.
    Firstly, we can transform our proof problem into:

{NS.SLEN ε SEQLEN}
with NS do begin
    . . . <with body> . . .
end
{ISIN = ∃ i ε 0. .(NS.SLEN−1): NS.SEQSP[i] = N}

Strictly, we have made a big leap by substituting ISIN(N,NS) with its body in which (in effect) formal parameter names have been replaced by actual parameter names. We will again assume without proof that, in the case of a function like ISIN, this is a valid manoeuvre, regardless of what actual parameters are involved (the strong typing of Pascal of course guarantees their domain compatability with ISIN's declared interface).
    The proof problem can now be reduced further to:

{SLEN ε SEQLEN}
    . . . <with body> . . .
{ISIN = ∃i ε 0. .SLEN−1: SEQSP[i] = N}

since the **with** clause is merely a notational device for avoiding direct reference to a record variable. From here, we can make rapid progress by applying the assignment axiom in 'forward' mode to the first two assignments, and in 'backward' mode to the last assignment, giving:

{SLEN ε SEQLEN and (FOUND = FALSE) and POS = 0}
while . . . do . . .
{FOUND = ∃ POS ε 0. .SLEN−1: SEQSP[POS] = N}

where we have used consistent name substitution in the consequent to replace *i* by POS (it is valid to apply name substitution to any logical expression whenever convenient to do so). We shall refer to this last consequent as CNSQ1.

(Note: we shall drop parentheses, providing readability is not sacrificed, where interpretation of an expression is unambiguous according to the decreasing priorities: *not*, all relations not on Bool, *and,or*, =>, Boolean =.)

By applying the inference rule for while-loops, our proof problem now reduces to finding an invariant LINV for the while loop such that we can prove the verification condition:

LINV and not (POS<>SLEN and not FOUND) => CNSQ1

or simplifying the antecedent (using deMorgan's law):

LINV and (POS = SLEN or FOUND) => CNSQ1

We shall refer to this verification condition as VC1.

Suppose we choose for LINV:

POS ε 0. .SLEN and (not FOUND or (POS ε 0. .SLEN−1
                                          and SEQSP[POS] = N))

Assume that LINV holds. Then, if POS = SLEN in the antecedent of VC1, POS ∉ 0. .SLEN−1 and so the inner conjunction in LINV cannot hold; thus, (not FOUND) must hold {i.e. FOUND = FALSE} if LINV overall is to be TRUE. Alternatively, if FOUND holds in the antecedent of VC1 {i.e. FOUND = TRUE}, then the right-hand expression of the disjunction in LINV must be TRUE if LINV overall is to be true. Summarizing these two results, we have deduced from the antecedent of VC1, given our choice of LINV, that if LINV is TRUE, then:

(not (POS ε 0..SLEN−1 and SEQSP[POS] = N) => (FOUND = FALSE))and
((FOUND = TRUE) => POS ε 0. .SLEN−1 and SEQSP   [POS] = N)

That is:

FOUND = (POS ε 0. .SLEN−1 and SEQSP[POS] = N)

and since:

(POS ε 0. .SLEN−1 and SEQSP[POS] = N) =
    ∃POS ε 0. .SLEN−1: SEQSP[POS] = N

therefore:

FOUND = ∃POS ε 0. .SLEN−1: SEQSP[POS] = N

which is CNSQ1. Therefore, the proof of VC1, which completes the proof overall, rests on verifying that LINV is indeed an invariant of the while-loop:

Induction basis

We already have:

(FOUND = FALSE) and (POS = 0)

which immediately implies LINV before the first iteration.

Induction hypothesis

Assume LINV holds before some arbitrary Kth. iteration of the while-loop body.

Induction step

We need to prove (from the inference rule for while-loops) that:

{LINV and POS <> SLEN and not FOUND} **if** ... {LINV}

Taking the two cases of the conditional separately:
(a) Suppose SEQSP[POS] = N; then in particular (using
    POS ε 0. .SLEN from LINV):
    {POS ε 0. .SLEN and POS <> SLEN and not FOUND
                                      and SEQSP[POS] = N}
    FOUND := TRUE
    {FOUND and POS ε 0. .SLEN and POS <> SLEN
                          and SEQSP [POS] = N}

The consequent follows by the assigment axiom and the fact that assignment to a variable leaves invariant all logical expressions not containing that (free) variable. Noting that:

POS ε 0. .SLEN and POS <> SLEN => POS ε 0. .SLEN−1

we can see that the consequent of FOUND := TRUE implies LINV (this deductive 'leap' could of course be formalized if required); hence:

{POS ε 0. .SLEN and ... etc ... } FOUND := TRUE {LINV}

(b) Suppose not(SEQ[POS] = N), then we have:

{POS ε 0. .SLEN and POS <> SLEN and not FOUND
                              and not (SEQ[POS] = N)}
    POS := POS + 1
{POS ε 0. .SLEN and not FOUND}

This consequent follows by the assignment rule and the fact that the first two conjuncts of the antecedent imply POS 0. .SLEN−1 (see above). However, the consequent also implies LINV (another 'leap' that could be formalized), and so :

{POS ε 0. .SLEN and ... } POS := POS+1 {LINV}

Therefore, using the inference rule for if-structures:

{LINV and ... etc ... } **if** ... {LINV}

This proves the induction step, which completes the proof that LINV is an invariant of the while-loop.

As explained above, proof of the invariance of LINV establishes the partial correctness of ISIN. To help the reader follow the verification argument, an overview of the above proof is given in the following 'proof tableau' (see Backhouse 1986). Here, the appropriate predicates have been inserted into the algorithm text; note that the juxtaposition of two predicates {A} {B} represents a verification condition A => B established in the proof.

```
{SLEN ε SEQLEN}
POS := 0;
FOUND := FALSE;
{SLEN ε SEQLEN and FOUND = FALSE and POS = 0}
{LINV ≡ POS ε 0..SLEN and (not FOUND or
                   (POS ε 0. .SLEN−1 and SEQSP[POS] = N))}
while POS <> SLEN and not FOUND do
   {LINV and (POS <> SLEN and not FOUND)}
   if SEQSP [POS] = N
   then {LINV and (POS <> SLEN and not FOUND) and SEQSP
                                                   [POS] = N}

        FOUND := TRUE
        {LINV}
   else {LINV and (POS <> SLEN and not FOUND)
           and not(SEQSP[POS] = N)}
        POS := POS + 1;
        {LINV}
   {LINV}
{LINV and not (POS <> SLEN and not FOUND)}
{FOUND = ∃ POS ε 0. .SLEN−1: SEQSP[POS] = N}
ISIN := FOUND
{ISIN = ∃i ε 0. .SLEN−1: SEQSP[i] = N}
```

To establish total correctness, we need to show that the while-loop halts in a finite number of iterations. We have:

{POS = 0} **while** . . .

and:

{POS = k−1} FOUND := TRUE {FOUND}
{POS = k−1} POS := POS+1 {POS = k}

hence:

{POS = k−1} **if** . . . {POS = k or FOUND}

by the inference rule for if-structures. Thus, if FOUND = TRUE after the kth iteration, the loop condition becomes FALSE and the loop halts; otherwise, by induction, after k iterations, POS = k. Substituting k by SLEN in the previous argument, we have:

after the SLENth. iteration, either FOUND = TRUE or POS = SLEN.

But POS = SLEN also halts the loop. Hence, after at most SLEN iterations, the loop will halt. Since SLEN ε SEQLEN, and therefore SLEN <= MAXSEQLEN, the loop must halt after a finite number of iterations, since MAXSEQLEN is a finite natural number.

Bibliographical note: for more on program verification, the reader is directed to the paper by Manna & Waldinger (1978) and the texts by Gries (1981) and Backhouse (1986).

5.4 METHODS, TOOLS, LANGUAGES

The reader may feel from the previous example that verification is hard work, even for simple realizations. Whilst this is undoubtedly true, the verification effort required can be offset against the fact that proof construction, like software construction, is a once-off task. Thus, if each operation in the realization NATST of our abstract data type is subjected to proof along the lines of ISIN, we would then have a verified module and hence confidence in the correctness of any of its components that were imported into larger programs. For example, wherever ISIN was applied in a program, we could take as proven that:

{pre_ISIN} ISIN(. . . . .) {post_ISIN}

and this would reduce the effort required in verifying the program itself. This integration or reuse of verified components could of course occur at higher levels, e.g. when building subsystems. Clearly, therefore, verification of bottom-up and reusable components is particularly worthwhile. The fact remains, however, that the effort required to verify even modestly sized programs is considerable. Can anything be done to reduce the intellectual and documentation load involved?

One way to reduce verification effort is to avoid *a posteriori* proofs, i.e. construction of proof following realization of software. To do this, verification needs to be integrated into the design process itself. One way this can be achieved is to use proof assertions themselves to steer the design. This kind of approach can be called *constructive* and can be achieved by the application of Dijkstra's 'weakest precondition' method (Dijkstra, 1976). Here, design synthesis takes place in 'backwards reasoning' mode thus:

Given the design objective of seeking a realization of S in the context:

$$\{P\} \ S \ \{Q\}$$

then we postulate a candidate for S and determine the *weakest precondition* of S with respect to Q, written *wp(S,Q)*; that is:

$$\{wp(S,Q)\} \ S \ \{Q\}$$

We also need to prove a verification condition, specifically the implication $P => wp(S,Q)$. We can then deduce that $\{P\} \ S \ \{Q\}$.

More formally, $wp(S,Q)$ is the precondition describing all possible states such that, when execution of S is begun in any one of those states, execution is then guaranteed to terminate in a state satisfying Q (i.e. weakest preconditions establish total correctness). Rules for defining $wp(S,Q)$ can be given for each type of statement S; for example:

$wp(V:=E,Q) \equiv Q(V:E)$
$wp(\textbf{if } C \textbf{ then } S1 \textbf{ else } S2 \textbf{ endif}, Q) \equiv (C => wp(S1,Q))$ and
$$(\text{not } C => wp(S2,Q))$$

etc.

The advantages of the approach are that:

★ Postconditions are generally more informative than preconditions about required program behaviour and therefore provide greater guidance in the discovery of design components.
★ Determining the *weakest* precondition allows any stronger assertion P to be used (provided that $P => wp(S,Q)$) in establishing the correctness of the design.
★ One arrives at designs with integral design-driving correctness proofs – no further verification is necessary; this is the effort-saving appeal of a constructive approach.

Another aspect of the weakest precondition method is that for a realized design D with implicit specification:

$$\{pre\_D\} \ D \ \{post\_D\}$$

it is possible algorithmically to construct a Hoare-style proof of conditional correctness using the *wp* transformation rules, provided that D is non-looping. If D contains loops, then, in addition, an invariant needs to be supplied for each loop within D. Automated proof construction will include generation of the necessary verification conditions whose proof, together with application of the Hoare axiomatic and inference rules, leads to the desired proof of conditional correctness. Automated support in fact represents the other, and most important way in which verification effort can be reduced.

Automated support for verification is usually but part of a more comprehensive 'support environment' for formal software development geared to a specific method and language(s). Typically, the main components of such a support environment are:

a specification language processor SLP;
a verification condition generator VCG;
a theorem prover TP;
other tools, e.g. syntax-directed editor.

The SLP performs various syntactic and semantic checks on a formal specification written in the formal descriptive language of the method being supported and transforms it into some suitable internal representation; depending on the system, it might also generate formulas to be used later by the TP. The VCG generates from some design or program description derived from the specification the verification conditions that need to be proved for partial correctness to be established. The proof is handled by a TP, which is usually interactive, needing guidance from users who supply additional axioms and lemmas to steer the proof process. The support system may also translate verified designs into a conventional target language such as Pascal. Examples of support system-based methods include:

★ *Gypsy*: The Gypsy system supports both specification and verification with a single description language that, in part, resembles Pascal. Development proceeds by way of writing a specification in the Gypsy language in terms of a collection of independently verifiable components. The specification of functions, etc. basically follows the implicit style. Specification components are then refined into implementations, also described in the Gypsy language. By use of the VCG and TP of the Gypsy system, proof of an implementation can proceed in parallel with its development. An important feature is that both concurrency and exception handling are catered for by the method.

★ *HDM*: The Hierarchical Design Methodology uses a description language SPECIAL to define a system in terms of a hierarchy of abstract state machines. The top-level state machine defines the system as it is visible to the user; the bottom-level state machine represents the layer to be implemented in the concrete language. Each layer is decomposed into a lower layer of modules – a module comprises data structures, and value-returning and state-changing functions – that provide the facilities for implementing the upper layer. HDM development is supported by a sophisticated interactive verification system (Halpern *et al.* 1987).

★ *FDM*: This system – Formal Development Methodology – also supports the state machine approach and is similar to HDM, though it employs an entirely different description language called *Ina Jo* [TM] (Berry 1987). For each specification decomposition level, the language processor generates theorems which establish that the decomposition correctly implements the level above and also preserves other correctness criteria. Verification is backed up by an interactive TP and a VCG at the bottom level specific to the concrete language in which the software will be written.

★ *Affirm*: The descriptive language directly supports specification in the algebraic equational style and implementation in a language that is a slightly cleaned-up, extended version of Pascal; however, specification in the abstract model style is also accommodated. The tool-kit includes a VCG for the implementation language using a 'predicate transformer' approach similar to Dijkstra's weakest preconditions and an interactive TP that makes use of equational substitution via a specification's axioms. Related to the Affirm system is the *Larch* project (Guttag *et al.* 1985). In Larch, specification occurs in two stages: (i) a first stage that is primarily algebraic and employs a 'shared language' common to any Larch-based development irrespective of concrete language; (ii) a second stage that employs an 'interface language' dependent on the concrete language and permits implicit-style specification. Interface languages for Pascal and CLU currently exist.

★ *OBJ*: We have already mentioned this system in Section 2.4. Supporting the algebraic equational approach with its own style of specification, it enables specifications to be animated by interpreting the axioms as rewrite rules when operations are applied to their inputs; this represents a valuable prototyping facility (see Goguen & Meseguer 1982). OBJ is in effect an executable subset of a more powerful specification language CLEAR.

The paper by Cheheyl *et al.* (1981) is well worth reading, as it compares and contrasts Gypsy, HDM, FDM, and Affirm by applying each to the problem of specifying and implementing a security model that provides data access protection in an operating system.

Another well-established development method that is currently being tooled up is VDM (Vienna Development Method) (Bjorner & Jones 1982, Jones 1986). This is a model-based approach in which, typically, the initial specification is expressed as a data abstraction modelled in terms of:

★ The rich supply of predefined primitive types (integer, Boolean, etc.) and abstract type structures (sets, sequences, mappings, etc.) provided by the VDM language (Meta-IV).
★ Operations, specified in the implicit style but with 'two-state' postconditions, on a 'state', i.e. one or more variables of the types being modelled.

VDM also permits specification of functions, which can be recursive, either in an implicit or explicit (operational) style. In conjunction with a state-based specification, they are generally used to simplify pre and postconditions. Subsequent development steps in the method involve:

(a) Reification of the data type(s) along with proof of adequacy of the representation via the specification of 'retrieve functions' (which show how the abstraction can be 'retrieved' from the representation).
(b) Decomposition of operations, with proof of correctness (including preservation of the state invariant) and consistency against the implicit specifications being achieved with inference rules similar to those discussed in Section 5.3 but adapted to take into account 'two-state' postconditions.
(c) Steps (a) and (b) are repeated, if refinement needs to be accomplished through one or more intermediate levels before the concrete level is reached.

Via an employment agency database example, Jackson (1985) shows how reification and decomposition of a VDM specification is facilitated by choosing Ada as the concrete representation.

Finally, another model-based approach is Z, whose language is based on set theory and first order predicate logic. Some non-trivial case studies using Z have been published, including the specification of the Unix [TM] file system (Morgan & Sufrin 1984). A description of Z and several case studies are collected together in Hayes (1987).

5.5 SOME CONCLUDING OBSERVATIONS

Few would argue about the potential benefits offered to software engineering by increased formality:

★ A disciplined, scientific framework for the production and documentation of quality software.

★ (Mechanically) verified, 'watertight' software exhibiting reliable behaviour and non-obscure structure.
★ Greater cost-effectiveness: concentration of effort occurs early in development but should pay for itself many times over in the testing and maintenance phases.

However, there are as yet certain problems, which some would consider are, and possibly always will be, prohibitive, to be overcome in achieving those benefits. These problems relate to certain difficulties associated with applying formal specification and verification techniques in practice. We shall begin with specification.

One problem that a formal specification language faces is that it should attempt to satisfy a number of possibly conflicting criteria. For example, it should:

be sufficiently rich to express all properties and constraints that might be determined by requirements analysis;

be sufficiently abstract not to constrain unnecessarily the characteristics of realizations (implementations);

facilitate the formal verification of realizations.

These are not the only properties that might be considered desirable in a specification language – one might add: support for modularity, parameterization, reusability and other such features that enhance the language's applicability to larger, system-sized problems. As yet, no current specification language performs well in all these areas.

Another difficulty is the domain of problems to which formal specification methods can be realistically applied. Many software development problems are still on a scale far greater than current formal specification technology can effectively deal with. Even with tractable problems, the skill and effort required in constructing a formal specification is at least the same as, if not greater than, that required in developing the program itself. Whilst this up-front expense may pay dividends later, the point is that there is no recipe for a specifier to follow that guarantees that a formal specification is in all senses 'adequate' or 'suitable'. Syntactic well-formedness and internal semantic consistency can be automatically checked for. However, adequacy of a specification with respect to user requirements relies mainly on inspection against a user requirements definition (unless specifications are executable); and suitability for implementation relies mainly on the skill and judgement of the specifier. With respect to the latter point, one might argue that it is a requirement of target languages that they should support the implementation of formal specifications, rather than vice versa.

A further problem with formal specifications is readability, which tends to vary from being acceptable to the trained, to being impenetrable to all but those few who are highly experienced in the technique/ language being used. Even for 'small' problems, formal specifications can be psychologically alarming, appearing as a dense, lengthy mass of arcane symbolism. Those mainly affected here are review personnel and implementors, who will clearly have to be people fully versed in the method being used. Certainly, it is wholly unrealistic to expect users to be able to peruse formal specifications to gauge whether or not requirements are being adequately captured – hence the need for review personnel who are adept at translating specifications back to users in terms the latter can comprehend.

Formal verification presents similar problems. Briefly, proof construction can be an extremely laborious, error-prone process; the skill/ effort factor required is very high – again, as great or greater than that needed to develop programs themselves. Proof lengths also are generally far longer than the programs whose correctness they verify. Readability alone, however, is not so problematic as with specifications; the logical theory employed by the mainstream verification methods is based on first order predicate calculus, with which the majority of software practitioners ought (in principle) to be familiar. It should be noted, however, that this calculus (and hence the methods that depend on it) does not facilitate satisfactory reasoning about all computational concepts; such aspects as exceptions, concurrency, network behaviour in distributed systems, etc. are less well handled, though progress is being made in these areas.

Perhaps the main problem with formal verification (implied in the preceding paragraph) lies with establishing that the proofs themselves are correct. Gerhart & Yelowitz (1976) identified errors in a number of programs that had supposedly been 'proved', as well as errors in specifications and systematically constructed programs. If proofs are expressed completely formally, they can be mechanically checked to verify that what was deduced was obtainable via application of the rules of inference of the logical theory to the axioms and previously proved theorems. However, proofs are generally presented with 'rigorous informality'; that is, they are not expressed completely in the language of the logical theory, but include narrative statements expressing implied reasoning that is deemed to be reasonably self-evident, and which has the effect of shortening the proof and making it more tractable. Despite this advantage, informality represents a potential source of error and increases the chance of applying the logical theory incorrectly. In addition, given the complexity of symbolism involved and the length of proof texts, the chance of making clerical errors must be considered relatively high. Since, however, proofs generally can be verified only by inspection, and given their complexity, the possibility remains that errors in a claimed 'proof' of correctness are overlooked.

The implication is that confidence in formal proofs needs to be enhanced by standard testing methods, and that the former, at present anyway, are not a total substitute for the latter.

Opinion about the role of formal methods in software engineering varies from the evangelical (... the only way out of the mess we are currently in ...) to the utterly sceptical and dismissive (... simply not cost-effective; will never be able to address real-life-sized problems ..); some would argue that formal methods are not even 'software engineering' anyway. However, it may be conjectured that neither extreme will ever hold true. That is, formal methods will play a highly significant, but not domineering, part in software engineering of the future. Even partial use only of formality should be beneficial. For example, by formalizing specifications, the specification 'sins' enumerated by Meyer (1985) are more likely to be highlighted; also, attempts at formalization will often provide a deeper insight into the nature of (the user's) problem and (possibly) its potential software solution. With (semi)informal specifications, attempting rigorously to verify a design may well show up design defects or inconsistencies between the design and the specification.

It should be appreciated that formal methods are already being practiced in production environments (see Hayes 1985, for example). Obviously, in order for the uptake of formal methods to increase, a great deal of retraining will be necessary, along with much inertia and pessimism to be overcome. This uptake will be aided by the availability of suitable tools, an area on which widespread adoption of formal methods will particularly depend. Ultimately, the success of any development method is mainly a function of:

its intuitive and/or theoretical appeal;
rational and convincing arguments for its adoption;
strong automated tool support.

As today's current practices are further refined and sharpened, they will gradually become more and more underpinned by a tool-supported formal, scientific basis that will impart much needed rigour to the whole process of specification, design, implementation, validation and verification (including inspections and reviews), and documentation also. Given the extent of the research effort into, and the amount of money invested in, formal methods, it is hardly conceivable that great strides will not be made in the future that will solve some of the problems that presently hinder the wholehearted acceptance of formal methods by the software engineering community.

Chapter 6

Implementation Techniques

6.1 IMPLEMENTATION – A TRANSFORMATIONAL VIEW

The implementation phase involves a number of activities that include
testing, debugging and integration. However, these aspects of implementation will be covered in Chapter 7. Before testing can ensue,
executable software products need to be generated. Our focus of
attention in this chapter will be a variety of techniques that map designs
into the concrete domains of target machine environments. In keeping
with the spirit of our general view of software development, our
descriptive approach will take a transformational standpoint.

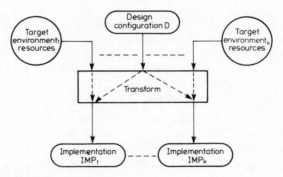

Fig. 6.1. The implementation process.

The relevant scenario should by now be familiar to the reader –
having constructed a design D, appropriate transformations must be
applied to D to obtain an implementation IMP of D, i.e. a product that
conforms to, and will perform acceptably under, the constraints imposed by the actual machine environment(s) within which the product
will operate; see Fig. 6.1. The transformations must therefore be
steered by those constraints, which will include available hardware
resources, operating systems and JCLs, file and database facilities,
and programming languages. The advantages of achieving this clean
separation of implementation domains from the abstract design domain

have been outlined previously but are worth restating here in more detail:

★ Since a design D relates to an abstract machine, it is thus maximally divorced from, and uncluttered by, the vagaries of any real machine environment. Therefore, changes to the latter will affect an implementation product, but not the design from which it is derived; the design will remain a correct transformation of the requirements specification.

★ Similarly, if a product is to be targeted towards several real environments, its design D remains the single abstract configuration from which all implementations are generated; it is only the transformations that need to be applied to D to create each IMPi that will be different in each case.

★ A consequence of these first two points is a potentially large saving in the effort and costs of reconfiguration caused by either modifications to a target environment or transportation of the product to other, dissimilar environments. This is because a large slice of the development effort is concentrated into constructing the specification and design, which, 'requirements drift' apart, should be a once-off task.

★ Further potential benefits are obtainable via software tools that automate various transformations applicable to designs. This improves efficiency of software development and minimizes the likelihood of introducing errors into an implementation derived from a correct design.

Most of what follows in this chapter will be concerned with describing a variety of implementation transformations of varying complexity, ranging from code level up to the level of system architecture. In addition, compilation and portability issues are also discussed.

6.2 CODING – LANGUAGE AND STYLE

Coding is the process of transforming design constructs into a machine-translatable form expressed in one or more target programming languages. Although often performed by hand, the process can easily be automated; naturally, this requires the design to be expressed in a formal notation. In some instances, the design and programming language are the same (as is often the case with step-wise refinement, say), so that there is no distinct coding phase in the development. Where this is not the case, the effort involved in hand coding depends to a large extent on the degree to which the constructs of the design and programming languages mirror each other – that is, the effort depends on the 'expressiveness gulf' that exists between them.

From a software engineering viewpoint, a programming language should ideally:

* Be very high level, partly because design languages tend to be, and partly because error-prone consideration of uninteresting, and usually irrelevant, machine-level detail is then avoided; assembly language or machine code should be used only where absolutely essential, e.g. when it is the only way to obtain the required performance from a time-critical section of a real-time system.
* Be extensible and directly support the various structuring mechanisms for achieving modularity, abstraction, etc.
* Provide other desirable support for software engineering such as separate compilation.
* Provide more specialized facilities that may from time to time be needed depending on application area, e.g. concurrency and exception handling if the language is to be used in the development of real-time software.

In practice, even given that there are several programming languages that would be suitable, other considerations such as customer requirements may limit this choice to a single possibility. Where choice and availability do exist, strong determinants are the application area, consistency with previously developed products and portability considerations.

The readability of coded software is largely a function of the stylistic standards adhered to within the syntactic constraints imposed by the chosen target language(s). Languages cover a whole spectrum from being 'fixed format' to 'free format' in layout with considerable variation in rules for identifier construction, significance of blanks and newlines, and placement of comments. Nevertheless, regardless of which language is used, few would quibble with the universality of the following minimum set of stylistic standards:

* Use meaningful identifiers, i.e. identifiers that convey the logical significance of the objects they name.
* Apply consistent indentation and alignment to reflect levels of structuring in the text of an algorithm; this is particularly important with free-format hierarchical languages, e.g. those of the Pascal family.
* Adopt a consistent usage of keyword patterns; for example, the following are some possible, sensible while-loop layouts in Pascal:

```
while C do              while C do              while C do begin
   begin                   begin                   S1;
      S1;                      S1;                   S2
      S2                       S2                 end
   end                     end
```

For each construct type, one form alone should be chosen and used throughout, apart from obvious exceptions, e.g. when the loop body is a single statement and the whole construct fits comfortably on one line.

★ Avoid cramped, unreadable text by making judicious use of blanks, newlining and blank lines to separate and spread out textual components.

★ Insert well-chosen commentary to inform, amplify and elucidate, but only where necessary, as there is no substitute for good structure and readable style. The danger here is to over, or inappropriately, comment, which could be worse than having no commentary at all. Sensible use of commentary would be to:

record documentation details, e.g. author, version etc.;
provide some global guidance on the structure and textual arrangement of the components of a large program;
provide a brief explanatory heading to a group of related subprograms;
provide an informal specification of each main subprogram;
augment the program text with invariants and pre and postconditions;
add explanation to aid understanding of a difficult algorithm;
record justification for a particular design decision in some part of the program.

Of course, management may impose prespecified coding standards on development personnel within the stylistic latitude allowed by a given language and then audit their use via quality assurance techniques. However, given the freedom of expression that is available, 'good coding style' is largely a matter of straightforward, commonsense application of the above guidelines.

6.3 OPTIMIZATIONS

Implementation transformations are frequently concerned with achieving optimization in target representations. The prevailing view of optimizations is that they should be avoided completely during design since they represent a threat to the preservation of correctness and good structure. Moreover, the essence of an optimization is either to reduce program size, increase execution efficiency or reduce data storage requirements. Hence, optimizations are basically implementation manoeuvres anyway and so should be considered only during the implementation phase. When a highly optimized program is an actual requirement, an unoptimized version can be retained for reference and maintenance purposes.

There exist a number of optimizing techniques, some of which are transformations that are within the capabilities of a software tool such as an optimizing compiler. The following is a representative selection of well-known possibilities that includes not only transformations but also sensible use of the target language. We restrict ourselves here to imperative languages. Other optimization techniques exist for programs written in; say, functional languages (Darlington 1982) or for transforming an executable formal specification into a conventional target language. These techniques will not be described here.

Optimizations on Selections

Factorization

The intention here is to avoid code duplication and thus make the program more compact. A general context where this arises is multi-choice selections; for example:

```
    if  C1 then A; B; X              if  C1 then A; B
  elseif C2 then F; X;   − − − >   elseif C2 then F
  elseif C3 then P; B; X           elseif C3 then P; B
            else  X                 endif;
    endif                               X
```

The tail action common to every 'arm' of the conditional has been factored out. Note that procedurization can achieve a similar effect (with B as well as X in the above). This type of optimization can be relatively sensitive to specification drift and so is 'unsafe' in terms of bug-generating potential if subsequent modification to the *optimized* product takes place – the modification might, for example, affect one of the original X's, but not the other three. The proper and save approach is to modify the design and then reapply any required transformations.

Ordering of predicate expressions

Suppose in the previous structure it is the case that:

$$p(C2) \ >>> \ p(C1) \ > \ p(C3)$$

where $p(Ci)$ is the probability that Ci is true. A reordering of the alternatives is thus likely to improve execution efficiency if, for example, the selection is embedded in an iteration of a large number of cycles:

```
    if  C2 then F; X
  elseif C1 then A; B; X
  elseif C3 then P; B; X
            else  X
    endif
```

Such optimization is unlikely to cause modification difficulties. However, care must be taken with the conditions in the reordered structure if they were not mutually exclusive in the original structure (we have assumed that they are in the example). If not mutually exclusive, the conditions will have to be re-expressed to preserve the semantics of the original selection; for example, if C1 was 'i < 0' and C2 'i < 10', the latter would need to be '(i < 10) and not (i < 0)' in the transformed structure.

Optimizing Logical Expressions

Efficiency improvements can sometimes be obtained in the evaluation of a logical expression, though this is target-language dependent. Given:

(a) **if** C1 **and** C2 **and** . . .
(b) **if** C1 **or** C2 **or** . . .

then:

in (a), the evaluation need proceed no further than the first Ci to yield false – the conjunction overall must be false;
in (b), the evaluation need proceed no further than the first Ci to yield true – the disjunction overall must be true.

Note that we have not specified the order in which the Ci are evaluated – this is of no consequence if the Ci are side-effect free. However, conditions with side effects would require a specified order of evaluation – typically left to right – to ensure determinism in the logical expression. Most target languages evaluate all operands of a conjunction or disjunction to decide its outcome – and in a non-specified order, making presence of side effects unsafe. One exception is language C, where evaluation proceeds from left to right and only as far as is necessary.

To provide for 'short circuit' evaluation as well as full evaluation of logical expressions, some languages (e.g. Ada) provide special logical operators in addition to the standard *and* and *or*. Thus, optimization is a matter of commonsense usage of the language – if short circuit logical operators are available, they can be used in conjunctions or disjunctions that are free of side effects; if side effects exist, a defined order of evaluation must operate.

Optimizations and Iterations

The standard situation is to avoid the re-elaboration of an expression with an invariant result within an iteration body:

iteration {of some kind}
    ... EXPR ...
end

where the result of evaluating EXPR is invariant over any number of cycles of the loop. The elaboration of EXPR can be removed from the body of the loop and placed before the start of the latter, using a working variable to hold the result.

Here is a related example; suppose we have:

for I **in** S **do**
    if B **then** P **endif**
enddo

Given that B is side-effect free and P has no effect on the state of B, then the structure can be transformed into the more efficient form:

if B **then**
    for I **in** S **do** P **enddo**
endif

Yet a further possibility is to transform recursive algorithms into iterative form; this is more efficient because of the avoidance of repeated procedure calling. However, whilst this is relatively easy for simple self-recursive algorithms, transforming more complex mutually recursive schemas into iterative form will require considerable effort.

Optimization of Data Storage

The aim of storage 'tuning' is to reduce program data storage requirements, albeit that this will involve an almost inevitable trade-off with execution efficiency. The possibilities here are very much target-language dependent. Here are two examples:

1. Suppose that, in a certain design, Boolean sequences are employed, with various logical-type operations applied to them. If the target language allows access to the bit level, possibly via a special data type, and provides associated bit-string operations, then it may be possible to transform the abstract Boolean data structures (with operations) into bit strings (with corresponding operations) in the implementation. This could, of course, result in a significant reduction in machine storage utilization compared to a more direct implementation of the design data structure.

2. The target language may provide optional storage attributes that have varying effects on storage requirements. For example, Pascal provides the attribute 'packed', which is specifically intended to reduce such

requirements without affecting program semantics in any way. In practice, what notice a Pascal compiler takes of usages of 'packed' in programs, and the storage organizations it subsequently effects, if any, is dependent on each Pascal system.

Optimizations via Target-Language Characteristics

A thorough knowledge of the target language, whilst in itself being obviously desirable, can also be of benefit from an optimization viewpoint. This includes knowledge of the idiosyncracies of the specific language system being used, which ought to be irrelevant, but acquaintance with which, in practice, can pay dividends. For example, the system's handling of certain language features may be known to generate gross run-time inefficiencies; such features are therefore worth avoiding if at all possible. As regards the language itself, its expressive power may be exploitable to advantage. Here is an example using Algol-68, one of the most 'orthogonal' – i.e. freely expressive – imperative languages ever devised:

```
x := x + 1;
if c <= 0
then write (y); a[x] := 0
else write (y); read ((a,b,c)); a[x] := c*2−1
fi
```

which can be transformed into:

```
a[x +:= 1] := if write(y); c <= 0
                 then 0
                 else read ((a,b,c)); c*2−1
              fi
```

This is marginally quicker and certainly more compact. The main danger of such expressive power lies in over-exploitation, yielding inscrutable code – as always, when there is power of any kind available, it needs to be used judiciously.

In conclusion, all optimizations should be placed in their proper context. With today's powerful hardware and large main storage capacity, there is little point in squeezing away a few milliseconds run-time or a meagre quantity of bytes from an application program – the net effect will not be 'user noticeable'. However, given the choice of several, otherwise equally acceptable, implementations, it would be perverse not to choose the most efficient. Also, situations do arise where storage constraints are imposed or response times are critical. So implementation efficiency is sometimes (vitally) important; but, all else being equal, it should never be regarded as an end in itself.

6.4   SEQUENTIAL STRUCTURES

Some sequential process structures may not be directly supported by a target programming language. Usually, this is because the latter's structuring power is inferior to the former, though the reverse can also be true. Thus, a variety of structural transformations can prove necessary when coding up designs.

Where the Target Language is Richer in Structure

To illustrate, we shall use JSP/JSD structure text as representative of a simple PDL. The sole iterative structure in this language is equivalent to the general-purpose while-loop. But there may be a more appropriate encoding in the target language. Suppose we have:

{Ei, Ef and Es are expressions}
V := Ei;
itr while (V <= {or >=} Ef) {Ef=vf, for some value vf, must be
                                        invariant}
.
.
.

V := V + {or −} Es; {Es=vs, for some value vs, must be
                                        invariant}
end

The iteration is then in fact determinate, and so transformation to a determinate loop in the implementation is superior. In FORTRAN 77, for example:

DO <label> V = Ei, Ef, Es
.
.
.

<label> CONTINUE

Of course, in languages like Pascal and Ada, where unitary incrementation and decrementation only are allowed, there is a little more work to do if the loop is numerically controlled and Es is not unitary; thus (Pascal):

```
V := Ei;
Vs := Es;
for I := 1 to {or downto} ABS (Ef–Ei) div Vs + 1 do
begin
    .
    .
    .
    V := V + {or −} Vs
end
```

Using brace brackets to denote '0 or more occurrences of' and square brackets to denote optionality, the JSP/JSD structure text for selections is equivalent to:

if ... **then** ... {**elseif** ... **then** ... } [**else** ...] **endif**

(Note, therefore, that the structure text form is ordered, whereas the diagrammatic form is not.) A more appropriate encoding, however, could be a case structure. One would identify the following kind of situation:

```
sel (V = X1 or V = X2) Pl
alt (V = X3) P2
alt (V = X4 or V = X5 or V = X6) P3
    .
    .
    .
end
```

Assuming the Xi are all values of a suitable type, then in Ada, say:

```
case V is
    when X1 | X2      => P1
    when X3          => P2
    when X4 | X5 | X6 => P3
        .
        .
        .
endcase
```

Where the Target Language is Structurally Inferior

The 'inferiority' could be relatively minor (e.g. having to transform a case structure in the design into a multi-choice **if** selection in the program), or it could be more substantial, necessitating the use of gotos. As regards the latter, it is essential that use of gotos, whenever unavoidable, should be disciplined – that is, the essence of the structure of the design should be preserved in the implementation, even though this will not be directly reflected at the superficial level of target code syntax. The following is a sample list of disciplined, transformational templates that can be adopted for different kinds of structure; in a top-down sense, they represent a final level of refinement:

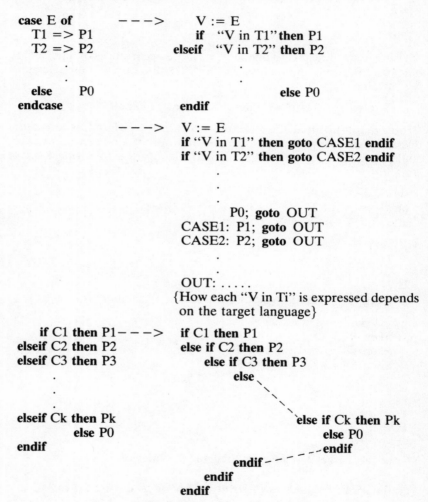

case E **of**   – – –>   V := E
  T1 => P1   **if**   "V in T1" **then** P1
  T2 => P2   **elseif**   "V in T2" **then** P2

          .   .
          .   .
  else   P0   **else** P0
endcase   **endif**

                        – – –>   V := E
                                 if "V in T1" **then goto** CASE1 **endif**
                                 if "V in T2" **then goto** CASE2 **endif**

                                         .
                                         .
                                         .

                                      P0; **goto** OUT
                                 CASE1: P1; **goto** OUT
                                 CASE2: P2; **goto** OUT

                                         .
                                         .

                                 OUT: . . . . .
                                 {How each "V in Ti" is expressed depends
                                 on the target language}

    if C1 **then** P1 – – –> **if** C1 **then** P1
 elseif C2 **then** P2   **else if** C2 **then** P2
 elseif C3 **then** P3   **else if** C3 **then** P3
          .   **else**
          .   ＼
          .   ＼
 elseif Ck **then** Pk   ＼ **else if** Ck **then** Pk
          else P0   **else** P0
 endif   – –**endif**
                                 endif – – – –
                                    endif
                                 endif

```
        ---->   if C1 then P1 endif
                if C2 and not C1 then P2 endif
                if C3 and not (C1 or C2) then P3 endif
                  .
                  .
                  .
                if Ck and not (C1 or C2 or ... Ck-1)
                  then Pk else P0
                endif
if C1 then P1 else P2 endif    ---->
                if not C1 then goto ELSE endif
                P1; goto OUT
                ELSE: P2
                OUT: .....
```

The general principle of simulating escapes is to use forward gotos that cause execution to continue from the point immediately following the process structure from which the escape is being effected. For example:

```
X: <start of some structure>   ---->    X: .....
  .....                                    .....
  leave X                                  goto OUT
  .....                                    .....
  end {of structureX}                      end
                                         OUT: .....
```

In the case of a subprogram, the jump would be effected to the end of the subprogram body.

Loops present no particular problems if they need to be 'refined down'. For example, the reverse of the transformation (described above) of a JSP/JSD-type iteration into a determinate loop indicates how a determinate loop in the design would be encoded as a while-loop in the implementation. Furthermore:

```
do P until C enddo    ---->  P
                             while not C do
                               P
                             enddo
while C do P enddo   ---->   LOOP:
                             if not C then goto OUT endif
                               P
                             goto LOOP
                             OUT: .....
```

In addition, by shifting the position of the conditional exit in the last template amongst P, one can encode any variation of the 'n+1/2 times' loop theme; there may be a construct in the target language specifically for expressing such loops.

The above are just basic schemas, but they can be utilized and adapted to cope with virtually any other variation and combination of selections, iterations and escapes that are encountered in practice. Furthermore, the templates involving gotos are those that can be used to transform structured designs into disciplined coding in assembly languages.

6.5 MODULES AND DATA ABSTRACTIONS

A programming language must possess something directly akin to the module structure illustrated in Sections 4.3 and 4.7 in order that it properly supports general bottom-up development, base-level enrichment, data abstraction and so on. Such a structure is not particularly prevalent amongst widely used programming languages, though examples include the 'classes' of Simula (Birtwistle *et al*. 1974), the 'modules' of Modula-2 (Wirth 1983), and the 'packages' of Ada (for an alternative to the Reference Manual, consult a text such as Barnes 1984). Shaw (1984) gives a more complete list, as well as a historical backdrop to the evolution and current state-of-the art of abstraction mechanisms in programming languages. Smalltalk-80 [TM] (Goldberg & Robson 1983) is the only language – more accurately, the only programming environment – purpose-built to support the object-oriented paradigm outlined in Section 4.2. However, hybrids of a few well-known languages exist, such as Objective-C (Cox 1986), that attempt to offer the best of both the 'object' and 'conventional' worlds. Cook (1986) assesses the suitability of the languages Simula, Ada and Clu for object-oriented programming. As he notes, data abstraction and encapsulation do not by themselves constitute support for the object-oriented paradigm (message sending, run-time binding, inheritance, uniformity of abstraction whether control or data), in respect of which all three languages are lacking.

Although Ada has attracted strong criticism from some quarters because of its large size, complexity, etc., it is likely to play a major role in large-scale (particularly real-time) software engineering projects of the future, and so we shall use Ada for illustrative purposes here. (For a vigorous defence of Ada, read Sammet 1986.) The structure of an Ada package is best understood by way of example. The following is a possible Ada declaration, including implementation of all exports, of the module QUEUE_SEQUENCE specified in Section 4.7:

```
package QUEUE_SEQUENCE is
   type QUEUE (MAXQLEN : NATURAL) is limited private;
   procedure ADDQ(Q : in out QUEUE; VAL : in QELEM);
   procedure REMQ(Q : in out QUEUE; VAL : out QELEM);
   function ISEMPTYQ(Q : in QUEUE) returns BOOLEAN;
private
   type QUEUE(MAXQLEN : NATURAL) is
   record
     FRONT : NATURAL := 0;
     REAR : NATURAL := 0;
     LENGTH : NATURAL := 0;
     QSPACE : array (NATURAL range 0..MAXQLEN−1) of QELEM;
   end record
end QUEUE_SEQUENCE

package body QUEUE_SEQUENCE is
   function ISFULLQ(Q : in QUEUE) returns BOOLEAN is
   begin
     return Q.LENGTH = MAXQLEN;
   end;
   procedure ADDQ(Q : in out QUEUE; VAL : in QUEUE) is
   begin
    if not ISFULLQ(Q) then
     Q.SPACE(Q.REAR) : = VAL;
     Q.REAR : = (Q.REAR+1) mod MAXQLEN;
     Q.LENGTH := Q.LENGTH + 1;
    end if;
   end ADDQ;
   function ISEMPTYQ(Q : in QUEUE) returns BOOLEAN is
   begin
     return Q.LENGTH = 0;
   end ISEMPTYQ;
   procedure REMQ(Q : in out QUEUE; VAL : out QELEM) is
   begin
    if not ISEMPTYQ(Q) then
     VAL := Q.SPACE(Q.FRONT);
     Q.FRONT := (Q.FRONT+1) mod MAXQLEN;
     Q.LENGTH := Q.LENGTH − 1;
    end if;
   end REMQ;
 end QUEUE_SEQUENCE;
```

An important first point to note is that, not only are package specifications and bodies (implementations) textually seperate but they can also be compiled disjointly from one another; this has definite advantages, as explained in Section 6.8. However, it does mean that, in order to enable full compile-time checking to be performed on compilation units making use of a package's exports, all representations of exported data types must be included in the package's specification section (this is necessary for determination of storage requirements). Hence, the representation of type QUEUE is specified in a special *private* section of the specification. The Ada qualification *limited private* is Ada's way of denoting an abstract data type; the qualification *private* on its own would permit also the operations of assignment and test for (in)equality. If, however, a data representation is included directly in the defining occurrence of a type rather than being 'privatized', then the representation is fully visible when the type name is exported. Note the useful feature in Ada of allowing field initializations to be specified in a record representation; thus, whenever QUEUE is applied to create a QUEUE object, the stated initializations automatically occur when the object is generated.

If there is no such module abstraction mechanism in the target language, then it can be simulated, though without the security and control over visibility that would otherwise be obtainable. The basic method can be found described in Coleman (1978). Essentially, an abstract data type becomes transformed into a procedure, in whose local environment are declared all the operations on the type, together with other subprograms required for the implementation of those operations. Using Pascal, our QUEUE abstract data type would become:

```
procedure QUEUEADT(var QADT : QUEUE);
   function ISFULLQ : BOOLEAN; .....
   procedure ADDQ(VAL : QELEM); .....
   procedure REMQ(var VAL : QELEM); .....
   function ISEMPTYQ : BOOLEAN; .....
   procedure INIT;
   begin
      with QADT do
         FRONT := 0; REAR := 0; LENGTH := 0
      end
   end;
begin
   {The body – see below}
end {QUEUEADT};
```

where QUEUE would be declared as:

```
type QUEUE =
record
    FRONT, REAR, LENGTH : INTEGER;
    QSPACE : array [0. .MAXQLENMINUS1] of QELEM;
    OP : (INITIALISE, ADDON, REMOVE, EMPTYTEST);
    VAL: QELEM;
    RES : BOOLEAN
end;
```

and type QELEM and the symbolic constant MAXQLENMINUS1 would also be appropriately declared. Note how the operations on the abstract type no longer have a QUEUE parameter – they now act on the 'transport' parameter QADT.

Thus, type QUEUE comprises the representation of the actual queue type, plus an operation 'flag' field (OP), plus fields for operation arguments and results to be passed to QUEUEADT and returned (VAL and RES). A user program would first declare, say:

var Q1 : QUEUE;

and then would be obliged to perform:

```
Q1.OP := INITIALISE
QUEUEADT(Q1)
```

before performing any actual operations on Q1 (data representation initializations have to become procedurized and explicitly instigated by the program). Thereafter, any manipulation on Q1 becomes:

```
with Q1 do
    OP := <appropriate enumeration literal>;
    set up argument field(s) if needed for operation
end;
QUEUEADT(Q1)
```

This all works because the body of QUEUEADT is coded as:

```
begin
    with QADT do
    case OP of
        INITIALISE : INIT;
        ADDON : ADDQ(VAL);
        REMOVE : REMQ(VAL);
        EMPTYTEST : RES := ISEMPTYQ
    end
end {QUEUEADT};
```

The QUEUE example in fact illustrates a standard abstraction-to-implementation reification for sequences – representing the latter as a fixed size array with associated length, head and tail information. An alternative is to use linked data structures, which involves extra run-time overheads but avoids an imposed upper bound on sequence length. These examples – reify queue as array, or reify queue as linked list – are the data structure equivalent of finding representations of abstract process structures in the target programming language. Another common example is implementing a set abstract data type; again, arrays, linked data structures or even bit strings in this instance can be used, depending on likely maximum set size, element type, etc.

Data transformations are not restricted just to structured types. For instance, suppose the design employs an enumeration type like that for OP in the above example, and such types are not part of the target language. In this case, symbolic constants ascribed to the integers 0, 1, 2, etc. would be an appropriate representation, as in FORTRAN 77, for example:

```
INTEGER ADDON, REMOVE, ETEST
PARAMETER (INTLSE = 0, ADDON = 1, REMOVE = 2,
                                      ETEST = 3)
```

6.6 CONCURRENCY

Here, we reach beyond the relative simplicity of dealing with the internal structure of single sequential processes to the more complicated realm of concurrent processes that system network architectures in particular can contain. The techniques we are concerned with here are those that map sets of concurrent processes into executable implementations of various kinds. The techniques described are applicable in any situation where the design structures dealt with arise.

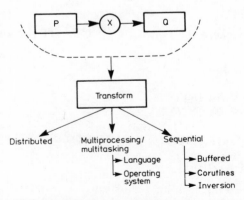

Fig. 6.2. Implementing asynchronous producer–consumer: some possibilities.

Producer-Consumer Connections

The basic structure is shown again in Fig. 6.2. Recall that process P generates a sequence of messages that are consumed by process Q, with P and Q operating at their own speeds. There are a number of possible ways in which this could be implemented, as Fig. 6.2 indicates:

In a distributed environment

P can be allocated to one node and Q to another; X now becomes a message stream transmitted by the network between P and Q. The implementation would thus be in the form of a mini distributed system, where P and Q run as truly parallel processes.

In a multitasking environment

P and Q can be run as separate tasks. The multitasking could be provided at the target language level, and in a variety of ways; compare, for example, the symmetric rendezvous capability of Occam[TM] (INMOS Ltd. 1984) with Ada tasks (the reader is referred back to Section 4.2). Alternatively, the processes could be encoded sequentially and run as separate tasks under a multitasking operating system; Unix[TM] 'pipes' (e.g. see Dunsmuir & Davies 1985) would be a possibility here, for example. In either case, it is the run-time system that handles all necessary mutual exclusion and synchronization, etc. between P and Q. Furthermore, on multiprocessor hardware, P and Q could again run as parallel processes.

In a uniprocessor, non-multitasking environment

It may be possible to implement P and Q as separate programs. They could then be scheduled to run sequentially, possibly on a repeated basis, with X being some suitable buffer such as a serial file. However, this implementation, even if it were feasible (it may not be – P and Q could be continuously running processes in a real-time system, say), would often be unacceptably inefficient.

To overcome these problems, it is necessary to 'multiprogram' P and Q so that they cooperate on a resume-and-suspend basis. More specifically:

When P has generated a message of X, it passes it to Q, which is resumed at the appropriate point (i.e. the point at which it was last suspended) whilst P now becomes suspended. Similarly, when Q has consumed a message of X, it resumes P to obtain a further message, whilst itself becoming suspended. Clearly, then, the resume and suspension points are associated with the original write and read operations in the processes P and Q respectively.

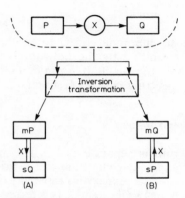

Fig. 6.3.   Simple inversion: two equivalent alternatives.

This resume-and-suspend multiprogramming can be realized directly with *coroutines* (see Grune 1977). However, coroutines are a rare facility in target languages, though both Simula and Modula–2 possess a coroutine capability. The mechanism normally has to be realized by appropriate transformations to the processes involved, in which one of the processes – it does not matter which one – becomes a conventional subprogram of the other. Diagrammatically, the two possible implementations are as in Fig. 6.3. The transformation required is called *inversion*. The changes that need to be made to the texts of P and Q are straightforward and mechanical. The precise details depend on the target language but a general prescription for either inversion case can be given. For example, for case (A):

Changes to P:
☆ alter P's text where appropriate to the correct syntax of a main program module mP;
☆ every 'write(X,message)' now becomes a conventional subprogram call with 'message' argument.
Changes to Q:
☆ code Q's text as a syntactically correct subprogram sQ with 'message' import parameter;

☆ delete the first 'read(X,message)', since the first message is transmitted to sQ via its parameter when it is first called by mP;

☆ every other ith. 'read(X,message)' is replaced by code equivalent to:

    TP := i

    return

  Li : . . . . . {next step after replaced read}

where TP is a new 'state variable', initialized to 1 before sQ is called for the first time;

☆ An initial step is inserted at the start of sQ which is equivalent to:

  case TP **of**

    1 => **goto** L1, 2 => **goto** L2, . . .

  endcase

where L1 labels what used to be the first step in Q's text. This, together with the previous modification, ensures that sQ is 'resumed' at the right point whenever it is called. If this would involve jumps into structures, which target languages normally disallow, those structures will have to be coded in 'destructured' form, e.g. using the coding templates given in Section 6.4. TP acts as a 'text pointer', i.e. an indication of the place in the text of sQ from which execution will proceed at its next resumption.

It is essential that all the local variables of sQ, which includes TP, are *own* variables so that their values are preserved from call to call of sQ. Also, the variable TP must be initialized appropriately before sQ is called for the first time. If the target language lacks an own variable facility (most widely used languages do), the variables of sQ must be declared, and TP initialized, in mP; these variables must be accessible to sQ, e.g. as non-local variables or structured into a record passed as an extra argument to sQ. There may be a few other 'housekeeping' details to take care of as well – see Jackson (1975). An inversion example is given below.

Process Multiplicities

A more complex situation, arising in JSD specifications (and JSP designs that resolve *interleaving* clashes), occurs when there exists a multiplicity of certain processes, usually to such an extent that even a distributed or multitasking environment could not possibly cope with the vast numbers of processes involved. In order to achieve a multiprogrammed implementation, the transformational technique of 'parallel' inversion is needed. The basic situation to be handled is described in Fig. 6.4. Each process Qi can be separated into two components:

★ A pure procedural component pQi, as represented by the text of Qi.

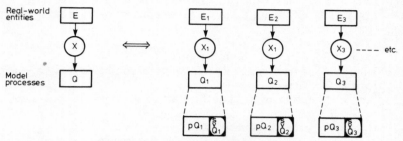

Fig. 6.4. Process multiplicity – the implementation problem.

★ A state component or 'state vector' svQi (see also Sections 3.8 and 3.9) comprising the local variable values of Qi and a 'text pointer'.

Note that the pQi are all identical, whereas each svQi varies dynamically and depends on the point which the execution of its particular Qi has reached; i.e. svQi reflects how much of its data stream the process Qi has consumed during its previous execution history. The parallel inversion transformation is as follows:

★ Invert (notionally) each Qi with respect to its data stream Xi to obtain a subprogram sQi.
★ Implement the sQi as a single re-entrant subprogram sQ (which represents all the identical pQi) by separating away the state vectors svQi.
★ Store the state vectors as components in a suitable file or database svdbQ to which a controlling process cP, or possibly sQ itself in some implementations, has single record read and write access.

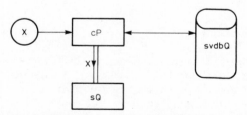

Fig. 6.5. Process multiplicity – parallel inversion implementation.

The implementation is shown diagrammatically in Fig. 6.5. Whenever cP resumes sQ, it transmits not only the next data message Xi.MES but also the appropriate state vector svQi (determinable from a field KEY of MES, say), which represents the current state of the conceptual process Qi about to be resumed. When sQ reaches a suspension point and return to cP is effected, cP writes back to the state vector database the (updated) svQi. Thus, each suspension point in cP, which is a resumption of sQ, looks like:

```
loadsv(MES.KEY,svQi)     {obtain the appropriate ith. state
                          vector}
sQ(MES,svQi)             {call − i.e. 'resume' − sQ}
storesv(MES.KEY,svQi)    {write back updated state vector}
```

cP's role is thus in effect to schedule, or interleave, the executions of the Qi processes on the single processor. An alternative implementation is to place the *loadsv* at the head of sQ itself before the multi-way goto and a *storesv* just before each suspension point in sQ, i.e. before each return instruction. The implementation of the database access primitives *loadsv* and *storesv* naturally depends on the implementation of the svdbQ database.

The following is an example of parallel inverted code. It is an implemented form of the STUDENT–2 multiple processes in the SUMS network (see Fig. 3.19 of Section 3.8) where STUDENT–2 has been inverted with respect to its SS&TS data stream. The reader should compare the inverted text, coded in Pascal, with the process text of STUDENT–2 derived in Section 3.9.

```
procedure sSTUDENT2(SSANDTSREC : SSANDTS;
                    var SVS12: STUDENTSTATEVECTOR);
   var SRREC : SR;
   label 1001, 1002, 1003, {the resume points}
         47, 48, 49,       {concerned with loop destructuring}
         555;              {end of procedure}
begin
   with SVS12 do begin
   case TPS2 of
    1: goto 1001; 2: goto 1002; 3: goto 1003
    end;
```

```
1001:
47: {STUDENT–2_BODY itr}
 TOTMCOMPS := 0; TOTMEDITS := 0;
 TOTMRUNS := 0; TOTMPTIME := 0;
 48: {cSS_BATCH itr}
  if SSANDTSREC.LOC_OR_TSM = TSRECMARK then goto 49;
  with SSANDTSREC do begin
   TOTMCOMPS := TOTMCOMPS + NCOMPS;
   TOTMEDITS := TOTMEDITS + NEDITS;
   TOTMRUNS := TOTMRUNS + NRUNS;
   TOTMPTIME := TOTMPTIME + PTIME
  end;
  TPS2 := 2; goto 555;
  1002: {cSS_BATCH end} goto 48;
 49: with SRREC do begin
     SRLOC := LOC;
     SRTOTMCOMPS := TOTMCOMPS;
     SRTOTMEDITS := TOTMEDITS;
     SRTOTMRUNS := TOTMRUNS;
     SRTOTMPTIME := TOTMPTIME
    end;
    WRITE(SRDATASTREAM,SRREC);
    TPS2 := 3; goto 555;
 1003: {STUDENT–2_BODY end} goto 47;
 555:
 end
end {sSTUDENT2};
```

We have assumed the following global declarations:

```
const TSRECMARK = ... ; {depends on type LOGONCODE}
type
LOGONCODE ... {some suitable representation} ...;
STUDENTSTATEVECTOR =
  record
    . . .
  LOC : LOGONCODE;
  TPS2 : 1..3;
  TOTMCOMPS, TOTMEDITS, TOTMRUNS, TOTMPTIME :
                                            INTEGER;
    . . .
  end;
```

```
SSANDTS =
  record
    LOC_OR_TSM : LOGONCODE;
    NCOMPS, NEDITS, NRUNS, PTIME : INTEGER
  end;
SR =
  record
    SRLOC : LOGONCODE;
    SRTOTMCOMPS, SRTOTMEDITS, SRTOTMRUNS,
                              SRTOTMPTIME : INTEGER
  end;
var SRDATASTREAM : file of SR;
```

In addition, we have assumed that a TS message is distinguished from an SS message by the LOC_OR_TSM field being set to a special value (TSRECMARK) – the values of the other four fields in this instance are immaterial.

Producer–Consumer Networks

There are of course arbitrarily many different networks that can be built from the basic data stream connection theme; the example in Fig. 6.6 is part of the SUMS system network. In general, there will be several ways in which inversion can be used to transform such a network into a multiprogrammed hierarchy implementation – see Fig. 6.7 for one

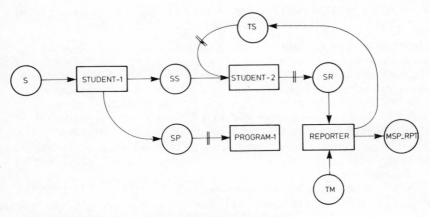

Fig. 6.6. A datastream subnetwork of the SUMS system.

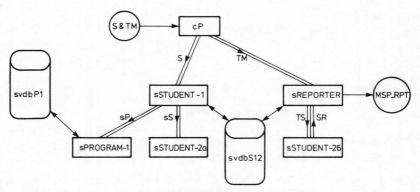

Fig. 6.7.   One possible implementation of the network in Fig. 6.6.

possible implementation of the network in Fig. 6.6. The implementation
is obtained by:

★ Having a control program cP handle all external input data streams (S
  and TM in this instance).
★ Inverting REPORTER with respect to the TM stream.
★ Inverting ('in parallel' because of the multiplicities involved in each
  case) STUDENT–1, STUDENT–2 and PROGRAM–1 processes with
  respect to their input data streams.
★ 'Dismembering' sSTUDENT–2 into two separate modules: one which
  is based on the portion of STUDENT–2 that deals with SS messages,
  and the other which is based on the portion of STUDENT–2 that deals
  with TS messages.
★ Inverting the TS-handling component of STUDENT–2 with respect to
  both the input TS data stream and output SR data stream.

Dismemberment is another form of transformation. The type of dismemberment involved here is equivalent to taking identical copies of
the complete inverted module and then deleting those parts that do not
apply in each case. In effect, the dismemberment is a consequence of
treating the rough merge of SS and TS as separate data streams.
The 'double inversion' giving sSTUDENT–2b as a subprogram of
sREPORTER happens to be very simple in this case – the arrival of a
TS message simply acts as signal to STUDENT–2 to write an SR
message back to REPORTER, which,, in the inverted form, is achieved
by parameter export.

Note that we have chosen to combine the state vectors of STUDENT–1
and STUDENT–2 processes and store them in a single database
svdbS12. sSTUDENT–1 and sPROGRAM–1 load and store their own

state vectors. Whenever sSTUDENT–1 or sREPORTER resumes its
dismembered module, it passes to the latter as a parameter the
STUDENT state vector that it has loaded from the svdbS12 database.

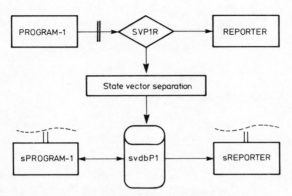

Fig. 6.8. Multiple asynchronous writer–reader implementation.

Writer–Reader Connections

The standard situation is shown in Fig. 6.8 (also taken from the SUMS
network). If there is a multiplicity of inspected processes as in the
example, then there will be a state vector database separated from a re-
entrant subprogram obtained by a parallel inversion transformation. If
sPROGRAM–1 and sREPORTER are implemented concurrently in a
distributed or multi-tasking environment, mutual exclusion must somehow be ensured between the critical sections of the two modules that
access svdbP1.

Module Hierarchies

The discussion has so far concentrated on transformations applied
to networks, but transformations are also applicable to process hierarchies. Consider the standard hierarchical structure and a typical
communication pattern that arises in Structured Design, as shown in Fig.
6.9. The top layer of the hierarchy can be 'flattened out' into a standard
producer-consumer connection. In other words, a distributed or multitasking implementation is possible (or, say, three sequential programs),
with the iterative control of process C being expressed locally within
each of P, T and Q. Note that inversion techniques would be of little use

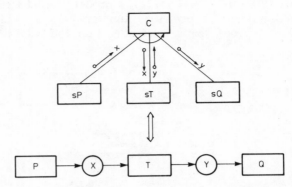

Fig. 6.9. Equivalence between an SD module structure and producer–consumer connectivity.

here – the effect would be to generate an implementation behaviourally very similar to the SD hierarchy. Nevertheless, the example illustrates how distributed or multitasking implementations are derivable from SD-type hierarchies as well as from networks.

6.7 SYSTEM IMPLEMENTATION

Overall, the problem of system implementation is to map an abstract system design on to a set of actual resource constraints, both hardware and software, in order to realize an executable product of acceptable performance. There are a variety of tools open to exploitation for implementation purposes – not just conventional programming and job-control languages, but also database management systems with query and update languages, transaction processing (TP) software, 4GL systems with associated tools, and so on. It is the responsibility of the developers to exercise their skill and judgement in deciding how to utilize available tools to best advantage, or whether to purchase or develop new tools, in order to achieve a given implementation. There are two major issues that must be addressed:

★ How to distribute system processes amongst the available processor resources; in particular, how to schedule several processes allocated to a single processor.
★ How to store system data in files and databases in order to realize all access pathways required to that data by system processes.

The decision-making involved is steered by the performance criteria with respect to storage and timeliness constraints expressed in the requirements.

Process Distribution and Scheduling

There may be a number of viable alternatives for process distribution, depending on how many processors (real and virtual) are actually available. If we use the network specification for the SUMS system (Fig. 3.19 in Section 3.8), then the following processes have to be allocated processors:

⋆ A multiplicity of STUDENT–1 model processes (with an embedded function).
⋆ A corresponding multiplicity of STUDENT–2 processes.
⋆ A multiplicity of PROGRAM–1 model processes.
⋆ The enquiry function ENLISTER, interactive function FLUSH and periodic information function REPORTER.

Suppose a multitasking environment is available. Part of the SUMS system could then be implemented by, say, running the STUDENT–1, STUDENT–2 and PROGRAM–1 processes as one task concurrently with another that handles the ENLISTER function. If, alternatively, a local area network of microcomputers of sufficient capacity were available, we would, say, partition the STUDENT–1, STUDENT–2 and PROGRAM–1 processes according to university faculty (let us suppose there are four in all), allocating each subset to a separate processor; other processors could be used to deal with the three functions. The result would then be a distributed implementation. In our actual example, it is required to implement the whole SUMS system on a single processor with neither multitasking operating system nor language system capable of expressing concurrency.

Scheduling becomes a consideration when more than one process is allocated to a given processor. A way has to be found of sharing process executions on the processor in order that system timeliness requirements are met. There are a number of scheduling techniques possible, which have already been covered by our discussions in the previous section:

⋆ Where acceptable, processes can be scheduled sequentially as programs or subprograms, communicating via intermediate files, database updates, program data structures, etc.
⋆ Multitasking, whether available via language or via operating system, allows all scheduling decisions to be left to the run-time environment.
⋆ Multiprogramming can be achieved either by coroutines, where the explicit suspend/resume mechanism is handled by the run-time environment, or by the inversion transformations, which create explicit suspend/resume scheduling via conventional subprogram call-and-return.

Of course, the total system scheduling can be realized by any mixture of the above, allowing the whole range of systems to be implemented – those that are purely 'detached' (batch, etc.), those that are part detached and part online, or those that are purely online or real time. Furthermore, part or all of the scheduling may be:

directly realizable by existing software; for example, transaction processing software may be available to schedule the online component of a system;
embodied in a (sub)program;
expressed in JCL;
carried out manually by an operator according to specified instructions;
achieved by any combination of these.

To illustrate, consider the implementation of our SUMS system on the Nirvana/STOPS machine. As regards timing constraints, we have:

★ MSP_RPT is to be produced once a month after 21.00 in the evening of the last working day of the month.
★ FLUSH is to be run any time when a member of staff wants the machine's filestore to be cleaned out.
★ The model part of the system (STUDENT–1, STUDENT–2 and PROGRAM–1), together with ENLISTER, is to be run online with the PATSY system.

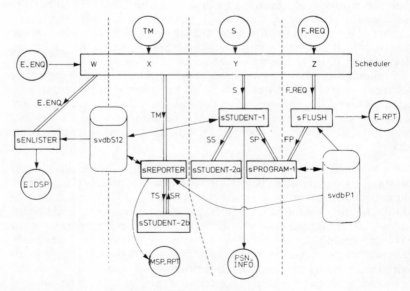

Fig. 6.10. One possible implementation of the SUMS system.

Conceptualizing the scheduling required as a single controlling process, and exploiting the transformation examples given in the last section, the implementation might be realized as given in Fig. 6.10. The following should be noted:

(a) Component W of the system deals with the ENLISTER function. Thus, this segment of the scheduler will be realized by instructions in the part of the PATSY system that has been modified to accept E_ENQ messages from a privileged user and call ENLISTER as a subroutine.

(b) Component X is the batch part of the system run once a month. The X portion of the scheduler in effect corresponds to an instruction carried out by someone to initiate sREPORTER on receipt of a TM message. Of course, the TM messages will be entirely notional – sREPORTER simply acts as the batch program that is initiated manually at the required monthly intervals.

(c) Component Y is the other online part of the system. This segment of the scheduler will be realized by subroutine calls of sSTUDENT–1 within the modified parts of PATSY that handle S messages.

(d) Component Z is a separate batch component run whenever desired. The scheduling is as for (b) – sFLUSH acts as the main batch program initiated manually by some member of staff (the scheduler segment Z) on receipt of the notional F_REQ message.

Storage of System Data

The basic issue here is: how should system data be stored, given the size and structural constraints imposed by the target environment, so that all access pathways to that data required by system processes are realized and performance criteria are satisfied? Solving this problem can involve considerable effort, since the system data, and access pathways needed to it, can be extremely complex in large systems. In our example, we have two databases – svdbS12 and svdbP1 – to realize along with several access pathways:

(a) The subprogram sENLISTER requires rapid read access to the svdbS12 database in a non-ordered manner but selective on the 'entered _PATSY' (= true) component of the state vectors.

(b) Access to the svdbS12 database needs to be rapid single record direct read-write access for the online sSTUDENT–1 subprogram. However, the efficiency of the same access pathway required by sREPORTER, being a batch program, is not so critical.

(c) Access to the database svdbP1 should be a rapid single record direct read-write access for the online copy of sPROGRAM–1, but the efficiency of the grouped, ordered, selective read access required by sFLUSH, being a batch program, is therefore a less important consideration. This latter point applies also to the grouped, ordered access pathway needed by sREPORTER to svdbP1.

System data implementation is a question of weighing up all such access requirements and coming to a satisfactory performance compromise. The tools and techniques available include:

★ Use of serial, sequential, index-sequential and direct-access files, with access primitives provided by the target language; any mixture of these may suffice without resort to databases.
★ Use of general-purpose database software, with access primitives supplied by the associated update and query language.
★ Special-purpose database design carried out as part of the implementation process in preference to utilizing existing database tools, which for some reason may be inappropriate in satisfying certain requirements.
★ Implementation of a simplified data design, realizing any access pathways that it does not directly satisfy by introducing extra processes into the implementation, e.g. an efficient sort routine to transform information as quickly as possible into the desired order.

Obviously, a given system data implementation might employ any mixture of appropriate methods to achieve a satisfactory operational product. Note that, although we are discussing the system data issue for convenience in the context of implementation, the exact distribution of the system data specification $->$ design $->$ implementation transformations over the development cycle is dependent on development method. To recap for comparison purposes:

★ In an 'information systems' approach wedded to data analysis techniques, conceptual and logical schema specification of data sit at the front end of development. Only thereafter are the functions specified, designed and implemented that realize user applications.
★ In an SSADM-based approach, logical specification of both system functions and system data stores and data structures occur together.
★ A process-oriented operational approach like JSD utilizes only simple abstract data objects in the pre-implementation phase. Thus, all file and database realization resides in the post-specification phase.
★ A formal approach like VDM regards choice of data abstraction as the first key decision in system development. The mapping of data abstractions on to target file and database structures will occur in later reification steps.

6.8   COMPILATION AND LIBRARIES

Compilers represent a subset of a variety of language translation tools that prove invaluable aids to the implementation process. Apart from compilers, there are:

★ Preprocessors to translate language extensions used in programs down into standard language constructs acceptable to a main compiler.
★ Macroprocessors, which are text substitution/expansion tools that can prove a useful adjunct to a main compiler system.
★ Code generators that produce machine code from intermediate code generated by a compiler.
★ Translators from an abstract design language (e.g. the structure text of JSP/JSD), a 4GL or a functional language, say, to some conventional high-level language.
★ Convertors between high-level languages, so that software written in one language can be easily sourced in another.

However, although compilers enable software expressed in high-level languages to be subsequently transformed to executable form, simple source-to-object code compilation on its own is insufficient to meet the needs of software engineering. What is also required is the ability to compile development units disjointly and to be able to store them in a library for future usage – either in a later integration phase of development, or for subsequent reuse in other applications. Without disjoint compilation in conjunction with a suitable library capability, recompilation costs would be enormous (since compilation units would often unavoidably be large 'monolithic' entities), the benefits accrued from applying a systematic development method (where component-wise construction and modularity are exploited) would largely be lost, and the concept of reusable software would be unrealizable in practice.

The simplest form of disjoint compilation is exemplified by FORTRAN systems. Here, a subprogram is compiled completely independently of other subprograms and can be entered in compiled form into a library if desired. However, there is a drawback in that full compile-time checking of subprogram references is not possible. Thus, if a subprogram being compiled contains a call to another – P, say – then it is not possible for the compiler to check that the supplied number and types of argument are consistent with P's (interface) specification as given in its declaration. Because compilation of modules is truly independent, the information required to carry out such checking is not available to the compiler.

There is a further difficulty that arises with hierarchical languages implemented with an associated conventional library system – compilation units must not contain references to globally defined variables.

Whilst such modularity is prerequisite for reusable software, it imposes restrictions on the kinds of development unit that can be stored in a library for integration into larger entities at some later point in time.

The separate compilation system of the kind associated with an Ada environment (DoD 1983) overcomes all these problems. Basically, two kinds of compilation unit can be placed in an Ada library:

Library units: These are compilation units that are self-contained, independent modules (subprograms or packages – possibly generic) that can act as reusable components or building blocks for other software.

Subunits: These are compilation units that belong to some specific enclosing lexical environment and can include Ada tasks as well as other module types.

A compilation in Ada can be made up of any number of compilation units. An important feature is that a compilation unit need comprise only the specification of an intended library unit if desired – the implementation (body) of the unit can be compiled and added to the library at a later date. This means that the implementation of a library unit, such as the body of a package, can be changed repeatedly without affecting any software that uses the unit, since using software is dependent only on the latter's specification; thus, there can be no 'ripple' effects if the library unit's implementation is modified.

Library units are incorporated into software by 'context specifications'; for example:

with X, Y;
use Y;
.
.

– – text of compilation unit
.

.

The **with** clause specifies which library units are being used, and enables the compiler to check use of those units in the compilation unit against their specifications in the library. The **use** clause is optional for packages, enabling package exports to be referenced directly by name in the program unit concerned, otherwise the syntax <name of package>. <name of export> would have to be used for every applied occurrence of an export. Naturally, the compilation unit could itself be destined for insertion in the library, and it is thus that library units provide the basic separate compilation support needed for general bottom-up software development.

Subunits, on the other hand, provide support for top-down development. Ada enables the compilation of units that contain *stubs* in their outermost declarative level. A stub takes the place of the full declaration of a subunit (subprogram, etc.) that is to be compiled separately from the enclosing unit at some later time. A stub provides the specification of a subunit without giving its body; for example:

```
procedure P . . . . . is
   procedure Q . . . . . is separate;  − − stub for subunit Q
   package X is
      − − the specification of X
   end X;
   package body X is separate;  − − stub for subunit X
− − etc.
end P;
```

The subunits would be supplied in subsequent separate compilations; for example:

```
separate (P);
procedure Q . . . . . is
   − − body of Q
end Q;
```

The **separate** clause specifies the enclosing lexical environment of the subunit – here, procedure P – which must of course already exist in the library. The compiler is now able to check the validity of any non-local names referenced within Q that (presumably) have been imported from its enclosing lexical environment. Note that: (i) subunit compilation can be taken down to any level, and (ii) subunits themselves can also make use of library units. So for example:

```
with A;
separate (P);
package body X is
   procedure R . . . . . is separate;
   − − rest of package body
end X;
```

When subsequently submitting subunit R for compilation, its **separate** heading would be:

```
separate (P.X);
```

In other words, the complete enclosing lexical environment hierarchy of a subunit must be specified. This allows non-local name referencing in subunits to be applied over as many levels as desired.

It should be apparent that an Ada library is far from being a simple sequential program library. Instead, it is a complex database of compilation units possessing a possibly intricate set of hierarchical dependencies. In practice, an Ada library system would preferably be augmented by additional tools and facilities, e.g. a library status and accounting subsystem, and a change-control subsystem, allowing control over revision and version creation of library components (see Section 8.4).

6.9 PORTABILITY

In transforming a design into implemented form, a number of characteristics may be acquired by the latter that relate to one specific operational environment, or one particular kind of environment as characterized by some operating system and target language, say. The *portability* of a product is related to its degree of environment independence, though this is purely relative. For example, a program meticulously written in standard PDL–86 is portable only to the extent that it can be run without modification in precisely those environments possessing a standard PDL–86 compiler – in all other environments, it is to varying degrees non-portable. However, if environments possessing standard PDL–86 compilers are widespread, then the portability of the product is greatly enhanced by writing it in that language; and if they are not widespread, the converse argument applies. Thus, the relative portability of a software product can be interpreted as the extent to which the totality of its implementation features are supported over a specified population of operational environments. If pEi (expressed between 0 and 1, say) is the portability of a product with respect to environment Ei of a population of N, then:

$$p = \sum pEi \,/\, N$$

represents the product's portability P relative to that population.

Portability may not be an important consideration, e.g. for bespoke software to be run only at one installation. However, for reusable software, it is clearly important to aim for high portability and for ease of modification to those dependencies that are unavoidable. The following is an enumeration of the main layers in an operational environment where dependencies can exist:

Operational	$--$> hardware
environment	$--$> operating system
	$--$> source language
	$--$> user

The more dependencies that exist in a product with respect to these layers, the more effort will be involved in porting the product between different environments. Some of the problems that can be encountered, and their solutions, are as follows:

Hardware Problems

These arise because different machines employ different conventions for the internal representation of data, as well as possessing unique processor instruction sets. The situation can be alleviated partly by manufacturers adhering to an established standard, e.g. ASCII for character sets. However, the basic remedy is to abstract software away from real machine architectures as much as possible by using high-level languages, although, depending on the application, even a high-level language may not be able to offer a completely effective shield. Nevertheless, a well-designed language can provide some measure of protection against machine dependencies in the following ways:

★ By 'parameterization' of dependencies wherever possible via pre-defined symbolic constants, e.g. *maxint* (maximum positive integer), *smallreal* (the smallest absolute real value that when added to, or subtracted from, 1.0 yields a result different from 1.0), etc. Floating-point arithmetic can be especially problematic in terms of accuracy and round-off error. Ada deals with this problem via the notions of 'model values', 'safe values', the DIGITS and MANTISSA attributes of real (sub)types and so forth (DoD 1983).
★ The language can provide built-in data type and operational primitives for bit-string representation and manipulation, address access and modification, as with C (Kerninghan & Ritchie 1978), for example.

Sometimes, hardware dependencies can be overcome by constructing the software so that it can be configured to particular hardware characteristics. Thus, a word processor might have built-in options to allow it to work with a variety of common terminal interface protocols – the user merely informs the software of the type of terminal being used. In addition, if the particular protocol in question is not directly catered for, the software may nevertheless provide means by which the user can supply the necessary configuration data in some suitable form.

Operating System

Different operating systems possess different JCLs for applying and scheduling user and operating system processes. The best solution to such portability problems is to construct software for a standard operating system that is available on a wide variety of machines. A good example here is Unix, which is available on a number of different makes of machine, from microcomputers to mainframes.

From within a program, operating system dependencies are most likely to concern file handling. Again, a well designed high-level language can substantially overcome this problem by providing a comprehensive, predefined I/O interface. For example, the program library of any Ada system will contain the standard packages TEXT_IO, SEQUENTIAL_IO and DIRECT_IO; Ada, of course, defines their specifications only, which must then be rigorously implemented in each different environment.

Source Language

A major reason for using a high-level language is to impart to a product a high degree of portability that it would otherwise not possess. Nevertheless, portability problems still persist with high-level languages – problems that are quite apart from those resulting from a language's inability totally to shield dependencies in lower layers. The reason is due to language 'dialects', i.e. language implementations containing specific features not shared across other implementations. The main culprits for this are lack of a standard definition of the language, or local extensions and modifications that are incorporated into the language according to the implementor's whims and fancies. Ways to ameliorate the dialect problem include the following:

★ Language design authorities should specify and enforce standards.
★ Implementors should exercise discipline in adhering to specified, or de facto, standards.
★ Where local modifications to a language are made, they should be downwards or upwards compatible with respect to the specified or de facto standard, i.e. so that dialects are strict subsets or supersets. In the case of a superset language, a preprocessor should exist to translate extensions into standard constructs.
★ Developers should avoid using non-standard features in source code as much as possible. This guideline also applies to those language features that are associated with dependencies in lower layers. However, where such features cannot be avoided, they should, as far as is possible, be encapsulated in appropriate modules so that subsequent modification is easily effected.
★ Compilers themselves should be made as portable as possible. To achieve this, a compiler should be written in some widely available high-level language and translate programs down into some intermediate object code. Each target environment now needs only a

specific interpreter or machine code generator to be developed (provided, of course, that it already possesses an implementation for the language used to source the compiler).

In the past, languages like FORTRAN have suffered considerably from 'dialectitis'. In contrast, the United States Department of Defense is rigorously enforcing one single Ada standard. This enforcement is essential to Ada achieving one of its major aims of being a main vehicle for establishing a quality-engineered, standard software components industry. However, care needs to be exercised even with a rigorously standardized language. Nissen & Wallis (1984) put forward a number of guidelines and recommendations for building maximum portability into Ada programs.

Users

Users at different installations may require essentially the same system with (possibly very) minor differences in their requirements. With product software, the solution is to make the product general enough without it being too complex and unwieldy, yet building in enough flexibility to allow users to tailor its facilities to suit their specific needs. Two main areas are involved here:

⋆ User interface, i.e. presentation of data between users and system: there should be means by which users can define their own input data formats, screen images, and so on, possibly overriding default displays.
⋆ Functionality: any product should be rich enough in its basic functionality to cater potentially for all conceivable user requirements. Ideally, this functionality should be extensible so that, via macros, command sequences and such like, the user can build new, more usable functions.

Almost by definition, portability considerations apply only to general product, as opposed to bespoke, software. Yet, analagously, an unexpected change in hardware or operating system should not wreak havoc on bespoke software in terms of the redevelopment subsequently needed. This requires a sufficiently clean separation between design and implementation, so that at least the former is maximally 'portable' across varying machine environments.

For an excellent, up-to-date comprehensive coverage of the topic of portability, the reader is referred to Lecarme & Gart (1986). A wealth of useful material on portability can also be found in Wallis (1982) and Brown (1978).

Chapter 7

Reliability and Quality Control

7.1 OVERVIEW

The purpose of this chapter is to discuss software reliability and techniques for validating and verifying the various deliverables, or work products, that software development generates. Reliability is clearly related to 'correctness', and correctness is the main concern of verification procedures that are carried out during a product's development. In fact, validation and verification (V&V) pervades the whole software life cycle because any work product generated by the cycle can be subjected to some form of validation, verification, or both.

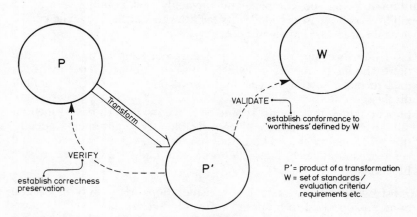

Fig. 7.1. Validation and verification: the difference.

There is no universally agreed definition of the terms 'validation' and 'verification' as they apply to software engineering, and they are often used loosely and interchangeably. One commonly accepted distinction is that validation is any activity that attempts to evaluate the worth, or fitness for intended purpose, of some artefact, whereas verification seeks to establish an artefact's correctness. The relationship between the two activities is expressed in general terms in Fig. 7.1. Note that neither 'worth' nor 'correctness' are meaningful qualities in an absolute sense. In the first case, a predefined set of requirements, standards or evaluation criteria is needed against which the worth of an artefact can be judged. In the second case, a definition or specification is needed, the extent of an artefact's conformance to which is to be established; thus, more generally, verification is an activity applied to the product of a transformation. Here are some specific V&V examples:

★ Requirements can be validated: (e.g.) is this what is really wanted from the system? A requirements specification can be verified: (i) does it capture stated user requirements precisely, i.e. without ambiguity, elaboration, deviation or omission? (ii) is it free of technical defects (in the syntax and semantics of the specification notations and language)?
★ A design can be validated: is this a sound design, or are there better alternatives (e.g. according to certain modularity criteria)? A design can also be verified by establishing whether the 'howness' it embodies correctly realizes the intended effect expressed in the requirements specification.
★ An implementation can be validated: does performance, usability, reliability and security meet user acceptance and specifications? Or it can be verified: is this product a correct realization of the design (or possibly specification)?

In the first example, correctness relates very much to stated human needs and objectives – an area rather fraught with difficulties when it comes to understanding, communicating and specifying what is required, and then determining whether what has been specified is a precise statement of what is deemed to have been communicated! In the second case, the situation is considerably different – there is now a formalized product whose correctness can, as a consequence, be argued against a precise, possibly formal, specification. The difference between this and the third case is that, in the latter, we are dealing with the observed behaviour of an operational product that is subject to the vagaries of hardware configurations, operating systems, compilers and so on. Thus, whilst the correctness of a program can in a formal sense be related back to a design and hence ultimately to a specification, in a concrete sense its correctness has to be judged with respect to the target environments in which it is operational.

There are a variety of V&V techniques that can be applied over the life cycle. These are described by Adrion *et al.* (1982). Boehm (1984a) discusses V&V techniques as applied to requirements and design specifications, and Deutsch (1981) concentrates mainly on testing and automated test tools. Another useful general reference is Hausen (1984). We shall broadly split up V&V into techniques that involve purely human effort, and those that involve the use of a computer. The latter are usually referred to collectively as 'testing', and some authors make a distinction between V&V and testing, retaining the former terminology specifically for those techniques that do not involve machine usage. Generally, we shall also follow this distinction.

Human-Oriented Techniques

There is a whole range of techniques that involves the scrutiny – or 'review' – of a work product by one or more individuals. These techniques can vary from the highly informal, as when one or more programmers perform a 'dry-run' on a section of code, to the completely formal, where there is a management function associated with the review and a fixed procedure and set of rules for carrying it out. For most V&V checkpoints in the life cycle, group activity rather than individual effort will be more appropriate and effective – there is a greater chance of a group of cooperative people detecting errors than one person working on his or her own. Group V&V activity is discussed in Section 7.3.

Techniques for formally verifying a design or implementation against a specification have already been covered in an earlier chapter; we merely reiterate their existence here for completeness. Note that correctness proofs themselves can be subjected to verification.

Machine-Oriented Techniques

We present a brief resumé here of techniques that have already been covered in earlier chapters:

★ Some requirements engineering methods facilitate requirements verification (of specification syntax and semantic consistency) via specialized software tools; see Section 2.3.
★ Executable specifications provide an automated means of requirements specification V&V; see Section 2.4.
★ Automated verifier tools for designs and implementations exist, though they are currently rather limited in scope; see Section 5.4.
★ The lexical and syntactic correctness of implementations is fully verified by language processor tools of various kinds (compilers, etc.).

However, of all the uses to which the computer is put in this context, it is the verification of operational correctness and validation of satisfactory operational capability that consumes most machine time. Testing will be discussed in detail in Section 7.4.

Product Quality Control and Product Assurance

V&V and testing form the basis of what can be regarded as product 'quality control'. *Quality control* (QC) collectively describes all life-cycle activities that attempt to detect defects at various stages of a product's formulation, development and maintenance. QC is strongly associated with other activities that, taken together, represent 'product assurance' – the overall life-cycle discipline that seeks to assure the customer of an acceptable, high-quality product that achieves conformance with requirements. In Chapter 8, we shall complete the picture by looking at product assurance from a project management viewpoint, specifically Configuration Management and Quality Assurance.

7.2 RELIABILITY

General Issues

Reliability is a quality measure that relates to the operational correctness of software. We can define a product to be operationally correct if its observed behaviour is always consistent with its requirements specification when it is executed within its stipulated target environmental characteristics and constraints. However, whilst it could be argued that 100% operational correctness must necessarily imply 100% reliability, a 'completely correct' system may not be an entirely meaningful or useful notion – for example, a system's real-world environment may not be sufficiently understood or stable. From a user viewpoint, reliability is not just related to how infrequently a piece of software 'falls down', but is also a measure of the product's continuing relevance and usefulness in the possibly ever-changing real world subdomain in which it is embedded. The reality is that users necessarily have to adopt a pragmatic attitude. A product that operates with perfect reliability, but at best only partially meets user requirements, can be worse than no product at all. On the other hand, users learn to tolerate relatively infrequent system failures if the services they get when the system is working are what they want. For example, it is better to have an operating system that provides good-quality service most of the time and only occasionally 'crashes', than to have no operating system at all.

Reliability, or lack of it, results from errors giving rise to failures. More specifically, a *failure* is any observable aspect of software operational behaviour that represents a departure from the requirements specification. A failure is by definition observable since, otherwise, software with 'non-observable failures' would always seemingly comply with its requirements specification and therefore be deemed to be perfectly reliable. Failures are caused by *errors* in operational software that result from *defects* in requirements, specification, design or coding, howsoever generated. Failures are also caused by hardware errors, i.e. *faults*, or human errors, i.e. *mistakes* (the emphasized terminology mostly follows that of Kopetz 1979). However, we shall be concerned only with software errors in this discussion.

Clearly, the greater the degree of failure-free behaviour exhibited by a system over its operational life, the more reliable it is. Therefore, a possible definition of reliability that also acts as a basis for reliability measurement is:

The reliability of a software system is the probability that it exhibits failure-free behaviour over a specified timespan within a specified operational environment.

Implicit in this definition are the assumptions that the hardware is fault-free, no mistakes are perpetrated and all inputs are 'tolerable' (see below). Obviously, if a system were run outside its operational limits, we would not be surprised, and could not complain too much, at a sudden increase in failure rate. It is an empirical observation, however, that probability of system failure tends to increase as operational limits (of storage occupancy, etc.) are approached, even though not exceeded. A typical example would be an operating system experiencing increasing load as more and more users log on demanding their share of machine resources.

When failure does occur, it is the symptoms or effects of the causing error that are observed, not the error itself. Since we wish the notion of failure to encompass any deviation from operational correctness, as well as the commonly understood sense of sudden and unspecified inoperability, observable failure modes include the following:

★ The software 'crashes', i.e. execution unexpectedly terminates in some indeterminate state outside specification.
★ Incorrect output is (eventually) generated.
★ Performance requirements are not satisfied, e.g. response times become slower than specified.
★ Operational behaviour becomes indeterminate, i.e. the software continues to execute but its observed behaviour is invalid in a 'pathological' sense (e.g. data in files might from time to time become corrupted).
★ The software exhibits non-pathological deviant functionality, e.g. it fails to provide a service expressed in, or provides a service not included in, the requirements.

Obviously, the exact nature of the failure observed is crucial information in aiding subsequent determination and rectification of the error(s) causing the failure (see Section 7.5).

One possible estimate of system reliability is in terms of MTBF (Mean Time Between Failure). This can be defined to be:

MTBF = MTTF + MTTR

where MTTF is 'Mean Time To Failure' and MTTR is 'Mean Time To Repair'. Such metrics are typically used to measure hardware reliability. Whilst the point is sometimes made that hardware suffers age degradation whereas software does not, this is only partially true. It is possible for software quality to degrade during its operational lifetime due to its suffering poor quality maintenance; this in turn is likely to increase the number of errors and hence decrease MTBF. (The apposite cynicism here is that 'hardware degrades despite maintenance, and software degrades because of it'.)

An operational characteristic closely allied to reliability is 'availability'. Whereas reliability has to do with failure frequency, availability is a measure of the likelihood of a system being in operation over a given period of time. Thus:

The availability of a system is the probability that the system is operating consistently with respect to its specification (again, within specified operational limits, etc.) over a given time interval.

One possible estimate of 'steady state' availability *Ass* is:

Ass = Tup/(Tup+Tdown)

where *Tup* and *Tdown* are respectively the total up-time and down-time of a system as measured over the given interval. Similarly, observational measurements of MTTF and MTTR can be made over a given period to estimate reliability. However, such measurements depend to a certain extent on the environmental conditions in existence, and the inputs handled, during the measurement period (a problem that predictive mathematical models of reliability attempt to overcome, e.g. see Shooman 1983). Thus, a bad (good) instance of a reliability measure may simply be due to the fact that, at the time, the environmental conditions and inputs just happened to be those that, for the most part, (do not) cause 'trouble'.

'Time between failure' metrics and 'number of failures in a specified time interval' metrics represent just two possible classes of reliability model. Two other types of model are: (i) the 'fault seeding' variety, where operational behaviour is observed before and after known errors have been introduced into the software; and (ii) models where reliability measurement is based on testing with samples from 'equivalence classes' of a software unit's input domain (see Section 7.4). This four-way categorization is given by Goel (1985), who provides a review and evaluation of software reliability models, including their assumptions and limitations. A comprehensive discussion of software reliability models can also be found in Dunn & Ullman (1982). The reader should also note that IEEE (1985) and IEEE (1986) are devoted to reliability in all its aspects.

Reliability implies 'robustness' – that is, the software does not immediately 'fall down' when an exceptional condition or event occurs. Obviously, robustness is a desirable feature of all software, although its importance increases considerably with real-time embedded and process control systems. As indicated in Section 1.6, systems of this kind interact with, control and monitor external environments in which, often, the safety of human life is ultimately at stake. Obviously, if any exceptional condition caused such a system to malfunction, thus leaving the external environment in an uncontrolled or unmonitored state, the result could be catastrophic. Fault tolerance is therefore a crucial characteristic of real-time software in particular and implies that, when an exception does occur, it is detected, reported upon if necessary, and the system either:

recovers from the exception and is able to carry on in a meaningful way; or

'dies gracefully' without subsequent harmful effects, if recovery is not possible.

Note that robustness of distributed systems is a double-edged consideration. In principle, reliability and availability are greater – the system can continue operating if a component goes faulty, possibly by software reconfiguration or having the faulty component replaced. However, there are more failure modes: communications links may drop, messages may become corrupted by, or get lost in, the network, and processing nodes may unpredictably go out of service for unknown amounts of time.

There are various ways of building robustness into software, and much depends on the type of error or exception involved and the facilities for exception handling offered by the target language.

Data Verification†

The largest slice of straightforward error handling lies in verifying imported data, i.e. ensuring that the data is consistent with an input specification (and, if not, taking appropriate action). Following Jackson (1975), a useful taxonomy is:

† It is perhaps more usual to speak of data *validation*, but we are being consistent with our earlier terminology.

★ *Tolerable data*: data that lies within a software unit's total input specification and hence will not of itself cause failure. This can be partitioned into:

> *intended data*: data that sources a unit's intended functionality;
> *error data*: data that lies outside the input domain of the unit's intended functionality but which the unit nevertheless handles in a prespecified manner without failure.

★ *Intolerable data*: data that lies outside a unit's specified total input domain (intended + error data) and which will therefore cause the unit to fail, as defined previously.

As a trivial example, consider a square root function SQRT. Tolerable input would be any member of the set of target machine reals Rm, of which the intended/error partition would be the non-negative/negative members of Rm respectively (we are assuming SQRT handles negative reals in a prespecified way, e.g. a suitable error message is generated and then execution closedown is initiated). Intolerable input would be any data not belonging to Rm.

The general implications for incorporating data verification into software designs are:

(a) The handling of error data should not be a late, 'add-on' (or *ad hoc*) modification to the main design but should be an integral part of the overall design in the first place. This maxim implies that a requirements specification should be as complete as possible with respect to exception requirements.

(b) Design should in general proceed on the basis that inputs are tolerable. This is because it is usually not cost-effective – from the point of view of design simplicity and elegance, or eventual performance – to attempt to trap all possible input anomalies. Also, strongly typed target languages will automatically provide a high level of checking for intolerable inputs to modules at compile-time anyway. Furthermore, a language system may apply type checking at run-time to detect certain type abberrations that cannot be trapped at compile-time. Some languages provide an exception-handling facility, much as discussed below, that is allied to program I/O; this enables intolerable inputs to be trapped and dealt with gracefully by the program itself (note that, in doing this, the intolerable data has become transferred to the domain of error data).

(c) In a structure of processes, the detection and then separation of error data from intended data should occur before reaching the central, functionally specific modules. This is essentially a matter of efficiency as well as sensible organization – error handling involves overheads and central functions tend to reside vertically at lower levels, or horizontally 'further in', and are called more often, than higher-level or 'outer' ones. Moreover, the more architecture that error flagging and recovery has to pass through, the greater the overheads. Despite this, users would normally expect reusable library modules to be robust, which means building into them the necessary checks for error inputs, as well as other types of exception as appropriate.

There are various classes of input error that can be handled by straightforward design methods, including:

* Lexical and syntax errors, e.g. an input command is not recognized from its constituent symbols.
* Semantic errors, e.g. an input value lies outside some permitted range (this is, in effect, a form of dynamic type checking).
* Corrupt data, i.e. as detected by parity checks, check-sum and check-digit methods.
* Misorderings, i.e. data arrives in an order that violates some ordering relation.
* Omissions, e.g. in the SUMS system, there is no matching QUIT record for the preceding ENTER record.
* Context errors, i.e. data (a user command, say) that would be valid in some circumstances arrives in a context in which it is not legal.

To what extent such errors can be filtered out or repaired, instead of the data being rejected, is problem-dependent. In terms of elegance and simplicity, however, there is a qualitative limit to what can be achieved with the use of conventional design structures. By 'conventional', we mean escape instructions and gotos to exit abnormally from loops, selections, subprograms, etc., and Boolean flags and parameter passing to communicate occurrence of an exception from one part of a software structure to another. To overcome these qualitative limitations, special exception handling mechanisms are necessary.

Exception Handling

This generalized facility, as found in Ada (DoD 1983), for example, enables exceptions to be defined, 'raised' and handled to facilitate recovery or graceful closedown as desired. There are two possible approaches to continuation of execution once an exception has been handled by an associated 'handler' routine: either (i) execution resumes from the point at which the exception was raised; or (ii) the unit in which the exception was raised is terminated, and execution proceeds from where that unit was initiated. There are advantages and disadvantages to both approaches and the reader is referred to Goodenough

(1975) for a general discussion of the issues involved. The resumption model (adopted by PL/1, for example) is more flexible as it subsumes the latter. Although Ada adopts the second approach, the effect of the first approach can still be achieved by appropriate coding. Goodenough recommends an approach that is a combination of the two models.

An exception in Ada is raised (enabled) thus:

```
    raise SOME_EXCEPTION_NAME;
e.g. raise CONSTRAINT_ERROR; − − which is a predefined exception
                             − − that the run-time system itself
                             − − will automatically raise under
                             − − certain conditions;
```

But program-defined exceptions are also possible:

```
    e.g. Q_EMPTY, Q_FULL : exception;
```

Handlers are defined via an optional exception section that is placed at the end of a unit, thus:

```
    e.g.   − − the body of some unit (block or subprogram, say)
           begin
           . . . . . − − assume Q_EMPTY and Q_FULL might be raised
           . . . . .
           exception
             when Q_EMPTY =>
               PUT("Attempt to retrieve from an empty queue");
             when Q_FULL =>
               PUT("Queue size has reached maximum limit");
           end; − − of unit body
```

An exception is automatically disabled when it is handled following the discontinuous jump from the raise to the handler; the unit containing the handler is then aborted and control returns to the next outer dynamic level. As many different exceptions may be handled via **when** clauses in a single unit as desired. There is also:

when others => . . . . .

by which all remaining exceptions not catered for in a unit can be associated with a common handler.

If there is no handler in a unit in which an exception is raised, the unit is aborted, control again returns to the next outer dynamic level, and the exception is automatically re-raised (though this does not apply to exceptions raised in Ada tasks). This process continues until either a handler is eventually encountered or the outer program environment is reached, in which case program termination then occurs. Furthermore, handled exceptions can also be explicitly re-raised at the next outer dynamic level if desired:

e.g. . . . . .
    exception
      when Q_EMPTY =>
        PUT("Attempt to retrieve from an empty queue");
        raise;   − − an "anonymous" raise, allowed only in
               − − handlers
    end;

Clearly, these mechanisms allow exceptions to be propagated upwards through as many dynamic levels as desired, thus enabling, where appropriate, each unit in a chain of calls to express its 'last wishes' before terminating.

As a final example, the exceptions Q_EMPTY and Q_FULL could be included in the specification of the package QUEUE_SEQUENCE given in Section 6.5. Suppose the implementation of REMQ is altered to:

procedure REMQ(Q : **in out** QUEUE, VAL : **out** QELEM) **is**
begin
  if not ISEMPTYQ(Q) **then**
    VAL := Q.QSPACE(Q.FRONT);
    Q.FRONT := (Q.FRONT+1) **mod** MAXQLEN;
    Q.LENGTH := Q.LENGTH − 1;
  else
    raise Q_EMPTY;
  end if;
end REMQ;

and similarly ADDQ. If either exception is raised during use of the package, it will be propagated upwards until a level is reached that contains a user-supplied handler for that exception. Note the gain in clarity compared to conventional techniques − in order for the user to handle such an unpredictable event, it has simply been necessary to specify an appropriate handler at the end of the desired unit (which could, of course, be the main program module). Also, different handlers could be specified for the same exception in different parts of the program.

The termination model of exception handling is not without its dangers. For example, it is possible to exit from a unit without first 'tidying up' partial side effects on global data objects that would otherwise leave the latter in an invalid state. However, it does provide a powerful, flexible and elegant way of building fault tolerance into systems.

7.3 VALIDATION AND VERIFICATION (V&V) TECHNIQUES

Reviews

If the term *review* is used in a general sense to describe any human-driven V&V activity, then 'walkthroughs' and 'inspections', described below, are simply special kinds of review. We shall equate a review here with two separate sets of activities that possess different objectives:

* A management review.
* A set of V&V procedures that is associated with a project milestone, which is a point in development when a major deliverable, or work product, is scheduled to be completed, documented and available for V&V and sign-off.

The first type of review is not a V&V activity as such but involves reviewing the development process itself; we include it here for the sake of completeness. Project management will hold regular meetings with senior project personnel (e.g. programming team leaders, quality assurance representatives) in order to:

* Monitor development progress and the teams and individuals responsible for carrying out the development work.
* Detect potential schedule slippage, cost overrun and other problems.
* Adjust plans associated with later development phases in the light of current circumstances.
* Be provided with all other relevant information that is needed to exercise proper control over the project.

Periodic meetings will also be held with customer representatives to report to them on progress and current state of the project, and to obtain from them appropriate input to the ongoing process of planning later phases.

In the second type of review activity, it is the product itself in its various stages of development that is being scrutinized. This type of review – milestone V&V – is our main concern here. Using the standard model of the development process, the reviewed milestone work products will be:

* Feasibility study report: validated.
* System definition and project management plan: both validated.
* Software requirements: validated and verified.
* Architectural specification/design: validated and verified; sometimes called the *preliminary design review*.
* Detailed design: validated and verified; sometimes called the *critical design review*.

★ Software test plan (for integration and acceptance testing – see Section 7.4): validated.
★ Project history document (recording all relevant data and facts about the project): validated.

Although the exact mechanics of a review procedure – before, during and after a review meeting – will depend on the deliverable in question and vary amongst different developer organizations, the following can be considered general features of V&V reviews of all kinds.:

★ No review can take place unless the deliverable to be reviewed is in a sufficient state of completion and properly documented.
★ The actual people taking part (and the V&V criteria they will use) will vary depending on the deliverable under review. However, one can assume at least the presence of:

> a chairperson to lead the review;
> a secretary to minute the review and its findings;
> the person(s), or appointed representative(s), responsible for the deliverable being reviewed;
> one or more reviewers;
> representatives of other interested parties, e.g. users.

These roles are not necessarily fulfilled by separate individuals – a given person might adopt multiple roles in some situations, e.g. be the secretary, a reviewer and an 'interested party'. Customer involvement in reviews will be concentrated at the front end of the project, namely:

> project feasibility review;
> system definition review;
> software requirements review.

However, there might also be customer involvement in major design reviews in order to obtain verification of the design from a customer perspective. Customer/user participation will also occur during acceptance testing of the executable end-product, but we are concerned only with reviews at the moment.

★ The purpose of a review is to detect, though generally not correct, defects or inadequacies in the deliverable to be reviewed. However, the action needed to correct some minor defects, such as typographical errors in documentation, may be trivial and so can be recorded at the time of the review.
★ The mechanism of the overall review procedure must include as appropriate:

> predistribution of relevant documentation to attending parties to allow sufficient time for study prior to the review taking place;

a follow-up procedure for corrective action of recorded deficiencies and subsequent revalidation and/or reverification.

★ The end result of a successful review will be customer sign-off, where formal customer approval is needed, and sign-off by relevant project personnel certifying that the deliverable has passed the V&V checkpoint and is now 'frozen'.

With this latter point, we are beginning to encroach upon configuration management. As will be seen in Chapter 8, a development model with defined milestones and review points can be integrated with configuration management and quality assurance into a coherent structure for product assurance (or 'quality management') covering the whole life cycle.

A general reference on formal (= providing management information), technical (= work product V&V) reviews – how to plan and conduct them, report their results, etc. – is Freedman & Weinberg (1982).

Walkthroughs

A *structured walkthrough*, as described by Yourdon (1979b), is based on the 'detect but not correct' principle mentioned previously. Most of the features of reviews enumerated above apply to walkthroughs, but the latter possess additional characteristics:

★ A walkthrough is intended to be a general-purpose mechanism that can be adopted for reviewing any intermediate work product – anything from a major deliverable (e.g. architectural design) to a 'small' item (e.g. the specification of an individual module).
★ It is a peer-group review technique – the work of the 'presenter' is examined by persons of equal status, typically colleagues from the same team or development function, although other individuals (e.g. a quality assurance representative) might take part as and when deemed appropriate. Thus, the minimum number of people needed for a walkthrough is two, though slightly larger numbers up to a recommended maximum of about six will be involved from time to time, particularly when more major items are being reviewed. Because of their peer-group nature, walkthroughs are an excellent vehicle for fostering team spirit amongst team members – the work of each team member will periodically undergo examination by his or her colleagues, and thus there is no sense in which a walkthrough is being used as a means of singling out the work of any one individual for particular attention. Indeed, it is important that walkthroughs are

conducted in a constructive, non-hostile atmosphere, since their broader objectives are to improve communication, openness and cooperation amongst team members, with consequent improvement in job satisfaction, work product quality and productivity.
★ A walkthrough is a review of a work product, and it is important for its effectiveness that it be nothing more than that. It is not a mechanism for personnel assessment, either in terms of the technical competence of individuals or their ability to perform well in a group situation.

The name 'walkthrough' derives from the fact that the presenter at the review verbally 'walks through' his or her work product, describing, explaining, justifying, clarifying, etc. The other attendees, whose responsibility it has been to give the predistributed documentation adequate prior study, concentrate on the major issues to be addressed by the review and constructively comment, criticize, etc. At the end of the walkthrough, a decision is made as to whether the work product is to be accepted as it stands, accepted after the suggested minor modifications have been carried out, or reworked as suggested and then submitted to a further walkthrough.

Inspections

The purpose and mechanics of *inspections* are similar to walkthroughs – an inspection is also a review of a work product. One distinction that can be drawn between the two techniques is that an inspection is a more formal review procedure with a definite process management function – that is, data derived from inspections is used to aid project management decision-making, both in the short and long term. Although inspections were originally reported upon by Fagan (1976) in the context of design and code reviews, the inspection technique, like the walkthrough technique, can be adopted as a review mechanism for any work product of the development and maintenance process.

The size of an inspection team is generally three or four people, particularly for design and code reviews. However, larger numbers could be involved when inspecting other types of work product, where it is important that the interests of all relevant parties are represented. The basic inspection team make-up is:

★ A 'moderator': usually a peer of the work product author(s), who is responsible for arrangement of the inspection and follow-up, as well as acting as chairperson and producer of the inspection report.
★ Two or three other participants – the inspectors – who are closely associated with the work product, one of whom could be (a contributory) author of the work product. For example, in a module design

inspection, the inspectors would usually be the person responsible for the design and two other persons who will be subsequently involved in coding and testing the module.

Between planning an inspection (materials to be used; group availability; date, time, place, etc. of inspection) and a preparatory period prior to the inspection meeting during which participants familiarize themselves with their forthcoming inspection duties, an overview meeting might take place to educate the participants in the work product to be inspected and to assign to them specific inspection roles. An inspection has a more formal structure than a walkthrough in the sense that:

(a) A work product is not submitted for inspection until it has satisfied its 'entry criteria'. Basically, these ensure that the work product is in a proper state of completion and documentation for inspection; for example, one entry requirement for a code inspection would be that the code in question has achieved clean compilation.

(b) A checklist of features to be scrutinized during the review is used to steer the inspection process. For example, a verification checklist for a code inspection would include typical logical errors not detectable at compile time.

(c) The work product must then satisfy its 'exit criteria' in order to formally pass the inspection process; thus, all detected defects must be subsequently resolved either to the satisfaction of the moderator or, if appropriate because of the severity of the defect(s), a further inspection.

As Weinberg & Freedman (1984) point out, it is a checklist of features that drives an inspection, whereas with a walkthrough it is the work product itself. Furthermore, the danger with inspections is that defects will not be trapped by the checklist (i.e. because it is not thorough enough); in contrast, walkthroughs are fine for broad issues (e.g. justifying design approach) and lots of detail skipping, but less suitable for detecting defects of detail.

Useful data derived from inspections would include counts of defects, defect severity ratings and categorization, time spent in inspection preparation and actual review, etc. Ackerman *et al.* (1984) indicate how such data can be used on a feedback, feed-into and feed-forward basis for exercising project control. Examples are:

* *Feedback*: architectural design inspections may reveal over a period of time a worse than expected defect rate, suggesting that a tightening up of technique is needed in that phase of development.
* *Feed into*: again over a period of time, experience with inspections may result in the development of more efficacious checklists.
* *Feed-forward*: a module found to be problematic during design

and code inspections may be subjected to more rigorous testing subsequently.

In fact, inspection data can be used as a primary source of input to the quality assurance function, as will be discussed in Chapter 8.

Some ten years on from his first paper, Fagan (1986) reports on the continuing success and increased usage of the inspection approach to V&V over the whole life cycle. Fagan estimates that design and code inspections typically amount to some 15% of total project cost and quotes two examples where inspections detected 82% and 93% respectively of life-cycle defects that would have caused failure. For maximum inspection effectiveness, Fagan recommends training for:

management: in the benefits of inspections etc.;
moderators: in generating group synergy;
participants: in inspection roles.

Audits

Audits are checks carried out by agents who are independent of the development personnel involved. We are not concerned here with audits performed by organizations external to the enterprise of which the developers are part – such audits are rarely cost-effective – but rather audits carried out in-house by a separate project management function. Just as any major deliverable or intermediate work product can be reviewed, so it can be audited. In fact, the in-house auditing functions are precisely configuration management and quality assurance, and inspections and similar review mechanisms represent an important vehicle for enabling these management functions to carry out their auditing role.

7.4 TESTING

Purpose and Limitations

A machine test is the submission of a software unit to a trial run under actual or simulated operational conditions with one or more carefully selected inputs in order to observe the unit's subsequent behaviour. The purpose of this is to arrive at inductive inferences regarding the operational correctness or acceptability of the unit concerned. There are two main points to appreciate:

★ Testing should be essentially a *destructive* activity, i.e. the aim of testing should be to detect errors by attempting to cause the unit to fail. Thus, as Myers (1979) states, a 'successful' test should be regarded as one that *does* show up the presence of errors, rather than vice versa. Therefore, tolerable test-case input data should be chosen that is the most likely to produce failure. How this might be done is discussed in 'Test Case Design' below.

★ Testing can be used only to detect the presence of errors. It cannot be used to achieve the opposite – to prove conclusively their absence – for one simple practical reason: to do so would require exhaustive testing of the unit with all members of the unit's tolerable input domain. Exhaustive testing is in general completely impractical, even for the most trivial of units. *Example*: Suppose a new integer addition function has been constructed that will operate in a target environment whose integer range is $[-8388608..8388607]$. Then exhaustive testing, leading to proof of correctness, would involve 33,554,432 separate integer-pair test cases.

It follows that testing is incomplete and inconclusive, hence inadequate, as a verification technique. However, since formal verification is still somewhat limited in its application, particularly to large-scale software, the practical reality is that establishing confidence in the operational correctness of software still lies very much with machine testing techniques. Therefore, it is essential that testing, like any other life-cycle activity:

is thoroughly planned in advance and documented;
is carried out methodically using well defined, rational strategies and techniques;
in particular, involves the design of test cases judiciously chosen so that eventual failure-free behaviour (unsuccessful testing!) is indicative of a high probability of operational correctness.

One of the main reasons for the release of low quality 'buggy' software is inadequate testing in the implementation phase of a project (often coupled with poor change control – see Section 8.4). The following sections indicate the various ways in which software can be tested in a thorough, methodical manner.

Testing Units as 'Boxes'

By 'unit', we mean here any self-contained software item that forms an integral component of a total system. Hierarchically, these units are:

System $->$ Subsystems $->$ Programs $->$ Modules $->$ Subprograms

Simplistically, any such unit can be regarded as a 'box', knowledge of which can exist at two levels of detail:

(a) The specification of the unit is known, i.e. its function and interface, but not its internal HOW detail – the unit is a 'black' box.
(b) As well as its specification, the unit's internal details are also visible – the unit is a 'white' box.

Thus, functional or 'black-box testing' attempts merely to check out a unit's behaviour with respect to its specification – that functionally 'from the outside' it operates correctly, generating expected outputs from tolerable inputs, including updates to externally accessible data objects. On the other hand, structural or 'white-box testing' concentrates on a unit's internal logic, such as the conditions controlling selections and iterations that together define the total number of different execution pathways through the unit. In practice, testing is a combination of the two approaches:

★ Subprogram and module testing: white box emphasis, concentrating on internal structure of units.
★ Program testing: more 'grey box' in nature, with emphasis not only on overall logical structure of the program, but also exercising the various incorporated subprograms and modules as black boxes.
★ Subsystem testing: concerned more with the correct interface behaviour between the black boxes from which the subsystem assembly is built.
★ System testing: primarily involves demonstrating that the overall operational capability of the system – its functionality and performance – is consistent with its specification.

This enumeration of broad qualitative differences in test objectives at different levels is not intended to imply a particular order of testing units, for which there are several strategic choices.

Testing Strategies

It is obvious that a once-off 'monolithic' approach to testing would present insurmountable problems with respect to adequacy of error detection and correction, even for relatively small programs. A rational test strategy must be 'step-wise', i.e. testing at some stage must involve a step by step iteration of BUILD $->$ TEST $->$ DEBUG. Thus, as each new unit of software is incorporated into the test entity, the latter in its new form is tested and debugged, and the cycle repeated until construction plus testing plus debugging of the total entity is complete. The integration strategy adopted can take several forms, two of which mirror and complement the two basic methods of hierarchical construction – decomposition or synthesis. To illustrate, consider the unit hierarchy depicted in Fig. 7.2.

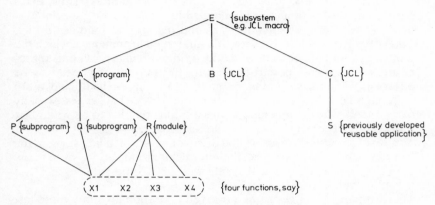

Fig. 7.2. Example of a unit hierarchy in a software subsystem.

Bottom-up integration

As the name implies, units are first of all tested individually in isolation before being combined one by one into higher-level assemblies which themselves then undergo upwards integration testing until the top-level target entity is reached. In fact, this is the 'classic' approach to software testing, being applied right through the subprogram-to-system hierarchy described previously. In terms of unit E in Fig. 7.2, one possibility would be to:

test X1–X4;
test P and Q, both using R[X1–X4];
test A[P,Q,R[X1–X4]], B and C[S] {no need to test S itself};
test E[A[P,Q,R[X1–X4]],B,C[S]].

Advantages:

Units can be handled independently of one another, and thus a high level of confidence in the correctness of modules can be achieved. Also, errors are well isolated in the early stages, which facilitates debugging.
As the test entity grows unit by unit, any new errors discovered will tend to indicate interface problems associated with inclusion of the new unit (though not necessarily caused by the new unit itself), giving more focus to the difficult task of error isolation and correction.

Disadvantages:

At the lowest levels, units are not stand-alone entities. Thus, extra development effort must be channelled into constructing special 'test beds' or test 'driver' software for subprogram and module testing. This software in effect simulates the kind of environment in which the unit will eventually become embedded, in particular providing appropriate test-case inputs and generating the outputs that need to be observed. Test drivers may be considerably non-trivial, and more than one may be needed for a large module, say, that possesses many components whose implementations are too complex to be white-box tested comprehensively via a single test driver.

Top-level structural errors will be discovered only at a late stage in the strategy. This could prove costly in terms of modification, since many critical design decisions will reside well above the subprogram and module level.

The complete product can be observed operationally only in the last stage. There has been no previous opportunity to test the product in a simplified, more primitive form (except via prototyping, say), which would prove useful for early evaluation purposes.

Top-down integration

The top-level structure of the entity is first tested, and then subordinate units are gradually incorporated one by one, level by level down through the hierarchy until the target entity in its entirety is built and tested. As each subunit is incorporated, the new partial entity is subjected to testing. The integration can occur either horizontally, vertically or a mixture of the two. For example (see again Fig. 7.2):

test E
test E with A, then also B, then also C[S];
test E[A,B,C[S]] with P, then also Q;
test E[A[P,Q],B,C[S]] with R[X1−X4].

Note that the horizontal integration approach in bottom-up and top-down integration focuses on pathways through an entity.

Advantages:

Problematic, costly errors such as high-level structural errors are much more likely to be detected sooner rather than later.

A prototype version of the eventual product is available at an early stage for testing, demonstration and possibly even limited use.

Top-down testing is a natural accompaniment to decompositional design techniques, forming together an overall coherent development strategy ('top-down development'). Thus, a system architecture (say) can be specified, and modules designed, coded, integrated and tested in the top-down manner.

Disadvantages:

In order to have a working whole to test at any stage prior to completion, extra effort is required to develop 'stubs' to replace lower-level units that have yet to be incorporated. For example, in the previous unit hierarchy, to test E requires stubs for A, B and C; then to test E[A], say, requires new stubs for P and Q etc. Obviously, a stub should:

   possess precisely the same interface as the actual unit it is temporarily replacing;

   behave functionally in an indistinguishable manner to the eventual unit.

To achieve the latter, the stub will, where appropriate, need to generate typical export values, and execute typical updates on globally accessible data objects. The difficulty of black-box simulation by the stub is thus directly related to the complexity of the actual unit it is replacing. In fact, at high levels, it may be impractical to attempt stub construction. Note that it may be useful to include additional actions in the stub that will not be part of the eventual unit, e.g. message output to facilitate execution tracing and error diagnosis.

Testing is useful only if it generates observable output that enables inductions to be made about the test entity's (lack of) operational correctness or acceptability. Because the functionality of a system that calculates results and generates output often resides at low levels, meaningful test output may be difficult or even impossible to obtain at high levels of top-down testing.

Sideways-on integration

The architecture of an implemented system does not necessarily correspond to a tree structure, and so a hierarchical integration strategy would not be acceptable. Even with hierarchies, though, horizontal integration is not the only possibility. For example, if the implementation structure of the subsystem E in Fig. 7.2 is examined, it can be seen overall to be a sideways-on composition of three main segments with roots A, B and C, respectively. This suggests a complementary integration approach towards system testing, in which the full system is built by adding on one main vertical segment at a time and retesting. The decision-making involved here would concern the order of integration of the vertical increments. This could be driven by functional considerations, e.g. one segment of the system must necessarily be operational before others can be added. In addition, practical considerations such as user requirements may be involved – the system segments are integrated according to user-stated priority of operational capability of the system. Of course, each vertical increment itself can be integrated according to the preferred hierarchical method.

Advantages:

The system can be readily implemented in functional increments according to, say, user preference. This facilitates early acceptance testing (see below) of priority parts of the system.

The integration of each vertical slice exercises both top and bottom levels of the system.

Disadvantages:

Horizontal communication across system slices via updates to global system data may not be fully exercised until late in the integration.

With complex hierarchical system structures, it may be difficult to vertically slice the system without the need for stubs at various levels.

In practice, some mixture of the three strategies can be adopted, in order to enjoy the advantages of, and minimize the problems associated with, each strategy. Bearing that in mind, an overall phased test strategy can be visualized as follows:

Unit testing

Testing of individual subprograms, modules and possibly programs.

Software integration testing

Combinations of bottom-up, top-down and sideways-on integration, as appropriate, of subsystem assemblies. Note that, regardless of strategy used, there is always some scope for overlap with unit testing – units can undergo testing whilst others already tested are integrated.

Software system testing

This is the culmination of the integration phase. At this stage, the testing – still purely software based and under control of the developers – is mainly performance and 'stress' oriented. Whereas performance testing checks out a system's time responses, run-time storage demands, load handling capabilities, etc., stress testing is designed deliberately to overburden the system in some way to see how it copes, e.g. by increasing the data input rate beyond the maximum stipulated level. In this way, the limits of the operational capability of the system can be probed.

Qualification/acceptance testing

Independent validation of the software system by the quality assurance management function to obtain formal in-house certification that the system satisfies its specified requirements.

System integration testing

The delivered software may consist of one or more 'configuration items' that are but components of a larger system involving processor hardware and other instrumentation in which the software is to be embedded. A further integration phase to full system is thus needed as a preliminary to final acceptance.

Installation (site)/acceptance testing

Under mainly customer control, the system is installed and run 'live' within the wider system of which it is a component. Such validation can span a considerable period of time (weeks or months) before the system finally obtains formal customer approval that it exhibits the required functionality and acceptable usability, and adequately meets contractually specified levels of performance and reliability. The timespan for acceptance can be lengthy because introduction of the new system may involve considerable change for the customer in terms of new work practices and operational procedures, staff training and acclimatization, etc. If the new system is replacing a previous computerized system, there may be considerable conversion work involved, e.g. on existing databases. Acceptance might also be staggered if the system is released incrementally via sideways-on production.

Not all of the above tests necessarily occur. For example, the delivered product may be purely non-embedded software, there being no requirement for any system integration testing. For stand-alone software, the customer will accept the product on the basis of satisfactory completion of qualification testing, in which the customer will participate. Special tests may be required for certain types of system. For example, the testing of real-time and distributed systems can pose particular problems, for obvious reasons. Here, software system testing will often involve simulation testing; the processor hardware, peripherals and external equipment being controlled may have to be simulated by program (which also generates whatever inputs are necessary) in order to make a 'safe' system test possible. It is hardly conceivable that rocket guidance software, say, encounters its first system test under live conditions!

An Example: Testing the SUMS System

(Reference to Fig. 6.10 of section 6.7 will help considerably in reading this section.)

There might be many sensible alternative ways in which a system could be tested and integrated; the following is only one viable possibility for the SUMS system:

(Phase MO)
(a) Unit test sSTUDENT–1 with trivial stubs for sSTUDENT–2a and sPROGRAM–1 using carefully constructed test input representative of data stream S. The test driver could be a small program along the following lines:

```
READ(S_REC)
while not at end of test stream do
   sSTUDENT–1(S_REC)
enddo
inspect svdbS12 database
```

The svdbS12 database need exist only as a simplified version of its eventual realization. If this is the case, the implementations of *loadsv* and *storesv* called within sSTUDENT–1 will be different to their eventual form.
(b) Unit test sSTUDENT–2a with a representative SS data stream. The test driver, and other comments, are similar to (a).
(c) Unit test sPROGRAM–1 with a representative SP data stream. Again, the test driver is similar to (a) and (b). The same comments apply here to the svdbP1 database as to the svdbS12 database.
(d) Integrate the three modules and exercise via a test driver with a representative S data stream followed by inspection of the two databases.

(Phase EN)
Provided that a suitable svdbS12 test database exists (the one generated in Phase MO could be utilized), sENLISTER can be unit tested. The test driver for sENLISTER need only call sENLISTER once.

(Phase FL)
Similarly for the svdbP1 database and sFLUSH. sFLUSH can function as its own test driver, with a trivial stub for sPROGRAM–1 that, say, simply outputs FP messages transmitted to it. Later, the tested sPROGRAM–1 and sFLUSH can be integrated – now we also need to inspect the svdbP1 database to check that DELETE actions have been properly effected.

(Phase LS)
When segments W and Y of the system have been thoroughly tested and debugged, they can be integrated into the PATSY system itself (recall that these two components represent the online portion of the SUMS system). This will also exercise the modified fragments of PATSY that support this online component. The net result will be a subsystem test under live conditions. If simplified databases are in use and would be unable to cope with the possible demands of live conditions, this subsystem test must wait until the actual database package has been designed, implemented and tested.

(Phase MR)
sSTUDENT–2b is simple enough to be tested along with sREPORTER. sREPORTER will function as its own test driver. Suitable test databases for svdbS12 and svdbP1 will be needed.

(Phase DB)
At some point the two actual database implementations must be fully tested. The minimum set of access primitives that need to be exercised in both cases will be:
createsv (see below)
deletesv (see below)
getsv
loadsv
storesv

The primitives *creatsv* and *deletesv* are needed respectively for state vectors to be created (students by REGISTER, programs by CREATE) and deleted (students by DEREGISTER, programs by DELETE). These primitives can be inserted into model subprograms at the appropriate entity action points.

The two databases can be implemented and exercised in parallel. The test of each database is in effect the test of an encapsulated data object. Each module of primitives needs to be exercised as fully as possible by test driver programs and specially constructed test data.

(Phase SX)
Full system test will be needed on actual databases. It will be necessary

to run sFLUSH live with PATSY to check that the operating system is handling mutual exclusion of access to the svdbP1 database correctly by the two copies of sPROGRAM–1. The same comments apply to sREPORTER and PATSY as regards both databases.

There is clearly considerable potential for overlap and parallel development and testing of the SUMS system, since the four main segments are largely orthogonal. For example, phases MO, EN, FL and MR could be scheduled to take place in parallel, though of course LS must follow both MO and EN, and SX must follow both FL and LS. It would be prudent to schedule DB at the earliest opportunity, as this would minimize or obviate the need for unit, subsystem and system retesting on actual, as opposed to simplified, databases. Although the above phase sequence is not intended to imply the actual order in which testing would have to take place, it seems natural to test (most of) the model part of the system before any of its functions.

Test Case Design

The crucial factor in *test case* design is the set of criteria used to select test case inputs. This set determines what features of the test entity will be covered, hence the extent of the test and the degree of confidence that can be attached to the entity's correctness if no failures are observed. The test case inputs – or *test set* – form part of a *test specification*, which comprises:
(a) The tolerable input data to be used – the test set.
(b) The features of the test entity that the test set will exercise, e.g. in white-box testing, the program pathways covered; in black-box testing, the functionality being exercised.
(c) The expected behaviour, particularly the outputs that should be generated.
It is deciding upon (b) that enables (a) to be designed and (c) worked out. In the discussion that follows, the following symbols will be used with the stated meaning:
   E is a test entity (subprogram, module, program, etc.);
   D is E's total input domain;
   C is a test selection criterion;
   T is a test set, being a subdomain of D; i.e. $T \subseteq D$;
   S is some arbitrary subdomain of D;
   Q is some subdomain of D that is a (potential) 'equivalence class' (defined below).

The design of adequate test cases is in general a highly non-trivial matter. The basic difficulty is that exhaustive testing is nearly always totally impracticable because of the large cardinality of D. Thus, the union of all test sets used must necessarily be a subset of D. The objective, then, is to make the totality of test sets used as thorough as is practicable. This requires that each T should be designed so as to obtain a specified coverage of E's features with a high probability of detecting errors in those features if they exist. Whilst randomized selection from D may represent the best possible choice of T on some occasions, e.g. at the system level with real-time software, generally design of T must be based on analysis of E's specification and structure.

We can discuss test case design on a rigorous basis as first established by Goodenough & Gerhart (1975, 1977). A test set T is said to be *successful* if E executes correctly for every test case input *t* of T (note that this definition of 'successful' is the opposite of Myers'). T is selected so that it satisfies some specified C (examples of what C might be are given later on). In general, there may be many T satisfying a given C. C is said to be *reliable* for E if the T selected by C are either all successful or all unsuccessful; that is, C gives consistent results no matter what T we choose that satisfies C. A further notion is that of 'validity'. C is *valid* for E if there exists at least one T satisfying C that will be unsuccessful if E is defective in any way. Of course, using C does not mean we actually select a T that will detect errors if they exist – validity merely expresses the fact that C possesses the potential for revealing errors if they are present in E.

The following now results: if C is both reliable and valid, and some T satisfying C is successful, then E is guaranteed correct (the reader should be able to see that this must follow from the definitions of *reliable* and *valid*). Any T satisfying a reliable and valid C is said to be *thorough*. A thorough test is an *ideal test*, i.e. if E is failure-free under T, E's correctness is proven. The objective for test case design is thus to find some selection criterion C that can be shown to be reliable and valid (note that the exhaustive test criterion T = D is reliable and valid!). Weyuker & Ostrand (1980) show that the properties of reliability and validity are interdependent and in general unrealizable in practice. They derive a more practical alternative in terms of the notion of 'revealing'. A test selection criterion C is *revealing* with respect to some S of D if, given that S has at least one unsuccessful member, any test set T satisfying C selected from S will also be unsuccessful. Further, the subdomain S is *revealing* if any subset of S selected as a test set is unsuccessful; the implication is then that all members of S are unsuccessful and no C is therefore needed to select a test set from S to reveal errors. Hence, the objective for test case design is to identify test selection criteria or input subdomains that stand a good chance of being revealing.

The 'revealing subdomain' concept represents one way of attempting to identify within a test entity E's total input domain a reliable 'equivalence class' of test inputs. We can define an *equivalence class* Q of D to be any subset, each of whose members exercises the test entity E *in the same specified way* – either functionally or structurally (path-wise). Note that this is not the same as saying that Q is 'reliable', i.e. each member of Q as a separate test case is behaviourally consistent in the sense defined above. However, the idea behind selecting a candidate Q is induction on the reliable behaviour of Q's members – that is, if E exhibits certain behaviour for some member of Q, then it can reason-ably be induced that it will exhibit exactly the same behaviour for all members of Q. Thus, in particular, if E is (un)successful for any member of Q, then it will be (un)successful for all members of Q. Clearly, equivalence classification enables test sets to be reduced to manageable proportions, since only one random test input need be selected from each equivalence class.

Equivalence classes can be formulated in a number of ways. For black-box testing, equivalence classes are derived from the test entity's functional specification; for white-box testing, from the test entity's structure. The effect of forming equivalence classes is to partition the input domain (and output domain – see below). Suppose Xi are a partitition of the input domain D derived from the specification of E, and Yi are another partition of D derived from some particular analysis of E's structure. Weyuker & Ostrand (1980) suggest that the intersec-tions of the Xi and Yi should be used as revealing subdomain candidates.

Determination of equivalence classes for black-box testing is based on selecting sufficient test data such that all 'typical' inputs are processed, all 'typical' outputs are generated and the complete range of function-ality desired to be exercised by the test is covered. All this is gleaned both from the test entity's specification and from exercising judgement as to what would constitute a behaviourally consistent (reliable) subset of the input domain. To illustrate this, consider testing the integer addition function mentioned in 'Purpose and Limitations':

Input domain: [−8388608..8388607] x [−8388608..8388607]
Output domain: [−8388608..8388607, OVERFLOW]

Obviously, treating the whole input domain as a reliable equivalence class and therefore exercising the function with just a single pair of integers would hardly be deemed to constitute a thorough test. We need a finer partition of the input and output domains. An obvious partition of each integer subrange is:

[−ve.integers, 0, +ve.integers]

The following are then functional equivalence classes of inputs and outputs:

Inputs: I1) +ve., +ve.
         I2) +ve., 0
         I3) 0, +ve.
         I4) +ve., −ve.
         I5) −ve., +ve.
         I6) −ve., −ve.
         I7) −ve., 0
         I8) 0, −ve.
         I9) 0, 0
Outputs: O1) OVERFLOW
         O2) +ve.
         O3) 0
         O4) −ve.

Our test selection criterion C is the one generally used in equivalence class black-box testing: choose sufficient members from each Ik, k=1, ... such that one representative output from each possible Oj, j=1, ... derivable from Ik is generated. Note that both I4 and I5 can yield O2, O3 or O4 and so should be partitioned further accordingly. Also, both I1 and I6 can generate O1 as well as O2 or O4 respectively; again, further partitioning should occur. It follows that C selects a test set T comprising fifteen test case input pairs in all – one randomly selected from each candidate input equivalence class. Our hope is that C is revealing with respect to D: if the addition function is defective in any way, it will fail on at least one of the fifteen test input pairs, whichever ones are chosen; if, however, it succeeds, we induce it is correct. This in turn rests on the assumption that each equivalence class is reliable.

Should C, hence T, be regarded as thorough enough? It will be recalled that the main objective of testing is to attempt to cause failure in the test entity by selecting what are judged to be potentially problematic test inputs. Such tests often tend to involve inputs or outputs that lie at the boundaries or extremes of equivalence classes. With the addition function, the two obvious extremes are −8388608 and 8388607 (−1 and 1 are also boundary values but can be judged to be non-problematic in this instance). Thus, these values should be used in the test, and this can be done without the number of additional test cases rising dramatically. For example, the following extra tests would be justified:

using 8388607 in I2 and I3;
generating 8388607 in I1;
using −8388608 in I7 and I8;
generating −8388608 in I6;
using 8388607 and −8388608 together in I4 and I5.

Chapter 7

Incorporating these extra five test cases into T would increase confidence in the efficacy of the test.

It should be appreciated that black-box testing of units alone is insufficient – it is easy to construct examples of units possessing internal defects that black-box testing would detect only if one was extremely lucky with the test inputs selected. White-box testing is needed to increase the probability of detecting various kinds of structural error. The standard way to identify equivalence classes and formulate test selection criteria in white-box testing is to examine control flow through the test entity. One way to do this is to represent such flow via a directed graph. Figure 7.3 gives an example of a trivial algorithm and its directed graph. Inspection and analysis of such graphs can then be used to determine what pathways need to be exercised to ensure various degrees of coverage. In fact, path analysis can be used to define equivalence classes. For example, suppose p is some particular pathway through (a part of) E. If some S comprises precisely those members of D that cause p to be exercised, then S is an equivalence class. Ideally, we would like to find some C on S such that any test set T satisfying C will find any errors in p if they exist. In general, this is not possible.

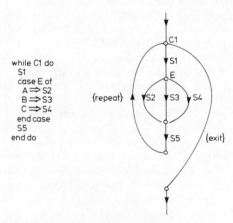

Fig. 7.3. Simple algorithm and its directed graph.

Typical examples of white-box selection criteria/coverage are:

all specified pathways to be exercised;
all statements performed at least once;
all selection expressions and iteration conditions exercised;
all possible alternatives (branches) of each selection exercised;
all loops exercised at least one cycle.

Rapps & Weyuker (1985) have suggested that data flow analysis (e.g. tracking the use of a variable in a program), in addition to path flow analysis, should be used to select fruitful program paths to test. Data flow analysis also figures in the functional approach to testing advanced by Howden (1986), where a program is viewed as an interacting collection of functions for the purposes of test data selection and coverage.

Having decided upon the degree of coverage required, it is then necessary to devise test sets that will provide that coverage; this may require several test runs to achieve. Naturally, the larger and more complex the unit, and the greater the coverage required, the more difficult and time-consuming the path analysis and determination of selection criteria. To see why exhaustive path testing is in general impractical, consider the graph in Fig. 7.3. There are three possible pathways through the loop. Thus, an iteration of N cycles represents 3^N different possible pathways in total; e.g. 6561 pathways for $N = 8$. However, a given test set that causes this structure to be exercised will exercise only one of these pathways. In a large program, of course, the total number of different pathways will be enormously large. Note that exhaustive path testing is not the same as exhaustive testing (of all inputs), since the equivalence class for any given path may be a (large) non-singleton subdomain. Hence, exhaustive path testing could not guarantee to reveal all errors anyway.

The above examples are of course only 'toy' examples but they serve to emphasize that test case design is not necessarily trivial even for functionally or structurally trivial modules. In practice, of course, the situation is far worse. For non-trivial units, test case design is extremely difficult and tedious. It involves a lot of judgement, experience and insight – commensurate with that required in software specification and design itself – to formulate and specify a set of adequately effective test case selection criteria, whether for black box or white box testing. Furthermore, ideal tests and related notions are generally unrealizable in practice, although such theories do provide much-needed guidance in the construction of tests and evaluation of test adequacy. It is these practical realities that expose the true limitations of testing, and the high probability that a lot of software in use today has been inadequately verified. Facts such as these are alone a strong argument for continuing research into establishing formal specification and verification techniques as a practical, (cost−) effective weapon in the armoury of the software engineer.

Test Specification and Planning

The testing involved in large-scale system development is clearly a complex ongoing activity that requires rigorous advance planning and specification. This requirement applies to the integration phase on-wards, as it is normal project discipline for unit testing to be specified and carried out by the individual or team responsible for the unit's design and implementation (recall that white-box testing in particular requires detailed knowledge of a unit's internal characteristics). There are a number of important considerations:

* Overall approach: how the testing will be divided into separately identifiable phases; how these phases will be scheduled.
* Coordination: what units, and when, should be tested and debugged ready for integration testing.
* Integration strategy: what mix of bottom-up, top-down and sideways-on integration will be employed; the order in which specific modules and subsystems will be integrated; specification of additional software – stubs and drivers – that will be required.
* Test specifications: for each distinct test, as described previously.
* Resources and any special tools required.

Such requirements as these should be rigorously defined in a *test plan* document. This document will then be used by a team of testers, possibly independent of the other development staff, to carry out the required integration and system testing. The test plan should, of course, be constructed as early as possible in the development cycle, so that project schedules can be adhered to. In fact, the overall software system test specification can be developed as soon as a definitive requirements specification exists. Similarly, integration test specifications can be developed as specification of the system architecture in terms of subsystems and modules ensues and becomes 'frozen'. If subsequent redesign occurs, the test specifications and plan will have to be corre-spondingly modified; this is another aspect of configuration manage-ment, which is discussed in Sections 8.4 and 8.5.

The test results themselves, as well as the test specifications, should be documented. This naturally requires the test documentation to be structured in such a way as to facilitate cross-referencing between test cases and the results of the test runs. This information is needed for maintenance purposes to record bugs and anomalies that still exist when the software is released. It is also needed for *regression testing*, i.e. when system test, say, has revealed defects that require modification and retest through part of the integration phase; then, ensuring repeatability of test cases may be vital. As regards acceptance test planning and specification, this is a matter for the customer organization that has commissioned the system. This acceptance test plan should be drawn up and agreed upon with the developers during the requirements analysis phase.

Software Tools for Testing

The testing process is a costly, time-consuming activity that can devour as much as 50% of development costs. Like any other activity in the development process, it is also error-prone. For example, it is all too easy mistakenly to omit a critical test input or overlook an anomalous value in a mass of generated test output. To ameliorate these problems, a number of automated aids for testing exist. The following is a brief summary of some of the main types of test tool available:

Static analysers

Although strictly not a testing tool, in the sense that code is not exercised, we include this category here for completeness. A static analyser carries out an analysis of the source text of the program – its control flow, declared identifiers, etc. – and reports on any defects detected, such as type incompatabilities that a main compiler would let through, use of uninitialized variables, instances of blocks of unreachable code, etc. It may also report on violations of coding or language standards as stipulated for the project or by some external authority.

Symbolic evaluators

Symbolic evaluation involves assigning symbolic names to inputs and then executing pathways through the program by interpreting statements on those paths. In doing so, intermediate values that are computed along a path are expressed in terms of the original symbolic inputs. Furthermore, at each decision point, an (in)equality, or *path constraint*, can be determined for each possible branch from the branch condition; since the values of all variables are expressions of the symbolic inputs, so too are the path constraints. The conjunction of all constraints along a path gives the *path condition* – a predicate that the input data must satisfy in order that the path is covered. Symbolic execution can be used to derive test data, detect infeasible paths (i.e. paths that no input data would exercise) and aid in the generation of verification conditions for formal verification. Further details can be found in Howden (1978) and Clarke & Richardson (1984).

Test file generators

Test file generators (TFGs) are useful when large quantities of test data, such as simulated transactions in a database environment, are needed to achieve a realistic test. A TFG will need to be supplied with data specifications – formats, ranges, etc. – in order to generate the required test data.

Test data generators

Test data generators (TDGs) are a more sophisticated form of tool. A TDG accepts a program as input and selects paths for testing, based on coverage criteria of the kind mentioned earlier. Symbolic execution is then used to determine path constraints, and hence path conditions. The test data is then automatically generated from the path constraints.

Test monitors

These tools analyse and report upon the flow coverage obtained on exercising a test entity, and hence are a useful adjunct to white-box testing. The analysis is obtained either via interpretive execution, or by instrumentation of the code with extra instructions – software 'probes' – inserted by a preprocessor or the compiler at various appropriate points in the test entity's code.

Output comparators

An output comparator, as the name implies, checks actual output obtained from a test run against pre-prepared expected output. This obviously helps overcome the error-proneness of manual checking, particularly where large volume output is involved or several regression test runs are involved.

Test harnesses

A test harness is controlling software that provides a total test environment in which units can be embedded for testing along with test tools of the kind just mentioned. Typically, a test harness is link-edited with the test entity and is interactive, providing online control over test inputs and outputs and coverage obtained.

7.5 DEBUGGING

Debugging is the activity of locating and rectifying an error after testing has indicated an error's presence by causing failure. Once modification has taken place to eradicate the error, regression testing follows. This DEBUG $->$ (RE)TEST sequence is often iterated over many cycles, because typically the removal of one error highlights others that the previous error was shielding. This in turn is why inspections and similar review techniques are a valuable adjunct to testing – a single inspection meeting can detect a number of defects that might only have shown up over a series of regression tests.

The philosophy to be applied to all debugging is: 'Whenever there is failure, it is always the software that is guilty – the probability of defect-free software is in effect zero.' Of course, there are rare occasions when the hardware is transiently faulty (say) but to debug on the premise of software innocence is not to debug at all. The amount of rework needed after debugging depends to some extent on the kind of error detected. For example, it is far less likely that rectification of a pure coding defect will have further side effects on the software than removal of a design defect. Good-quality structure and modularity are essential in order that design modification, if it is needed, will have localized perturbations. Design modification to poorly structured and modularized software can lead to one modification generating the necessity for others in a disastrous 'ripple' effect.

The hardest part of debugging is the first phase – locating the actual error. Again, it should be emphasized that it is the effect of an error that is observed (the mode of failure), not its cause. So, for example, the statement at which the program 'crunches' is not necessarily where the error actually exists. Clearly, it is important to have as much useful information as possible in order to facilitate bug detection. This information mostly centres on:

(a) Symbolic dump information: the names and values of (relevant) data objects at the time of failure, particularly:

☆ those variables, and parameters if appropriate, in the most local environment – e.g. block, subprogram, module – surrounding the point of failure;
☆ as a special case of the first, the values of control identifiers of loop structures, and the values of selecting expressions in multi-choice structures, that surround the point of failure;
☆ those non-local data objects accessible at the point of failure.

(b) Tracing information: various aspects of the execution history up to the point of failure, particularly:

☆ trace of statement sequence execution;
☆ trace of subprogram calls (particularly useful for tracing mutual recursion calling sequences);
☆ the extent to which each input stream has been consumed and each output stream generated.

Debugging information of this kind can be obtained by a variety of methods, as described below.

Special-purpose diagnostic aids built into the target language for user-selective dumping and tracing. This is a rather rare facility to find in a language (Snobol 4 is an example), and other approaches to obtaining diagnostic information are more usual.

The target language run-time system. This will normally provide symbolic dump and tracing information when a catastrophic error occurs (together with an error message of course – hopefully meaningful and relevant!). The quantity of such information generated may be fixed by the system, or the user may have some control via language system parameters. For example, various trace mechanisms may be on-off switchable, such as checking for out-of-bounds array indices. There may also be different trace level options providing varying amounts of detail. Since dynamic tracing adds significant run-time overheads, debugged in-use software will usually be run at minimum trace level.

Debugging tools integrated into the host development environment. A number of debugging tools exist to provide symbolic dump and program trace/flow analysis information that can be used to augment what is obtained via other sources. Perhaps the most sophisticated form of debugging tool is that which provides an interactive debugging environment – the user is able to perform debugging tasks as the program is being executed (or interpreted). A central feature is the ability to insert one or more *breakpoints* into the program. Execution is suspended when a breakpoint is reached, and the environment allows the user to carry out a number of activities, e.g. inspect the contents of specified variables/locations, perform modifications to the program, continue execution (possibly on a statement-by-statement basis), etc. Conditional breakpoints may be allowed; that is, execution halts only if a certain set of associated, user-specified conditions are satisfied at the breakpoint (e.g. the value of a particular variable has exceeded K, a specified loop has executed X cycles, and so on). More generally, it may be possible, prior to program execution, to specify certain sets of conditions, such that suspension of program execution is triggered *whenever* any one of the condition sets is satisfied.

Designed-in debugging statements. This is a programmer-effected instrumentation technique, involving the insertion of extra output operations generating useful diagnostic information at appropriate points in the software. These operations can perform dumping where desired and/or act as a means of execution flow tracing. Since it is unlikely that this information will be wanted when the software is operational, yet it may be desirable to retain the diagnostic statements in the source code, a simple means of switching them on and off is needed. This can be accomplished at compile-time if conditional compilation is available or at run-time by some global variable initialized appropriately by a user input parameter. If the reduction in efficiency with the latter method is unacceptable, then two versions of the software can be maintained – one with the diagnostics retained, the other with them removed.

Exception handling. As discussed in Section 7.2 with respect to Ada, such a facility provides a means of recovering or gracefully dying from an error condition. In particular, an exception handler can be used to generate meaningful error messages and useful sumbolic dump information.

Naturally, all tools have their limitations. In the last resort, successful debugging reduces to the application of 'raw' human intelligence and know-how acquired through experience. Whether one has available a powerful interactive debugging environment, or merely pen and paper, it is important to attempt to:

★ Gather and organize as much relevant data about the bug as possible.
★ Form one or more plausible hypotheses as to the cause of the bug (sometimes there can only be one possible cause, sometimes many).
★ Check out each hypothesis in decreasing order of likelihood.
★ Be humble and seek help from colleagues when all else fails. Unfortunately, counterproductive psychology can operate here in two ways:
    having to reveal that one's work is defective;
    having to admit defeat in being unable to solve a debugging problem.

Automated tools should be used cost-effectively to aid the debugging process appropriately, not to act as a substitute for it. In reality, it may take several days to track down an elusive bug in a few thousand lines of code that turns out to be due to a trivial coding mistake. The author remembers one such instance where a large Algol–68 program cleanly compiled but mysteriously kept failing during execution. The error was eventually tracked down to an assignment step where the colon of the assignment symbol had been accidentally omitted. The result of this mistake, syntactically, was a Boolean 'unitary clause' that the compiler, quite correctly, was happy to accept but which generated a subtle error during execution. The result in human terms, however, was several days of (sometimes intense) frustration.

Chapter 8

Project Management
and Related Topics

8.1 THE PROBLEMS

A large-scale software project is an exceedingly complex task to carry out:

> comprising a number of individually complex and interacting, sometimes parallel, activities (analysis, specification, design, implementation) ...
> carried out by possibly large numbers of people working over lengthy time spans (e.g. years) ...
> developing a highly complex product that should conform to prescribed, sometimes stringent, requirements and standards.

Clearly, then, if software projects are to have any chance of successfully delivering quality products on time within budget, they must be thoroughly planned in advance and effectively managed as they are executed.

We have already indicated in Section 2.1 the main elements that need to be incorporated into a project management plan. In this chapter, we shall expand upon four essential ingredients of project management – *estimation*, *organization*, *configuration management* (including *maintenance*) and *quality assurance*; we shall also deal with a fifth associated topic, namely *documentation*. Respectively:

★ Project planning involves estimating effort, time, cost and staff resources needed to execute the project. It also requires scheduling the various deliverables, review points, etc. according to the phases of the development model that will be used to impart an overall structure to the project. Furthermore, re-estimation and rescheduling must occur throughout the lifetime of the project in order to adjust previous estimates to the more accurately quantifiable data that emerges as project execution moves through its various phases.

★ Some kind of organizational structure must exist within which all staff involved on a project can effectively carry out the work they are required to perform.

★ Mechanisms are needed to control and keep track of the configuration – loosely, the 'state' – of the product, both as it is developed and during its operational lifetime.

★ Procedures are needed to ensure as far as is possible that quality practices, and standards in emerging product and associated documentation, are being adhered to.

★ Reliable information concerning the state of a project must at all times be available; this requires appropriate documentation to be generated and maintained as part of the software configuration.

In fact, sound management in these areas is just as crucial to the success of a software project as any other aspect of software engineering that has been discussed in previous chapters. Many a 'software crisis' can be attributed not only to the non-application of principle and method, but also to inadequate project management caused by lack of recognition and understanding of what the real problems are in carrying out large-scale software development (quite apart from the intellectual difficulty involved). As a documented example of what can, and did, happen in real life, and what can be deduced from the experience, Brooks (1975) should be read.

Project management has to do with *monitoring* and *control* – control of what is happening now and what will happen in the future. There is a fundamental principle here:

What is not (or cannot) be evaluated, measured or estimated cannot be controlled.

Thus, all forms of control presuppose a disciplined, well-defined framework within which the object(s) under control function or exist and can be monitored. Monitoring supplies the necessary tracking, evaluation and measurement (on which estimations, where needed, can be based) that is required as input by the management decision-making processes in order to exercise effective control. In terms of our above enumeration of 'essential ingredients':

★ Line management controls, and monitors adherence to, all timescales and budgets.

★ Project management controls and monitors the progress of a particular project and the staff involved.

★ Configuration management controls and monitors software configurations.

★ Quality assurance controls and monitors quality.

★ Documentation describes and records all that is relevant; without it, control and monitoring would be impossible.

It is when projects go 'out of control' that disasters ensue. Loss of control can occur to the software (its configuration – this includes documentation), its quality, the people producing it or the resources (time, money) needed to produce it. Severe project slippage and budget overshoot then loom on the horizon as severe 'technical hitches' are encountered during software development or original planning estimates are found to be wildly optimistic. We shall now take each of the above five aspects of project management in turn and discuss how loss of control can be avoided.

Bibliographical note: two general texts on project management the reader is encouraged to consult are:

Metzger (1981): provides general coverage and advice on project management worded in a practical, down-to-earth manner;
Bruce & Pederson (1982): includes thorough coverage of the major topics discussed in this chapter, as well as V&V, testing, etc.

8.2   RESOURCE ESTIMATION AND SCHEDULING

Resource estimation and scheduling is concerned with the management of time, money and personnel that will be needed to execute a project, broadly from the project planning stage up to product release and thereafter during maintenance. In particular, it involves estimating effort and time needed to accomplish the development work so that a realistic budget can be determined and a schedule for the various development activities worked out. Clearly, this is one of the most difficult areas of project planning, since estimations have to take place at the start of a project when least is known about the development task. Firstly, broad estimates of budget and timescale will need to be made at the feasibility stage. Assuming that the project then passes its feasibility review and go-ahead is formally approved, more refined estimates will need to be included in the project management plan. Since preliminary budget and schedule estimates will inevitably be subject to considerable uncertainty and risk, they will generally have to be revised at appropriate points during project execution. There are several reasons why such revision may be necessary:

★ The inaccuracies in the original estimates may be too gross (usually too optimistic) to be tolerated. Some possible causes are:
    attempting to undercut the competition when tendering for development work;
    poor judgement;
    poor calibration of estimation method used (see below);
    lack of experience in project problem domain.
★ Life is unpredictable – things can, and do, go wrong. For example, the host environment may become unreliable due to an intermittent

hardware fault; staff may fall ill, change jobs, etc. Lack of continuity in development resource availability and personnel can impede development and lead to slippage. Thus, estimation should attempt to incorporate an extra X% as contingency planning.

★ Users change their minds. The later that requirements drift occurs in the development process, the greater in general will be the effort required to accommodate it. Whereas in the previous two cases, extended deadlines and consequential additional costs would be borne by the developer, here the customer organization would be responsible for meeting such increases, unless considered small enough to be absorbable.

A further, though less problematic, consideration is the hardware and software tools needed to support the work involved. Usually, the developers are already in possession of a suitable basic host development environment (i.e. virtual machine – hardware of adequate size and power plus operating system), and so large expenditures in that area are avoided. This basic environment obviously needs to be augmented by various utility and support software: editors, compilers, DBMS, life-cycle support tools, etc. It may be that essential software needs to be purchased from other sources, or possibly developed in-house. Either way, extra costs will be incurred that need to be included in budget estimates. However, if a certain facility is desirable but not essential, trade-offs can be examined. For example, if in-house tool development will add a further estimated $X to the budget but the envisaged increase in productivity in the current and possible future projects will quickly recoup the extra investment, then the tool development represents a worthwhile risk to undertake.

Note: 'development environment' and 'target environment' are not necessarily the same. This is commonly the case with process control and embedded systems, where the target environment is typically a small microprocessor that is incapable of hosting the development work itself. In such circumstances, a suitable development system is required that not only provides standard software tools but also cross-compilers, microprocessor emulators, test harnesses and so on.

Estimation of Effort and Time

If the effort and timescale needed up to product release can be estimated, then this provides a means of deriving overall cost, work breakdown schedules and staffing resources distributed amongst the development phases. As a preliminary step, various relevant attributes of the development task need to be evaluated and fed into the estimation process. At project inception, the estimation process may consist of little more than a combination of 'expert judgement' (possibly the consensus judgement of several individuals) and comparison with past experience. The reliability of the estimates will be mainly a reflection of the extent to which the project represents familiar territory to the developers – the more the project is similar in type, complexity, scale, etc. to past projects, the more accurate are the estimates likely to be. Note that it is incumbent upon developers to maintain relevant historical data of past projects – a vital task, because historical data is a crucial input to the management of future projects, not just for preliminary estimation, but for other reasons discussed later on. Compensation can be exercised for differences that presently exist (e.g. better development tools are now available, which will have a reducing effect on effort, time, etc.) to arrive at final figures that can form the basis for contractual agreement.

Expert judgement and historical analogy may produce reasonably reliable estimates on relatively small projects with mainly familiar characteristics, but on large projects possessing much hitherto 'untrodden ground', something better is needed. The main alternative is to use an algorithmic cost estimation technique. Important publications in the arena of cost estimation include Wolverton (1974), Putnam (1978) and Boehm (1981). A brief description of several algorithmic cost estimation techniques is given in Boehm (1984b). Typically, such techniques employ equations of the form;

$$E = f(S), \text{ often } a*S^b$$
$$T = g(E), \text{ often } c*E^d$$

where:

E, the development effort (expressed in person-months, say) is some function f (usually exponential) of project size S;
T, the development time, is some function g (usually exponential) of effort:
a,b,c, and d, are constants determined empirically from analysis of past projects and chosen to reflect project characteristics.

Thus, project size S is a pivotal 'cost driver', i.e. a variable on which cost is dependent. The problem, therefore, is how to measure and determine S.

One of the simplest measures of project size is an estimation of the number of lines of source code (LSC) that will eventually be delivered. To determine LSC, appeal can again be made to expert judgement and historical comparison. However, by the time the requirements definition milestone has been reached, there exists a better basis for project size estimation – the requirements themselves or, more accurately, those requirements that will lead to generated code:

the system functions;
user interface;
error and exception handling requirements;
performance constraints.

DeMarco (1982) shows how the complexity of an SSA-based design can be analysed to provide a measure of project size on which to base cost estimation. Albrecht & Gaffney (1983) propose a 'function points' metric, which is a measure of the amount of 'function' the software is required to satisfy, expressed in terms of the data the software is to consume or produce at its external interface; the metric can then be used to estimate LSC. If no specific size estimation model is used, then the amount of code that will result from satisfying each requirement must be gauged by again using judgement and analogy, though on a smaller scale compared to a single overall estimate and with the possibility of any inaccuracies to some extent cancelling out; an aggregated LSC figure can then be derived. There are, however, certain problems associated with determining LSC figures, whether estimating them at the start of development or on completion when 'precise' LSC can be counted:

★ It is not altogether obvious what constitutes an LSC. Does it mean physical line, or source language instruction, of which there may be many to one physical line or one spreading over several physical lines? Should only executable statements be included? Whatever interpretation of LSC is adopted, it should be used consistently in all estimations.
★ Should only *delivered* source code be estimated/counted or should other code be included that contributes to project effort, e.g. that required for test stubs and drivers?
★ Should reusable code be included in the figures? It is certainly part of the delivered LSC figure, but it will also reduce the effort that would otherwise be needed to develop the code from scratch.
★ An LSC figure is a rough estimate of the target size of the product, and hence only crudely indicative of the amount of effort needed for development. There exist many other factors that influence effort needed, including staff experience and familiarity (e.g. with the application area), performance constraints (the more, and the tighter, the greater the effort), and availability of support tools (basically, the more, the better).

Nevertheless, despite certain problems associated with LSC estimation, LSC is still the measure of project size most commonly used by algorithmic cost estimation techniques. The COCOMO (COnstructive COst Model) model of Boehm (1981) is no exception. It is currently one of the most highly developed cost estimation models available, which, in its most basic form, provides nominal estimates for E (in person-months – PMs) and T (in months) according to the following equations:

$$E = k1*KLSC^{k2}$$
$$T = 2.5*E^{k3}$$

where KLSC = the number of 1000's of LSC (where LSC are physical lines of source code, not source code instructions) and k1, k2, k3 are constants that depend on the type of software project.

Software projects are divided into three categories – hence there are three pairs of equations, i.e. a different set of constants for each project category. This categorization can be regarded as an attempt to reflect three different levels of 'project complexity'. The categories are termed *organic*, *semi-detached* and *embedded* and in part reflect decreasing degrees of staff familiarity and experience with the problem domain. For example, a 'we've done many of these before' applications project would slot into the first category, development of a more demanding utility program (e.g. compiler) would belong to the second category and an innovative application involving real-time constraints would go into the third category. In the basic COCOMO method, the project is fitted into one of the three categories and then the relevant pair of equations is applied to obtain effort and development time estimates.

The nominal values obtained by the basic COCOMO method may be useful as rough indicators, but project planning would normally require values that are more reflective of other factors that affect effort, etc. The intermediate version of COCOMO defines fifteen further cost drivers allocated to four project attribute categories. With each cost driver is associated a range of 'effort multipliers' – values that define different ratings for the cost driver. For example (EMR stands for 'effort multiplier range'):

★ Required reliability (a *product attribute* cost driver): EMR is 0.75 (very low) to 1.40 (very high); i.e. the higher the reliability required, the greater the effort needed.
★ Storage constraints (a *machine attribute* cost driver): EMR is 1.00 (nominal) to 1.56 (extra high); i.e. the tighter the storage constraints, the greater the effort needed.
★ Programming language experience (a *personnel attribute* cost driver): EMR is 1.14 (very low) to 0.95 (high); note the decrease here – for obvious reasons.
★ Use of software tools (a *development environment* attribute cost driver): effort multipliers range from 1.24 (very low, i.e. only basic tools available, e.g. editor, compiler) to 0.83 (very high, i.e. sophisticated tools available, e.g. integrated program development environment – see Section 9.2).

Obviously, each EMR is an empirical quantification of the expected effect the associated cost driver could have on project effort. The intermediate COCOMO method is thus:

★ Obtain a nominal effort value from the appropriate basic equation.
★ Nominate a rating for each of the fifteen cost drivers that as accurately as possible reflects project attributes.
★ Select the corresponding multipliers from the EMR tables (see Boehm 1981) and adjust the effort figure accordingly.
★ Now derive a development time estimate from the appropriate equation.

Of course, the COCOMO model can be tuned to reflect the local conditions of a particular development environment, e.g. by omitting or adding further cost drivers, or by using different EMRs to those supplied by Boehm. Mohanty (1981) lists overall some forty-nine cost drivers taken into account by a sample of cost estimation methods.

The basic/intermediate COCOMO method is a 'top-down' method in the sense that it first calculates an effort value for the whole project that is then subsequently distributed across various phases (see below). The advanced version of COCOMO takes a bottom-up approach by initially requiring a preliminary architectural system design to be performed. The size, effort and development time for the total system is then built up by firstly applying intermediate-type COCOMO estimations to each module and using this data as input to calculating the size, effort and development time for each subsystem along intermediate COCOMO lines. The total system size, effort and development time is then a summation of subsystem values. The model can be further refined by taking each phase of development separately into account.

Costing

Although cost estimates may stem from a cost driver associated with delivered source code, it would be wrong to assume that total project cost is merely the capital needed to fund those activities directly concerned with producing the code. Project cost is a function of:

★ The resources and personnel needed to carry out:
 planning, analysis and requirements definition;
 specification, design, coding and unit testing;
 integration and system testing;
 configuration management (CM);
 quality assurance (QA);
 reviews and other V&V activity not covered by CM and QA.
★ The generation and publication of documentation.

* Extra staff enrolment, possibly on a short-term contract basis, and in-house training as necessary.
* Acquisition of new equipment, software, etc.
* Additional in-house support, e.g. tool development.
* Miscellaneous administrative and operational support.
* Installation of system, training of users.

It is therefore important to know which costs are, and are not, covered by the cost estimation method being used. Bearing that in mind, total development cost can be obtained by:

* Taking the effort estimate E (in PMs), an averaged cost per unit effort R in $/PM and computing C = E*R; R can be computed from the staff salaries of the developer organization.
* Adding on to C estimates of all other costs not covered in the estimation of E.

Given the variety of cost estimation techniques that are available, it is not surprising that each will tend to give different estimates for the same project task; again, see Mohanty (1981) for the wide variation that can be obtained from different algorithmic cost models. The safest approach in practice is not to rely solely on a single type of estimation method. So a strategy for cost estimation might be:

* Adopt an algorithmic estimation model and tune the various coefficients, etc. used in its equations to achieve as good a fit as possible with historical data and to reflect current local conditions.
* Also obtain cost estimates via a non-algorithmic approach. There are several ways this could be achieved. For example, if a cost per delivered KLSC is available from historical data, then multiplying this with estimated total KLSC will yield a cost figure. Note that, in this simple method, the $/KLSC figure used may have been averaged out over *all* system development costs and not just (say) design through to acceptance testing. However, care must be exercised in using such figures. It is important that the $/KLSC figure used relates to past projects of a similar nature. It would be meaningless to use a figure derived from past data processing applications, say, on a current project with real-time attributes. Equally, a sophisticated tool such as a 4GL system (use of which would tend to decrease development costs) would make past $/KLSC figures (when the tool was not available) also inapplicable, though it might be possible to adjust them to take the effect of current tool availability into account.

If the two sets of estimates are in broad agreement with one another, say within 15%, then they can be taken as a basis for project costing. If not, some iterative reappraisal should be applied until the desired tolerance between the two estimates is achieved. For example: is the algorithmic model sufficiently precisely calibrated? are inappropriate $/KLSC figures being used?

People and Productivity

Given effort and time figures, a nominal staff requirement for a project can be estimated by dividing the former by the latter. For example, if E is 55 PM and T is 15 M, then staff requirement is about four persons. What this estimate ostensibly tells us is that approximately four people working over one and a quarter years should be adequate to complete the project. However, suppose that there are more staff available to work on the project – eight, say. Can T apparently be cut to about seven months? Unfortunately, the facts of life for software projects are not as simple as that. Past experience has demonstrated that 'throwing more people at a project' does not necessarily have a beneficial effect on development time. In fact, the observed effect can be to make 'a late project later' (again, see Brooks 1975). The reader should also note that development time in COCOMO and other cost models is not a function of staff numbers.

The problem is that the relationship between staff requirement, schedule, work effort and development phases is much more complex than may at first appear:

★ Staff requirement is not constant across the development period. For large projects, relatively few people will be needed in the early phases of specification and architectural design, but the staff requirement will begin to rise as detailed design, coding, etc. gets underway, peaking during integration and system testing
★ The greater are staff numbers, the greater too are the number of possible communication channels between them. This can have a deleterious effect on work rate since people will tend to spend more time communicating – not necessarily effectively either – than doing useful work.
★ The more staff there are, the more difficult it is to organize them into structures that promote productive software development.
★ All tasks have their saturation levels, i.e. the number of people working on a particular problem may already be such that adding further 'brain power' will in no way speed up the achievement of a solution and may be a positive hindrance.

Also, for a given project, the more productive staff are, the less staff will be needed in principle to complete the project in a given timespan (or equally, for a given level of staffing, the less time will be needed to complete the project). It follows that some productivity element should enter into effort-time-staffing estimations. This is done explicitly in the COCOMO model via effort multipliers that take into account staff skill levels and experience, etc. In a study by Walston & Felix (1977), twenty-nine separate factors were identified as having a significant effect on productivity, including user-product interface complexity, use of structured programming and number of pages of delivered documentation per KLSC. User-product interface complexity had the greatest single effect – the more complex it was, the less was productivity (as would be expected). The study also showed that greater use of both structured programming and top-down development had beneficial effects on productivity. However, some trade-offs are inevitable. For example, increased user participation in requirements definition led to a marked decrease in productivity. Such a finding has to be weighed against the fact that high levels of user participation are generally considered very desirable, and the productivity cost incurred should pay for itself many times over later on, e.g. in reduced maintenance.

Despite the problems involved in defining what constitutes an LSC (see above), the most widely used measurement of productivity is LSC/PM or similar, which can be calculated at project completion; note that, although the LSC figure pertains to the final, implemented product, the PM component represents the total development effort from requirements definition onwards. Productivity measurements are useful from at least two points of view. Firstly, a productivity measure P can be used in the estimation of effort; that is, effort = $1000*KLSC/P$. This provides yet another route to cost estimation, though care should be taken to use a meaningful P figure, i.e. one that relates to past projects of similar attributes. Secondly, productivity figures can be used to demonstrate to management the efficacy, or otherwise, of applying particular tools and methods. Obviously, the more such figures are available from past projects, the greater can be the reliance placed on productivity estimates employed in cost and time projections. However, productivity figures should be interpreted with caution. Developing quality products takes more time and effort than churning out poor quality code. Thus, acknowledgement of a high productivity figure should be tempered by the fact that quantity does not necessarily imply quality, though it is difficult to see how evaluation of the latter (in terms of the quality criteria defined in Section 1.4, say) can be reflected in productivity figures. This is an area for further research.

Scheduling and Resource Distribution

The scheduling component of project planning involves two main tasks:

(a) Breaking the development down into well-defined phases that encapsulate major activities and associating with each a proportion of the estimated total effort and development time; from this distribution, a breakdown of the staff requirement per phase can be derived.

(b) For each phase or activity, carrying out a more detailed work breakdown and scheduling.

In Section 7.3, we implied a breakdown of the development process in terms of major activities, the culmination of each of which was a major deliverable and associated review point. This breakdown can be used as a macroscopic structure on which to base resource distribution. However, as we have already stated, the distribution of effort over the development cycle is certainly not linear; this also applies to time. To some extent, these distributions depend on the type of project involved. For example, greater expenditure of effort would be expected in the integration and testing stages of a life-critical, real-time embedded system than in the comparable stages of an information system. Likewise, different development methods may demand emphasis in different parts of the development process. Thus, generalized effort distributions are of limited value. Some possibilties are given in Fig. 8.1.

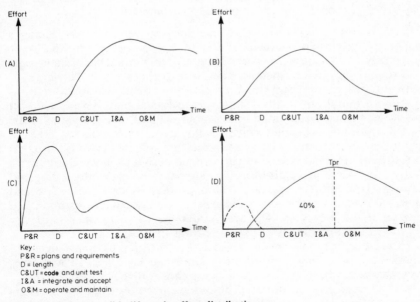

Key:
P&R = plans and requirements
D = length
C&UT = code and unit test
I&A = integrate and accept
O&M = operate and maintain

Fig. 8.1. Some possible life-cycle effort distributions.

Distribution (A) can be regarded as correlating with 'software crisis management': little effort is expended in requirements, specification and preliminary design; more and more effort is ploughed in as problems begin to escalate during the coding and testing phases; thereafter, a continual high level of effort is required to maintain a poor-quality product. Distribution (B) might be typical of a medium-scale 'organic-mode' project executed with sound software engineering technique. Distribution (C) has a profile that might be consistent with applying a formal development method. The reason is that we would expect a far greater slice of the effort to be shifted to the front-end of development due to emphasis on specification and verification-driven design. This would be coupled with greater use of automated implementation tools, less reliance on traditional V&V procedures and a predicted decrease in corrective maintenance.

Distribution (D) is based on the so-called Rayleigh curve as adapted by Putnam (1978) to reflect the general characteristics of large-scale software development and maintenance. It is part of the SLIM cost estimation model, whose central equation is:

$$E = LSC^3 / (C^3 * T^4)$$

where E = effort (in person-years)
     T = development time (in years)
     C = a constant whose magnitude reflects the quality and sophistication of the development environment

The technical derivation of this equation will be found in Putnam's paper, but its main characteristic is that E is highly sensitive to T (inversely to the fourth power). Thus, compressing development time will require far greater increases in effort to compensate. However, as with any such model, care should be taken not to apply it too literally to the interpretation of reality. Thus, it is reckoned that there is a cut-off point in practice – estimated to be about 86% of nominal value in the SLIM cost model – beyond which development time cannot be reduced, regardless of how many extra resources are injected into the project. Note that Putnam's curve starts at detailed design from which there is a fairly rapid build-up of effort as development proceeds into coding and testing. The effort peaks at around product release time *Tpr* and thereafter decays more slowly during the operational and maintenance phases of the life cycle. The area under the curve to the left of *Tpr* represents approximately 40% of the total E value.

Effort distributions can be estimated in practice by firstly deciding upon the model distribution that is judged to have best fit with project characteristics. Again, past experience will be invaluable here, especially if effort distribution profiles have been recorded for previous projects of various types. The same applies to time distribution profiles across development breakdown structure. A hypothetical resource distribution estimate is given in Table 8.1 with respect to our milestone breakdown structure for a 110PM project with nominal development time of fifteen months. The last column in the table, the full-time staff requirement FTSR for each phase, is obtained by computing E/T per phase.

Table 8.1: Effort, time and staff requirement breakdowns for a 110PM, 15M project with the given hypothetical effort and development time distribution profiles

Phase	Effort dist.%	Time dist.%	E	T	FTSR
Plans & reqs.	5	10	5.5	1.5	4
Arch. design	15	20	16.5	3.0	6
Detailed design	20	20	22.0	3.0	8
Code & unit test	40	25	44.0	3.75	12
Integrate & accept.	20	25	22.0	3.75	6

In order to schedule development within phases, the granularity of work breakdown must be finer still. Thus, for example, one might take the modules in an architectural design and individually schedule their detailed design, coding and then testing. With each activity there needs to be assigned an estimate of the time required to carry it out, e.g. as obtained from estimated size of module. The two important aspects of a collection of activities to be scheduled are to identify:

which activities are orthogonal and therefore can be scheduled in parallel;
which activities are dependent on each other

Potential parallelism in scheduling can be exploited to advantage, since it provides a degree of flexibility in deciding when to initiate, or require the completion of, the activities involved. However, where there are activity dependencies, it is important to understand fully the dependency relationships that exist so that, for example, the effect of delays can be determined. A PERT network (e.g. Wiest & Levy 1977) is a directed graph representation in which each node represents a point at which a work product is expected. The arcs are labelled with the activities contributing to the generation of those work products. Furthermore, each activity is given a worst-case, expected and best-case estimate for time duration. Such a graph provides a way of determining total time lapse for the work package covered by the graph and facilitates identification of the possible effects that would ensue if a particular activity became delayed. In fact, given the difficulty of project scheduling and the high probability of changes (usually delays) to original estimates as development proceeds, it is important to be able to handle unexpected schedule changes effectively. A PERT network aids 'real-time' scheduling by enabling the consequences of an actual delay to be traced through and dependent activities to be rescheduled accordingly.

During and After Development

So far, we have been discussing resource estimation mainly as it applies to the project management planning milestone and the requirements definition milestone, when enough detail is then known about the software to obtain sufficiently reliable estimates of KLSC, etc. However, estimation should not stop there. Once a preliminary design has been carried out to arrive at a module structure for the system, more accurate estimates can be computed; indeed, the advanced, bottom-up version of the COCOMO model needs a preliminary design on which to base its calculations. Note that a preliminary design need not be the definitive architectural design of the system. In fact, a preliminary design performed to refine estimates can act as a 'trial run' providing valuable insight into the problems and possibilities associated with the internal system architecture.

Once detailed design is underway, highly accurate estimates of eventual system size, etc. can be obtained. These would hardly be used as a basis for contractual agreement, though the customer might contract to accept a series of cost and schedule refinements from the planning stage to preliminary design inclusive. However, estimates based on detailed design could be used to carry out late tuning to budget management and schedules for testing.

Cost estimation also needs to be applied to the maintenance phase of a project as well as to the mainstream development period. This is a much more problematic area of estimation for many reasons:

★ Maintenance costs can fluctuate considerably from project to project and, for a given project, from year to year. One main reason for this is that many factors that initiate post-release change to software are unpredictable – user requests, environment changes, etc.
★ Maintenance effort is a complex function of both size, type and quality of released software and the familiarity, skill, experience, etc. of the staff assigned to carry out maintenance.
★ Degradation of software quality over the maintenance part of the life

cycle will have an adverse affect on maintenance effort, but the extent to which this will occur (e.g. as a product of suspect quality is made worse by *ad hoc* modifications) and the effect it will have is very difficult to quantify.

Nevertheless, cost models like COCOMO do provide a means of maintenance cost prediction. The basic formula advanced by Boehm (1981) for computing maintenance effort ME (in PMs) is:

$$ME = E * K$$

where E (the actual development effort) is multiplied by a constant K that reflects the expected number of LSC to be added or modified over a given time period expressed as a fraction of product size. Thus, if K relates to expected annual fractional change, ME is the annual maintenance effort. ME can also be adjusted by appropriate effort multipliers to take into account some of the project factors mentioned previously.

Ultimately, project resource planning and management can only be as good as the past experience and data on which it is based. The experience gained from executing each project should be recorded in a project history document to be archived for future reference. The document will record what went well, what went wrong and why, evaluate the efficacy of new tools and techniques tried out, etc. Equally importantly, it will record relevant quantitative data connected with the project. This data should be entered into a project histories database that is maintained and continually updated precisely for the purposes of future project planning and other management-related activities. It is this database that provides the crucial input to estimation, calibration, etc. and to achieving accuracy therein.

A major implication is that measurement is an activity that must permeate the whole life cycle in order to gather the desired quantitative data. The following list is a sample of what can, and ought to, be measured, not all of it directly connected with resource management:

★ Size, effort, cost, time and staff requirement estimates and their subsequent refinements at various points during development.
★ Actual effort, time and staff requirement expended:
   per phase/activity of macroscopic breakdown of development structure;
   per component of detailed work breakdown structure, e.g. for design, code and test of each module, integration of each subsystem, system testing; for each review, inspection, etc.;
   for configuration management, quality assurance;
★ Actual LSC sizes per module, subsystem, total system.
★ Budget expenditure profile over breakdown structure; actual total cost incurred.

★ Documentation profile: amount generated per category (system, user, etc.); effort, time, cost and staff that was required.
★ Defect history: defect counts per review/work product, defect categorization (we shall return to this aspect of project measurement in Section 8.6).

In conclusion, software engineering, and project management and control in particular, must learn and improve by experience. The basic method is: *measure*, *record* and *feed into* the future.

8.3 ORGANIZING PEOPLE

Management of people partly involves motivating and guiding them in their day-to-day working environment and dealing with their needs, ambitions, personalities and personal difficulties. As such, successful management requires a great deal of subjectivity and judgement infused with an understanding of human psychology and the ability to communicate. Moreover, 'programmers' might be deemed to be a unique breed of individual working in an environment that demands its own special considerations as regards human relationships. Nevertheless, we shall concentrate mainly on organizational aspects of the software engineering work environment here.

Given that there will be a minimum of (say) four or five staff, and possibly numbers vastly in excess of this, working on a software development project, then some form of organization – that is, some form of team framework – will be needed to structure staff into effective work groups. This is necessary to avoid the chaos that would inevitably arise if staff were working more or less in isolation on a project – there would be a general lack of coordination, control and integration across the whole development effort. Furthermore, the larger the project or the larger the number of staff involved, the more severe these problems would become. Thus, it is generally acknowledged that a team approach is necessary in order to create for software personnel a disciplined, successful work environment.

A further reason for adopting team structures is that many software engineering activities require a team structure or are team oriented anyway. For example, the V&V processes of inspection and walkthrough are group activities. Also, a team framework fits in naturally with typical breakdown structures of development work. Thus, for example, it is eminently sensible to allocate the development of a complex subsystem to a group of tightly-knit, cooperating individuals rather than spreading it across an amorphous collection of largely autonomous people.

Team Functions

Figure 8.2 depicts a generalized functional model down to team level that could be adopted by an organization carrying out one or more software development projects at any given moment and practising systematic software engineering techniques. The team functions depicted in the model are as follows.

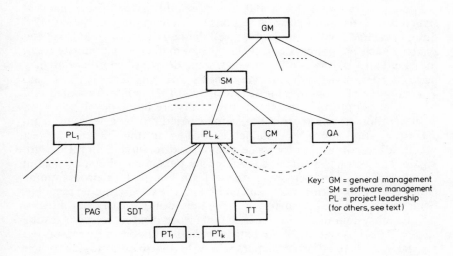

Fig. 8.2. Software personnel: a generalized functional model.

Each project has a separate project leader, answerable to general software management, who is responsible for overall control, monitoring and coordination of the project from the planning stage through to product release. The project leader will control budget, scheduling, staff requirement allocation, etc. and monitor both overall project progress and progress of individual teams or team members by holding regular reviews with team leaders. Although the project leader's function is primarily one of management, he or she might be actively involved in some of the more 'senior' activities such as project planning, requirements specification or system testing. The project leader might also participate in critical inspections and other types of formal review.

Planning, system definition and software requirements analysis is carried out by a group PAG of senior planners, analysts and requirements engineers who specialize in those functions across projects. Group size would be a function of project scale, complexity and criticality. On small software-only projects, a single person might be sufficient.

We have shown architectural design to be carried out by a separate team SDT of senior software engineers. This would almost certainly be the case on large-scale projects, but for small-scale development work, it could be allocated to a senior individual in the programming team involved. The SDT team would also be responsible for constructing integration test specifications.

Each programming team PT, the possibilities for whose internal structure is discussed below, is responsible for carrying out the detailed design, coding and testing of a well-defined functional unit of the system, such as a subsystem. Thus, programming teams mostly work independently of one another, though some degree of coordination may have to operate across teams via reviews involving team leaders, say. The number of programming teams needed (one might suffice) would be commensurate with the scale of the software being developed.

Integration testing is shown as being carried out by a separate team TT of quality control personnel according to the integration test specifications drawn up by those responsible for architectural design. Again, the testing might be conducted by personnel who specialize in that function, or by personnel drawn from the SDT or programming teams once unit testing has been completed. If a programming team has been responsible for a subsystem, say, then it might carry out integration to subsystem test before releasing its work product for later testing stages. This has one main advantage – the likelihood of increased job satisfaction, as team programmers will be less inclined to feel that their sole function is limited to designing, coding up and unit testing modules.

The configuration management CM and quality assurance QA teams are separate software management functions that interact across all projects. These management functions are discussed respectively in subsequent sections. In practice, depending on the developer organization, QA and CM may be larger in scope than Fig. 8.2 indicates, carrying out product assurance not just on software, but on hardware, etc. as well.

Team sizes, particularly programming teams, should be small – no more than eight, say. This minimizes communication problems and fosters group working or – as Weinberg (1971) calls it – 'egoless' programming, the psychology of which is that all work generated is regarded as the public property of the team, and not the private products of particular individuals. This helps reduce the problems that might otherwise arise with ego-centred individualism. (Weinberg's advice is that any 'indispensable' programmer should be dispensed with as quickly as possible!).

The above model of managerial organization and team functional responsibility is intended only to give a general appreciation of a disciplined framework for software engineering projects. The theme of Fig. 8.2 can be tailored to suit the preferred work practices and actual structures of individual organizations.

Programming Team Structures

Within a programming team, a team leader may exist – someone with a certain degree of seniority and experience – who allocates work to individual members, possibly carries out critical parts of the team's task, and generally controls and oversees the development activities of the whole team. This team structure might be termed *controlled* (by an authoritative individual) *decentralized* (tasks delegated to junior team members). As Mantei (1981) indicates, there are other possible variations on the status of individuals relative to one another within each team. For example, all control and creative development might be vested in one senior individual, with other members occupying supporting roles – the *controlled centralized* team structure. Alternatively, consensus decision-making takes place and team leadership might rotate amongst members from time to time – the *democratic decentralized* team structure, based on the 'egoless programming' concept of Weinberg (1971).

The main problem with programming teams is deciding upon the staff experience and skill-level profile of each team and the allocation of programming functions to individual members. One possibility is that team members are largely junior staff carrying out design, coding or unit-testing tasks depending on level of expertise. This means that the team's development task is distributed across a number of people who are not necessarily very experienced or skilled. This lack of experience in software personnel is not too difficult to understand. Very often, 'programming' is viewed as, and in practice actually is, the first lowly rung of a career pathway that quickly transforms 'programmers' into 'engineers' and 'analysts' and eventually management, with significant increases in status and reward along the way. Also, because promotion is rapid, programming staff turnover is high, which can create lack of continuity on long-term projects. Arguably, therefore, quality software is much more likely to result from individuals who are not only highly skilled, but who are also highly dedicated and receive sufficient motivating incentive and reward to keep them in the job at which they are best. A *chief programmer team* (CPT) organization, a particular form of controlled centralized structure, attempts to create such a work environment.

The CPT concept is described by Brooks (1975), and has been subject to experimentation in actual production environments (see Baker 1972; also 1975), from which substantial increases in productivity and reduction in defects have been documented. The pivotal member of a CPT is a *chief programmer* – a talented individual who is skilled at the craft of programming, i.e. specifying and designing non-trivial software. Thus, in a CPT, software development basically emanates from a single, highly productive expert. The functions of the other members of the team are to support this expert. These members include:

* A backup programmer: another experienced individual who can take over the chief programmer's role whenever necessary; his or her main supporting role is to verify the chief programmer's work and construct test specifications.
* A librarian: looks after the team's development support library (DSL); in effect, the librarian is the team's local 'configuration controller' (see Section 8.4).
* An editor: prepares documentation drafted by the chief and backup programmers.

A CPT might also include a project administrator, a programmer assigned to tool development and support, and other support programmers, e.g. to code up and unit test modules in large-scale designs. Note that a central theme of a CPT is to allocate members highly specific duties in such a way that the chief programmer is relieved of all tasks that would otherwise prove a burden to his or her prime function: generating high-quality software.

There are clearly many variants of team structure, and individual roles within such a structure, that could be devised. Each will have its own advantages and disadvantages. Mantei (1981) suggests that controlled centralized teams are best suited for a 'simple, well-structured programming task with rigid completion deadlines and little individual interface with the client', whereas democratic decentralized teams are most effective on a 'difficult task of considerable duration which demands personal interaction with the customer'. For controlled decentralized teams, she suggests large, reasonably straightforward, short-lived projects. For any software development organization, what is important is that it adopts its own particular team method that is found to function satisfactorily in practice. The issue is not whether to follow a team approach to software development, but how.

8.4   CONFIGURATION MANAGEMENT

Introduction

One of the vital product assurance tasks of software engineering involves keeping track of the emerging product itself, or its 'configuration'

– that is, the form in which the product exists at any stage of development as defined by various documentation (detailing requirements, specifications, designs, etc.) and actual implemented software (source and object code) as maintained in files and project development libraries. *Software configuration management* (SCM) is an integrated set of techniques designed to exercise effective control over a software product's evolving configuration so as to provide a firm basis for assuring quality of product both during its development and throughout its operational lifetime during maintenance. From this brief description, the following have already emerged:

★ SCM is a global life-cycle activity and is not localized just to (say) source and object code housekeeping. SCM therefore encompasses all life-cycle documentation as well as compilable or executable program entities.
★ SCM is closely allied to the quality assurance (QA) function. Logically, it could be regarded as being subsumed by QA. We shall prefer to regard SCM as a separate product assurance function that strongly interacts with QA.

The primary aims of CM (we shall assume the S in front of CM from now on) are captured by the following three terms:

Visibility

The software configuration must at all times be available with the appropriate degree of visibility (depending on role and status) to all those whose responsibilities demand access to it.

Traceability

The software configuration must be such that the origins of all configuration elements can be determined, e.g. so that a coded module can be traced back to a design element, the design element back to a specification element and the specification element back to a particular requirement.

Integrity

The software configuration must at all times be up to date, complete, consistent and relevant.

To realize these aims, the major activities carried out by the CM function are:

baselining and identification;
auditing;
change control;
library management;
status reporting.

We shall now examine each of these activities in turn. The reader is referred to the texts of Bersoff *et al.* (1980), Buckle (1982) and Babich (1986) for an in-depth treatment of the subject.

Baselining and Identification

In a general overview of software CM, Bersoff (1984) defines it to be 'the discipline of indentifying the configuration of a system at discrete points in time for the purpose of systematically controlling changes to the configuration and maintaining the integrity and traceability of the configuration throughout the system life cycle'. Thus, a software configuration continually evolves throughout its life cycle. If this evolution is not to be riddled with uncertainty, chaos and possible collapse, it must be 'discretized' into a sequence of well-defined steps in such a way that the software configuration, at the accomplishment of a given step, represents an absolutely secure springboard for achieving the next step. In CM terminology, the discrete states of a software configuration that chart its evolution are called *baselines*. A baseline is a secure specification of the software in its most recent state. It is secure because, once established, a baseline is placed under CM control and becomes 'frozen'. Thereafter, updates to an established baseline can be made only via the proper procedures (described later). Baselines are thus the reference points that guarantee the necessary certainty in configuration required for controlled development and maintenance.

The required baselines for a given project must be defined from the outset – that is, they must be part of the CM plan drawn up during the project planning phase. Although the baselines to be used could vary somewhat from project to project, the following is a list that would suit CM practices on most projects (the major components introduced into the configuration at each new baseline are also indicated):

Computing Subsystem Baseline

System Definition and Project Management Plan, including software development, CM and Quality Assurance plans, any of which might function as separate configuration elements.

Software Requirements Baseline

Software requirements specification, acceptance test plan, preliminary user manual.

Preliminary Design Baseline

Architectural design components (subsystems, networks, hierarchies, data objects, etc. as per design method employed), integration test plan.

Detailed Design Baseline

Specifications/designs of modules, stored data, data flows, etc. as per development method used.

Product Baseline

(i.e. unit and integration testing are complete and a working software product now exists that has passed QA and acceptance testing): Source code listings and files, relocatable object code files, executable code files and 'build maps' (arising from integration testing), test reports.

Operational Baseline

(i.e. the product has undergone any remaining system integration, has passed all installation test prodecures and is now operational): Installation and training documentation.

We have used our own terminology here. The first baseline, containing definition of system requirements and plan for project management, is sometimes called the *functional baseline*; the second baseline is also known as the *allocated baseline*. In a purely 'soft' development, these two baselines would fuse together, with the software requirements definition and project management plan being the two main configuration elements. In some baseline plans, there may be a single design baseline, or even none at all, between the allocated and product baselines. Furthermore, the product and operational baselines would merge in the release of a software-only, stand-alone product. The reason for our choice of baseline plan is that it corresponds closely with the milestone and major review point breakdown of development given in Section 7.3. The fact is that the two can be meshed together harmoniously in a way that

provides structure and discipline to product assurance in the general
software engineering framework.

Each baseline thus comprises a number of elements, or, using fairly
standard terminology, *software configuration items* (SCIs). An SCI is a
separately identifiable unit in the configuration that is subject to CM
mechanisms; it could correspond to a document or a module of code,
say. Thus, successive baselines add one or more new SCIs to the
configuration. Once an SCI has entered the configuration, it remains as
part of the configuration; this might be a slight simplification of what
happens in practice, but there is no harm in permanently retaining
under CM control all documentation generated during product development and maintenance.

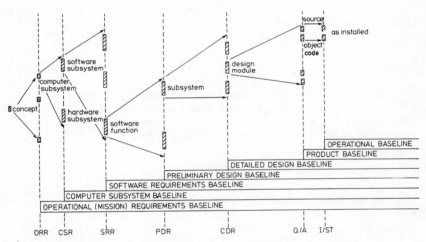

Fig. 8.3. Configuration management: baselines, configuration items and audits.

Generally, new SCIs will be related in some way to existing SCIs
introduced in previous baselines. In fact, the relationships form a
natural tree structure as Fig. 8.3 illustrates; to complete the picture, we
have included a seventh 'operational requirements baseline' that will
exist in projects where one or more computer subsystems are themselves only elements of an overall operational concept. Achieving
traceability through this complex structure necessarily requires a
method of uniquely naming SCIs in such a way that appropriate
relationships are indicated, i.e. a systematic scheme of *identification* is
needed. The actual naming scheme used does not matter – it is merely
necessary that an SCI name conveys all that is required of it to

characterize it fully in the configuration. For example, consider a source code module in the product baseline. Its CM identification should convey the following:

the name of the module;
the fact that it is source code and not, say, object code or some other type of SCI;
its version code (several versions of a module may exist);
the SCI (a module design) to which it relates in the detailed design baseline (a single design module might be implemented as several physical source code segments, as is possible with some separate compilation systems – see Section 6.9).

Auditing

Before a prospective baseline, or baseline update, is established, it must be subjected to appropriate V&V or test procedures. Once it has passed these procedures, it is placed under control of the CM authority. Verification is the process of ensuring that a prospective baseline is completely consistent with respect to the previous baseline; validation ensures that the configuration properly satisfies the original software, system or operational requirements. In fact, we have already covered the processes of verification and validation in Chapter 7. From a CM viewpoint, the sanctioning of each of the seven baselines in Fig. 8.3 corresponds to successful completion of the following product assurance checkpoints (also shown in Fig. 8.3):

ORR: operational requirements review;
CSR: computer subsystem requirements review;
SRR: software requirements review;
PDR: preliminary design review;
CDR: critical design review;
Q/AT: qualification and acceptance tests – validation against software requirements;
I/ST: integration/site tests – validation against (computer sub) system requirements;
FT: field testing – validation against operational requirements (not shown in Fig. 8.3).

CM therefore represents one of the main 'interested parties' at each of these milestone checkpoints. CM auditing might be carried out by QA or separate V&V and test teams. However, in a computer system development organization where CM is firmly established as the main product assurance function alongside Quality Assurance, the above checkpoints are fundamentally baseline audits, and CM will play a leading role in their execution. Once each new baseline, or baseline update, is established and sanctioned by the appropriate audit procedure, CM is then formally in control of it.

Baseline audit and sanctioning can thus be seen to be one of the major planks of assuring product integrity in computer system and software development. In fact, Bersoff *et al.* (1980) assert that 'life cycle management is principally baseline management'.

Change Control

As development proceeds, circumstances inevitably arise that necessitate modification to the baselined configuration. This can arise for two main reasons: either the current development phase has picked up a defect not detected at a previous baseline audit, or a requirements change has been requested by users. If such modification is not to cause loss of control by being arbitrary, unrecorded, unfollowed-through or undisseminated to those who need to be aware of the change, then it must be effected and documented in a rigorous manner. This is the function of *change control*. In order to provide an effective framework for change control, certain CM procedures (laid down in the CM plan) will be provided:

★ Firstly, a procedure for precipitating a change must be followed. Generally, this involves preparing an appropriate form or document detailing the need for the change, etc. There are two main types of form that will be used:

Change requests: a change request (CR) form will be used to detail a proposed change to requirements;

Software problem reports: a software problem report (SPR) is used during the establishment of the product and operational baselines, and during operational lifetime, to document software failures that need corrective action to be taken. It could also be used to report documentation defects, though a separate type of form might be used specifically for this purpose.

An SPR or CR received by CM is then passed on to the appropriate personnel for analysis, e.g. software developers who will assess potential schedule and budget impact of rectifying a software deficiency. The result of the analysis will be the production of a *formal change proposal* (FCP). FCPs are the documentation mechanism by which all configuration change proposals are formally specified to CM.

★ Each FCP will be submitted to the *change control authority* (CCA) – the major CM subfunction that oversees configuration changes. The FCP will detail as necessary:

a description of the proposed change and its rationale;
urgency of change;
the baselines and SCIs that will be effected;
any significant cost and schedule implications.

On receipt of an FCP, the CCA will evaluate it and either approve or disapprove it. Assuming the former, those who will be responsible for effecting the change(s) then receive authorization from the CCA to go ahead. Once a change has been accomplished and the appropriate audit procedures have passed the modified items, the CCA commit the update to the baseline(s) involved. In so doing, a new version of at least one existing baseline is generated.

The procedures associated with controlling changes to code are more complex than those associated with documentation changes. A documentation change is precipitated, formally requested, etc. in the manner described above and then, once effected, it is disseminated by CM to all those who need to be informed. This process holds, regardless of which baseline is affected. However, code changes are concentrated in the complex development phase between the design and product baselines when, particularly due to human error, oversight or mismanagement, a lot more can go wrong. Library management is an integral component of CM that acts as the code change control subfunction.

Library Management

A configuration can easily go out of control as development progresses between the detailed design and product baselines for a number of possible reasons:

★ The wrong source code version or revision of a module is released for integration testing.
★ The object code of a module does not correspond to its source (someone has performed a quick binary 'patch' without informing anyone).
★ Integration testing goes awry (the wrong object code modules are being integrated).

In order to avoid these kinds of problem, a subfunction separate from the main CM authority is needed during the integration and qualification test phases. This revolves around the management of source and object code held in a controlled development library. Of particular importance is a comprehensive identification scheme, since there may be a proliferation of different versions, and revisions to versions, of various modules in the configuration. The main features of the library management subfunction are as follows.

Up to the release of a module for integration testing, the individual or team who produced it has the responsibility of keeping track of its various versions, etc. and associated unit test data (the data might vary from version to version, for example). In a team structure incorporating a librarian, he or she will act as the team's local configuration controller.

Once a module, or possibly subsystem, has passed its inspections and testing, it is released for integration. At the same time, control of the module is transferred to library management. Thereafter, changes to an integrated module's source can be effected only by library management. Specifically, we suppose the existence of a project librarian whose function is to act as code configuration controller for the complete validation test phase, i.e. from integration through to qualification and acceptance inclusive. The project librarian's duties will include:

★ Maintaining source code modules released for integration testing and controlling all subsequent changes to them as and when necessary.
★ Generating relocatable object code modules with correct identification from compilation of source code modules.
★ Maintaining master and backup libraries of source modules and corresponding relocatable modules. These represent a code baseline in its most recent state evolving towards the product baseline as integration testing proceeds towards full software system validation.
★ Performing link-edit of relocatable modules into executable integration test entities and maintaining build maps of the latter; a test entity and its corresponding build map will need to be appropriately identified.

If a code change is needed as a result of detection of a defect during integration testing onwards, an SPR is prepared to initiate the change control procedure desribed above. Once the resulting FCP has been approved, the CCA will issue a *software change notice* authorizing the change, and there are several ways in which the defect might then be rectified:

★ The librarian performs the specified change, the change needed being sufficiently trivial to allow this.
★ A quick binary patch is authorized and made to some object code. Patches must be documented on special *software patch forms* and subsequently reflected back into source code; inherently, patches are the most dangerous form of code revision and need to be strictly controlled.

★ The modification required is serious enough to require regress back into what is effectively the unit code and test stage; software developers now take over, possibly the individual or team originally responsible for the module in question.

Changed modules must of course undergo thorough V&V and retesting before being copied as updates into master and backup libraries and subjected to repeated integration testing, etc. Naturally, if a code change requires a consequent documentation change, the latter is taken care of by existing documentation change control procedures.

The library management function serves its purpose until the product baseline is established, at which point the software product has been integration-tested to full product status and has passed its qualification test and, if appropriate, customer acceptance test.

Status Reporting

A CM database must be maintained so that at all times the following information is available:

★ The software configuration in its most recent baselined state.
★ The history of the evolution of the configuration.

Thus, whereas baselining, identification, auditing, change control and library management are primarily concerned with the security and integrity of the configuration, maintenance of a CM database provides the necessary visibility and traceability required to manage the configuration. A CM database will therefore record:

★ A catalogue of SCI's and baselines, and identification and description of each.
★ CRs, SPRs, FCPs and other CM documentation.
★ The dates on which baselines were established, updates committed.

Because of the quantity and complexity of information that needs to be recorded, a manual or 'paper' database will be inefficient and cumbersome to use. Automated support for effective CM is therefore an almost mandatory requirement.

CM Tools

An appropriate database management system with data dictionaries represents a major tool for providing automated support for CM. In the ECLIPSE 'Object Management System' OMS (Alderson *et al.* 1986) a derivation network of object hierarchies is maintained, where an 'object' is a CM element that is deemed to be created by some transformation (e.g. designing, compiling, etc.). By relating the output objects of one transformation as the input objects of others, OMS provides complete traceability of components throughout their life-cycle development, as well as the necessary mechanisms for controlling and recording the history of modifications to those components.

A tool like OMS covers the whole life cycle. Other tools have been developed to support a more specific part of the development process, particularly library management. Examples include SCCS (Source Code Control System; Rochkind 1975) and MAKE (Feldman 1979); these tools are also described in Babich (1986). SCCS is in effect a version tracker – it maintains records of revisions made to source code modules when new releases or new versions of a system are being generated in such a way that any version can be frozen, tested and subsequently reconstituted whenever desired. MAKE complements SCCS in the sense that it is a consistency controller – it ensures that object code corresponds to source code; it does this by recording the dependencies that exist amongst files so that when source code is changed, corresponding object code is recreated. It is tools such as these that help to provide the necessary degree of control over the configurational complexities of production between the design and product baselines.

8.5 MANAGING MAINTENANCE

General Issues

'Maintenance' is a blanket term used to cover all those activities associated with the reconfiguration of software that takes place once a product has passed its operational baseline. There are a number of different reasons why such 'post-release reconfiguration' may be necessary:

★ To eradicate errors that come to light during product usage, or that were known to exist anyway when the product was initially released; this is *repair* or *corrective* maintenance.
★ To modify the software to accommodate changes in factors external to, but impinging upon, it; this is *adaptive* maintenance. There exist many possible causes here, among them being alterations in:

    resources, e.g. secondary storage;
    hardware and/or operating system;
    file/database organization.

These factors are concerned with the target machine environment, changes to which are not readily predictable in general.

★ To increase the acceptability of the product; for example:

accommodate new or modified requirements;
upgrade performance, e.g. faster response times;
improve person-product interface.

This is *perfective* maintenance, or *enhancement*. Enhancement should be regarded as small-scale ongoing development. This is different from large-scale ongoing development where a system is released in prototype form and subsequently undergoes a series of radical, mainly additive alterations over an extensive time interval, resulting in a number of different versions of increasing complexity and sophistication. Such development should be regarded as 'planned evolution' rather than maintenance.

By way of analogy, some authors argue for the non-inclusion of enhancement in defining what constitutes 'maintenance'; e.g. repairing cracks in the wall of a house would certainly be regarded as maintaining the property, but converting the loft into a fifth bedroom would not be. If, however, maintenance means 'maintaining usefulness', then the analogy is less strong – presumably, the occupants of the house need a fifth bedroom, otherwise the property's usefulness (= adequacy in satisfying user requirements) will decrease; if a fifth bedroom is not needed, the modification is unnecessary 'gold plating' – something that can occur to software as well. The fact is that no complex product, particularly a large computer system, can remain static over its lifetime. In true Darwinian style, it has to evolve, be enhanced and adapt successively to changing circumstances as they arise, otherwise it will 'fall over', die and be replaced by something that should be fitter to satisfy the need at hand.

One of the most extensive analyses published of software maintenance is Lientz & Swanson (1980). Some of the main findings of their study of some 487 data processing organizations are as follows:

★ Only 16.2% organized maintenance as a separate activity from new applications development.
★ About 75% of applications were maintained by the equivalent of one full-time person or less.
★ Of the total time allocated to maintenance, just over 20% was taken up by corrective work, just under 25% by adaptive work and over 50% by perfective work; user enhancements in particular accounted on average for 42% of the total maintenance effort.
★ The six most severe problems encountered in maintaining software were judged by data processing managers to be: quality of

documentation; user demand for enhancements, etc.; competing demands for maintenance personnel time; meeting schedules; inadequate user personnel training; staff turnover in user organization.

Although specifically concerned with data processing applications software, the results obtained by Lientz & Swanson provide considerable insight into the 'maintenance problem' in that domain. It is unlikely that much has changed since their study took place; a more recent look at software maintenance can be found in IEEE (1987).

Being by far the costliest phase of the software life cycle, one of the main objectives of software engineering is to reduce maintenance costs. This can be achieved by:

(a) Reducing the need for maintenance in the first place.
(b) Building 'maintainability' into software, i.e. facilitating any maintenance that is necessary.

Achieving (a) and (b) basically revolves around quality – see Section 1.4. Quality software implies that it has been developed by properly identifying and defining requirements, systematically applying disciplined methods of specification, design, implementation, validation and verification, etc. and that this development has taken place within a controlled environment. This reduces the likelihood of perpetrating defects and helps trap as early as possible those defects that do occur; this therefore cuts down maintenance of the corrective kind in particular (essentially, point (a) above). However, expecting complex large-scale development to be defect-free is completely unrealistic; and maintenance of the adaptive and enhancing kind is virtually inevitable anyway. Thus, maintenance must be looked upon as an unavoidable activity, which leads to point (b) above.

In Section 1.4, the major characteristics of maintainability are stated as being modifiability, understandability and testability. Perhaps the most important element that affects all three characteristics is that of 'structure' (hierarchy, modularity, abstraction). Moreover, since structure is a product of specification and design, these two activities are of pivotal importance to the whole software development process. Although methods like SSADM, JSD/JSP and VDM take quite different approaches to design and the structural characteristics that software needs to possess for it to be modifiable, etc., nevertheless each method in its own way addresses the problem of building maintainability into software.

A further important point is that no software can be properly maintained if it is not adequately documented for maintenance staff, who are rarely the original development personnel. In any case, a few months' lapse is all that is needed for a programmer to return to some code that he or she was responsible for and experience difficulty in understanding what certain parts of it are supposed to be achieving, or how. Given also that there is often considerable turnover amongst programming and maintenance personnel, leading to unfamiliarity with established methods and products, the need for quality documentation to complement quality software is of paramount importance. Thus, it is essential for documentation also to be maintained and kept up to date in line with the software – which returns us to configuration management and the problems to be addressed in maintaining product integrity during the operational phase.

Post-Release Configuration Management

The essential ingredients of CM apply just as much to the operation and maintenance of a product, as to its development. However, there are certain additional factors that have to be dealt with. For example, there must be appropriate mechanisms by which users can report detected bugs, performance anomalies, changed requirements and so on, back to the developers. Similarly, once the appropriate change control procedures have taken place and the update(s) effected, users will need to be supplied with the modified software (or parts thereof) together with any documentation changes that are necessary – this applies, of course, whether the update is user or developer initiated. To help keep track of the evolution of a system configuration, Narayanaswamy & Scacchi (1987) propose the use of a special 'system configuration description language' (NuMIL), with which a system can be described as an evolving ensemble of subsystems; NuMIL is in fact a form of module interconnection language – an idea first propogated by DeRemer & Kron (1976) as an aid to 'programming in the large'.

CM is, however, potentially more complicated in the operational phase because of the possibility that a multiplicity of versions and variants of versions of a basic system may exist; i.e. there may exist concurrently a number of different operational baselines. Different *versions* of the same product may have been implemented and released, each tailored to the non-identical requirements of different sets of customers. Thus, we are defining a 'version' here as a manifestation of a product satisfying one specific set of requirements. Each version will satisfy a slightly different set of requirements, the differences arising in functionality, interface, performance or whatever. However, for each version there may exist a number of different *variants*. A set of variants will map back to some parent version but differ because they are installed in different operational environments.

Determining the scope of changes – enhancements, corrections, etc. –

to operational baselines thus applies to all user or developer initiated changes. A formal change proposal prepared for submission to the CCA (who, in granting the proposal, must then issue the appropriate authorizing documentation, e.g. a software change notice), must therefore specify as appropriate whether the change affects:

only a local variant;
a parent version, thus requiring all variants of that version to be updated;
some versions but not others;
the common, reusable parts of all versions, hence all variants, in use.

Thus, each new *revision*, or release, of the software may affect all versions, some versions, one version or one or more variants of a particular version. It is an important part of the CM baselining and identification process that exact details are maintained of the revision status and version and variant of the system installed at each operational site.

8.6 QUALITY ASSURANCE

'Quality assurance' is a term frequently used in software engineering literature, though not always with exactly the same connotation. Clearly, quality assurance has to do with attempting to ensure that a product will satisfy prespecified levels of performance, reliability, etc. and will gain user acceptance in terms of its usability. As such, therefore, it is possible to equate quality assurance partly with (i) defect prevention – applying development principles and techniques of the kind covered in previous chapters of this book, and partly with (ii) defect detection and rectification – applying the V&V processes of review, inspection etc. and machine testing: the *quality control* (QC) activities of software development.

However, there is a 'meta' level at which quality assurance can be viewed. Quality can be attained only if effective standards, techniques and procedures *exist* to be applied, are *seen to be* properly and rigorously applied, and their efficacy is continually monitored and, where necessary, improved. This represents the management function of *Quality Assurance* (QA), and we shall discuss the topic from this viewpoint.

In what follows, we shall assume that some separate QA function exists within the developer organization. It is preferable that the QA function is carried out by a specialist section of personnel who are entirely separate from other functions – effective QA rests on integrity, impartiality and independence. We can regard QA, QC (V&V and testing) and CM as the 'product assurance' disciplines of software development. The interaction between product development and product assurance is shown in Fig. 8.4 as a product engineering matrix. Although each assurance discipline is a separate function spanning the life cycle and interacting with each of its phases, there is inevitably some coupling between the assurance disciplines themselves. For example, there would probably be QA representation on the CCA (change control authority) of CM. Moreover, since QA represents the independent, audit function over the life cycle, QA might be responsible for CM audits. Also, as we shall see, QA will be strongly associated with QC activities. In fact, in some organizations, QA would be equated with QC, or QA would carry out QC, but this is not the position we are taking.

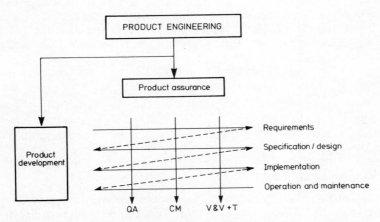

Fig. 8.4.   Product engineering = product development + product assurance.

To reiterate, QA:

(a) Requires the existence of, and where appropriate establishes, standards, conventions, techniques and procedures for software development.
(b) Verifies proper and rigorous adherence to those standards etc.
(c) Monitors their efficacy and effects improvement where necessary.

Dunn & Ullman (1982) identify three major roles of QA, one of which is captured by the above three aspects of QA, namely:

★ QA is the mechanism for creating and improving quality.

In addition:

★ QA is a process management tool: QA is a main vehicle for providing control and visibility of a project over the entire life cycle. It provides real measurement data concerning the state of health of a project – progress (work completed, resources spent), current defects and their implications, and data for refining resource and schedule estimates for the work yet to be carried out. In particular, it acts as an early warning system for possible impending problems. It can also act as resource controller, e.g. by holding back release of all funds allocated to the next phase until the previous phase has been completed to its satisfaction.

Last, but not least:

★ QA serves the interests of users. QA can act as an early warning system for customer as well as for management, e.g. if agreed schedules are likely to have to be extended. It can also be seen both as an independent validation mechanism, thus increasing user confidence in being assured of a satisfactory end-product, and as a receptacle after product release for user-suggested improvements to usability, etc.

Effective QA must be planned in advance like any other management function. The QA plan will define:

the formal reviews, inspections and audits to take place: what, when and who;
the mechanisms for defect reporting, defect removal and assurance of the latter;
other QA functions such as qualification: in-house certification of the product's validity with respect to requirements.

QA's involvement in product development is mainly effected via interaction with QC and CM activities. This can be achieved directly, e.g. QA is represented at a formal review either as moderator, secretary, inspector or observer; or indirectly, e.g. a report of a review is written by the moderator on standard QA documentation and sent to QA for analysis and archive. However, by direct involvement, QA carries out part of its audit responsibility – to ensure independently that a QC activity is performed according to specified procedural standards and that the activity functions effectively in detecting the kinds of defect appropriate to the work·product in question. Specifically in the testing phases, QA will spot check that unit and integration tests are being performed according to plan and specification. QA will also audit change control procedures during the integration phase when rigorous CM is of the utmost importance.

The reports of formal reviews and inspections, howsoever obtained, will form the basis of QA's future decision-making. It is by constructing a defects database over the history of several projects that QA can monitor the efficacy of standards and procedures, identify areas for improvement and thereby propose and justify adjustments to those standards and procedures. Thereafter, QA can monitor the effect of the introduction of a new work practice. For example, QA might propose a modification to existing inspection procedures in an attempt to increase defect detection success rate and reduce total time spent on preparation, review and follow-up. Or it might propose the introduction of a new software tool in order to achieve increases in productivity.

Areas for improvement are identified by defect classification. There are many ways in which this could be done, but one possible scheme is to classify defects:

by phase, i.e. when introduced;
by nature, e.g. if requirements, is it domain, functional, interface, exception, performance ?;
by KLSC;
by time slice (for reliability measurement);
by severity on a prespecified scale.

Note that defects also include those that are reported by users after product release. Whilst post-release defects are inevitable, the report rate is to some extent an indication of QA's own performance – QA, in particular, is responsible for, and carries out, the formal in-house validation test before product release is effected (recall that this may function as the acceptance test according to user agreement, or that separate user acceptance tests might be carried out afterwards).

Effective QA needs to be underpinned by standards. If none exists, then one of QA's first priority tasks, on being created, will be to establish appropriate standards in cooperation with software management. Enforced standards minimize unnecessary variability, and this adds its own contribution to quality improvement. A standard can exist in a variety of forms; for example:

★ Quantifiable standards: a standard can define a range, limit, tolerance or norm of some measurable attribute against which compliance can be judged.
★ Procedural standards: a standard can represent a prescribed way of doing something (rules, steps, guidelines, plans).
★ Definitional standards: a standard can represent an authoritative definition of terminology, language, etc.

In fact, procedural standards already exist for CM and QA themselves (IEEE 1983 and ANSI/IEEE 1981 respectively). There is also a definitional standard for software engineering terminology (ANSI/IEEE 1983) in which QA, for example, is defined to be: 'A planned and systematic pattern of all actions necessary to provide adequate confidence that the item or project conforms to established technical requirements.'

One problem with establishing standards for software engineering projects is the enormous diversity of the latter. Branstad & Powell (1984) give some general suggestions, but it seems likely that no detailed standards can be laid down that will be universally adoptable. In other words, detailed standards relating to QA will be a matter for each developer organization to define, document, and (with QA's help) assure compliance to and improve. Examples of such 'local' standards could be:

* A procedural standard for conducting a requirements inspection from preparation through to follow-up and completion.
* A set of coding standards for identifier construction, layout, use of commentary, etc.
* A set of standards for the preparation of design documentation in terms of structure, content, etc.
* A procedural standard for library management, identification and change control during integration and system testing.

Quality Metrics

Software metrics provide QA with a further means of obtaining quantitative data relating to quality that will enable it to track and manage quality more effectively. Software metrics – estimations of quantifiable characteristics of software – is an area that the reader can obtain general coverage on by consulting Perlis *et al.* (1981) and IEEE (1983c), for example. According to Perlis *et al.* software metrics addresses the question: 'Is it possible to define indices of merit that can support quantitative comparisons and evaluations of software and the process associated with its design, development, use, maintenance and evolution?' Two major branches of software metrics that we have already dealt with in the text are:

* Reliability: the bases of different kinds of approach to the measurement of reliability have been briefly described in Section 7.2.
* Size/effort/cost metrics relating to software development have been discussed in Section 8.2.

Obviously, the first category is relevant to QA; in particular, predictive estimations of reliability provide quality indicators prior to product release. To what extent obtaining accurate quality indicators early in the life cycle is feasible is a moot point; certainly, as we have noted above, quality can begin to be evaluated both qualitatively and quantitatively as defect data is gathered by QA from V&V reviews, inspections, etc.

One approach to assessing quality quantitatively is to decompose high-level quality characteristics of the kind comprising the 'quality tree' of Fig. 1.3 in Section 1.4 into more tangibly measurable attributes of software. This is the approach adopted by Boehm *et al.* (1978), who express their higher levels of quality characteristics ultimately in terms of a basis set of quality primitives – legibility, structuredness, consistency, etc. With each primitive they associate one or more metrics, the effectiveness of each of which is evaluated against certain criteria, e.g. the metric's quantifiability and its perceived indicativeness of the quality characteristic being measured.

In contrast to Boehm *et al.*'s approach, DeMarco (1982) takes a more global, development-oriented view of quality. DeMarco defines quality as the 'absence of spoilage', where 'spoilage' is the money and effort spent over the life cycle rectifying defects (DeMarco distinguishes defects – avoidable inadequacies – from 'bugs', which are unavoidable and the result of purely human mistakes). More specifically, DeMarco's quality metric is:

$$\frac{\text{Total cost of rectifying all defects}}{\text{Product size (in bytes, say)}}$$

Obviously, the smaller the value obtained, the better. Clearly, DeMarco's metric cannot be accurately computed until the product is at least ready for release (although it could be computed and repeatedly updated during development as defect data is collected and estimates are made of eventual product size). However, note that quality indicator computation also occurs late in development in the approach of Boehm *et al.* (1978), where quality is primarily measured in terms of source code characteristics.

Two influential past works on software metrics are McCabe (1976) and Halstead (1977). Both approaches in effect measure software 'complexity', though the former is a graph-based technique (e.g. relates to control flow complexity in a program) whereas the latter is based on counts of operators and operands in a program. Note, therefore, that the former could be applied in development phases preceding coding where specifications and designs are expressed in graphical formalisms. The usefulness of these metrics has been the subject of much scrutiny and debate over the years, but correlations have been observed between the Halstead metric and, for example, program clarity (Gordon 1979). McCabe and Halstead metrics have also been used to measure the 'psychological complexity' of software from a maintenance standpoint (Curtis *et al.* 1979). Recently, the usefulness of seven different complexity metrics, including McCabe's and Halstead's, has been assessed with respect to the maintenance task by Kafura & Reddy (1987). Their findings also indicate a good correlation between the metrics and the ease of understanding of to-be-maintained software. They also observe that complexity metrics can be used to identify improper integration of enhancements, e.g. if large increases in complexity are measured in modules peripheral to the enhancement.

Kaposi & Kitchenham (1987) have proposed a general 'architecture' for system quality that they consider is applicable to hardware, software and hybrid systems, and which consists of three main components:

* 'Transcendental' properties: properties relating to innate excellence that can be experienced but not quantified.
* Merit indices: quantities computed from subjective ratings of quality characteristics (e.g. 'appropriateness of error messages' might be rated on a scale from 0 to 10 inclusive).
* Quality factors: quantities computed from two sources of objective, repeatable measurement – 'attributes' (an attribute is not quantified but is merely designated as being present or absent; e.g. inclusion of verified, reusable components in the product) and 'metrics' (this term being specifically applied to quantities that characterize the extent to which some property is present; e.g. operand and operator counts used in the computation of Halstead's metric).

The development and success of a generalized model of system quality such as this is yet to be seen. It would seem that some quality characteristics could be assigned to either of the latter two categories, depending on preference. For example, 'readability' could be a merit index that is assessed subjectively; alternatively, it could be computed as a quality factor from (in part) the number of spaces and blank lines used to separate out various program text components. Presumably, 'meaningfulness of identifiers used' would be another property to be incorporated into computation of a readability quality factor, yet this could be only subjectively rated. This suggests that the model should be developed to permit parameter overlap between categories. Nevertheless, to paraphrase Kaposi & Kitchenham, QA is at present unable to apply tests based on objective quality measures to assess the effectiveness of its own defined procedures and standards. Their model can be seen as an attempt to provide a more effective viable framework within which QA can operate.

8.7   DOCUMENTATION

Although the activity of documenting is not itself a management process, nevertheless documentation pervades the whole life cycle and is the visibility 'glue' that holds the management process together:

★ It provides reference points for standards, procedures, plans, requirements etc.
★ It represents the 'window' on the emerging or emerged product and the track record of its development.
★ It is the indispensable material on which many activites directly depend; e.g. the V&V activities of review, inspection and audit.
★ It can describe and record what happened and why, and so provide a historical database on which future improvement can be founded.

Without appropriate quality documentation, effective project management would be impossible. Other things would be impossible too, or nearly so. All too frequently, end-users have the unenviable task of making use of a software product via documentation that is frustratingly inadequate in various ways, or even non-existent. It is also not unknown for maintenance programmers to be faced with the task of maintaining large chunks of undocumented (as well as unstructured) source code. It is not too extreme to state that undocumented, or very badly documented, software development or operational software is virtually unmanageable or 'useless' from every conceivable point of view. Quality documentation can demand just as much discipline, organization, effort and attention to detail to produce as the very software that it complements. There are three basic issues to be addressed:

How can 'documentation quality' be characterized?
How can documentation quality be assured?
What documentation needs to be produced?

Documentation Quality

Although there are many different kinds of documentation, which are discussed below, the author would like to proffer the view that documentation quality in general very closely parallels that of software quality – that is, the former can be expressed in terms very similar to the latter (see Section 1.4). The following description of documentation quality follows this analogy (the reader should try to keep track of the quality characteristics tree discussed in Section 1.4):

Documentation must above all be USEFUL; that is, it must precisely, clearly and competently serve the purpose for which it is intended.

This covers not only the usefulness of the document in its current state, but the extent to which that usefulness can be preserved if changing circumstances affect the document's content.

Current usefulness

Reliability (Integrity)

To echo what is stated in Section 8.4, a document must be up to date, complete, consistent and accurate.

Efficiency

A document's text should not occupy more space than is necessary, i.e. it should be concise (not verbose) without sacrificing clarity, and it should be relevant (not contain extraneous detail).

Usability

A reader should be able to find what he or she wants to know easily and quickly. A good interface between document and reader is essential; readers will expect to find appropriate contents descriptions, sensible headings and section numbering, indexes, cross-referencing, etc. Also, the document's 'functionality' must be tailored to the particular type of reader at which it is aimed. Thus, for example, a novice user studying a user guide would not expect to find advanced facilities described in what is supposed to be an introductory manual.

Security

Documentation should be used to convey only that information needed by people to carry out their roles effectively. For example, a user library catalogue should not give implementation details of any library modules (this would be for the user's good as much as anyone else's).

Potential usefulness

Reconfigurability

It is important that documentation can be readily adapted so that it is always up-to-date, relevant, etc.

* Documentation obviously must be understandable, otherwise bug-free changes to it will be difficult to accomplish.
* Small changes in factors which impinge upon what a document describes should not necessitate large rewrites – documentation must be easily modified by the insertion, alteration or deletion of words, sentences, paragraphs, (sub)sections, diagrams etc.
* As regards 'testability', documentation needs to be subjected to V&V (inspection, etc.) like any other product of software engineering, and its style and structure should facilitate this.

Reusability

Just as it is a waste of resources in software development to 're-invent the wheel', so it is also wasteful to redescribe it:

* Documentation should display modularity. Each (sub)section should be highly cohesive (topics should not be lumped together that were entirely separate in the first place) and (sub)sections should display a minimum of coupling (high degrees of coupling would be manifested by a lot of cross-referencing).
* Documentation must be sufficiently general. For example, suppose several customized versions of a system exist with a large common basis. It should then be possible to write documentation in a 'generic' manner so that corresponding customized versions of it can easily be generated by substitution of version-dependent features.
* Documentation should be structured so that it is easy to alter, add or remove components as circumstances demand.
* Where separate documentation describing different subsystems, say, potentially could be integrated along with those subsystems in the formation of a new product, then there should be no 'intercommunication clashing'; i.e. the separate documents should use the same terminology, diagrammatic conventions, etc.
* Documentation should be written so as to avoid reference to target – environment dependent features as much as possible. However, where non-portable features need to be described, they should be readily identifiable in the document text so that appropriate changes can be made easily. This identification might be accomplished by separating out such features into separate sections (in the manner of modularization), or by providing a list of references to their positions in the text.

As with software, a factor which underpins most of these desirable features is good structure – structure that is appropriately modular and hierarchical to facilitate the lucid description of complex topics. Indeed, the production of good documentation could be seen to be very much a mix of top-down (getting the overall structure right) and bottom-up (designing individual 'functional' units) followed by integration of the two. Naturally, some low-level topics may need to be referred to more than once, which is analogous to bottom-up procedurization.

Finally in this analogy, one reaches the 'coding' level. The elements of good writing style are well known and generally agreed upon. Browning (1984) contains a useful chapter of guidelines on documentation readability. Suffice it to say here that use of itemization and diagrams wherever possible to avoid narrative is generally beneficial for clarity, conciseness and communication of facts and ideas.

Documentation Assurance

This has already been covered! Documentation software is just as much subject to the product assurance disciplines as program software. Thus, documentation assurance is achieved by:

QA: standards, guidelines etc.;
CM: configuration control;
V&V: inspections, audits etc.

It might be added that quality will improve if staff take documentation seriously – it is often regarded as a kind of tedious add-on activity that is grudgingly accepted as being necessary, though not worth too much effort. This is a matter for developer organizations to instil into staff via training, work practices and appropriate management attitude; even better if a developer organization has a separate, specialized documentation function.

Types of Documentation

There are various kinds of documentation associated with software engineering. The following is a reasonably comprehensive classification:

Project documentation

By project documentation, we mean documentation that charts the development of software from inception through to maintenance inclusive. It should be remembered that preliminary systems analysis (feasibility studies, etc.) alone can generate a large quantity of information that needs to be recorded. General categories of documentation included under the 'project' heading are:

(a) project plans: QA, CM, V&V, test, work breakdown structure, training, installation and operation etc.;
(b) requirements definition: system, software;
(c) specification and design of system architecture;
(d) detailed designs, formal verifications;
(e) source code listings, build maps, library status accounting reports;
(f) test specifications, test reports;
(g) V&V documentation: review, inspection and audit reports;
(h) CM documentation: problem reports, change proposals, configuration status accounting reports, release notices;
(i) QA documentation: standards, procedures, defect reports.

The exact nature and form in which this documentation exists will depend on many factors, including:

★ Development method, which affects (b), (c) and (d); e.g. in an SSADM project, there would be a logical data flow diagram, function specifications (as structured English, decision trees, decision tables), data dictionary containing data flow and data store specifications, structure charts, etc.
★ Working practices, which will affect the way in which information is physically presented; e.g. standard forms (for QA, CM, V&V), programmer notebooks or 'unit development folders' recording the specification, design, coding and unit testing of modules, etc.

Installation and Operation Documentation

This documentation supplies the information necessary to install and operate a software product in a target environment. The details it provides would include:

minimum hardware resources required;
system files and databases that need to be generated;
installation parameters that steer the system's performance or configure the system to the particular characteristics of the target environment;
changes that need to be made to source code, system macros, etc. to achieve complete compatibility with the target environment;
operator instructions, e.g. what to do when the system issues various messages at the console, when to schedule the running of certain programs, how to restart the system if necessary.

procedures to follow if failure occurs, including defect reporting to developers.

User documentation

Such documentation enables users to make effective use of a product once it has been installed and is operational. It can exist in a variety of forms, amongst these being:

★ Full user manual, which will provide complete and comprehensive details of:

> purpose of product;
> each facility provided by the product and how to use and converse with it – parameters, formats, commands, menus, response sequences, etc.;
> how to recover from mistakes made and what the consequences of those mistakes will be;
> outputs generated by the product, including error messages and what they mean;
> a liberal quantity of well-thought-out, illustrative examples of usage, possibly including examples of whole sessions with the product that the user can try out;
> how to interface, if necessary, between the product and the target environment (operating system).

★ Simplified or introductory user manual, being a subset of a full user manual intended for inexperienced and casual users. This type of manual would concentrate only on those basic facilities that such users are likely ever to need.
★ Independently written and published comprehensive guide to a particular system or applications package, containing a liberal supply of examples and exercises, both theoretical (with correct answers, explanations) and practical (to be actually tried on the product) with expected responses, etc.

The importance of user documentation is not only that it exists in appropriate forms and is of good quality, but also that it is readily accessible to the people who need it. Availability can be enhanced by maintaining computerized online versions, sometimes within the product itself in the form of a 'help' subsystem.

There is relatively little literature available on the subject of documentation production. Stuart (1984) is concerned with user and reference manuals, the latter for programming languages and operating systems, for example. Browning (1984) concentrates on the production of project documentation but includes a section on user manual writing. Price (1984) deals specifically with writing manuals for 'ordinary folk' (users).

Documentation Tools

Large-scale software engineering projects generate voluminous quantities of information that need to be documented, stored, maintained and accessed. The advantages of computerization in this respect are obvious, not the least of these being the wide availability of software tools for the preparation and manipulation of text, diagrams, tables and so on. These tools include various kinds of editor, text formatters, word processors, spelling/typography checkers and graphics systems, as well as database and document retrieval systems for general storage and access purposes. Some sophisticated applications tools allow the separate facilities of word processing, graphics, database and spreadsheet (for table production), for example, to be combined in the generation of documentation. This kind of tool integration is an important consideration for software engineering environments and is discussed in the final chapter. One example of a purpose-built documentation support tool is SODOS (Horowitz & Williamson 1986a and 1986b) which has a built-in DBMS and takes an object-based view of the software life cycle; documents are stored as sets of structured components using an extended relational model.

Chapter 9

Perspectives – Past, Present and Future

> ... building software will always be hard.
> There is inherently no silver bullet.
> *F.P. Brooks Jr. (1986)*

9.1 THE PAST

As Was

The two NATO conferences on software engineering of 1968 and 1969 (Naur *et al.* 1976) were held nearly two decades ago. The problems being discussed then – for example (not in any particular order):

  problems of scale;
  what order to do things in;
  strategies and techniques to use;
  how to specify software systems;
  project planning and control;
  proliferation of unreliable software;
  gap between expectation and achievement (software never seemed to be produced on time or meet its specification, and always exceeded its estimated cost);
  etc.

are still the problems that are being grappled with today. It is recorded in the 1968 proceedings that there was general agreement amongst participants that, compared to other engineering disciplines, software engineering was at a very rudimentary stage of development. Has anything changed for the better over these past two decades?

Advances

The answer must be a definite, though qualified, YES. In a sense, some sort of past software 'crisis' was perhaps inevitable – problems invariably lead the tools and techniques that are eventually devised to solve them. However, such factors as lack of foresight, conservatism and slowness to recognize and respond to the situation, can also be identified as root causes of the problem. Fortunately, since the late 1960s, great strides have been made that have helped to crystallize the concept of software *engineering* into a well defined, constantly evolving discipline. Some areas where progress has especially been made are:

* Modelling: requirements, systems.
* Formalization: specification, verification.
* Computer science: languages, software concepts such as modularity and abstract data types.
* Method/design paradigm: structured programming, SSADM, Jackson methods, object oriented design, etc.
* Support: databases, tools, software development environments.
* Human factors: user participation, project management, person-software interface.
* Metrics: quality, reliability, costing.

Nevertheless, despite such advances, there is still no room for complacency; and if Brooks (1986) is right (see quote at head of chapter), there never can be. We shall explain and expand upon Brooks' statement in the last section.

9.2 THE PRESENT

As Is

The 'software problem' still exists today. Despite advances of the kind listed in Section 9.1, and despite a much wider awareness of, and sense of urgency about, the nature of the problem across the whole professional computing community, there is still a lot of low-quality software being produced. The spectres that continue to haunt software engineering are:

schedule slippage;
budget overrun;
unmet specifications;
inadequate performance;
unreliable systems;
costly, cascading maintenance

There are many causes of the persistence of this undesirable situation, among them being:
* Straightforward lack of a methodical, disciplined engineering approach, i.e. inexcusable sloppiness.

* Vested interest in adhering to outdated, *ad hoc*, ineffective or inappropriate tools and techniques.
* Inertia to change, e.g. change (to a new development approach, say) considered too radical or costly.
* General scepticism of the claimed benefits of modern principles and practice.
* Constant pressure to generate working code in ever-decreasing time-scales.
* Lack of proper training; general prevailing ignorance and lack of skills and expertise amongst workers and management.
* Demand for quality software products far outstripping even our *potential* ability to supply them (i.e. potential that could be realized given that other inhibiting factors in this list did not hold).

This is not to say that the situation is as bad as it used to be in all respects – simply that some of the problems are far more acute than they were, e.g. demand exceeding ability to supply. We can at least say that software engineering has at last arrived in the minds of growing numbers of software practitioners. Looking at employment opportunities in the computing press, it is 'software engineers' that commerce and industry predominantly advertise for these days, not 'programmers' or 'analysts'. In fact, rather like 'structured programming' or 'object oriented', the term 'software engineering' is in danger of being misused and abused, being applied to contexts where a narrower term would be more apposite (e.g. program design).

In order to improve and advance further the state of software engineering, there is now a tremendous amount of research and development going on, some of it on a national and international basis. Examples of this scale of enterprise are:

* In the USA, the STARS (Software Technology for Adaptable, Reliable Systems – see IEEE 1983b) program: this is a DoD research and development program designed to improve software practice, with emphasis on software reusability and the environments in which software is developed and supported. Naturally, Ada figures strongly in the program.
* In the UK, the Alvey intitiative: this is a government and industry sponsored program covering a number of 'enabling technologies' – VLSI (Very Large Scale Integration), AI (Artificial Intelligence), HI (Human Interface), etc. – and includes a major software engineering component. Also in the UK, the STARTS program (Crinean & Baguley 1986) funded by the Department of Trade and Industry has as its main objective the improvement of the real-time software industry via the adoption of appropriate software engineering principles, methods and tools.

★ In Europe, the ESPRIT project: this project, similar in nature to Alvey, is sponsored by the Council of European Communities and also receives funding from a number of multinational companies.

★ In Japan, the Fifth Generation Project: a coordinated, concerted national effort to realize AI technology as the foundation of the next generation of machines and computing environments. The concept of 'software factories' (see below) is also in prominence.

Naturally, these programs tend to possess different emphases. For example, a survey of current software engineering projects associated with the UK Alvey initiative (Alvey 1986) will reveal a definite leaning towards the formal methods area. However, the programs share one common objective and, overall, one common means of achieving it: the advancement of software practice by 'tooling up' to transform it from being a cottage industry into an efficient, productive, reliable, mechanized technology. In fact, if one was to attempt to characterize currently world-wide a common dominant theme in the advancement of software engineering, it would be 'tool building'.

Software Tools and Support Environments

Any complex development activity will be facilitated by the availability of appropriate quality tools. In preceding chapters at various points, mention has been made of tools that aid components of the software engineering process – requirements definition tools, implementation tools and testing tools to name but some. Before continuing, we should attempt to characterize more precisely what is meant by a 'software tool'. In its broadest sense, a software tool can be defined to be any software product, the purpose of which is to aid a practitioner in some area of endeavour in effecting the execution and accomplishment of his or her tasks. In the specific area of software development, Riddle & Fairley (1980) define three broad tool categories:

★ Cognitive: these tools aid intellectual activity in the analysis and construction of solutions to problems. A design method such as object-oriented design could be classed as a cognitive tool.

★ Notational: these tools provide vehicles for the communication and expression of ideas. Examples here would be the data flow graphs and structure charts of SSADM.

★ Augmentive: these tools increase the practitioner's 'reach' or effectiveness, either by providing support for tasks that would otherwise be unproductive, extremely laborious or even virtually impracticable, or by providing a new or enhanced capability in some area. Examples would be tools to execute specifications and tools to perform implementation transformations on specifications.

Note that, in this taxonomy, the first two categories are not themselves software. Moreover, the categories are by no means disjoint; for example, an augmentive software tool might contain cognitive or notational elements. However, for the purposes of this section, 'software tool' will be taken to mean a software product that is intended to aid (some part of) the software engineering process.

Clearly, the construction of quality software tools should be one of the central concerns of software engineering – in itself an interesting notion, since the very process that requires tool support is the main instrument in developing the tools needed. Inevitably, the issue of quality arises again. Quite apart from the characteristics of quality discussed in Section 1.4, a quality software tool will:

★ Serve a perceived need; automation for its own sake is rarely, if ever, beneficial.
★ Improve the productivity of users, for otherwise it will be difficult to justify the possibly high cost and effort required to develop the tool.
★ Improve the quality of products that are generated by using the tool.
★ Enhance the job satisfaction of tool users, e.g. by making the task less error-prone, less tedious, etc.

These advantages that are derivable from a well-engineered tool must be set against possible disadvantages, e.g. the high cost of the tool's development, the fact that the tool is restricted to use within a particular development environment, the possibility that the user learning/training curve will be extensive. Factors such as these must be considered in advance of tool development; and a sophisticated person-tool interface should not be used to mask the fact that the tool itself possesses little, if any, usefulness, augmentive or otherwise.

Software tools of some description have been in existence for a long while. Largely, they have been applicable to the 'back end' of program development (i.e. the implementation phase) and have included:

assemblers, compilers, preprocessors;
link-editors and loaders;
text editors (line, screen etc.);
program text beautifiers ("prettyprinters") and listers;
program analysers, e.g. to provide execution flow summaries etc.

Tools like these can be largely independent of one another, forming a useful, albeit *ad hoc*, tool-kit for the program developer, i.e. they simply 'hang' from the host operating system. However, the trend nowadays is, and will continue to be, towards more integrated tool-kits.

An integrated tool-kit is where the tools have been designed deliberately as connected components making up a larger whole – they cooperate and interface with each other cleanly, consistently and reliably, and present the same logical interface to all users, regardless of the actual host machine being used. Integrated tool-kits occur in various manifestations; here are some examples:

(a) The tool-kit might support one specific component activity of software engineering. An example would be requirements specification and SREM or PSL/PSA; each method provides a language processor, database, report generators, etc. (see Section 2.4). A non-method-specific example would be a comprehensive test tool-kit offering various forms of static and dynamic analysis, symbolic execution, test data generation, etc.

(b) Integrated tool-kits exist for particular development methods such as SSADM. The tool-kit provides tools geared to the specific characteristics of the method, enabling the (graphical and/or textual) input, editing etc. of specifications, designs and other associated documentation, plus other appropriate tools for transforming designs to source code, say. Such a 'development method' tool-kit could form the front end to a *programming support environment* (PSE).

(c) An example of an integrated programming support environment is CEDAR (Teitelman 1985), comprising sophisticated graphics, editing and documentation preparation facilities, as well as tools for program development and debugging. Although not strictly an 'integrated' support environment, nevertheless the rich supply of separate software tools for program development, document preparation and such like that are an established part of the Unix system environment represents an excellent example of a widely available coherent, and eminently successful, tool-kit – the 'programmer's workbench' PWB (Ivie 1977).

(d) Some tool-kits support the whole of software development from specification to executable programs according to a particular development approach. Two contrasting examples are

☆ 4GL systems or application generators, particularly suited to database and data processing applications (see Section 2.4).

☆ Formal development environments, typically comprising specification language processor, verification condition generator and theorem prover (see Section 5.4).

(e) On a larger scale than Unix/PWB is the envisaged Ada Programming Support Environment (APSE – see McDermid & Ripken 1984). As well as comprising an Ada compiler, editors, tools for cross development work, testing/debugging tools, specification tools, etc., an APSE would need a comprehensive set of tools to implement and manage Ada's sophisticated program library support. These latter tools would facilitate:

the creation of new libraries;
the addition, recompilation and deletion of library components;
the transfer of components from one library to another;
inspection of library contents and status accounting;
revision/version control.

Many of these functions are of course essential components of source and object code configuration management.

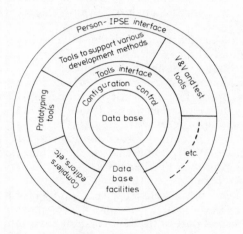

Fig. 9.1. One possible overall IPSE architecture.

The ultimate concept in support environments is the IPSE – *Integrated Project Support Environment* – which provides support for the whole software life cycle, and is neither development method specific, nor language specific (though a language like Ada might play a significant role). Figure 9.1 gives an impression of the possible outline architecture of an IPSE. At the 'outer edge' of an IPSE is the person-IPSE interface, which gives users the appropriate degree of access to, and visibility of, IPSE facilities and IPSE data, be they tool-users, managers, analysts, designers, programers or whoever. At the heart of the IPSE lies a database that will contain all deliverables relevant to a particular project (requirements, specifications, designs, coded modules, etc.). Naturally, the database will be supported by the usual set of facilities – query language, data dictionaries, etc. – that are standard features of data management systems. Those involved in tool-building and usage will manipulate the database via a standard tools interface, which itself will interact with an inner subsystem providing essential configuration control on constituents of the database. The available tools themselves will be split up into a number of different subsystems – an APSE, say, tool-kits for different development methods, a prototyping subsystem, and so on. Naturally, it would be expected that in the course of time an IPSE would grow as more and more tools become available and are added to it. Indeed, because of the potentially vast size of an IPSE, a distributed implementation is likely to be more cost-effective than a centralized one. A further advantage of a distributed IPSE would be that it would enable multi-site working on a given project at workstations spread over a geographically wide area. An IPSE would be the production machine driving a 'software factory' – a manufacturing concern cost-effectively, productively generating high-quality software products. However, as Dell (1986) points out, introducing an IPSE into the work environment is not necessarily an easy task. As well as requiring a lot of computing power, senior management need to be made aware of exactly what an IPSE is intended to do, and users need hands-on experience and familiarity with its underlying concepts; perhaps more importantly, an IPSE must be seen as a tool only – it cannot create quality practices and procedures where they do not exist already.

A number of projects are already well underway in developing 'first and second-generation' IPSEs that should become available in the late 1980s. A first-generation IPSE is based around existing tools provided by an established operating system such as Unix. Second-generation IPSEs will be centred on a database (as described above and illustrated in Fig. 9.1), and third-generation IPSEs are envisaged as incorporating AI components. The ECLIPSE project (Hutchison & Walpole 1986) is one example of the effort being put into IPSE development, as is the ASPECT project; both are reported upon in McDermid (1985) along with other support environments. Other examples of program development and software engineering support tools and environments can be found in Huenke (1981) and ACM (1984).

9.3 THE FUTURE

As Might Be

Arguably (and pessimistically), a software crisis of some sort will always exist, given that the past and present have set a pattern for the future. Software practice will always lag behind in exploiting the technologies – hardware, languages, development techniques – of whatever next generation is just around the corner. If one accepts this future perspective, then one might well comment on the irony that any book such as this is discussing present solutions to what are really yesterday's problems that are likely still to be plaguing us tomorrow when the next technological leap occurs. Optimistically, however, given the current degree of awareness of the importance of software engineering and the research, development and educational effort being put into its advance and promulgation, this augurs well for the future, and one can look forward with greater confidence to the arrival and establishment of fifth-generation technologies. Yet it is a brave person who predicts how long it will be before users are articulating their requirements to 'intelligent' front-end analysis tools, programmers at large are using functional languages to develop software verified (mainly automatically) against formal specifications, and software practitioners in general are using large distributed IPSEs.

Some of the main areas in which the advancement of software engineering will be concentrated in the next decade or more are:

* Framework: increasing adaptation of the traditional life-cycle structure and its associated techniques (top-down decomposition, etc.) using more effective models on which to base software development, e.g. incremental, evolutionary/prototyping approaches.
* Formal methods: further development of formal specification and verification and their scaling up to cope with large 'real-life' problems, particularly via increased tool support.
* Metrics: improved methods for estimating cost, and software quality and reliability.
* Reuse: software reusability will represent a major way of effecting desperately needed increases in productivity, if software practice is going to have any chance of coping with the demand for software products that will continue to escalate in the next decade.
* Management: more reliable, more effective techniques for managing the life cycle in all respects.
* Tool support: increased provision of automated software tools for supporting all activities of software engineering, both on an individual basis and as integrated support environments; again, increase in productivity is the key objective.
* Languages: greater emphasis on the development and use of functional and other kinds of non-imperative language, particularly (amongst other benefits) with respect to their far better fit with formal methods of specification and verification.
* Implementation: increased exploitation of data flow and parallel architectures, and of networks and distributed implementations.
* Person-product interface: continuing improvements in the human-machine interface and the means by which people can articulate their problems, requirements and desired services to machines.

★ Applied technologies: application of other techniques, e.g. AI, to the general enhancement of software engineering.

The relationship between AI and software engineering is worth examining, particularly in the light of the Fifth Generation project currently underway in Japan.

AI and Software Engineering

The subject of artificial intelligence tends to promote heated debate, polarizing people into two opposing camps – those vociferously for it, and those who strongly doubt whether it has delivered, or ever will deliver, the goods it has promised. Parnas (1985) distinguishes two kinds of AI:

★ Software that solves problems that originally only people could solve.
★ Software that solves problems (via knowledge bases, heuristics, inferential reasoning, etc.) in a way that mimics how people solve problems.

An example in the first category would be a speech recognition system; the second category is occupied by *expert systems*. Whilst it is difficult to see how the first example could contribute *fundamentally* to software egineering – it could be part of an exotic user interface, but that does not in itself advance software engineering – expert systems hold greater promise. The reader who wishes to know more about expert systems without getting immersed in a textbook is recommended to read Hayes-Roth (1984).

Simon (1986) is in no doubt about AI's relationship with software engineering: '. . . software engineering and Artificial Intelligence are either going to have to join hands or software engineering people are going to have to reinvent artifical intelligence'; i.e. the two disciplines need each other. Simon sees their progress as complementary and mutually enriching. Certainly, AI techniques have already filtered into software engineering. Frenkel (1985) takes a look at how expert systems technology is being applied in the development cycle to improve productivity, including compiler code generation and real-time debugging.

Probably the first really significant advance in the application of knowledge representation and expert system AI to software engineering will be in the area of requirements engineering. Borgida *et al.* (1985) argue for a requirements method that constructs dynamic world models; they describe a language (RML) for requirements specification that has been influenced by AI knowledge representation techniques. More ambitiously, user requirements are a fertile field for expert system technology with their fuzziness, inconsistencies, conflicts, ambiguities, etc. Thus, we can envisage intelligent requirements engineering tools conversing with users, extracting and analysing their requirements, examining the implications, and identifying and (where feasible) resolving conflicts, contradictions and impossibilities, possibly via some kind of direct requirements execution. This future scenario is articulated by Kowalski (1984). Brooks (1986) takes a slightly different view of what the main contribution of expert systems will be – '. . . to put at the service of the inexperienced programmer the experience and accumulated wisdom of the best programmers'.

Whatever contribution AI makes to software engineering in the future, it is hard not to disagree with the other half of Simon's (1986) view. AI software production needs software engineering . . . but in some tailored form? There has been surprisingly little written about this topic. Mostow (1985) states that 'the development of an AI program can be viewed as an accelerated form of perfective maintenance involving frequent specification changes'. The general approach is akin to implementing before specifying. Partridge (1986) examines in depth the differences between AI and non-AI software engineering, which are mainly caused by the accentuation of certain characteristics of problems in the AI domain compared to the non-AI domain, e.g. AI problems tend not to be completely specifiable, are performance-mode oriented (concerned with the HOW of human behaviour), and are tightly coupled to context (problem environment), etc. Partridge sees machine learning (self-adaptive software), 'step-wise abstraction' (moving from the concreteness of behaviourally inadequate programs to more abstract representations – the reverse transformation of conventional software engineering approaches) and 'structured incremental programming' as possible elements of the required software engineering paradigm for AI.

The Way Forward – Two Views

In a paper likely to become a minor classic in the footsteps of his earlier work (Brooks 1975), Brooks' view of the future for software engineering (Brooks 1986) is captured in the quote at the start of this chapter. Translated, it means that there is not, and never will be, any single 'magic solution' (silver bullet) to the software crisis (the werewolf). The main reason is the inherent conceptual complexity of software – its 'essence' – and the difficulty involved in specifying, designing and testing its abstract structures. Past breakthroughs have really only tackled the 'accidents' of software engineering, e.g. the representation of abstract structures and the speed and time constraints imposed by machines. Brooks considers that current developments such as Ada, AI, object-oriented programming, tools and environments, etc. still mainly address the accidental problems left in software engineering and will have a marginal effect on the essential ones, which is where the attack should be concentrated. However, depite there being no silver bullet, Brooks sees four major fronts on which the complex essence of software can be tackled:

★ The software marketplace, i.e. buy existing software instead of building it (which is cheaper as well as easier); here, the essence is tackled by avoiding the need to construct software through customized utilization of available generalized packages.
★ Adopt approaches and tools for prototyping and iterative refinement of requirements; requirements are the hardest part of any system to get right and have a crippling effect if they are later found to be defective.
★ Software should be 'grown' rather than 'built' because its conceptual structures are too complex to specify accurately in advance and build without defect. Brooks argues for a top-down approach to software growing as it facilitates backtracking and early prototyping.
★ Nurture great designers (Brooks suggests ways in which organizations can do this) – it is only they who possess the inspirational creativity needed to construct great designs.

B.W. Boehm, another highly respected figure in the software engineering arena, focuses on the enormous cost of software production in Boehm (1986); example projection – software cost in the USA will be of the order of $125 billion by 1990. Basically, Boehm sees productivity as the key issue and advances a 'software productivity improvement opportunity tree' to define ways in which real gains in productivity can be achieved. In all, he identifies six different 'opportunities':

★ Make people more effective with appropriate incentives, working conditions, etc.
★ Make production steps more efficient via tools, support environments, work stations, etc.
★ Eliminate steps, e.g. via automatic programming – generating programs automatically from their specifications (see Balzer 1985).
★ Eliminate rework by making the right decisions first time with the aid of expert systems, for example, or controlling the effect of requirements volatility through incremental development.
★ Write less code: reusability!
★ Build simpler products, i.e. avoid software 'gold-plating' – overburdening the product with unnecessary functionality.

There is largely common ground underlying the views of Brooks and Boehm. The lessening of the 'software problem' in future years will surely come from improvements in at least some of the areas they have between them identified.

Epilogue

There is no doubt that software engineering is alive, reasonably well and making significant inroads into some of the real, very difficult problems that arise in large-scale software development. There is also no doubt that the impetus built up over the last decade or so will continue to grow, and the problems will be tackled with increasing vigour and effectiveness as further advances are made. We have already indicated above that productivity will be one of the key issues, perhaps *the* key issue, as the gap between demand and ability to supply grows ever wider. The situation is exacerbated by the lack of qualified personnel with the right skills. Boehm & Standish (1983) estimate that, by 1990, the USA could be suffering a shortfall of 800 000–1 000 000 software personnel. Thus, the success or failure of software engineering, probably more than anything else, depends upon appropriate education and training, as well as the will to try new principles and methods where others have manifestly failed in the past. It is hoped that this book has made its own small contribution to the educational objective.

Appendix

Case Study

This appendix consolidates the various major components of the case study developed in the text. For ease of reference, the section of the text in which each component appears is also indicated.

A.1 PROBLEM DESCRIPTION (SECTION 2.1)

Outline Scenario

The University's computer science department possesses a Nirvana hypermini that can support a large number of online users. The machine is used primarily for teaching purposes, especially to support Pascal programming courses which form part of several first-year undergraduate degree programmes. The Pascal system implemented on the Nirvana, named PATSY (PAscal Teaching SYstem), includes a special-purpose screen editor. The editor accepts Pascal source online, generates an internal, tokenized representation (from which the original source is easily recompiled), and in so doing carries out simple low-level syntax checking. Tokenized forms, correct or otherwise, whether of partial or complete programs, are automatically saved by PATSY for future editing. Complete tokenized programs can be translated down to machine code by the main compiler and optionally run if a clean compilation is obtained.

At a departmental staff meeting, it is decided that it would be worthwhile developing a system to monitor student performance and usage of PATSY.

Brief Analysis

★ At present, there is absolutely no feedback about usage of the PATSY system, either in general terms (e.g. patterns of loading throughout the day, or on different days of the week), or specifically with respect to individual students. The latter is seen as particularly desirable when judging a student's perceived performance (via coursework, say) against his or her actual usage of the system. The only way to obtain the desired information would be by implementing a 'big brother' monitoring system on the Nirvana.

★ The new system, codenamed SUMS (Student Usage Monitor System), would obviously impose additional overheads on an already heavily used machine. However, estimates suggest that SUMS will be relatively small (at most a few thousand lines of high-level source code) and could be scheduled to run, in part, at times of low volume Nirvana usage.

★ SUMS will clearly need to interact with the PATSY system, which will therefore have to be modified with possible consequent degradation in its performance. However, the source code of PATSY (written largely in Pascal) is available for maintenance purposes; and the modifications required are envisaged as being relatively minor. Furthermore, any performance degradation is likely to be apparent only during peak loads, and is considered to be worth the price.

★ The development task, which is completely 'soft' and requires no additional equipment, is estimated to be about 1 person-year. Two of the department's research assistants are requested to carry out the development work in order that it is completed well before the start of the next academic session, when the department wants SUMS operational. The research assistants involved are capable, experienced with Pascal and STOPS – the Nirvana's Single Tasking OPerating System – and familiar with the idiosyncracies of the Nirvana and PATSY.

A.2 EXAMPLE REQUIREMENTS FOR THE SUMS SYSTEM (SECTION 2.3)

Real World Domain – JSD Modelling

Entities and actions

Entity type STUDENT

REGISTER {become an allowed user of the Nirvana machine in general, and hence the PATSY system in particular}
  name, date, department, course, log_on_code
TERMINATE {cease to be an allowed user of the Nirvana machine}
  name, date, log_on_code
ENTER {initiate use of PATSY}
  log_on_code, date, time
QUIT {leave PATSY}
  log_on_code, date, time

CREATE {create a new program within the PATSY system}
    log_on_code, prog_idr, date
EDIT {use the PATSY editor to alter an existing program}
    log_on_code, prog_idr, date
COMPILE {request a program to be compiled}
    log_on_code, prog_idr, date
RUN {request a cleanly compiled program to be executed}
    log_on_code, prog_idr, date
DELETE {erase a program from the PATSY system}
    log_on_code, prog_idr, date

Entity type PROGRAM

CREATE {the program comes into existence via use of the PATSY
        editor}
    log_on_code, prog_idr, date
DELETE {the program is erased from the PATSY system}
    log_on_code, prog_idr, date
COMPILE {the program is compiled}
    log_on_code, prog_idr, date
RUN {the program is executed}
    log_on_code, prog_idr, date
EDIT {the program is modified}
    log_on_code, prog_idr, date

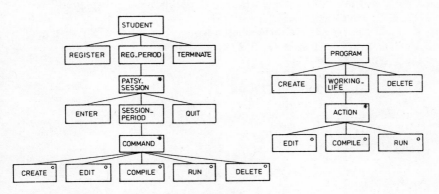

Fig. A.1. Entity structures for STUDENT and PROGRAM.

Time-Ordered Entity Structures

Four functions

function FR1 **is**
  descr
    "Whenever a student quits PATSY, the totals of compilations
    and runs performed during that session by the student, together
    with the session time length, are to be appended to a file
    QLOG_LIST"
  on STUDENT.QUIT =>
    write STUDENT.PSN_INFO **asin** OUTR1 **to** QLOG_LIST
    where PSN_INFO **is**
      {log_on_code,
        NCOMPS   **descr** "the no. of compilations initiated by the
                              student during the PATSY session just
                              quit",
        NRUNS   **descr** "the number of executions initiated . . .
                              ditto . . . ",
        PS_LENGTH **descr** "the length of the PATSY session just
                              quit in minutes and seconds"
      }
  constraints PR1
end FR1;

function FR2 **is**
  descr
    "On enquiry from a terminal, the number of students currently
    within PATSY, and who they are, should be displayed"
  on E_ENQ **asin** INR1 **from** USER =>
    let SN **be** STUDENT[N] **selectedby** entered_PATSY = **true**
    write E_DSP **asin** OUTR2 **to** USER
    where E_DSP **is**
      {N, SN.LOGINFO
        where LOGINFO **is**
          {name, dept, course, log_on_code}
      }
  constraints PR2
end FR2;

function FR3 **is**
  descr
    "On request, automatically delete all program files not accessed
    within the last 180 days. List to a file FLUSH_REP the names
    and last access dates of all such files deleted. The files listed
    should be grouped according to student owner, the latter being
    identified by log_on_code. Groups should be lexicographically
    ordered by log_on_code, and program file names within each
    group should be ordered by decreasing last access date"
  on F_REQ **asin** INR2 **from** USER =>
    let
      SP **be** PROGRAM **selectedby**
        (F_REQ.date − last_access_date)>180
      GSP **be** SP **groupedby** log_on_code
    do SP.DELETE
    write F_RPT **asin** OUTR3 **to** FLUSH_REP
    where F_RPT **is**
      GSP.GRP_DESCR **orderedby** (+)LOC
        where GRP_DESCR **is**
          {#LOC,
           PROGSET.PROG_DESCR
             orderedby (−)last_access_date
           where PROG_DESCR **is**
             {prog_idr, last_access_date}
        }
  constraints PR3
end FR3;

function FR4 **is**
  descr
    "At the end of each month, print out certain details of each student currently registered on the Nirvana machine. Per student, these details are to comprise:
      – the student's name, course and log_on_code;
      – the total number of compilations, edits and runs initiated, and total PATSY time consumed, during the past month;
      – the names, lexicographically ordered, of all program files owned by the student.
    These details are to be alphabetically ordered by student name"
  on TM **asin** INR3 **is monthly** =>
    let GPROGS **be all** PROGRAM **groupedby** log_on_code
    write MSP_RPT **asin** OUTR4 **to** PRINTER
    where MSP_RPT **is**
      all STUDENT.ST_DETAILS **orderedby** (+)name
      where ST_DETAILS **is**
        {name, course, log_on_code,
        NCOMPS **descr** "total no. of compilations initiated by student during the last time grain interval",
        NRUNS **descr** "total number of executions initiated ... ditto ... ",
        TP_TIME **descr** "total amount of time spent in PATSY during ... ditto ... ",
        (GPROGS#log_on_code).prog_idr
         orderedby (+)prog_idr
        }
  constraints PR4
  end FR4;

A.3 SUMS SPECIFICATION

JSD Model Processes (Section 3.7)

Real-world connection

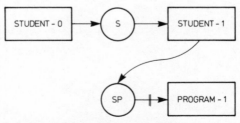

Fig. A.2. Connection of model processes to real world.

Process texts

STUDENT–1 **seq**
  read S;
  REGISTER; read S;
  REG_PERIOD **itr while** (not terminate)
    PATSY_SESSION **seq**
      ENTER; read S;
      SESSION_PERIOD **itr while** (not quit)
        COMMAND **sel** (create)
          CREATE; write CREATE to SP[prog_idr]; read S;
        COMMAND **alt** (edit)
          EDIT; write EDIT to SP[prog_idr]; read S;
        COMMAND **alt** (compile)
          COMPILE; write COMPILE to SP[prog_idr]; read S;
        COMMAND **alt** (run)
          RUN; write RUN to SP[prog_idr]; read S;
        COMMAND **alt** (delete)
          DELETE; write DELETE to SP[prog_idr]; read S;
        COMMAND **end**
      SESSION_PERIOD **end**
      QUIT; read S;
    PATSY_SESSION **end**
  REG_PERIOD **end**
  TERMINATE;
STUDENT–1 **end**

PROGRAM–1 **seq**
  read SP;
  CREATE; read SP;
  WORKING_LIFE **itr while** (not delete)
    ACTION **sel** (edit)
      EDIT; read SP;
    ACTION **alt** (compile)
      COMPILE; read SP;
    ACTION **alt** (run)
      RUN; read SP;
    ACTION **end**
  WORKING_LIFE **end**
  DELETE
PROGRAM–1 **end**

JSD Network with Functions (Section 3.8)

(Note: data stream PSN_INFO realizes requirement FR1;
      ENLISTER realizes requirement FR2;

FLUSH realizes requirement FR3;
REPORTER and STUDENT–2 realize requirement FR4.)

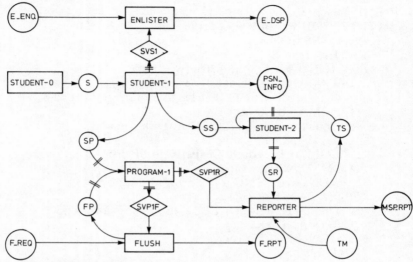

Fig. A.3. The SUMS system network.

A.4 EXAMPLES OF FUNCTION DESIGN

Requirement FR1 (Section 3.8)

(Text of STUDENT–1 elaborated to accommodate FR1 as an embedded function.)

```
STUDENT–1 seq
  read S;
  REGISTER; read S;
  REG_PERIOD itr while (not terminate)
    PATSY_SESSION seq
      ENTER seq
        entertime := ENTER.time;
        ncomps := 0; nruns := 0;
      ENTER end
      read S;
      SESSION_PERIOD itr while (not quit)
        COMMAND sel (create)
          CREATE; write CREATE to SP[prog_idr]; read S;
        COMMAND alt (edit)
          EDIT; write EDIT to SP[prog_idr]; read S;
        COMMAND alt (compile)
          COMPILE seq
            ncomps := ncomps + 1;
          COMPILE end
          write COMPILE to SP[prog_idr];
          read S;
        COMMAND alt (run)
          RUN seq
            nruns := nruns + 1;
          RUN end
          write RUN to SP[prog_idr];
          read S;
        COMMAND alt (delete)
          DELETE; write DELETE to SP[prog_idr]; read S;
        COMMAND end
      SESSION_PERIOD end
      QUIT seq
        sessionlength := QUIT.time − entertime;
        write log_on_code, ncomps, nruns, sessionlength to
        PSN_INFO;
      QUIT end
          read S;
    PATSY_SESSION end
  REG_PERIOD end
  TERMINATE;
STUDENT–1 end
```

Part of Requirement FR4 (Section 3.9)

(JSP design of STUDENT–2 : structure and operations.)

1. read SS&TS	6. totmptime := 0
2. write SR_REC to SR	7. totmcomps := totmcomps + ncomps
3. totmcomps := 0	8. totmedits := totmedits + nedits
4. totmedits := 0	9. totmruns := totmruns + nruns
5. totmruns := 0	10. totmptime := totmptime + ptime

```
STUDENT–2 seq
  read SS&TS;
  STUDENT–2_BODY itr {for lifespan of system}
    cMONTH_BATCH seq
      totmcomps := 0; totmedits := 0;
      totmruns := 0; totmptime := 0;
      cSS_BATCH itr while (not TS message)
        cSS_REC seq
          totmcomps := totmcomps + ncomps;
          totmedits := totmedits + nedits;
          totmruns := totmruns + nruns;
          totmptime := totmptime + ptime;
          read SS&TS;
        cSS_REC end
      cSS_BATCH end
      cTSgSR_REC seq
        write SR_REC to SR; read SS&TS;
      cTSgSR_REC end
    cMONTH_BATCH end
  STUDENT–2_BODY end
STUDENT–2 end
```

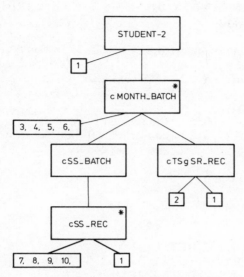

Fig. A.4. Structure of STUDENT–2 with operations allocated.

Requirement FR3 (Section 3.9)

(JSP design of FLUSH – structure text.)

```
FLUSH seq
  read F_REQ;
  FLUSH_BODY itr {for the lifespan of the system}          (a)
    cFL_RECgF_REP itr while (not end of log_on_codes)       (b)
      gF_SGROUP seq
        write S_HEADER to F_RPT;
        getsv(P1F);                                         (c)
        gD_BATCH itr while (not end of P1Fs)                (c)
          cP1FgD_REC&DELETE seq
            write P1F_details to F_RPT;
            write DELETE to FP[progidr];
            getsv(P1F);                                     (c)
          cP1FgD_REC&DELETE end
        gD_BATCH end
      gF_SGROUP end
    cFL_RECgF_REP end
    read F_REQ;
  FLUSH_BODY end
FLUSH end
```

A.5 IMPLEMENTATION OF SUMS SYSTEM JSD/JSP SPECIFICATION

(a) Pascal Encoding of Inverted STUDENT–2 (Section 6.6)

```
procedure sSTUDENT2(SSANDTSREC:SSANDTS;                    •
                         varSVS12      :STUDENTSTATEVECTOR);
    var SRREC : SR;
    label 1001, 1002, 1003,    {the resume points}
        47, 48, 49,            {concerned with loop destructuring}
        555;                   {end of procedure}
begin
  with SVS12 do begin
  case TPS2 of
    1: goto 1001; 2: goto 1002; 3: goto 1003
  end;
    1001:
    47: {STUDENT–2_BODY itr}
      TOTMCOMPS := 0; TOTMEDITS := 0;
      TOTMRUNS := 0; TOTMPTIME := 0;
        48: {cSS_BATCH itr}
          if SSANDTSREC.LOC_OR_TSM = TSRECMARK then
                                                    goto 49;
          with SSANDTSREC do begin
            TOTMCOMPS := TOTMCOMPS + NCOMPS;
            TOTMEDITS := TOTMEDITS + NEDITS;
            TOTMRUNS := TOTMRUNS + NRUNS;
            TOTMPTIME := TOTMPTIME + PTIME
          end;
          TPS2 := 2; goto 555;
          1002: {cSS_BATCH end} goto 48;
    49: with SRREC do begin
            SRLOC := LOC;
            SRTOTMCOMPS := TOTMCOMPS;
            SRTOTMEDITS := TOTMEDITS;
            SRTOTMRUNS := TOTMRUNS;
            SRTOTMPTIME := TOTMPTIME
          end;
          write (SRDATASTREAM, SRREC);
          TPS2 := 3; goto 55;
    1003: {STUDENT–2_BODY end} goto 47;
    555;
    end
  end {sSTUDENT2};
```

We have assumed the following global declarations:

```
const TSRECMARK = ... ; {depends on type LOGONCODE}
type
LOGONCODE ... {some suitable representation} ... ;
STUDENTSTATEVECTOR =
  record
    . . .
    LOC : LOGONCODE;
    TPS2 : 1 . . 3;
    TOTMCOMPS, TOTMEDITS, TOTMRUNS, TOTMPTIME :
    integer;
    . . .
  end;
SSANDTS =
  record
    LOC_OR_TSM : LOGONCODE;
    NCOMPS, NEDITS, NRUNS, PTIME : integer
  end;
SR =
  record
    SRLOC : LOGONCODE;
    SRTOTMCOMPS, SRTOTMEDITS, SRTOTMRUNS,
    SRTOTMPTIME : integer
  end;
var SRDATASTREAM : file of SR;
```

In addition, we have assumed that a TS message is distinguished from an SS message by the LOC_OR_TSM field being set to a special value (TSRECMARK) – the values of the other four fields in this instance are immaterial.

(b)Implementation Diagram of Complete System (Section 6.7)

(Note: system segments W and Y are online, X and Z are batch.)

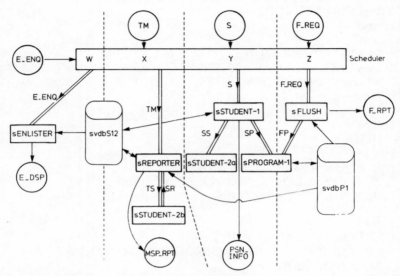

Fig. A.5.   An implementation of the SUMS system.

A.6 TEST AND VALIDATION – ONE POSSIBLE APPROACH (SECTION 7.4)

(Phase MO)

★ Unit test sSTUDENT–1 with trivial stubs for sSTUDENT–2a and sPROGRAM–1 using carefully constructed test input representative of datastream S. The test driver could be a small program along the following lines:

```
read(S_REC)
while not at end of test stream do
    sSTUDENT–1 (S_REC)
enddo
inspect svdbS12 database
```

The svdbS12 database need exist only as a simplified version of its eventual realization. If this is the case, the implementation of *loadsv* and *storesv* called within sSTUDENT–1 will be different to their eventual form.

* Unit test sSTUDENT–2a with a representative SS datastream. The test driver, and other comments, are similar to (a).
* Unit test sPROGRAM–1 with a representative SP datastream. Again, the test driver is similar to (a) and (b). The same comments apply here to the svdbP1 database as to the svdbS12 database.
* Integrate the three modules and exercise via a test driver with a representative S datastream followed by inspection of the two databases.

(Phase EN)
Provided that a suitable svdbS12 test database exists (the one generated in Phase MO could be utilized), sENLISTER can be unit tested. The test driver for sENLISTER need only call sENLISTER once.

(Phase FL)
Similarly for the svdbP1 database and sFLUSH. sFLUSH can function as its own test driver, with a trivial stub for sPROGRAM–1 that, say, simply outputs FP messages transmitted to it. Later, the tested sPROGRAM–1 and sFLUSH can be integrated – now we also need to inspect the svdbP1 database to check that DELETE actions have been properly effected.

(Phase LS)
When segments W and Y of the system have been thoroughly tested and debugged, they can be integrated into the PATSY system itself (recall that these two components represent the online portion of the SUMS system). This will also exercise the modified fragments of PATSY that support this online component. The net result will be a subsystem test under live conditions. If simplified databases are in use and would be unable to cope with the possible demands of live conditions, this subsystem test must wait until the actual database package has been designed, implemented and tested.

(Phase MR)
sSTUDENT–2b is simple enough to be tested along with sREPORTER. sREPORTER will function as its own test driver. Suitable test databases for svdbS12 and svdbP1 will be needed.

(Phase DB)
At some point the two actual database implementations must be fully tested. The minimum set of access primitives that need to be exercised in both cases will be:

createsv (see below)
deletesv (see below)
getsv
loadsv
storesv

The primitives *createsv* and *deletesv* are needed respectively for state vectors to be created (students by REGISTER, programs by CREATE) and deleted (students by DEREGISTER, programs by DELETE). These primitives can be inserted into model subprograms at the appropriate entity action points.

The two databases can be implemented and exercised in parallel. The test of each database is in effect the test of an encapsulated data object. Each module of primitives needs to be exercised as fully as possible by test driver programs and specially constructed test data.

(Phase SX)

Full system test will be needed on actual databases. It will be necessary to run sFLUSH live with PATSY to check that the operating system is handling mutual exclusion of access to the svdbP1 database correctly by the two copies of sPROGRAM–1. The same comments apply to sREPORTER and PATSY as regards both databases.

There is clearly considerable potential for overlap and parallel development and testing of the SUMS system, since the four main segments are largely orthogonal. For example, phases MO, EN, FL and MR could be scheduled to take place in parallel, though of course LS must follow both MO and EN, and SX must follow both FL and LS. It would be prudent to schedule DB at the earliest opportunity, as this would minimize or obviate the need for unit, subsystem and system retesting on actual, as opposed to simplified, databases. Although the above phase sequence is not intended to imply the actual order in which testing would have to take place, it seems natural to test (most of) the model part of the system before any of its functions.

References and Bibliography

ACM (1984) Proceedings of the ACM SIGSOFT/SIGPLAN Software Engineering Symposium on Practical Software Development Environments, *ACM SIGPLAN Notices*, **19**(5).

Ackerman, A.F., Fowler, P.J. & Ebenau, R.G. (1984) 'Software Inspections and the Industrial Production of Software'. In *Software Validation* (Ed. by H.L. Hausen), pp. 13–40. North-Holland, Amsterdam.

Adrion, W.R., Branstad, M.A. & Cherniavsky, J.C. (1982) 'Validation, Verification, and Testing of Computer Software', *ACM Computing Surveys*, **14**(2), 159–192.

Albrecht, A.J. & Gaffney, J.E., Jr. (1983) 'Software Function, Source Lines of Code, and Development Effort Prediction: A Software Science Validation', *IEEE Transactions on Software Engineering*, **SE–9**(6), 639–648.

Alderson, A., Bott, M.F. & Falla, M.E. (1986) 'The Eclipse Object Management System', *IEE Software Engineering Journal*, **1**(1), 39–42.

Alexander, H. (1986) 'Specifying and Prototyping Human-computer Interaction'. In *Software Engineering 86* (Ed. by D. Barnes & P. Brown), pp. 336–351. Peter Peregrinus Ltd, London.

Alford, M.W. (1977) 'A requirements engineering methodology for real-time processing', *IEEE Transactions on Software Engineering*, **SE–3**(1), 60–69.

Alford, M.W. (1985a) 'A Graph Model Based Approach to Specifications'. In *Distributed Systems. Methods and tools for specification. An Advanced Course*, pp. 175–176. Springer-Verlag, Berlin.

Alford, M.W. (1985b) 'SREM at the Age of Eight; The Distributed Computing Design System', *Computer*, **18**(4), 36–46.

ALVEY (1986) *Alvey Programme, Annual Report 1986, Poster Supplement*. IEE Publishing Dept, Stevenage, Herts.

Andrews, G.R. and Schneider, F.B. (1983) 'Concepts and Notations for Concurrent Programming', *ACM Computing Surveys*, **15**(1), 3–43.

ANSI/IEEE (1981) *IEEE Standard for Software Quality Assurance Plans, Std. 730–1981*. IEEE Computer Society, New York.

ANSI/IEEE (1983) *IEEE Standard Glossary of Software Engineering Terminology, Std.729–1983*. IEEE Computer Society, New York.

Appleton, D.S. (1986) 'Very Large Projects', *Datamation*, **32**(2), 62–70.

Avison, D.E. (1985) *Information Systems Development: A Data Base Approach*. Blackwell Scientific Publications, Oxford.

Babich, W.A. (1986) *Software Configuration Management: Co-ordination for Team Productivity*. Addison-Wesley, Reading, Mass.

Backhouse, R.C. (1986) *Program Construction and Verification*. Prentice-Hall, Englewood Cliffs, N.J.

Backus, J. (1978) 'Can Programming be Liberated from the Von Neumann Style? A Functional Style and Its Algebra of Programs', *Comm.ACM*, **21**(8), 613–649.

Baker, F.T. (1972) 'Chief Programmer Team Management of Production Programming', *IBM Systems Journal*, **11**(1), 56–73.

Baker, F.T. (1975) 'Structured Programming in a Production Programming Environment', *IEEE Transactions on Software Engineering*, **SE–1**(2), 241–252.

Balzer, R.M.(1985) 'A 15 Year Perspective on Automatic Programming', *IEEE Transactions on Software Engineering*, **SE–11**(11), 1257-1268.

Balzer, R., Goldman, N. & Wile, D. (1982) 'Operational Specification as the Basis for Rapid Prototyping', *ACM SIGSOFT Software Engineering Notes*, **7**(5), 3–16.

Barnes, J.G.P. (1984) *Programming in Ada*. Addison-Wesley, Reading, Mass.

Bell, T.E., Bixler, D.C. & Dyer, M.E. (1977) 'An extendable approach to computer-aided software requirements engineering', *IEEE Transactions on Software Engineering*, **SE–3**(1), 49–60.

Ben-Ari, M. (1982) *Principles of Concurrent Programming*. Prentice-Hall, Englewood Cliffs, N.J.

Berg, H.K., Boebert, W.E. Franta, W.R. & Moher, T.G. (1982) *Formal Methods of Program Verification and Specification*. Prentice-Hall, Englewood Cliffs, N.J.

Berry, D.M. (1987) 'Towards a Formal Basis for the Formal Development Method and the Ina Jo Specification Language', *IEEE Transactions on Software Engineering*, **SE–13**(2), 184–201.

Bersoff, E.H. (1984) 'Elements of Software Configuration Management', *IEEE Transactions on Software Engineering*, **SE–10**(1), 79–87.

Bersoff, E.H., Henderson, V.D. & Siegel, S.G. (1980) *Software Configuration Management: An Investment in Product Integrity*. Prentice-Hall, Englewood Cliffs, N.J.

Birrell, N.D. & Ould, M.A. (1985) *A Practical Handbook for Software Development*. Cambridge University Press, Cambridge.

Birtwistle, G.M., Dahl, O–J., Myhrhaug, B. & Nygaard, K. (1974) *SIMULA Begin*. Wiley, New York.

Bjorner, D. & Jones, C.B. (1982) *Formal Specification and Software Development*. Prentice-Hall, Englewood Cliffs, N.J.

Boehm, B.W. (1976) 'Software Engineering', *IEEE Transactions on Computers*, **C–25**(12), 1226–1241.

Boehm, B.W. (1981) *Software Engineering Economics*. Prentice-Hall, Englewood Cliffs, N.J.

Boehm, B.W., (1984a) 'Verifying and Validating Software Requirements and Design Specifications', *IEEE Software*, **1**(1), 75–88.

Boehm, B.W. (1984b) 'Software Engineering Economics', *IEEE Transactions on Software Engineering*, **SE–10**(1), 4–21.

Boehm, B.W. (1986) 'Understanding and Controlling Software Costs'. In *Information Processing 86* (Ed. by H.–J. Kugler), pp. 703–714. North-Holland, Amsterdam.

Boehm, B.W., Brown, J.R., Kaspar, H., Lipow, M., MacLeod, G.J. & Merritt, M.J. (1978) *Characteristics of Software Quality*. North-Holland, Amsterdam.

Boehm, B.W. & Standish, T.A. (1983) 'Software Technology in the 1990's: Using an Evolutionary Paradigm', *Computer*, **16**(11), 30–37.

Bohm, C. & Jacopini, G. (1966) 'Flow Diagrams, Turing Machines and Languages with only Two Formation Rules', *Comm. ACM*, **9**(5), 366–371.

Booch, G. (1983) *Software Engineering with Ada*. Addison-Wesley, Reading, Mass.

Booch, G. (1986) 'Object-oriented development', *IEEE Transactions on Software Engineering*, **SE–12**(2), 211–221.

Borgida, A., Greenspan, S.J. & Mylopoulos, J. (1985) 'Knowledge Representation as the Basis for Requirements Specification', *Computer*, **18**(4), 82–90.

Branstad, M. & Powell, P.B. (1984) 'Software Engineering Project Standards', *IEEE Transactions on Software Engineering*, **SE-10**(1), 73–78.

Brooks, F.P., Jr. (1975) *The Mythical Man-Month: Essays on Software Engineering.* Addison-Wesley, Reading, Mass.

Brooks, F.P., Jr. (1986) 'No Silver Bullet – Essence and Accidents of Software Engineering'. In *Information Processing 86* (Ed. By H.–J. Kugler). North-Holland, Amsterdam.

Brown, P.J. (1977) *Software Portability; An Advanced Course.* Cambridge University Press, Cambridge.

Browning, C. (1984) *Guide to Effective Software Technical Writing.* Prentice-Hall, Englewood Cliffs, N.J.

Bruce, P. & Pederson, S.M. (1982) *The Software Development Project: Planning and Management.* Wiley, New York.

Buckle, J.K. (1982) *Software Configuration Management.* Macmillan, London.

Budgen, D. (1985) 'Combining MASCOT with Modula-2 to Aid the Engineering of Real-time Systems', *Software Practice and Experience*, 15(8), 767–793.

Burns, A. (1985) *Concurrent Programming Ada.* Cambridge University Press, Cambridge.

Cameron, J. (1983) *Tutorial: JSP and JSD – The Jackson Approach to Software Development.* IEEE Computer Society Press, Washington, DC.

Cameron, J. (1986) 'An Overview of JSD', *IEEE Transactions on Software Engineering*, SE–12(2), 222–240.

Cardelli, L. & Wegner, P. (1985) 'On Understanding Types, Data Abstraction, and Polymorphism', *ACM Computing Surveys*, 17(4), 471–522.

Ceri, S. (1986) 'Requirements Collection and Analysis in Information Systems Design'. In *Information Processing 86* (Ed. by H.–J. Kugler), pp. 205–214. North-Holland, Amsterdam.

Chand, D.R. & Yadav, S.B. (1980) 'Logical Construction of Software', *Comm. ACM*, 23(10), 546–555.

Cheheyl, M.H., Gasser, M., Huff, G.A. & Millen, J.K. (1981) 'Verifying Security', *ACM Computing Surveys*, 13(3), 279–339.

Clarke, L.A. & Richardson, D.J. (1984) 'Symbolic Evaluation – An Aid to Testing and Verification'. In *Software Validation* (Ed. by H.L. Hausen), pp. 141–166. North-Holland, Amsterdam.

Claybrook, B.G. & Claybrook, A–E. (1985) 'Defining Database Views as Data Abstractions', *IEEE Transactions on Software Engineering*, SE–11(1), 3–14.

Clocksin, W.F. & Mellish, C.S. (1984) *Programming in Prolog*, 2nd edn. Springer-Verlag, Berlin.

Cohen, B., Harwood, W.T. & Jackson, M.I. (1986) *The Specification of Complex Systems.* Addison-Wesley, Wokingham, Berks.

Coleman, D. (1978) *A Structured Programming Approach to Data.* Macmillan, London.

Cook, S. (1986) 'Languages and Object-oriented Programming', *IEE/BCS Software Engineering Journal*, 1(2), 73–80.

Cox, B.J. (1984) 'Message/Object Programming: An Evolutionary Change in Programming Technology', *IEEE Software*, 1(1), 50–61.

Cox, B.J. (1986) *Object Oriented Programming: An Evolutionary Approach.* Addison-Wesley, Reading, Mass.

Crinean, K. & Baguley, L. (1986) 'The STARTS Programme', *IEE/BCS Software Engineering Journal*, 1(6), 207–211.

Curtis, B., Sheppard, S.B., Millman, P., Borst, M.A. & Love, T. (1979) 'Measuring the Psychological Complexity of Software Maintenance Tasks with the Halstead and McCabe Metrics', *IEEE Transactions on Software Engineering*, SE–5(2), 96–104.

Dahl, O–J., Dijkstra, E.W. & Hoare, C.A.R. (1972) *Structured Programming.* Academic Press, London.

Darlington, J. (1982) 'Program Transformation'. In *Functional Programming and Its*

Applications (Ed. by J. Darlington, P. Henderson & D.A. Turner), pp. 193–215. Cambridge University Press, Cambridge.

Date, C.J. (1986) *An Introduction to Database Systems, Vol. I*, 4th edn. Addison-Wesley, Reading, Mass.

Davis, R.E. (1982) 'Runnable Specification as a Design Tool'. In *Logic Programming* (Ed. by K.L. Clark & S.–A. Tarnlund), pp. 141–149. Academic Press, London.

Dearnley, P.A. & Mayhew, P.J. (1983) 'In Favour of System Prototypes and their Integration into the Systems Development Cycle', *Computer Journal*, **26**(1), 36–42.

Dell, P.W. (1986) 'Early Experience with an IPSE', *IEE/BCS Software Engineering Journal*, **1**(6), 259–264.

DeMarco, T. (1978) *Structured Analysis and System Specification*, Yourdon Inc., New York.

DeMarco, T. (1982) *Controlling Software Projects: Management, Measurement and Estimation*. Yourdon Inc., New York.

DeRemer, F. & Kron, H.H. (1976) 'Programming-in-the-large versus Programming-in-the-small', *IEEE Transactions on Software Engineering*, **SE–2**(2), 80–86.

Deutsch, M.S. (1981) 'Software Project Verification and Validation', *Computer*, **14**(4), 54–70.

Dijkstra 'Cooperating Sequential Processes'. In *Programming Languages* (Ed. by F. Genuys), pp. 43– 112. Academic Press, New York.

Dijkstra, E.W. (1975) 'Guarded Commands, Nondeterminacy, and Formal Derivation of Programs', *Comm.ACM*, **18**(8), 453–457.

Dijkstra, E.W. (1976) *A Discipline of Programming*. Prentice-Hall, Englewood Cliffs, N.J.

DoD (1983) *Reference Manual for the Ada Programming Language*. United States Department of Defense.

Dunn, R. & Ullman, R. (1982) *Quality Assurance for Computer Software*. McGraw-Hill, New York.

Dunsmuir, M.R.M. & Davies, G.J. (1985) *Programming the Unix System*. Macmillan, Basingstoke, Hants.

Fagan, M.E. (1976) 'Design and Code Inspections to Reduce Errors in Program Development', *IBM Systems Journal*, **15**(3), 182–211.

Fagan, M.E. (1986) 'Advances in Software Inspections', *IEEE Transactions on Software Engineering*, **SE–12**(7), 744–751.

Fairley, R.E. (1985) *Software Engineering Concepts*. McGraw-Hill, New York.

Feldman, S.I. (1979) 'MAKE – A Program for Maintaining Computer Programs', *Software Practice and Experience*, **9**(4), 255–265.

Freedman, D.P. & Weinberg, G.M. (1982) *Handbook of Walkthroughs, Inspections and Technical Reviews: Evaluating Programs, Projects, and Products*, 3rd edn. Little, Brown & Co., Boston, Mass.

Frenkel, K.A. (1985) 'Toward Automating the Software-Development Cycle', *Comm. ACM*, **28**(6), 578–589.

Gaines, B.R. & Shaw, M.L.G. (1984) *The Art of Computer Conversation*. Prentice-Hall, Englewood Cliffs. N.J.

Gane, C. & Sarson, T. (1979) *Structured Systems Analysis: Tools and Techniques*. Prentice-Hall, Englewood Cliffs, N.J.

Gardner, A.C. (1981) *Practical LCP*. McGraw-Hill, Maidenhead.

Gehani, N.H. (1982) 'Specifications: Formal and Informal – A Case Study', *Software Practice and Experience*, **12**(5), 433–444.

Gehani, N. & McGettrick, A.D. (Eds) (1986) *Software Specification Techniques*. Addison-Wesley, Wokingham, Berks.

Gerhart, S.L. & Yelowitz, L. (1976) 'Observations of Fallibility in Applications of

Modern Programming Methodologies', *IEEE Transactions on Software Engineering*, **SE-2**(3), 195–207.

Glaser, H., Hankin, C. & Till, D. (1984) *Principles of Functional Programming*. Prentice-Hall, Englewood Cliffs, N.J.

Goel, A.L. (1985) 'Software Reliability Models: Assumptions, Limitations and Applicability', *IEEE Transactions on Software Engineering*, **SE-11**(12), 1411–1423.

Goguen, J.A. (1984) 'Parameterized Programming', *IEEE Transactions on Software Engineering*, **SE-10**(5), 528–543.

Goguen, J.A. (1986) 'Reusing and Interconnecting Software Components', *Computer*, **19**(2), 16–28.

Goguen, J.A. & Meseguer, J. (1982) 'Rapid Prototyping in the OBJ Executable Specification Language', *ACM SIGSOFT Software Engineering Notes*, **7**(5), 75–84.

Goguen, J.A., Thatcher, J.W. & Wagner, E.G. (1977) 'An Initial Algebra Approach to the Specification, Correctness and Implementation of Abstract Data Types'. In *Current Trends in Programming Methodology, Volume IV: Data Structuring* (Ed. by R.T. Yeh), pp. 80–149. Prentice-Hall, Englewood Cliffs, N.J.

Goldberg, A. & Robson, D. (1983) *Smalltalk-80: The Language and its Implementation*. Addison-Wesley, Reading, Mass.

Goldsack, S.J. (Ed.) (1985) *Ada for Specification: Possibilities and Limitations*. Cambridge University Press, Cambridge.

Gomaa, H. (1983) 'The Impact of Rapid Prototyping on Specifying User Requirements', *ACM SIGSOFT Software Engineering Notes*, **8**(2), 17–28.

Goodenough, J.B. (1975) 'Exception Handling: Issues and a Proposed Notation', *Comm.ACM*, **18**(12), 683–696.

Goodenough, J.B. & Gerhart, S.L. (1975) 'Toward a Theory of Test Data Selection', *IEEE Transactions on Software Engineering*, **SE-1**(2), 156–173.

Goodenough, J.B. & Gerhart, S.L. (1977) 'Toward a Theory of Testing: Data Selection Criteria'. In *Current Trends in Programming Methodology, Volume II: Program Validation* (Ed. by R.T. Yeh), pp. 44–79. Prentice-Hall, Englewood Cliffs, N.J.

Gordon, R.D. (1979) 'Measuring Improvements in Program Clarity', *IEEE Transactions on Software Engineering*, **SE-5**(2), 79–90.

Gould, J.D. & Lewis, C. (1985) 'Designing for Usability: Key Principles and What Designers Think', *Comm.ACM*, **28**(3), 300–311.

Green, T.R.G. (1980) 'Programming as a Cognitive Activity'. In *Human Interaction with Computers* (Ed. by H.T. Smith & T.R.G. Green), pp. 271–320. Academic Press, London.

Gries, D. (1981) *The Science of Programming*. Springer-Verlag, Berlin.

Grune, D. (1977) 'A View of Coroutines', *ACM SIGPLAN Notices*, **12**(7), 75–81.

Guttag, J.V. & Horning, J.J. (1978) 'The Algebraic Specification of Abstract Data Types', *Acta Informatica*, **10**(1), 27–52.

Guttag, J.V., Horning, J.J. & Wing, J.M. (1985) 'The Larch Family of Specification Languages', *IEEE Software*, **2**(5), 24–36.

Halstead, M.H. (1977) *Elements of Software Science*. North-Holland, Amsterdam.

Halpern, J.D., Owre, S., Proctor, N. & Wilson, W.F. (1987) 'Muse – A Computer Assisted Verification System', *IEEE Transactions on Software Engineering*, **SE-13**(2), 151–156.

Hausen, H–L. (Ed.) (1984) *Software Validation: Inspection, Testing, Verification, Alternatives*. North-Holland, Amsterdam.

Hayes, I.J. (1985) 'Applying Formal Specification to Software Development in Industry', *IEEE Transactions on Software Engineering*, **SE-11**(2), 169–178.

Hayes, I. (Ed.) (1987) *Specification Case Studies*. Prentice-Hall, Englewood Cliffs, N.J.

Hayes-Roth, F. (1984) 'The Knowledge-Based Expert System: A Tutorial', *Computer*, **17**(9), 11–28.

Henderson, P. (1980) *Functional Programming: Application and Implementation*. Prentice-Hall, London.

Henderson, P. (1986) 'Functional Programming, Formal Specification, and Rapid Prototyping', *IEEE Transactions on Software Engineering*, **SE–12**(2), 241–250.

Heninger, K.L. (1980) 'Specifying Requirements for Complex Systems: New Techniques and Their Applications', *IEEE Transactions on Software Engineering*, **SE–6**(1), 2–13.

Hoare, C.A.R. (1969) 'An Axiomatic Basis for Computer Programming', *Comm.ACM*, **12**(10), 576–580, 583.

Hoare, C.A.R. (1974) 'Monitors: An Operating System Structuring Concept', *Comm. ACM*, **17**(10), 549–557.

Hoare, C.A.R. (1978a) Keynote address, IEEE Proceedings 3rd. International Conference on Software Engineering, Atlanta.

Hoare, C.A.R. (1978b) 'Communicating Sequential Processes', *Comm.ACM*, **21**(8), 666–677.

Hoare, C.A.R. (1985) *Communicating Sequential Processes*. Prentice-Hall, Englewood Cliffs, N.J.

Horowitz, E., Kemper, A. & Narasimhan, B. (1985) 'A Survey of Application Generators', *IEEE Software* **2**(1), 40–54.

Horowitz, E. & Williamson, R.C. (1986a) 'SODOS: A Software Documentation Support Environment – Its Definition', *IEEE Transactions on Software Engineering*, **SE–12**(8), 849–859.

Horowitz, E. & Williamson, R.C. (1986b) 'SODOS: A Software Documentation Environment – Its Use', *IEEE Transaction on Software Engineering*, **SE–12**(11), 1076–1087.

Howden, W.E. (1978) 'An Evaluation of the Effectiveness of Symbolic Testing', *Software Practice and Experience*, **8**(4), 381–397.

Howden, W.E. (1986) 'A Functional Approach to Program Testing and Analysis', *IEEE Transactions on Software Engineering*, **SE–12**(10), 997–1005.

Howe, D.R. (1983) *Data Analysis for Data Base Design*. Edward Arnold, London.

Huenke, H. (Ed.) (1981) *Software Engineering Environments*. North-Holland, Amsterdam.

Hutchison, D. & Walpole, J. (1986) 'Eclipse – A Distributed Software Development Environment', *IEE/BCS Software Engineering Journal*, **1**(2), 88–92.

IEE/BCS (1986) *Software Engineering Journal*, **1**(3).

IEEE (1983a) *IEEE Standard for Software Configuration Management Plans, Std. 828–1983*. IEEE Computer Society, New York.

IEEE (1983b) *Computer*, **16**(11).

IEEE (1983c) *Transactions on Software Engineering*, **SE–9**(6).

IEEE (1984) *Transactions on Software Engineering*, **SE–10**(5).

IEEE (1985) *Transactions on Software Engineering*, **SE–11**(12).

IEEE (1986) *Transactions on Software Engineering*, **SE–12**(1).

IEEE (1987) *Transactions on Software Engineering*, **SE–13**(3).

Ingevaldsson, L. (1979) *JSP: A Practical Method of Program Design*. Chartwell-Bratt, Bromley, Kent.

Inmos Ltd (1984) *Occam$^{(TM)}$ Programming Manual*. Prentice-Hall, Englewood Cliffs, N.J.

Ivie, E.L. (1977) 'The Programmer's Workbench – A Machine for Software Development', *Comm.ACM*, **20**(10), 746–753.

Jackson, M.A. (1975) *Principles of Program Design*. Academic Press, London.

Jackson, M.A. (1983) *System Development*. Prentice-Hall, Englewood Cliffs, N.J.

Jackson, M.I. (1985) 'Developing Ada Programs Using the Vienna Development Method (VDM)', *Software Practice and Experience*, **15**(3), 305–318.

Jensen, R.W. & Tonies, C.C. (Eds) (1979) *Software Engineering*. Prentice-Hall, Englewood Cliffs, N.J.

Jones, C.B. (1986) *Systematic Software Development Using VDM*. Prentice-Hall, Englewood-Cliffs, N.J.

Kafura, D. & Reddy, G.R. (1987) 'The Use of Software Complexity Metrics in Software Maintenance', *IEEE Transactions on Software Engineering*, **SE–13**(3), 335–343.

Kaposi, A. & Kitchenham, B. (1987) 'The Architecture of System Quality', *IEE/BCS Software Engineering Journal*, **2**(1), 2–8.

Kernighan, B.W. & Ritchie, D.M. (1978) *The C Programming Language*. Prentice-Hall, Englewood Cliffs, N.J.

King, M.J. & Pardoe, J.P. (1985) *Program Design Using JSP: A Practical Introduction*. MacMillan, Basingstoke.

Kitchenham, B.A. & Walker, J.G. (1986) 'The Meaning of Quality'. In *Software Engineering 86* (Ed. by D. Barnes & P. Brown), pp. 393–406. Peter Peregrinus Ltd, London.

Knuth, D.E. (1974) 'Structured Programming with go to Statements', *ACM Computing Surveys*, **6**(4), 261–301.

Kopetz, H. (1979) *Software Reliability*. Macmillan, London.

Kowalski, R. (1984) 'Software Engineering and Artificial Intelligence in New Generation Computing', *Future Generations Computer Systems*, **1**(1), 39–49.

Lecarme, O. & Gart, M.P. (1986) *Software Portability*. McGraw-Hill, New York.

Lehman, M.M. (1980) 'Programs, Life Cycles and Laws of Software Evolution', In *Proceedings IEEE Special Issue on Software Engineering*, **68**(9), Sept. 1980, 1060–1076.

Lehman, M.M. & Belady, L.A. (Eds) (1985) *Program Evolution: Processes of Software Change*. Academic Press, London.

Lientz, B.P. & Swanson, E.B. (1980) *Software Maintenance Management*. Addison-Wesley, Reading, Mass.

Lindsey, C.H. & Meulen, S.G. van der (1977) *Informal Introduction to Algol 68*, revised edn. North-Holland, Amsterdam.

Linger, R.C., Mills, H.D. & Witt, B.I. (1979) *Structured Programming: Theory and Practice*. Addison-Wesley, Reading, Mass.

Liskov, B.H. & Zilles, S.N. (1974) 'Programming with Abstract Data Types', *ACM SIGPLAN Notices*, **9**(4), 50–59.

Liskov, B.H. & Zilles, S.N. (1975) 'Specification Techniques for Data Abstractions', *IEEE Transactions on Software Engineering*, **1**(1), 7–19.

Luckham, D.C. & von Henke, F.W. (1985) 'An Overview of Anna, a Specification Language for Ada', *IEEE Software*, **2**(2), 9–22.

Macro, A. & Buxton, J. (1987) *The Craft of Software Engineering*. Addison-Wesley, Wokingham, Berks.

Manna, Z. & Waldinger, R. (1978) 'The Logic of Computer Programming', *IEEE Transactions on Software Engineering*, **SE-4**(3), 199–229.

Mantei, M. (1981) 'The Effect of Programming Team Structure on Programming Tasks', *Comm.ACM*, **24**(3), 106–113.

Martin, J. (1985) *Fourth Generation Languages: Volume 1*. Prentice-Hall, Englewood Cliffs, N.J.

McCabe, T.J. (1976) 'A Complexity Measure', *IEEE Transactions on Software Engineering*, **SE-2**(4), 308–320.

McCracken, D.D. & Jackson, M.A. (1982) 'Life Cycle Concept Considered Harmful', *ACM SIGSOFT Software Engineering Notes*, **7**(2), 29–32.

McDermid, J. (Ed.) (1985) *Integrated Project Support Environments*. Peter Peregrinus Ltd, London.

McDermid, J. & Ripken, K. (Eds.) (1984) *Life Cycle Support in The Ada Environment*. Cambridge University Press, Cambridge.

Metzger, P.W. (1981) *Managing a Programming Project*, 2nd edn. Prentice-Hall, Englewood Cliffs, N.J.

Meyer, B. (1985) 'On Formalism in Specifications', *IEEE Software*, **2**(1), 6–26.

Mills, H.D. & Linger, R.C. (1986) 'Data Structured Programming: Program Design without Arrays and Pointers', *IEEE Transactions on Software Engineering*, **SE–12**(2), 192–197.

Mohanty, S.N. (1981) 'Software Cost Estimation: Present and Future', *Software Practice and Experience*, **11**(2), 103–121.

Morgan, C. & Suffrin, B.A. (1984) 'Specification of the UNIX File System', *IEEE Transactions on Software Engineering*, **10**(2), 128–142.

Mostow, J. (1985) 'What is AI? And What Does It Have to Do with Software Engineering?', *IEEE Transactions on Software Engineering*, **SE–11**(11), 1253–1255.

Mullery, G.P. (1979) 'CORE – A Method of Controlled Requirements Specification', *Proceedings 4th International Conference on Software Engineering*, 126–135.

Mumford, E. (1980) 'Social Aspects of Systems Analysis', *Computer Journal*, **23**(1), 5–7.

Mumford, E., Land, F. & Hawgood, J. (1978) 'A Participative Approach to the Design of Computer Systems', *Impact of Science on Society*, **28**(3), 235–253.

Myers, G.J. (1975) *Reliable Software Through Composite Design*. Van Nostrand Reinhold, New York.

Myers, G.J. (1978) *Composite/Structured Design*. Van Nostrand Reinhold, New York.

Myers, G.J. (1979) *The Art of Software Testing*. Wiley, New York.

Narayanaswamy, K. & Scacchi, W. (1987) 'Maintaining Configurations of Evolving Software Systems', *IEEE Transactions on Software Engineering*, **SE–13**(3), 324–334.

Naur, P. (1969) 'Programming by Action Clusters', *BIT*, **9**(3), 250–258.

Naur, P., Randell, B. & Buxton, J.N. (Eds.) (1976) *Software Engineering Concepts and Techniques*. Petrocelli/Charter, New York.

Nissen, J. & Wallis, P. (1984) *Portability and Style in Ada*. Cambridge University Press, Cambridge.

Parnas, D.L. (1972a) 'On the Criteria to be used in Decomposing Systems into Modules', *Comm.ACM*, **15**(2), 1053–1058.

Parnas, D.L. (1972b) 'A Technique for the Specification of Software Modules with Examples', *Comm.ACM*, **15**(5), 330–336.

Parnas, D.L. (1985) 'Software Aspects of Strategic Defense Systems', *Comm.ACM*, **28**(12), 1326–1335.

Partridge, D. (1986) 'Engineering Artificial Intelligence Software', *Artificial Intelligence Review*, **1**(1), 27–41.

Perlis, A., Sayward, F. & Shaw, M. (Eds) (1981) *Software Metrics: An Analysis and Evaluation*. MIT Press, Cambridge, Mass.

Peterson, J.L. (1977) 'Petri Nets', *ACM Computing Surveys*, **9**(3), 223–52.

Peterson, J.L. (1981) *Petri Net Theory and the Modelling of Systems*. Prentice-Hall, Englewood Cliffs, N.J.

Pressman, R.S. (1982) *Software Engineering: A Practitioner's Approach*. McGraw-Hill, New York.

Price, J. (1984) *How to Write a Computer Manual: A Handbook of Software Documentation*. Benjamin/Cummings, Menlo Park, CA.

Putnam, L. (1978) 'A General Empirical Solution to the Macro Software Sizing and Estimating Problem', *IEEE Transactions on Software Engineering*, **SE–4**(4), 345–361.

Ramamoorthy, C.V., Prakash, A., Tsai, W–T. & Usuda, Y. (1984) 'Software Engineering: Problems and Perspectives', *Computer*, **17**(10), 191–209.

Ramamoorthy, C.V., Garg, V. & Prakash, A. (1986) 'Programming in the Large', *IEEE Transaction on Software Engineering*, **SE–12**(7), 769–783.

Rapps, S. & Weyuker, E.J. (1985) 'Selecting Software Test Data Using Data Flow Information', *IEEE Transactions on Software Engineering*, **SE–11**(4), 367–375.

Rentsch, T. (1982) 'Object-oriented Programming', *ACM SIGPLAN Notices*, **17**(9), 51–57.

Riddle, W.E. & Fairley, R.E. (Eds) (1980) *Software Development Tools*. Springer-Verlag, Berlin.

Rochkind, M.J. (1975) 'The Source Code Control System', *IEEE Transactions on Software Engineering*, **SE–1**(4), 255–265.

Roman, G–C. (1985) 'A Taxonomy of Current Issues in Requirements Engineering', *Computer*, **18**(4), 14–23.

Ross, D.T. (1977) 'Structured Analysis (SA): A Language for Communicating Ideas', *IEEE Transactions on Software Engineering*, **SE–3**(1), 16–34.

Ross, D.T. & Schoman, K.E. (1977) 'Structured Analysis for Requirements Definition', *IEEE Transactions on Software Engineering*, **SE–3**(1), 6–15.

Ross, D.T. (1985) 'Applications and Extensions of SADT', *Computer*, **18**(4), 25–34.

Sammet, J.E. (1986) 'Why Ada is Not Just Another Programming Language', *Comm. ACM*, **29**(8), 722–732.

Scheffer, P.A., Stone, A.H. & Rzepka, W.E. (1985) 'A Case Study of SREM', *Computer*, **18**(4), 47–54.

Shaw, M. (1984) 'Abstraction Techniques in Modern Programming Languages', *IEEE Software*, **1**(4), 10–26.

Shooman, M.L. (1983) *Software Engineering: Design, Reliability and Management*. McGraw-Hill, New York.

Simon, H.A. (1986) 'Whether Software Engineering Needs to be Artificially Intelligent', *IEEE Transactions on Software Engineering*, **SE–12**(7), 726–732.

Simpson, H.R. & Jackson, K. (1979) 'Process Synchronisation in MASCOT', *Computer Journal*, **22**(4), 332–345.

Sommerville, I. (1985) *Software Engineering*, 2nd edn. Addison-Wesley, Wokingham, England.

Stevens, W.P. (1981) *Using Structured Design. How to Make Programs Simple, Changeable, Flexible, and Reusable*. Wiley, New York.

Stevens, W.P., Myers, G.J. & Constantine, L.L. (1974) 'Structured Design', *IBM Systems Journal*, **13**(2), 115–139.

Stuart, A. (1984) *Writing and Analyzing Effective Computer System Documentation*. Holt, Rinehart and Winston, New York.

Swartout, W. & Balzer, R. (1982) 'On the Inevitable Intertwining of Specification and Implementation', *Comm.ACM*, **25**(7), 438–440.

Teichrow, D. & Hershey, E.A. (1977) 'PSL/PSA: A Computer-Aided Technique for Structured Documentation and Analysis of Information Processing Systems', *IEEE Transactions on Software Engineering*, **SE–3**(1), 41–48.

Teitelman, W. (1985) 'A Tour Through Cedar', *IEEE Transactions on Software Engineering*, **SE–11**(3), 285–302.

Tsichritzis, D.C. & Lochovsky, F.H. (1982) *Data Models*. Prentice-Hall, Englewood Cliffs, N.J.

Turner, D. (1986) 'An Overview of Miranda', *ACM SIGPLAN Notices*, **21**(12), 158–166.

Vessey, I. & Weber, R. (1984) 'Research on Structured Programming: An Empiricist's Evaluation', *IEEE Transactions on Software Engineering*, **SE–10**(4), 397–407.
Vick, C.R. & Ramamoorthy, C.V. (Eds) (1984) *Handbook of Software Engineering*. Van Nostrand Reinhold, New York.

Wallis, P.J.L. (1982) *Portable Programming*. Macmillan, London.
Walston, C.E. & Felix, C.P. (1977) 'A Method of Programming Measurement and Estimation', *IBM Systems Journal*, **16**(1), 54-73.
Warnier, J.D. (1981) *Logical Construction of Systems*. Van Nostrand Reinhold, New York.
Wegner, P. & Smolka, S.A. (1983) 'Processes, Tasks, and Monitors: A Comparative Study of Concurrent Programming Primitives', *IEEE Transactions on Software Engineering*, **SE–9**(4), 446–462.
Weinberg, G.M. (1971) *The Psychology of Computer Programming*. Van Nostrand Reinhold, New York.
Weinberg, G.M. & Freedman, D.P. (1984) 'Reviews, Walkthroughs and Inspections', *IEEE Transactions on Software Engineering*, **SE–10**(1), 68–72.
Weinberg, V. (1978) *Structured Analysis*. Yourdon Inc., New York.
Weyuker, E.J. & Ostrand, T.J. (1980) 'Theories of Program Testing and the Application of Revealing Subdomains', *IEEE Transactions on Software Engineering*, **SE–6**(3), 236–246.
Wiener, R. & Sincovec, R. (1984) *Software Engineering with Modula-2 and Ada*. Wiley, New York.
Wiest, J.D. & Levy, F.K. (1977) *A Management Guide to PERT/CPM*. Prentice-Hall, Englewood Cliffs, N.J.
Winters, E.W. (1979) 'An Analysis of the Capabilities of Problem Statement Language: A Language for System Requirements and Specifications'. In *Proceedings of the 3rd International Conference on Computer Software and Applications*, 283–288. IEEE Computer Society Press, New York.
Wirth, N. (1971) 'Program Development by Stepwise Refinement', *Comm.ACM*, **14**(4), 221–227.
Wirth, N. (1974) 'On the Composition of Well Structured programs', *ACM Computing Surveys*, **6**(4), 247–259.
Wirth, N. (1983) *Programming in Modula-2*, 2nd edn. Springer-Verlag, Berlin.
Wolverton, R.W. (1974) 'The Cost of Developing Large Scale Software', *IEEE Transactions on Computers*, **C-23**(6), 615–636.
Wood-Harper, A.T. & Fitzgerald, G. (1982) 'A Taxonomy of Current Approaches to Systems Analysis', *Computer Journal*, **25**(1), 12–16.

Yourdon, E.N. (1975) *Techniques of Program Structure and Design*. Prentice-Hall, Englewood Cliffs, N.J.
Yourdon, E.N. (Ed.) (1979a) *Classics in Software Engineering*. Yourdon Inc., New York.
Yourdon, E.N. (1979b) *Structured Walkthroughs*. Yourdon Inc., New York.
Yourdon, E.N. (Ed.) (1982) *Writings of the Revolution: Selected Readings on Software Engineering*. Yourdon Inc., New York.
Yourdon, E.N. & Constantine, L.L. (1979) *Structured Design: Fundamentals of a Discipline of Computer Program and System Design*. Prentice-Hall, Englewood Cliffs, N.J.

Zave, P. (1982) 'An Operational Approach to Requirements Specification for Embedded Systems', *IEEE Transactions on Software Enginnering*, **SE–8**(3), 250–269.

Zave, P. (1984) 'The Operational Versus the Conventional Approach to Software Development'. *Comm.ACM*, **27**(2), 104–118.

Zave, P. & Schell, W. (1986) 'Salient Features of an Executable Specification Language and its Environment', *IEEE Transactions on Software Engineering*, **SE–12**(2), 312–325.

Zelkowitz, M. (1978) 'Software Engineering Perspectives', *ACM Computing Surveys*, **10**(2), 197–216.

Subject Index

Author Index